ZAPATISMO BEYOND BORDER.
NEW IMAGINATIONS OF POLITICAL POSSIBILITY

On 1 January 1994, in the far south-east corner of Mexico, a guerrilla army of Indigenous Mayan peasants calling itself the Zapatista Army of National Liberation rose up in rebellion against five hundred years of colonialism, imperialism, genocide, and racism, and decades of neoliberal capitalism. *Zapatismo beyond Borders* examines how Zapatismo, the political philosophy of the Zapatistas, crossed the regional and national boundaries of the isolated indigenous communities of Chiapas to influence diverse communities of North American activists.

Drawing on a year of fieldwork with activists and personal experience with social justice struggles, Alex Khasnabish examines the 'transnational resonance' of the Zapatista movement. He shows how the spread of Zapatismo has unexpectedly produced new imaginations and practices of radical political action in diverse socio-political movements throughout North America.

Zapatismo beyond Borders provides a close look at a radical political philosophy that has been a model of grass-roots organizations and a rallying call for members of the anti-globalization movement. Rigorously argued and engagingly written, this study is essential reading for anyone interested in Indigenous rights movements, political philosophy, and the recent history of political activism.

ALEX KHASNABISH is an assistant professor in the Department of Sociology and Anthropology at Mount Saint Vincent University.

ALEX KHASNABISH

Zapatismo beyond Borders

New Imaginations of Political Possibility

UNIVERSITY OF TORONTO PRESS
Toronto Buffalo London

ISBN 978-0-8020-9830-6 (cloth)
ISBN 978-0-8020-9633-3 (paper)

Library and Archives Canada Cataloguing in Publication

Khasnabish, Alex, 1976–
    Zapatismo beyond borders : new imaginations of political
possibility / Alex Khasnabish.

    Includes bibliographical references and index.
    ISBN 978-0-8020-9830-6 (bound). – ISBN 978-0-8020-9633-3 (pbk.)

    1. Social movements – Mexico – Chiapas – History.   2. Social movements –
North America – History.   3. Political activists – Mexico – Chiapas.
4. Political activists – North America.   5. Ejército Zapatista de Liberación
Nacional (Mexico).   6. Chiapas (Mexico) – History – Peasant Uprising,
1994–.   7. Social justice – North America.   8. Indigenous peoples – Civil
rights.   9. Anti-globalization movement.   I. Title.

HM881.K48 2008   322.4   C2008-903156-3

University of Toronto Press acknowledges the financial assistance to its
publishing program of the Canada Council for the Arts and the Ontario
Arts Council.

University of Toronto Press acknowledges the financial support for its
publishing activities of the Government of Canada through the Book
Publishing Industry Development Program (BPIDP).

For Indra and Candida,
bright lights in the darkness.

Contents

Acknowledgments   ix

Introduction: Bridges of Imagination, Spaces of Possibility   3

1 Power, Democracy, and (Re)shaping the Terrain of
   Political Struggle   29

2 Northern Struggles, Northern Histories   55

3 Dreams of Revolution, Myths of Power: Mexican
   Revolutionary Histories   84

4 Echoes and Openings: Resonance   122

5 Imagining Struggle/Struggling to Imagine: Imagination
   and Political Action   152

6 New Horizons: Resonance and Political Action   186

7 New Terrains: Mapping Emerging Possibilities in a
   Transnational Field of Action   233

Conclusion: Globalizing Hope   271

References   281

Index   295

Acknowledgments

This book is the product of the efforts of a multitude of individuals and here I want to acknowledge as many of these important people as possible. I would like to begin by thanking my doctoral supervisor and mentor, Dr Petra Rethmann. An incredible scholar, supervisor, and friend, her insights, provocations, and tremendous support have deeply informed my understanding of what it means to be an engaged and critical academic. I also want to warmly thank Dr Harvey Feit and Dr Richard Roman, both of whom put considerable time and energy into advising me at a critical time in my academic career.

I owe a great debt to my research partners who shared their thoughts, insights, and experiences with me and without whom this work would not have been possible. For all those people working to build dignified, democratic, just, and sustainable alternatives to the terror of global capitalism, patriarchy, racism, sexism, imperialism, heterosexism, violence, exploitation, and suffering, (y)our struggles are an endless source of hope, joy, and possibility. Of course, in this respect, I owe my deepest gratitude to the Zapatistas, whose struggle for democracy, liberty, and justice, for a world where all worlds fit, remind me and so many others that there are always possibilities, that there is always hope if we choose to fight for it.

Funding research is always challenging, particularly when it does not fit easily into 'market-driven needs' and sincere thanks need to go to my sponsors. My research was made possible by the generous support of the Social Sciences and Humanities Research Council of Canada, the Institute on Globalization and the Human Condition, and the School of Graduate Studies at McMaster University.

To Virgil Duff, executive editor at the University of Toronto Press, my sincere gratitude in assisting me at each stage of the publication process and for fighting for this book in difficult times. I would also like to thank both Beth McAuley, who thoroughly copy-edited this book, as well as my anonymous reviewers whose thoughtful feedback contributed greatly to this work.

For all their support and encouragement I would like to thank my family. To my mother, Ingrid, my father, Kai, my sister, Krista, and my uncle, Bob, I want to offer my deepest appreciation and love. To the Hadleys, and especially to Brian and Margie, I also want to offer my warmest love and respect. Your kindness and generosity have brought so much to my life and I sincerely hope my work honours that gift. To Chris, my oldest and closest friend, thanks for keeping me grounded and for always doing it with laughter and music.

Finally, I want to express my deepest love and gratitude to those who touch my life profoundly every day. To Bast and Yorba, my constant companions during the writing of this book, thanks for making writing a much less solitary process. To Candida, my partner and my inspiration, I owe more than I can possibly say. You bring wonder, passion, and meaning into my life. Your intelligence, strength, and dedication remind me every day that this work and the politics it embodies are fundamentally acts of love. To Indra, the newest member of our family, you are absolute joy. You remind me that hope, possibility, and love are not things to be given or taken away, they are experiences we bring into being, give shape to, and nurture collectively.

ZAPATISMO BEYOND BORDERS:
NEW IMAGINATIONS OF POLITICAL POSSIBILITY

Introduction: Bridges of Imagination, Spaces of Possibility

The new distribution of the world excludes 'minorities.' The indigenous, youth, women, homosexuals, lesbians, people of color, immigrants, workers, peasants; the majority who make up the world basements are presented, for power, as disposable. The new distribution of the world excludes the majorities.

The modern army of financial capital and corrupt governments advance conquering in the only way it is capable of: destroying. The new distribution of the world destroys humanity.

The new distribution of the world only has one place for money and its servants. Men, women and machines become equal in servitude and in being disposable. The lie governs and it multiplies itself in means and methods.

A new lie is sold to us as history. The lie about the defeat of hope, the lie about the defeat of dignity, the lie about the defeat of humanity. The mirror of power offers us an equilibrium in the balance scale: the lie about the victory of cynicism, the lie about the victory of servitude, the lie about the victory of neoliberalism.

Instead of humanity, it offers us stock market value indexes, instead of dignity it offers us globalization of misery, instead of hope it offers us an emptiness, instead of life it offers us the international of terror.

Against the international of terror representing neoliberalism, we must raise the international of hope. Hope, above borders, languages, colors, cultures, sexes, strategies, and thoughts, of all those who prefer humanity alive.

The international of hope. Not the bureaucracy of hope, not the opposite image and, thus, the same as that which annihilates us. Not the power with a new sign or new clothing. A breath like this, the breath of dignity. A flower yes, the flower of hope. A song yes, the song of life.

Dignity is that nation without nationality, that rainbow that is also a bridge, that murmur of the heart no matter what blood lives it, that rebel irreverence that mocks borders, customs and wars.

Hope is that rejection of conformity and defeat.   .

'The First Declaration of La Realidad for Humanity and against Neoliberalism,' Subcomandante Insurgente Marcos (1998)

In his essay 'A Storm and a Prophecy – Chiapas: The Southeast in Two Winds,' Subcomandante Insurgente Marcos, spokesperson and a military leader of the Zapatista Army of National Liberation (EZLN) in August 1992, writes:

Everyone is dreaming in this country. Now it is time to wake up ...
The storm is here. From the clash of these two winds a storm will be born. Its time has arrived. Now the wind from above rules, but the wind from below is coming ...
The prophecy is here: When the storm calms, when the rain and fire again leave the country in peace, the world will no longer be the world, but something better. (2001a, 36)

These words, written almost two years before the Zapatista uprising of 1 January 1994 speak of a new world, a world ushered in by a storm born of a clash between two winds, the wind from above and the wind from below. What kind of world did the combatants and support bases of the Zapatista Army of National Liberation hope to see brought into being? In what way did they hope others would respond to their collective cry of '¡Ya basta!' – 'Enough!' – which issued from the mouths of masked Indigenous guerrillas of the EZLN on 1 January 1994? What reply did the Zapatistas expect to hear? While the uprising which began on 1 January 1994 apparently bore many of the marks of a traditional guerrilla insurgency, the ultimate arc of the Zapatista struggle would be quite different. Similarly, while the Zapatistas called for a national uprising in order to establish 'justice, democracy, and liberty' for all Mexicans, the response articulated by national and international civil society would also be quite different. Rather than inspiring a nation-wide insurgency, the Zapatista uprising instead galvanized people throughout Mexico and around the world to become participants in a shared struggle not to conquer the world but to make it anew.

In 2001, Subcomandante Insurgente Marcos would reflect:

> Our army is very different from others, because its proposal is to cease being an army. A soldier is an absurd person who has to resort to arms in order to convince others, and in that sense the movement has no future if its future is military. If the EZLN perpetuates itself as an armed military structure, it is headed for failure. Failure as an alternative set of ideas, an alternative attitude to the world ... You cannot reconstruct the world or society, or rebuild national states now in ruins, on the basis of a quarrel over who will impose their hegemony on society. (García Márquez and Pombo 2004, 4–5)

An armed insurgency aimed at deposing the Mexican federal executive, defeating the Mexican army, and allowing for all Mexicans to realize an authentic democracy became a movement aimed not at conquering society but at reimagining and reconstituting it. The Zapatista rebellion was not only challenging the power of the ruling regime in Mexico but also the very idea of power itself.

In the years since the Zapatista Army of National Liberation rose up in arms in the most south-eastern Mexican state of Chiapas on the very day that the North American Free Trade Agreement came into effect, much has been written by authors within and beyond Mexico about the Zapatistas' origins, agenda, structure, history, tactics, and ultimate goals as well as those of their most public mask, Subcomandante Insurgente Marcos (Arquilla et al. 1998; Collier and Quaratiello 1999; Harvey 1998; Hernández Navarro 2002; Kingsnorth 2003; Klein 2002; Leyva Solano 1998; Monsiváis 2002; Nash 2001; Ross 2000; Rus, Castillo, and Mattiace 2003; Stephen 2002; Weinberg 2000; Womack Jr. 1999). Yet in all of this, the question of why their cry of '¡Ya basta!' and their ensuing struggle has resonated so strongly with people beyond the borders of Mexico remains largely unconsidered.

In this work, I consider the significance of the Zapatista struggle within the broader context of North American political activism since 1994. How and why did people from outside of the Zapatista communities of Chiapas, Mexico, come to not only hear the Zapatistas' words but to actually begin to listen to them and then to formulate their own responses, to add their voices to a transnational dialogue? How and why has the Zapatista struggle resonated so powerfully beyond the borders not only of Chiapas but also of Mexico? What have been the reasons for and consequences of this transnationally resonant political imagination of Zapatismo? These questions serve as the guiding principles for my analytical engagement throughout this work.

In invoking the 'transnational,' I do so cognizant of the tremendous amount of scholarship and debate this phenomenon has generated, particularly since the early 1990s (see, for example, Evans 2000; Glick Schiller 2005; Kearney 1995; Mintz 1998; Olesen 2005b; Portes, Guarnizo, and Landolt 1999; Roudometof 2005; Vertovec 2001, 1999; Yegenoglu 2005; Yeoh, Willis, and Fakhri 2003). It is not my contention that we are living in a 'transnational age,' that locality has disappeared or become irrelevant, or that all identities are 'hybridized.' However, I would assert that it is a mistake to regard current social, political, and economic relations – and radical challenges to them – as *merely* a continuation of processes that have been going on for centuries or millennia (see Miyoshi 1993; Robinson 2005). My own use of the term is a reference to a political space which, if not yet properly 'global,' is nevertheless constituted as beyond the more familiar constructions of the national and the international. The phenomenon of resonance that I explore here and the forms of political action and imagination to which it has given rise are not predicated on the assumption that the nation-state system is in decline or that national politics serves no constructive purpose. Rather, they are lines of flight that seek to bring into being a political space of practice and imagination that transverses, transgresses, and lies beyond the hegemony exercised by dominant conceptions of the state, the nation, and the current world (dis)order they constitute. It is in this sense that I refer to the transnational character of Zapatismo's resonance as well as the political imaginations to which it has given rise.

The types of activism I refer to here span a range from individuals and organizations focusing upon human rights issues to those deeply involved in what has become known as the global anti-capitalist movement. Yet all these individuals and organizations are outside of 'mainstream' channels of political participation. I use the term 'significance' here purposefully – only peripherally will issues of movement infrastructure and networks enter into this analysis – instead, I focus upon the processes of transmission, translation, and resonance in relation to how Zapatismo has become meaningful for activists located within their own particular contexts and engaged in the dynamics of their own particular struggles, and what the consequence of this emergent 'political imagination' is.

I use the term 'political imagination' in my work very deliberately. While I explore the phenomenon of the 'political imagination' extensively later in this work, for now I simply wish to explain that I use it as a reference to imagination as an integral part of radical political practice. I use the term referring to both the impetus and processes involved in envisioning and articulating political projects that have emerged, directly and indirectly, due to the influence of Zapatismo. In many ways this political imagination is the force that fuels the transnational resonance of Zapatismo that I explore throughout this work. In this sense, the political imagination is both an act and a constellation of political projects.

The Dimensions of Resonance

What is 'resonance'? At its most fundamental level resonance is the non-linear and unpredictable dynamic by which meaning made in a particular context becomes significant in another. But this is not all. Once meaning finds significance in another context it provokes effects both predictable and unanticipated. It is these unanticipated but often powerful effects to which the concept of resonance draws attention. Much like a voice reverberating in a cave, environment is intrinsic to the existence and character of an echo, but the echo's *significance* rests ultimately with its perception and interpretation by a receptive actor. Rather than 'diffusion,' which signifies the migration of things (both material and immaterial) across boundaries, resonance signifies movement and mutation. As a dynamic, resonance implies not only the spread of ideas, tactics, or imaginations, it also implies that these things take on new meanings and produce unpredictable effects once they find spaces and actors amenable to them. While diffusion is a dynamic constituted by processes of transmission, distribution, and adoption, resonance is a dynamic constituted by processes of transmission, translation, and reception. While diffusion is often conceived of as a *relatively* static process of interaction between innovators and adopters, resonance is inherently fluid and unpredictable, relying as it does not only upon senders and receivers but upon the dialogic processes of communication and translation.

In terms of socio-political analysis, the concept of resonance draws attention to those interactions, engagements, and effects that often go unnoticed by analyses emphasizing causality and correlation. While much contemporary social movement analysis demonstrates 'robustness' through recourse to causality, correlation, and concreteness, what such analysis fails to grasp is the deeper truth that contentious sociopolitical and cultural action aimed at radical change frequently overflows the boundaries of these analytical boxes. This is so because committed resistance to the status quo and the active building of alternatives to it do not emerge as a consequence of singular events that provoke them, they emerge out of a confluence of events, inspirations, encounters, imaginations, desires, movements, and individuals. In ways that confound prediction, radical social imaginations and action are not simply consequences of grievances articulated in response to a perceived injustice, they are rather intelligible only as manifestations of dense, rhizomatic networks of connections amongst 'the real' (individuals, movements, systems of power) and 'the more-than-real' (imaginations, languages, and repertoires embodying new political horizons). In this sense, the emergence of new political imaginations and collectivities in action are not simply outcomes of or responses to empirically verifiable systems of power, they are partial, precarious, and potentially liberatory signposts marking the way towards new terrains of political possibility. It is within this complex socio-political and cultural landscape that resonance operates both as a generative phenomenon and an analytical concept.

In Canada and the United States, the resonance of Zapatismo has given rise not only to a diversity of organizations expressing direct solidarity with the Zapatistas but also to movements, organizations, and forms of political activism that overflow the bounds of solidarity and that have yielded new and unanticipated results. It should be noted that one of the most obvious and widespread symptoms of the resonance of Zapatismo transnationally is the adoption of its rhetoric, most frequently conveyed via the writings of Subcomandante Insurgente Marcos and disseminated globally not only via printed form but also via the Internet, CD-ROMs, DVDs, and audio and video tapes. The resonance of Zapatismo is one born of poetry; it is a resonance that inspires rather than leads, a resonance that speaks the audacious language of creativity, imagination, laughter, and hope rather than that of tactics, dogma, and structure. In many ways, the manifestation of this resonance points quite precisely to the growing dissatisfaction with established political traditions (from the teleologies of Marxism to the empty promises of liberal democracy) and practices (from political parties to the labour movement to lobby politics) on the part of many individuals who believe in the necessity of realizing meaningful socio-political and economic change. But much more than a marker for failure or disillusionment with other political traditions the resonance of Zapatismo transnationally signifies new political possibilities and potentials.

It is of vital importance to recognize that the resonance of Zapatismo is by no means identical to active solidarity with the concrete struggles of Zapatista communities in Chiapas. In large part this is due to the fact that the Zapatistas themselves have explicitly reconfigured the meaning of 'solidarity' and worked to reconceptualize the nature of radical and revolutionary political action, a fundamental shift which I will discuss at greater length shortly. While solidarity work is indeed carried out by a wide range of collectives and organizations throughout the United States and Canada, the resonance of Zapatismo has also stimulated a tremendous variety of politically engaged action from the formation of transnational anti-capitalist networks of coordination and communication to the production of 'tactical media' aimed at telling new stories of struggle and possibility. This resonance alludes to the presence of Zapatismo as a sign in a globalized field of meaning that emerges from but is not limited to any specific context. This is not to say that Zapatismo is an 'empty' or 'co-opted' political project, on the contrary, it is a project that overflows with meaning from the perspective of many activists involved in the search for new political spaces and practices both in Canada and in the United States. Indeed, the phenomenon of resonance itself implies that a sound resonates within a given space only because the characteristics of that space allow it to do so. The echoes produced by the act of resonance are not identical to the original sound but neither are they entirely separate from it. Resonance is thus characterized both by affinity and difference, politically as well as aurally.

Rather than an act of appropriation, the transnational resonance of Zapatismo represents a reimagining of political struggle that has at once reinvigorated the search for new kinds of socio-political possibilities not limited to variations of capitalist or socialist ideologies, stimulated a renewed discussion surrounding the character and potential of political action and solidarity, and brought to light powerful bases of connection amongst diverse groups of political activists. Perhaps most significantly, this transnational resonance of Zapatismo has provoked an explicit consideration of phenomena such as hope, dignity, and imagination and their relationship to radical socio-political change. Reso-

nance is thus not at all an end it itself; rather, it is perhaps best understood as a beginning, an opening onto a new terrain of possibility and
connection. The political consequences and opportunities of this resonance transnationally are my points of focus here.

Researching Resonance, Exploring the Imagination

Taking phenomena such as the 'political imagination' and 'transnational resonance' as the conceptual hubs of my research involved fash-
ioning methodologies that would accommodate such points of focus.
Imagination and resonance do not occupy physical space, although they
may indeed make use of such physical spaces or temporarily manifest
themselves in such places, and as such my research has focused on issues of consciousness, interconectedness, communication, and points
and means of connectivity. While planning and preparation for this
project began in March 2003, my active research phase began in September 2003 and continued until September 2004. During this period I conducted in-depth and open-ended interviews with more than thirty
political activists living and working in Canada and the United States
and whose work engaged Zapatismo and the Zapatista struggle.

Although I argue that the resonance of Zapatismo is a transnational
phenomenon, I chose to focus upon the north of the Americas in my
research for several interrelated reasons. First, there is the matter of
political geography. While the elite-driven nation-state projects of Canada and the U.S. have often been explicitly and implicitly linked to a civ-
ilizational legacy shared with western Europe, these nation-states and
the populations who inhabit them are nevertheless physically, historically, politically, economically, and socially part of the Americas. Of
course, Canada and the U.S. also share a continent with Mexico, and it
is this fundamental connection that makes exploring the resonance of
Zapatismo in the north of the Americas particularly relevant. The political, economic, social, and environmental challenges facing peoples
around the world today necessitate critical thinking and action that recognizes a global sense of interconnection while remaining constantly
aware of the shared spaces and places we inhabit. This brings me to my
second reason: the significance of socio-political context. As I argue
throughout this work, resonance can never be divorced from the context
within which it occurs, and in this sense exploring the transnational resonance of Zapatismo amongst communities of activists in Canada and
the U.S. allows for a much richer consideration of the role of context and

history than a wide-ranging, globe-spanning overview might. Finally, my focus upon the U.S. and Canada in relation to Zapatismo's resonance also derives from the pre-eminent position of both these states with respect to the post–Cold War New World Order and globalized neoliberal capitalism. The elites and populations of both these states are deeply implicated – willingly or not – in the dynamics of power, exploitation, and domination on a global scale in the twenty-first century. As Vinay Lal (2002) has remarked with respect to the terror induced by the gross global imbalance of power and the ideology of affluence that underlies it in places like Canada and the U.S., 'It has been the American way of life to assume that one can live without fear; indeed, that one is entitled to live with as much security as a multicultural democracy can promise, while being perfectly free to inflict, through one's representatives in government, fear and terror upon others' (195). The resonance and concrete manifestations of alterative imaginations amongst the populations of these countries is profoundly significant with regard to the possibilities for envisioning and articulating socio-political and economic alternatives at a time when they are so clearly desperately needed.

It is in light of these intersecting reasons that I chose my focus. Specifically, I sought to engage activists who had experienced the resonance of Zapatismo and translated it in ways that were meaningful and powerful within the socio-political and cultural contexts where they live and work. The activists I interviewed are involved in a diversity of organizations and projects, including Big Noise Tactical; Building Bridges; the Chiapas Media Project; Food for Chiapas; Global Exchange; 'hacktivists' from the University of Toronto; Mexico Solidarity Network; the Ontario Coalition Against Poverty; Peoples' Global Action; the smartMeme Strategy and Training Project; activists involved in planning the Third Intercontinental Encuentro for Humanity and Against Neoliberalism; and a variety of activists involved in political projects ranging from Latin American solidarity to community capacity-building projects.

The process used to identify and engage potential participants in this research in many ways reflects some of the challenges of doing research with people involved in transnational anti-capitalist activism. There are no 'centres' for this activism; it occupies no permanent spaces. This in fact tends to be one of the strengths of the contemporary global justice/anti-capitalist movement – it is characterized by decentralization, an absence of permanent structures and hierarchies, and few formal channels and spaces of interaction and communication. Compounding this is the fact that many of these activists are extremely busy and over-committed and live and work in widely separated urban areas. This often makes it difficult to attempt to reconcile these commitments and realities with the demands of a research schedule. In order to identify relevant groups, I began by conducting a broad-ranging Internet search for groups identifying themselves as being involved in Zapatista solidarity work, using both keyword searches through search engines and employing the links provided by reliable Zapatista solidarity sites such as Chiapas-95 (www.eco.utexas.edu/Homepages/faculty/Cleaver/chiapas95 .html) and ¡Ya basta! (www.ezln.org).

What quickly became obvious was that while many of these groups once existed many had long since disappeared with only outdated Web presences testifying to their past existence. Nevertheless, there remained a wide range of active Zapatista solidarity groups in the United States and Canada and upon identifying them, introductory e-mails were sent explaining the project and my academic, personal, and political interests in it and in working with them. Initially, I attempted to target the most prominent and well-known organizations such as Mexico Solidarity Network and Global Exchange, but I quickly expanded my scope to include smaller, lesser-known Zapatista solidarity groups. Some groups never responded to my requests, a circumstance I had anticipated given the academic interest in these types of movements and the meagre return social movements often receive as a result of their participation. It seems a sad truth that few academics contribute meaningfully to the struggles of the social movements and organizations which they seek to study, but it is not my purpose to consider this point here.

My search also convinced me of the value of branching out to explore some of the more unexpected manifestations of the resonance of Zapatismo. Rather than focusing only upon Zapatista solidarity organizations, I began to search for groups which had found inspiration in Zapatismo but had sought to interpret it according to their own contexts and to materialize it accordingly. Again, I almost always made initial contact with groups via e-mail and if they expressed interest in the project I proceeded to make further connections with activists outside of the immediate contact people. While thirty may not seem to be an overwhelming number of research partners, I would suggest that given that many of the groups with whom I worked function with very small bodies of full-time activists, thirty is indeed a significant number. This is particularly so considering that the work of many of these activists is disseminated to much wider circles of people and the impact of this activism often has social and political repercussions far beyond the core group of activists involved in the day-to-day work of any given project. Throughout this work, I draw extensively from the conversations and encounters I had with my research partners in order to explore the reasons for and consequences of the transnational resonance of Zapatismo. Before proceeding to this however, a brief overview of these organizations and collectives is necessary in order to establish a context for what follows.

In a more 'traditional' vein, organizations such as Building Bridges based in Vancouver, British Colombia, and Global Exchange based in San Francisco, California, have perhaps responded to the Zapatistas in more familiar solidaristic capacities; Building Bridges through the training and accreditation of human rights observers who then travel to Chiapas to live in Zapatista communities and Global Exchange through the building of 'people to people ties' through facilitating reality tours to Chiapas and other places. Not disimilarly, Zapatismo inspired the work of three 'hacktivists' from the University of Toronto to travel to Guatemala City, Guatemala, and Chiapas, Mexico, in the summer of 2003 in order to provide their technical expertise to organizations working to support Indigenous struggles, a journey which was documented in the film *Hacktivista*. In a more explicitly political manner, the Mexico Solidarity Network (MSN) in the United States grouped over ninety organizations together and emerged initially in the aftermath of the Acteal massacre in 1998 in order to support the Zapatistas. MSN has since expanded its focus considerably to include an emphasis on trade agreements and on U.S. militarism. In Canada, Food for Chiapas emerged in Toronto in April of 1994 in order to respond to the needs of the Zapatista communities in Chiapas.

Yet if these organizations could be said to represent a more 'traditional' political response to Zapatismo, there are most certainly individuals and organizations in Canada and the U.S. which have felt the impact of Zapatismo and translated its meanings in other ways as well. Radical filmmakers such as members of Big Noise Tactical – who produced the films *This Is What Democracy Looks Like*, *Zapatista* and, most recently, *The Fourth World War* – locate a large part of the inspiration for their work in the resonance of Zapatismo. Filmmakers and activists working with the Chiapas Media Project, a bi-national project between the U.S. and Mexico, provide the resources and training to Indigenous communities in Chiapas, Oaxaca, and Guerrero, so that they can tell their own stories about their own struggles. The Third Intercontinental Encuentro for Humanity and Against Neoliberalism – an initiative inspired by and modelled on the original Zapatista Intergalactic Encuentro held in the jungles of Chiapas in 1996 – was to be held in the summer of 2003 in Ontario and was to bring together Indigenous peoples, academics, labour activists, people involved in Latin American solidarity movements, and others in an effort to see it realized. While the Encuentro did not materialize ultimately, the vision which inspired it nevertheless stands as a testament to the resonance of Zapatismo.

Related to the Zapatista Encuentros is the transnational network of anti-capitalist coordination and communication known as Peoples' Global Action (PGA), which has been at the heart of the majority of anti-capitalist spectacles and mass demonstrations since its formation in 1998. It emerged as a direct response to the Zapatistas' call for a transnational network of communication 'for humanity and against neoliberalism,' and has been an effective coordinating and communication tool for a multiplicity of distinct struggles globally without having become an 'organization' itself. The smartMeme Strategy and Training Project is aimed at grassroots movement building and the injection of new ideas into culture, to intervene in capitalism 'at the point of assumption.' While the project itself is not directly related to Zapatismo, those lessons and examples have resonated strongly with its founding members. Finally, the Ontario Coalition Against Poverty, although by no means a Zapatista-inspired organization, displays a commitment to grassroots community organizing and its explicitly revolutionary and anti-capitalist stance demonstrate its affinity with groups such as the Zapatistas, a resemblance which OCAP's own organizers and members assert.

In addition to these interviews and engagements, during the course of my fieldwork I participated as a member of a solidarity delegation organized by the Mexico Solidarity Network to Zapatista communities in August 2004 and spent an additional four weeks conducting research in Chiapas, Mexico. My research also involved extensive analysis of the mechanisms and means facilitating the transnational transmission, translation, and resonance of the political imagination of Zapatismo. Such mechanisms and means include the communiqués issued by the EZLN as well as the writings of Subcomandante Marcos; the abundance of DVDs, videos, and photographic material circulated about the Zapatistas and their struggle as well as their connection to the global anti-capitalist and global justice movement; virtual methods of communication linked to the Zapatistas and to the activist groups they have engaged in Canada and the U.S. such as websites and e-mail distribution lists; and, finally, the plethora of writings that has emerged from the global anti-capitalist/justice movement and that has served to explicitly affirm the significance of Zapatismo and the Zapatista uprising with respect to this 'movement of movements.'

Theoretically, I draw upon a diverse group of scholars in order to explore the terrains of the political imagination and resonance. Rather than focusing on an established body of work or school of thought, I instead engage a variety of theoretical traditions, including autonomist Marxism, the Frankfurt School, globalization, post-structuralism, and social movement analysis. While I recognize the considerable diversity of this theoretical terrain, I have drawn upon these traditions precisely because they offer powerful conceptual tools for illuminating the contours and dimensions of phenomena like resonance and political imagination. In engaging such thinkers as Arjun Appadurai, Roland Barthes, Ernst Bloch, Guy Debord, Gilles Deleuze and Felix Guattari, John Holloway, Michael Hardt and Antonio Negri, as well as a selection of anthropologists and cultural writers, I acknowledge that these theoretical and analytical fields by no means necessarily form a coherent or singular terrain, nor do they always agree with one another. I do not, however, see contradiction or an uneven terrain as inherently problematic. Indeed, for my purposes here I contend that only an eclectic group of scholars representing a variety of traditions is suited to informing an exploration of the phenomenon of resonance, the field of the political imagination, and the socio-political consequences and possibilities they engage.

Echoes That Re-Echo: The Bases and Consequences of Resonance

The connections of each of these organizations to the Zapatista movement varies greatly as do the experiences of the individuals involved with respect to Zapatismo. Certainly, no consideration of the transmission and reception of the Zapatista struggle can avoid acknowledging the fact that pre-existing political solidarity networks focused on Latin America, Indigenous peoples, and human rights played a significant role in the transmission and translation of the struggle (see Arquilla et al. 1998); however, beyond issues of pre-existing infrastructure and an activist community which had some familiarity with the region, what could account for the significance attributed by U.S. and Canadian supporters to Zapatismo in the aftermath of the uprising in 1994? This question should be considered in relation to the fact that the EZLN is far from the only, let alone the most dangerous, armed insurgent organization in Mexico. In fact, in the years following the Zapatista uprising, the Popular Revolutionary Army (EPR) staged a series of bold and violent attacks on police and military installations, demonstrating a willingness and proficiency with respect to violent action that the Zapatistas never approached (see Ross 2000). Unlike insurrectionary movements of the past such as the Sandinistas under Carlos Fonseca and Daniel Ortega and the Cuban revolutionaries under Fidel Castro and Che Guevara, the Zapatistas did not attempt to capture the state and its infrastructure for their project nor have they managed to force significant concessions from the Mexican government.

As I will argue throughout this book, the transnational resonance of Zapatismo is a complex and multifaceted phenomenon, and its bases of emergence are equally so. I explore these bases explicitly in this work, but by way of an introduction to the analysis that follows, it is important to realize that these bases are intimately connected to the realities within which activists themselves live and work. Notions of hope, creativity, human dignity, communication, democracy, and what could be termed an intellectual and political cosmopolitanism occupy places of prominence with respect to the landscape of this transnational resonance of Zapatismo. These elements, I would argue, are most certainly present in Zapatismo, all the more so with respect to the communiqués and communicative actions directed towards supporters transnationally, but they also speak to needs (a powerful rejection of neoliberalism; affirmation of human dignity; peace; autonomy and interconnectedness; the desire to speak and be heard as well as to listen) and means (communicative and symbolic rather than violent action) familiar to people struggling within 'First World' or 'post-industrial' societies like Canada and the United States. Less apparent, but by no means always absent, from this perspective on Zapatismo are the complexities of the Zapatista struggle on the ground in Chiapas, the mundane work of building relations of 'good government' amongst the communities and municipalities in rebellion, and the unavoidable contradictions that occupy the sphere of human action.

As I will discuss in the following chapters, to a certain extent this 'discrepancy' in the 'content' of Zapatismo between the on-the-ground experience in Chiapas and its transnationalized manifestation indicate almost a double movement with respect to the political imagination of

Zapatismo. This is not, however, a matter of labelling one of these move-ments 'authentic' and the other 'inauthentic.' Resonance and the politi-cal imagination are by no means uncomplicated phenomena, they are practices and processes deeply enmeshed in terrains of communication and experience and as such they reflect the intentions, hopes, and desires as well as the mistakes, miscommunications, and failures of all parties in this encounter. This of course means that power relations and issues of privilege are always present, but it also means that these reso-nances and their consequences are also not reducible simply to them.

Information about the Zapatista struggle has been transmitted via information technologies such as the Internet and the production of vid-eos and DVDs as well as through the movement of activists across bor-ders (primarily from North to South) in roles ranging from casual 'Zapatouristas' to human rights observers to peace campers to solidar-ity delegations. Yet it should be clear that such 'flows' of people, images, and information are by no means neutral and rely upon the character-istics, both social and technological, often attributed to so-called post-industrial societies such as Canada and the United States. In fact, while much has been made of the Zapatistas' presence on the Internet and the media-savviness of their spokesperson Subcomandante Marcos, many Zapatista communities lack basic utilities such as electricity and running water, let alone access to the Internet or international travel. Michael Hardt and Antonio Negri state in *Empire* (2000), today 'the imaginary is guided and channeled within the communicative machine,' a process resulting not simply in the imaginary and the sym-bolic being put at the service of power but rather 'actually integrating them into its very functioning' (33). The very channels used to deploy and engage these Zapatista-inspired political landscapes are simulta-neously deeply linked to other processes that form a significant portion of the Zapatistas' rationale for rising up in rebellion in the first place.

I do not hold, however, a reductive or deterministic view of this dis-crepancy in wealth and access. Much as the impact of Zapatismo has all too often been reduced to Marcos's communicative abilities, valid criti-cisms of aspects of the international response to Zapatismo have been turned into sweeping denunciations of the international solidarity movement. In these analyses, North American and European support-ers of the Zapatista movement have been criticized for a number of unfortunate and even damaging tendencies, including a facile romanti-cism of Indigenous peoples and armed insurgency; an overreliance on 'virtual' as opposed to 'real' images of the struggle in Chiapas; a desire to look for revolution 'somewhere else' rather than facing issues of concern 'at home'; and an obsession on the part of foreign supporters of the Zapatista movement with the 'trope' of Chiapas (see Hellman 2000; Meyer 2002). Once again, this is not to say that such assertions are not accurate with respect to some elements of the international solidarity movement. It is to say, however, that just as pointing to Marcos's writing or the Internet does not explain why Zapatismo has resonated beyond Chiapas neither does focusing on criticisms of elements of a tremendously diverse network of supporters offer a complete or convincing picture of why people paid attention to the uprising initially, nor does it account for the deep impact Zapatismo has had upon the emergent global social justice and anti-capitalist movement.

As for Subcomandante Marcos himself, his literary voice can be found throughout this work in the form of excerpts from interviews and communiqués. But the presence of Marcos's voice should not be mistaken for an identification of Zapatismo with Marcos. As the EZLN's military strategist and spokesperson, the figure of Marcos and his prolific writings have become well known both within and beyond the borders of Mexico. However, the survival and successes of the Zapatista movement is indisputably due not to any single individual's creative capacities but to the collective efforts of men, women, and children engaged in the daily struggle to build a new world. While Marcos has received substantial praise – and criticism – for various actions engaged in by the EZLN and the Zapatista movement since 1994, this personalistic identification says far more about the focus, frames, and narratives adopted by often distanced analysts than it does about the movement itself. Furthermore, while Marcos has achieved a considerable level of notoriety – some might even say 'celebrity' – amongst certain sectors of the international community, this phenomenon is by no means identical with the resonance of Zapatismo that I seek to trace and illuminate here. Indeed, while the majority of activists with whom I worked recognized the significance of Marcos as a communicator and strategist, their experiences of resonance and the consequences that derived from it clearly and explicitly exceeded any narrow cult of personality.

Communication and Rhizomes of Struggle

In *Empire*, Michael Hardt and Antonio Negri (2000) offer a provocative analytical perspective with respect to the Zapatista uprising that provides a useful opportunity to explicitly address issues of circulation and communication with respect to political struggles. In their analysis, Hardt and Negri contend that the Zapatista rebellion was not able to stimulate other revolutionary struggles nor was it able to form a link in a chain of struggles because 'the desires and needs [it] expressed could not be translated into different contexts' and thus people in other parts of the world could not recognize it as their own struggle as well (54). Contemporary struggles such as that of the Zapatistas, Hardt and Negri maintain, have become 'incommunicable and thus blocked from travelling horizontally in the form of a cycle,' for two primary reasons: first, because the 'nature of the common enemy is obscured'; and second, because 'no common language exists to translate the particular language of each struggle into a "cosmopolitan" language' (ibid., 57). This notion of a cycle of struggle thus extends beyond a politics based in solidarity to metaphorically resemble 'a virus that modulates its form to find in each context an adequate host' (ibid., 51), and this is precisely what Hardt and Negri contend that contemporary political struggles have been unable to achieve. Yet while it is not clear that all U.S. and Canadian activists inspired by the Zapatista movement would articulate the Zapatista struggle as their own struggle, it is also difficult not to take issue with Hardt and Negri's assessment that Zapatismo has remained somehow 'incommunicable.' Communication, sustained by more traditional sources such as the Mexican newspaper *La Jornada* as well as e-mail distribution lists such as Chiapas-95 and the Web presence of activist independent media such as Indymedia Chiapas, has played a key role in the transmission of Zapatismo transnationally. Furthermore, and contrary to Hardt and Negri's assertions, Zapatismo and the language and iconography of the Zapatista movement itself have come to occupy an increasingly important place within the repertoire of global anti-capitalist and social justice activism. While this convergence has by no means resulted in the emergence of the 'cycle of struggle' that Hardt and Negri discuss, nor has it even necessarily led to a drastic improvement in the lives of Zapatistas on the ground in Chiapas, the impact of Zapatismo upon the scope of struggles elsewhere has certainly not been insignificant.

Gilles Deleuze and Felix Guattari engage many of the issues later picked up by Hardt and Negri in *A Thousand Plateaus: Capitalism and Schizophrenia* (1987), particularly with respect to concepts such as imagination, communication, and the dynamics of political struggle. One of the core concepts deployed by these scholars is the notion of the 'rhizome,' which is, strictly speaking, a tuber or bulb possessing both shoots and roots (3). Yet the rhizome is also a new way of thinking about realities, particularly when counterposed to the image of the tree or the root; in fact, I would argue that the notion of the rhizome not only provides a new way of thinking about realities writ large but also provides a new way of thinking about such phenomena as social movements and the imagination. Composed of 'dimensions, or rather directions in motion,' the rhizome has no essential essence, it changes as the relations that comprise it change (ibid., 21), and it certainly bears a conceptual resemblance to the viral metaphor employed by Hardt and Negri with respect to a cycle of struggles. The rhizome is not a network, it is not a 'structure' of any kind, and as such, its application to such phenomena as the political imagination and social movements is profound and radical in its consequences. What the notion of the rhizome encourages is an explicit consideration of the dynamics of political struggle and the relationships between individuals and groups therein rather than focusing upon 'cause-and-effect' relations. Thus the rhizome as a conceptual and analytical tool should not be seen as a way of bypassing or replacing social movement theory so much as a metaphor through which to explore different dynamics and consequences of contemporary social movement activity.

In fact, as an explanatory tool in and of itself, the rhizome offers us very little; rather, its true value lies in conceptually re-mapping how social movements and their organizations 'fit together,' how they interrelate, and with what consequences. This reorients the analytical gaze from questions of resources or 'successes' and 'failures' to a focus on the complexity of socio-political struggle and its often unanticipated outcomes. I argue that transnationalized Zapatismo is rhizomatic, just as its impact upon U.S. and Canadian activists has rhizomatic qualities. It needs to be understood in this fashion precisely because the experience of it has been shaped not only by the concrete struggles of Zapatistas in Chiapas or by the eloquence and literary flair of Subcomandante Marcos but also by the actors who have taken up the challenge of communicating it, the technologies employed to disseminate it, and the desires, needs, and socio-political realities of those who have received it.

The relationship between Zapatismo and the rise of global anticapitalism is one which has been considered by several authors, including Naomi Klein (2002), Paul Kingsnorth (2003), and the editorial collectives Midnight Notes (2001) and Notes from Nowhere (2003). While it was initially the World Trade Organization (WTO) protests in Seattle in 1999 that garnered so much attention with respect to the emergence of this 'movement of movements,' it has since been much more widely acknowledged by those involved with the movement itself that 1 January 1994 and the Zapatista uprising is a much more significant moment in this history. Within Mexico, the works of Adolfo Gilly (1998), Xóchitl Leyva Solano (1998), Luis Hernández Navarro (2002), and Carlos Monsiváis (2002) provide excellent insight into the national resonance of Zapatismo. My own work on the intersection between Zapatismo and the independent labour movement in Mexico also contributes to this field of analysis (Khasnabish 2004, 2005). Yet transnationally, the resonance of Zapatismo and its consequences have remained largely unconsidered.

The Transnational Terrain of Resonance, Imagination, and Political Action: Organization and Overview

This book is organized into seven chapters, each addressing a specific thematic area; however, these chapters are by no means distinct or easily segregated from one another. In the first chapter, 'Power, Democracy, and (Re)shaping the Terrain of Political Struggle,' I provide an exploration of the theoretical perspective that shapes my analysis in this work. More than an interpretive framework, in this chapter I seek to situate my analysis of the transnational resonance of the Zapatista political imagination upon a terrain of political possibility marked by significant social, economic, and political transformations most often grouped together under the banner of 'globalization.' This terrain – and the political subjectivities that inhabit it – come to bear directly upon the political challenges and possibilities facing us today. While I argue strongly for this emergent terrain and these subjectivities, I do not contend that either of them are fully present. Rather, I contend that they are emerging tendencies and, like all social phenomena, will be imbued with force and presence only if dedicated human agency inspires them. Right now they are only vectors of possibility, not fully formed realities. Nevertheless, I argue that this is the space within which the transnational resonance of Zapatismo is best understood and within which its emerging consequences are best appreciated.

In the second chapter, 'Northern Struggles, Northern Histories,' I engage in an analysis of the histories of radical political activism in Canada and the United States, in general since the end of the Second World War but most specifically since the mid-1980s. By engaging these histories of northern activism, I seek not only to provide a context within which to situate the transnational resonance of Zapatismo but also to demonstrate that northern radical political action has its own histories that help to shape the possibilities for imagining and practising new kinds of politics. By invoking the term 'history,' I refer not only to authorized genealogies of socio-political resistance and alternative-building, much less to official narratives of social and political change. Instead, I seek to draw attention to the fact that these genealogies – whatever their political inclination – are never simply discrete or empirical accounts; rather, they are stories that are constantly reconstructed and retold from a multitude of perspectives and, in so doing, they form what I consider to be a body of mythological political history. This is not to say that these histories are somehow 'false' or 'untrue,' but rather that they are powerful vehicles for the creation of certain kinds of possibilities, terrains, and subjectivities. As Vinay Lal (2002) has argued with respect to history and the politics of knowledge, 'a critical interrogation of the received view of history calls for a hermeneutics which would bring us to the awareness that some forms of remembrance are but forms of forgetfulness' (121). I would contend, in a similar vein, that some forms of remembrance facilitate the capacity to recognize certain possibilities and radically foreclose upon others. It is these histories, and the possibilities and limitations they offer, that I explore in this chapter.

In the third chapter, 'Dreams of Revolution, Myths of Power: Mexican Revolutionary Histories,' I address the interlacing issues of the history of the Zapatista Army of National Liberation and the mythology of revolution in Mexico. Once again, by 'mythology' I do not mean to imply that the revolution in Mexico from 1910–17 did not occur. Rather, I seek to draw attention to the fact that the legacy of the revolution has become the target of appropriation, particularly on the part of post-revolutionary elites, in the service of a variety of socio-political and economic projects. In this sense, as with the histories of northern radical political struggles, the story of revolution has become a powerful interpellating myth in Mexico, a story which the Zapatistas have actively sought to contest and recapture. This chapter explores the history of the emergence of the EZLN as a 'reformulation' of various Mexican revolutionary trajectories infused with a new and powerful political critique of power; a history and critique that would significantly impact Zapatismo's resonance transnationally. This chapter also considers the bases of the resonance of Zapatismo within the Mexican national context.

In the fourth chapter, 'Echoes and Openings: Resonance,' I explore the

concept of 'resonance' as well as the evidence for and bases of the resonance of Zapatismo amongst activists in Canada and the United States.
This chapter focuses particularly on the resonance of Zapatismo with
respect to the global anti-capitalist/global justice movement and the
dynamics of the processes of transmission, translation, and resonance
that such a connection reveals. The fifth chapter, 'Imagining Struggle/
Struggling to Imagine: Imagination and Political Action,' explores the
concept of the 'imagination' as it relates to radical political projects, particularly in an increasingly globalized era. Engaging both scholarly
debates surrounding the imagination as well as my research partners'
reflections with respect to it, I seek to trace the powerful significance of
imagination as it relates to the political and particularly to the search for
new political spaces and practices.

   In the sixth chapter, 'New Horizons: Resonance and Political Action,'
I undertake an extensive analysis of some of the most powerful examples of the rhizomatic histories of political action to which the transnational resonance of Zapatismo has given rise in the United States and
Canada. In this chapter, my focus is limited to examples of resonance
that I consider to be closer to 'traditional' or more familiar solidaristic
modes of activism that have arisen as a result of the resonance of Zapatismo in the North. In addition, I also explore what I term the 'dark
side' of dynamics of resonance. Rather than subverting the significance
of resonance, in the second half of this chapter I seek to provide a constructive critique of some of the dangers, pitfalls, and failures of the
dynamics of transnational resonance with respect to meaningful political action. In the seventh and final chapter, 'New Terrains: Mapping
Emerging Possibilities in a Transnational Field of Action,' I continue to
develop the political terrain shaped by the transnational resonance of
Zapatismo but this time with an eye towards what I consider to be perhaps more 'innovative' or 'experimental' rhizomatic histories of resonance in Canada and the United States. The analysis I present here does
not aim to provide a comprehensive or definitive account of these new
terrains, subjectivities, and political imaginations; rather, it seeks to
offer an analysis of what I consider to be an emerging tendency, a possibility, rather than a picture of a fully formed reality.

   Notions of hope and inspiration are deeply implicated in understanding the impact of Zapatismo in Canada and the United States. Similarly,
the resonance of Zapatismo cannot be understood outside of the specific
contexts within which those who respond to it live and work. So in 1994,
at a time when neoliberal capitalism appeared uncontestedly globally

ascendant and the organized left appeared in tatters, the Zapatista uprising burst explosively on to the horizon. Yet the image of armed rebellion was only as successful as the significance attributed to the Zapatistas allowed it to be. After twelve days of fighting, the EZLN had been brutally driven back into the Lacandón Jungle, the Mexican army appeared poised to eliminate them completely, and yet now more than a decade later the EZLN has survived, Zapatista communities in Chiapas continue to consolidate their autonomy, and the landscape of distinct forms of political activism in the United States and Canada has been indelibly marked by Zapatismo.

So how can this resonance be explained? This question lies at the heart of this project and I will explore it thoroughly in what follows. Here I merely wish to offer some introductory thoughts to structure the analysis to come. The transnational resonance of Zapatismo emerges from many interconnected bases and has produced consequences both diverse and interrelated. For many of the activists with whom I spoke both in Canada and in the U.S., Zapatismo offered precisely what mainstream channels of political participation do not: hope, creativity, imagination, poetry, dialogue, and space. Rather than rallying people with calls for state socialism, the Zapatistas instead took up arms and then took the path of transnational dialogue under such banners as 'democracy, liberty, and justice,' a life lived with dignity, commanding by obeying, and walking questioning. They said they masked themselves in order to be seen, armed themselves in order to be heard, and fought not to kill or be killed but to live a life worth living. For activists disillusioned by the defeat of state socialism and numbed by capitalism's ascendancy, the radically democratic and dignified spirit of Zapatismo was infectious and inspiring. Perhaps even more significantly, even as the Zapatistas sought support and recognition for their own struggle, they simultaneously acknowledged and supported the struggles of others both in Mexico and around the world.

. As the Zapatista communities in Chiapas continued to struggle against a state of low-intensity war while building autonomous and sustainable communities, Subcomandante Insurgente Marcos continued to engage national and international civil society in a dialogue about building a new kind of world. This dialogue resulted in the First Intercontinental Encuentro for Humanity and Against Neoliberalism in the jungles of Chiapas in August 1996, which drew thousands of participants from around the world and which would culminate in a call for the realization of an 'International Order of Hope' to build resistance and alternatives to global neoliberal capitalism. The following year, the Second Encuentro would be held in Spain and would serve as the springboard for the emergence of Peoples' Global Action. More recently, the Zapatistas held another Intercontinental Encuentro in the highlands of Chiapas in December 2006 in order to discuss the contours of global resistance to neoliberal capitalism, and yet another was held in the summer of 2007. But aside from the numerous encounters and spectacles organized by the Zapatistas since 1994, it has been the ways in which people in their own places have responded to Zapatismo which has been most telling. As North American political channels become ever more professionalized, rationalized, and remote, alienation and disillusionment become defining characteristics of social engagement and political responsibility. As measures of political participation and confidence throughout the U.S. and Canada continue to fall (Crotty 1991; Nevitte 1996) and for many people already dissatisfied with the corporate liberal democracy in those countries, the issue becomes not how to take power but rather how to change the world without taking power. In this sense, the Zapatista struggle for autonomy and their commitment to direct democracy resonate far beyond the borders of Chiapas.

Without exception, the activists with whom I have spoken all cite personal and profound experiences with diverse forms of injustice as essential elements in provoking their desire to act politically in the world. Furthermore, the vast majority of these activists also cite their deeply held belief that in order to address the various sources of social injustice, one needs to operate outside of official channels of political action. Compounding this is a sophisticated and thoughtful awareness of several interlacing factors: first, the connections between contemporary neoliberal capitalism and existing structures of political and economic power and long-standing historical systems of oppression such as racism, patriarchy, colonialism, and imperialism; secondly, an intellectual and personal awareness of the contemporary dimensions of violence and inequality generated by neoliberal capitalism both at home and globally; thirdly, a rejection of structures of political action that rest upon imposing new structures of domination and violence as well as a rejection of pre-fabricated plans for post-capitalist society; fourthly and finally, a commitment to taking personal responsibility to realize change, often through diverse forms of direct action, and to challenging the legitimacy of existing systems of power and privilege. This is not to say that the political activists who have shared their thoughts and experiences with me have not encountered moments of contradiction or that they have been unequivocally successful in achieving their aims, far from it. In fact, several of my research partners have commented on what politely might be called the 'disjunctures' between the predominantly white global justice movement and resistance communities in the global South and on the creation of an 'institutionalized solidarity sector' that actually participates in the further subordination of peoples in the South.

Often, and sometimes accurately, these activists are accused of having 'romanticized' struggles in other places, particularly those in the South, and often to the detriment of the very people engaged in those struggles. It must be acknowledged that this 'romanticism' has certainly come into play with respect to northern activists' views of the Zapatista movement and has indeed had negative consequences in some instances, yet I wish to posit a different interpretation of this romantic sentiment. Is the desire to romanticize not also linked to a desire to reinvigorate a world that has been sapped of its magic, vitality, and spirit? Certainly for the Romantic poets, playwrights, and authors of the late eighteenth and early nineteenth centuries, their work was inspired in part as a response to the epistemological violence of the Enlightenment, which had resulted in a profound disenchantment of the world – a disenchantment which they sought to contest and a world which they sought to reimagine through their writings.

Undoubtedly, the writings of Zapatista spokesperson Subcomandante Marcos strive to accomplish much the same ends, written as they are both in a style and substance that seeks not simply to provoke revolutionary fervour but a reimagining of the world, of its multiple realities, and of the dreams, hopes, and aspirations of the people who share it. This is also reflected in the carnival atmosphere that accompanies so many of the global anti-capitalist movement's protests. This is not to say that this romantic impulse is not problematic, nor is it to say that the intentions with which it is done are unselfish; rather, it is to say that this impulse needs to be considered in relation to the context in which it occurs and the relations and conditions which it seeks to resist and subvert.

An example of resistance; a thoughtful, democratic struggle for autonomy; a monumental gesture of defiance against the seemingly indomitable force of global neoliberal capitalism; a movement that cherishes life and laughter and connectedness; a demonstration of how tactics, strategies, and goals must always be considered in the context within which they are set and must always be subordinated to the will and the needs of the people they affect. These are but a few reasons why Zapatismo has resonated so profoundly within activist communities in the U.S. and Canada. They are issues that I will explore more fully in what follows. The Zapatistas offer an example, they offer hope, and they speak of the things that so many people living within the belly of the neoliberal beast are desperately seeking within their own lives: dignity, autonomy, justice, democracy, and liberty. As many of my research partners noted, the Zapatistas do not offer a template for struggle here in Canada or in the United States; rather, they offer a symbol of resistance and the creative search for alternatives which, despite dominant narratives to the contrary, is neither futile nor an anachronism.

Of course, this inspiration does not address the deep set inequalities between activists and organizations in the North and the South – many of my own research partners have commented on the fact that one of the most productive things northern activists and intellectuals could do is to help facilitate connections between movements in the South and to accompany their struggles rather than try to lead them. Furthermore, many, though not all, of my research partners also spoke of their belief that true challenges to neoliberal capitalism, empire, and injustice come, and will continue to come, from the South rather than from the North, principally because the success of neoliberalism here has foreclosed on so many spaces and alienated so many people from one another. Does this not itself reflect a decisive – and not unproblematic – reason for the resonance of Zapatismo transnationally? Zapatistas, distant and dramatic agents of revolutionary change, who embody the desire to rebel felt by those whose own lives – filled with complexity and contradiction – could not support the same radical action. Yet Zapatismo continues to inspire political activism in the U.S. and Canada in a diversity of forms, ranging from solidarity campaigns to direct action to information and image-based struggles. In many cases, this inspiration has been 'indirect,' that is, it has inhabited people who have not made the pilgrimage, as one of my research partners termed it, to Chiapas and who have never 'seen' a Zapatista. Instead, it has come via Marcos' writings, Zapatista communiqués, and images of struggle transmitted via solidarity networks, often employing technologies much more familiar and accessible to activist communities in the North than to Zapatista communities in the South. This inspiration has also filtered from one group to another, taking on different forms as it does so, and dialogically engaging other socio-political and cultural threads. These are complicated – and sometimes deeply conflicted – issues that I will address more fully shortly.

Aside from the communicative infrastructure and the often 'spectacular' nature of the Zapatista struggle, the kernels of transnationalized Zapatismo – a vision of a world in which many worlds fit, an image of connectedness and autonomy, an emphasis on dialogue with respect and peace built with dignity – rather than asserting a pre-fabricated solution to neoliberal capitalism or affirming a singular experience or essence as the 'true' one, speaks to a wide array of concerned citizens and political activists. In this sense, Zapatismo as a discourse is one which, particularly via the mediation provided by Subcomandante Marcos, is capable of effectively addressing the realities and struggles of northern activists in Canada and the United States by virtue both of its legitimacy as an Indigenous-based movement as well as its 'cosmo-political' sensibilities emphasizing a deep commitment to autonomy and self-determination while simultaneously pushing towards greater human interconnectedness, understanding, and co-operation. These are some of the most provocative contours of the transnational resonance of Zapatismo. In what follows, I will explore the complexity and power, the promise and the contradiction of these dynamics, and I will strive to illuminate not only their contemporary consequences but also the significance they hold for political horizons, terrains, and subjectivities that are only beginning to emerge.

1 Power, Democracy, and (Re)shaping the Terrain of Political Struggle

Durito says that all the multiple options being offered by the Powers conceal a trap.

'Where there are many paths, and we're presented with the chance to choose, something fundamental is forgotten: all those paths lead to the same place. And so, liberty consists not in choosing the destination, the place, the speed and the company, but in merely choosing the path. The liberty which the Powerful are offering is, in fact, merely the liberty to choose who will walk representing us,' Durito says.

And Durito says that, in reality, the Power offers no liberty other than that of choosing among multiple options of death. You can choose the nostalgic model, that of forgetting. That is the one which is being offered, for example, to the Mexican indigenous as being the most suitable for their idiosyncrasies.

Or you can also choose the modernizing model, that of frenetic exploitation. This is the one which is being offered, for example, to the Latin American middle classes as being the most suitable for their patterns of consumption.

Or, if not, you can choose the futuristic model, that of 21st century weapons. This is the one, for example, being offered by the guided missiles in Iraq and which, so that there may be no doubt as to their democratic spirit, kill Iraqis as well as North Americans, Saudi Arabians, Iranians, Kurds, Brits and Kuwaitis (the nationalities which have accrued in just one week).

There are many other models, one for almost every taste and preference. Because if there is anything neoliberalism is able to pride itself on, it is on offering an almost infinite variety of deaths. And no other political system in the history of humanity can say that.

Then Durito puts a vase with water on the little table, which is made of sticks, tied together with liana, and he says: 'The Powers tell us, for example, that we have to choose between being optimists or pessimists. The pessimist sees the glass as being half empty, the optimist sees the glass as half full. But the rebel realizes that neither the vase, nor the water which it contains, belong to them, and it is someone else, the powerful, who fills it and empties it at his whim. The rebel, on the other hand, sees the trap. But he also sees the spring from which the water issues forth.'

'And so, when the rebel faces the option of choosing between various paths, he looks further ahead and he looks twice: he sees that those routes lead to the same place, and he sees that there is no path to the place where he wishes to go. Then the rebel, instead of agonizing over polls which say that one path is better than the other because such and such a percent cannot be wrong, begins building a new path,' says Durito, while handing out many 'Nos' on little pieces of paper of all colors in front of North American embassies throughout the world, which, as everyone knows, look suspiciously like plastic burger shops.

'Durito and One about False Options,' Subcomandante
Insurgente Marcos (2004b)

I have chosen to begin this chapter with this tale by Zapatista spokesperson Subcomandante Insurgente Marcos for several reasons, which I hope will become clear as my narrative unfolds. For the purposes of clarity, and for those who are not familiar with Marcos's fables, Durito is 'sometimes a detective, sometimes a political analyst, sometimes a knight-errant as well as a writer of epistles' (Subcomandante Insurgente Marcos 2001e, 289). Durito, it should be noted, is also a beetle. Since 1995, Durito has travelled with Marcos, 'righting wrongs, rescuing damsels in distress, healing the sick, aiding the weak, instructing the ignorant, humbling the mighty, and exalting the humble' and 'holding up for us a mirror to the future, showing us what might be' (ibid., 289). Durito and his tales are a vehicle for the articulation of the political imagination inspiring Zapatismo, they are conduits for expression that need not conform to the discourse of the Zapatista declarations and communiqués. Durito and his stories – and 'Durito and One About False Options' is an excellent example of this – speak powerfully to the ways in which the transnationalized imagination of Zapatismo has sought to provoke a (re)shaping of the terrain of political struggle. But this assertion anticipates the analysis to come. Before considering specific issues of transnational resonance, its bases and consequences, and the concrete manifestations of the transnational resonance of the political imagination of Zapatismo in the North, there are northern histories of struggle and a shifting terrain of political action that require attention.

In the chapters to follow, I will explore some of the particular dynamics and consequences of the transnational resonance of Zapatismo amongst northern activists. Through this analysis, I seek to demonstrate that while the resonance of Zapatismo has inspired a wide array of political activism and the emergence of new collectives and organizations, perhaps the most significant contribution of Zapatismo transnationally has been the ways in which it has facilitated a radical questioning and reshaping of the grounds upon which radically democratic and anti-capitalist political struggle can occur. In this vein, I argue that the Zapatistas have provided not only a new language through which to express political alternatives, they have opened the possibility for the emergence of new kinds of political subjectivities. However, in order to undertake this exploration, it is first necessary to examine the two foundational elements upon which my analysis rests.

The first of these elements, and the one upon which this chapter is focused, is the theoretical framework within which my analysis of the transnational resonance of Zapatismo is situated. Drawing from a range of political theorists and philosophers – including Gilles Deleuze and Felix Guattari, Susan Buck-Morss, John Holloway, Nick Dyer-Witheford, Michael Hardt and Antonio Negri, Paolo Virno, and Richard Day – I situate my analysis of the transnational resonance of the Zapatista political imagination upon a terrain of political possibility marked by significant social, economic, and political transformations that have accelerated over the last twenty years. More than simply producing a new terrain, these transformations that also brought into being new kinds of subjectivities who inhabit it. This terrain and these political subjectivities come to bear directly upon the political challenges and possibilities facing us today. Here it is necessary to note that while I argue strongly for this emergent terrain and these subjectivities, I do not contend that either of them are fully present. Rather, I contend that they are emerging tendencies and, like all social phenomena, will be brought into being, aborted, maintained, altered, or abandoned depending upon the human agency that does – or does not – inspire them. Right now they are only vectors of possibility, not fully formed realities. Neverthe-

less, I argue that this is the space within which the transnational resonance of Zapatismo is best understood and within which its emerging
consequences are best appreciated.

The second foundational element of my analysis, which is the focus of
the chapter that follows, is formed by the histories of political activism
and radical political contestation as they have manifested themselves in
Canada and the United States, in general since the end of the Second
World War but most specifically since the mid-1980s. By engaging these
histories of northern activism I seek not only to offer a context within
which to situate the transnational resonance of Zapatismo but to demonstrate that northern radical political action has its own histories that
help to shape the possibilities for imagining and practising new kinds of
politics today. In invoking the historical, I am mindful of the potent critiques levelled by scholars such as Vinay Lal against the politics of
knowledge (who speaks, who writes, who decides, and with recourse to
what categories and disciplinary forms?) inherent in history-making
and the fact that 'some forms of remembrance are but forms of forgetfulness' (Lal 2002, 116–21). These critiques I contend are particularly
salient when it comes to ways of speaking that lie beyond the pale of conventional historiography, for example, when voices speak of pasts, presents, and futures in the language of prophecy, myth, or other ahistorical
forms. Can we take seriously voices that do not speak in authorized languages and the glimpses that they may provide of possible alternative
political landscapes? This question seems particularly relevant with
respect to the poetic and mythological interventions attempted by the
Zapatistas and their spokesperson Subcomandante Insurgente Marcos
since 1994, but it is also pertinent when considering the histories of political action and possibility narrated by activists in the North.

In this vein I contend that histories of political action in Canada and
the United States are narratives, sometimes authorized, sometimes not,
which are constantly reconstructed and retold from a multitude of perspectives. In so doing they form what I consider to be a body of mythological political history. By invoking the notion of the mythological, I do
not mean to imply that these histories are somehow false or untrue or
that they are merely constructed foundational stories; rather, as Roland
Barthes asserts, myth is a mode of signification consisting not just of
writing but also of other forms of representation (Barthes 1972, 109–10).
Myth is a kind of interpellating mode of signification or speech, it participates in the formation of subjects even as it engages them (ibid., 124).
In a sense, myth 'calls' to us and our subjectivity is shaped as we re-

spond to it. It is in this respect that I employ the notion of history to explore the constitutive aspects of these narratives and genealogies of radical political action in Canada and the United States. In chapter 3, I use the same concept of histories to explore the emergence of the Zapatista Army of National Liberation and the legacy of revolution in Mexico.

New Political Terrains, New Political Subjectivities

ONCE UPON A TIME there were three children. One was good, one was bad, and one was El Sup. Coming from different directions, they arrived at a house and went in. Inside the house there was only a table. On that table there was a plastic container, like the kind used for ice cream or slushies, one for each child. Inside each white plastic container (take note: they had no brand name or logo), there were two chocolate bunnies and a slip of paper. The slip of paper said:

Instructions for Using the Two Chocolate Bunnies

After 24 hours, this pair of chocolate bunnies will reproduce and make a new pair of bunnies. Every twenty-four hours thereafter, the pairs of chocolate bunnies inside this white plastic container will multiply into other pairs. In this way, the owner of this magic plastic container will always have chocolate bunnies to eat. The only condition is that there must always be one pair of chocolate bunnies inside this plastic container, like the kind used for ice cream or slushies.

Each child took his white plastic container.

The bad child couldn't wait twenty-four hours and ate his two chocolate bunnies. He enjoyed the moment, but he no longer had chocolate bunnies. Now he has none to eat, but he is left with the memory of and nostalgia for the chocolate bunnies. ·

The good child waited the twenty-four hours and was rewarded with four chocolate bunnies. After another twenty-four hours, he had eight chocolate bunnies. As the months passed, the good child opened a chain of chocolate bunny stores. After a year, he had branches all over the country. He was financed with foreign capital and began to export. He was eventually named 'Man of the Year' and became immensely rich and powerful. He eventually sold his shares in the chocolate bunny industry to foreign investors, and became a mere executive in the company. In order not to cut into the profits, he never tasted the chocolate bunnies. He no longer owns the magic white plastic container, nor does he know what chocolate bunnies taste like.

The child Sup, instead of chocolate bunnies, put walnut ice cream in the white plastic container, like the kind used for ice cream or slushies. Changing the whole premise of the story, he packed a half-liter of walnut ice cream between his chest and back, and ruined the moral of the story of the chocolate bunnies, deducing that all final options are a trap.

Neo-moral: Walnut ice cream has dangerous implications for neoliberalism.

From 'Another Cloud, Another Bottle, and Another Letter
from Durito,' Subcomandante Insurgente Marcos (2001b)

That the world is not the same place it was at the end of the Second World War or in the immediate aftermath of 1968 or after the fall of the Berlin Wall is not only axiomatic, it is a statement almost devoid of any significant meaning at all. While periodization may assist in providing historical and analytical frameworks, a fixation upon moments and events also draws the analytical gaze away from the fact that the world is never the same. Events are the products of relationships, interactions, movements, and as such the only constant state is that of flux. In order to understand the shape of political contestation and possibility, it is therefore necessary to first consider the ways in which the social itself is brought into being and the subjects to which it gives birth.

In *A Thousand Plateaus: Capitalism and Schizophrenia* (1987), Gilles Deleuze and Felix Guattari consider – amongst a tremendous variety of other things – the dynamics of the social, the articulation of subjectivity, and the implications of these processes for political possibility. In their work, Deleuze and Guattari reject the notion that subjects are ever fully formed entities; rather, they assert that 'bodies' are 'nothing but affects and local movements, differential speeds' distributed across a 'plane' (260). They contend that there are perhaps two planes, or two ways of conceptualizing the plane (there is, of course, no clear differentiation between or within these planes, they are constantly at work upon one another and within themselves). In the first instance, the plane is a 'plane of organization or development' and, while the 'plane' itself is hidden, it produces organizational and developmental principles which then structure the way that existence is experienced (ibid., 265). In the second instance, the plane is a 'plane of consistency' or 'immanence,' and in this plane 'there are no longer any forms or developments of forms; nor are there subjects or the formation of subjects.' Rather, this plane is marked only by 'relations of movement and rest, speed and slowness between unformed elements, or at least between elements that are relatively unformed, molecules and particles of all kinds' (ibid., 266). The plane of immanence is the plane of radical possibility, while the plane of organization corresponds to the desire to foreclose upon these possibilities, to impose a transcendental concept to establish order. I argue that the transnational resonance of the political imagination of Zapatismo has revitalized this plane of immanence or consistency precisely because it has led to a radical questioning not just of the dominant neoliberal capitalist order on a global scale but because the possibilities and alternatives it insists upon continually return to the notion of the radically unclosed nature of the world and of the subjectivities people have adopted in relation to it. This, however, is a point I will come to later, for now it is enough to appreciate that what Deleuze and Guattari suggest here is not a position predicated upon some apolitical postmodern relativism but rather a philosophical position that allows for a truly radical critique of hegemonic political systems and, simultaneously, facilitates an awareness that all subjectivity and all social experience is inherently and irreducibly relational.

The notion of 'immanence' is in fact a very fruitful notion to employ in exploring the possibilities with respect to contemporary social realities, particularly with regard to the experience of the social as it relates to the dynamics of 'globalization.' What is the connection between 'immanence,' contemporary geopolitical dynamics, and a politics of radical possibility? Susan Buck-Morss (2003) offers a compelling answer to this question by positing the following:

> Globalization is not new, but global 'immanence' is ... in our era of global capital, global production, global labor migrations, and global penetration by technologies of communication, there is no spatial outside, no 'other' of peoples, territory or environment against which some of us could conveniently define ourselves and, holding ourselves apart, control our fate. The global space that we inhabit in common is overdetermined, contradictory, and intractably diverse. Our lived experiences are simultaneous and incongruous, resisting division into distinct nationalities, pure ethnicities, or racial differences. We are morally accountable in a multiple world where no religion monopolizes in practice the virtue that would be needed to fight evil in its name, where there is no value-free, objective science that could ground universal, secular truth – just as there is no universal law of the market that can guarantee us a benevolent future. (93)

The immanent realities of the world described by Buck-Morss concretize the plane of immanence illuminated by Deleuze and Guattari. In this space of interconnection and incongruity, simultaneity and disjuncture, affinity and radical difference, the only assurance we have politically is that there are no singular routes to the realization of liberated, just, and dignified social realities. As the Zapatistas have sought to remind us, this openness need not be viewed with trepidation; rather, it can be seen as a source of hope, a promise that there are no final destinations, only multiple paths of possibility.

The plane of immanence, described by Deleuze and Guattari and whose contemporary contours are sketched above by Buck-Morss, is also a fundamental aspect of other critical analyses brought to bear upon the nature and consequences of globalized neoliberal capitalism. As Nick Dyer-Witheford asserts in *Cyber-Marx: Cycles and Circuits of Struggle in High-Technology Capitalism* (1999):

> This reductionism – the reductionism of capital – has today a totalizing grip on the planet. Other dominations, too, are reductive – sexism reduces women to objects for men, racism negates the humanity of people of color. But neither patriarchy nor racism has succeeded in knitting the planet together into an integrated, coordinated system of interdependencies. This is what capital is doing today, as, with the aid of new technologies, it globally maps the availability of female labor, entho-markets, migrancy flows, human gene pools, and entire animal, plant, and insect species onto its coordinates of value. (9–10)

And yet in so doing, capital helps shape the very terrain upon which new struggles capable of radically challenging and subverting it can emerge. In this sense, the possibilities for the transnational resonance of Zapatismo and the emergence of new political spaces, practices, and subjectivities are not in any way separate from capitalist processes or phenomena that seem to operate to block or capture such possibilities. The experience and recognition of 'immanence' is not inherently liberatory or oppressive, it merely points to a way of being in the world that implicates us as social beings capable of a multiplicity of relationships and bearing a limitless variety of obligations, responsibilities, and possibilities.

Concretely, the lack of separation between the realization of possibility and the processes that seek its curtailment or capture operates in clearly discernable ways. This is true in two distinct senses: first, in the sense that neoliberal capitalist processes have, and continue to be, directly implicated in constructing the reality of marginalization, exploitation, and oppression to which the Zapatistas and other contemporary anti-capitalist movements have responded; second, the global processes marshalled by neoliberal capitalism since the 1970s (such as the development and proliferation of communications and information technologies) have provided not only much of the 'infrastructure' necessary for the emergence of the possibility of transnational political resonances, but have also facilitated the articulation of what might be considered a 'global consciousness,' which has led many – although by no means all – people to conceive of the realities they inhabit as much more interconnected and mutually constitutive.

The Zapatistas have long asserted that the time and space within which we find ourselves now is that of 'the Fourth World War.' While the 'Third World War,' otherwise known as the 'Cold War,' ended with the collapse of the Soviet Union and the 'victory' of neoliberal capitalism over state-sponsored socialism, the 'Fourth World War' marks a time when global neoliberal capitalism ushered in 'a new framework of international relations in which the new struggle for ... new markets and territories' produced 'a new world war,' a war against humanity (Subcomandante Insurgente Marcos 2004d, 257). The socio-political challenge of our time thus becomes not one of capitalism versus communism but one of a geopolitical system and its agents, armies, and weapons (military, socio-political, economic) versus the vast majority of humanity who not only continue to be marginalized and targeted by this system but who are actively seeking to build alternatives to it. As Marcos (2002b) writes:

> The apparent infallibility of globalization comes up hard against the stubborn disobedience of reality. While neoliberalism is pursuing its war, groups of protesters, kernels of rebels, are forming throughout the planet. The empire of financiers with full pockets confronts the rebellion of pockets of resistance. Yes, pockets. Of all sizes, of different colors, of varying shapes. Their sole common point is a desire to resist the 'New World Order' and the crime against humanity that is represented by this Fourth World War. (282)

This is not a struggle engaged in by a homogeneous group of people; it is not a struggle built according to strict principles or a revolutionary blueprint; it is, rather, a struggle that is being joined by people all over the world seeking to affirm their autonomy and interconnectedness, their will to live in a world capable of holding many worlds.

Within this plane of immanence, now increasingly shaped by the dynamics of global neoliberal capitalism, how can radical possibilities come into being? While the fundamentally unclosed nature of the social may be acceptable in principle, how can alternatives manifest themselves in any coherent way within this space? In answer to this question, Deleuze and Guattari (1987) offer the concept of the 'war machine' that, despite its label, is in fact most often a generative rather than a destructive force. The war machine does not have war as its object but is rather directed towards 'the emission of quanta or deterritorialization, the passage of mutant flows,' and in this sense the 'war machine' is in fact generative of every creation (229–30). The 'war machine' is a 'war machine' in the sense that it is directed against the enclosures and dominance that are the fundamental characteristics of the state form precisely because its purpose is the generation of possibilities that escape this form. Socio-political possibilities and alternatives are thus the products of this 'machine' as it takes aim at the enclosures and transcendental principles that are so intimately a part of the state form and that seek to fence in these socio-political 'lines of flight' – mutations, possibilities, radical alternatives. Of course, the war machine is inherently neither good nor bad; it is the source of possibilities whose nature is not predetermined. What this means is that the realization of 'alternatives' or 'possibilities' can never be ends in themselves, nor can the status quo rely upon its own internal principles for its validation. Rather, the means by which the socio-political comes into being, the shape it takes, and the consequences it entails imply an irreducible and irrefutable sense of obligation and responsibility on the part of all of us who inhabit and constitute it.

Just as the lines of flight generated by the war machine hold out hope and danger simultaneously, so, too, does the war machine itself constitute both hope and threat. War becomes the primary object of the war machine if it is appropriated by the 'state apparatus' or if it has itself constructed its own 'state apparatus' (ibid., 230). As Deleuze and Guattari describe, 'When this happens, the war machine no longer draws mutant lines of flight, but a pure, cold line of abolition' (ibid.). When it becomes fixed, rigid, and entrenched, the war machine – the very source of possibility – reproduces the violence and enclosure against which it was originally directed. Rigidity and transcendence entrench order and absolute authority, impose inviolable limits upon alternatives, deny possibility, and seek to ensure the reproduction of the dominant socio-political order to the violent exclusion of all else. This is most certainly a warning to those who would believe the seizing of the power of the state – even on the most noble, hopeful, and revolutionary of principles – can result in anything but new forms of tyranny. As the Zapatistas have sought to remind us since 1994, what matters is not who holds power but how power is exercised. To replicate the form while seeking to substitute the principles that underlie it is to fundamentally misunderstand how power and violence operate.

Echoing warnings about the foreclosure of possibility, the capture of the war machine, and the state form issued by Deleuze and Guattari, autonomist Marxist theorist John Holloway (2002b) affirms that one of the most important contributions of Zapatismo to radical politics is that it 'moves us decisively beyond the state illusion,' which places the state at the centre of the project for radical change (157). Not only has a radical politics centred upon winning control of the state become increasingly problematic, according to Holloway – due to the movement of capital towards a global rather than national terrain of operation thus reducing the power of the state with respect to capital – the pre-eminent position of the state within radical politics has also been challenged because the forms of revolutionary action appropriate to winning control of the state (the party, the revolutionary vanguard, the leader) all serve to discipline class struggle rather than empower it (ibid.). The forms of discipline associated with the conquering of the state all serve to capture productive and radical energies – Deleuze and Guattari's war machine – and to bend them to a singular project intent on exercising 'power-over' the social rather than liberating people's 'power-to,' thus ushering in a new regime of domination. As Holloway notes, 'The state illusion penetrates deep into the experience of struggle, privileging those struggles which appear to contribute to the winning of state power and allocating a secondary role or worse to those forms of struggle which do not' (ibid.). Winning power is primary, empowering people so that they can liberate themselves from violence, exploitation, and subjugation becomes a goal to be achieved after the state and power have been seized.

Of course, none of this critique need imply that the state is no longer a significant locus of power or that meaningful socio-political victories cannot be won upon its terrain, it is to suggest however, that the concept of revolution and the projects of radical politics must be positioned differently if they are to overcome the failures of the past. As Holloway (2002b) affirms, 'The revolutions of the twentieth century failed because they aimed too low, not because they aimed too high' (158). Control of the state is simply not enough; as Holloway asserts, we need a new conception of revolution and a new kind of radical politics, one in which dignity operates as a central concept (ibid., 159). 'If dignity is taken as a central principle, then people cannot be treated as means: the creation of a society based on dignity can only take place through the development of social practices based on the mutual recognition of that dignity' (ibid.). In light of this, Holloway (2002a) claims the following: 'This, then, is the revolutionary challenge at the beginning of the twenty-first century: to change the world without taking power. This is the challenge that has been formulated most clearly by the Zapatista uprising in the south-east of Mexico' (20).

New Dynamics of Struggle

As should be obvious by now, there is no essential character to the generative engine of possibility that Deleuze and Guattari have named the 'war machine.' Indeed, as Deleuze and Guattari (1987) note, 'the very conditions that make the State or the World war machine possible ... constant capital (resources and equipment) and human variable capital, continually recreate unexpected possibilities for counterattack, unforeseen initiatives determining revolutionary, popular, minority, mutant machines' (422). This generative engine is always at work, but the outcomes it produces depend entirely upon the project with which it is associated and the ways in which the possibilities that emerge from it are approached.

The work of war machines – both that of neoliberal capitalism as well as those engaged in the generation of new and radical possibilities beyond current relations of domination – are explored by theorists of autonomist Marxism, albeit in a somewhat different lexicon, such as John Holloway, Nick Dyer-Witheford, Michael Hardt and Antonio Negri, and Paolo Virno. These scholars focus upon the primacy and generative power of labour rather than merely upon the domination of capital. As Dyer-Witheford (1999) explains, while capital and its war machine responds to workers' collectively articulated threats to it by 'constant revolutionizing of the means of production – by recurrent restructurings, involving organizational changes and technological innovations that divide, deskill, or eliminate dangerous groups of workers,' it can never entirely eliminate its antagonist precisely because capital only exists by virtue of its appropriation of people's productive capacities (66). Thus, at each point of restructuring 'new and different types of labor' must be recruited, yielding 'the possibility of working-class recomposition involving different strata of workers with fresh capacities of resistance and counterinitiative' (ibid.). The global plane of immanence and the world-war machine of neoliberal capitalism thus encounter the war machines of the global multitude engaged in the productive work of bringing the world into being, not merely those involved in the direct production of commodities. More than this, the encounter itself is overdetermined by the fact that the world-war machine of neoliberal capitalism is inextricably wrapped up in and fundamentally dependent on the productive capacities of those it seeks to dominate, thus opening the field of struggle far beyond the narrow parameters of 'domination' and 'resistance.' As Michael Hardt and Antonio Negri assert in *Multitude: War and Democracy in the Age of Empire* (2004), 'resistance is primary with respect to power' (64). Thus, it is power that attempts to capture the productive force of resistance rather than resistance merely being a reaction to power. Once again, it is the productive and creative capacity of humanity that is the only truly generative force here, power merely seeks to appropriate this force, to enclose and commodify it.

The important point here, aside from the fact that 'working class' in this sense thus expands to include forms of work far outside the factory or the shop floor, is that it is the counterinitiatives that drive the processes of capitalism itself, capital appropriates that which is created by people's creative capacity (Dyer-Witheford 1999, 66–7). This autonomist Marxist perspective views contemporary society itself as a factory, a factory directed towards the production and reproduction of life itself. The challenge of a revolutionary project becomes the achievement of an 'escape velocity' on the part of the circulation of people's struggles breaking the 'spiraling "double helix"' of capitalist recomposition and freeing labour from the wage relation that seeks to capture it (ibid., 68). In 'post-industrial' or 'late' capitalism, where information technologies have come to occupy a central role in capitalist accumulation, capital's own circuits actually become 'pathways for the circulation of struggles' (ibid., 93). Moreover, through its own global aspirations, neoliberal capitalism has actually facilitated an erosion of the barriers that once separated people from one another, allowing for a drastic increase in the speed of the circulation of struggles globally (ibid., 145). In this sense, there is no distinction between the 'machine' that dominates and exploits people and the one that allows for the possibility of the realization of new possibilities and subjectivities. This is so precisely because all creative power resides solely within humanity; all that capital, its agents, and its institutions accomplish is a temporary capturing or enclosure of this capacity. It is upon this terrain and with this same realization that Zapatismo has so successfully challenged the dominant myths of neoliberal capitalism and opened spaces for the construction of alternatives based in people's own creative and generative capacities.

This relationship between people's productive capacity, in its most radical sense, and the apparatuses deployed to effect its capture is particularly relevant when considered in light of the changing nature of the most significant – or hegemonic – sectors of the global neoliberal capitalist economy. In fact, Hardt and Negri (2004) argue that 'immaterial labor, that is, labor that produces immaterial products, such as information, knowledges, ideas, images, relationships, and affects,' is exercising a hegemonic influence not only over the contemporary scene of labour and production but also over society as a whole (65). One need look no further than the most advanced and lucrative sectors of the economies of the G8 countries to establish the veracity of this assertion. While this has led to 'new and intense forms of violation and alienation' such as the erasure of the distinction between 'work' and 'non-work' time and the increasing enclosure of every aspect of social life, it also means that 'immaterial labor ... tends no longer to be limited to the economic but also becomes immediately a social, cultural, and political force' (ibid., 65–6). The significance of this is that this labour becomes 'biopolitical,' oriented toward the production and reproduction of forms of social life, the 'production of subjectivity' itself, 'the creation and reproduction of new subjectivities in society' (ibid., 66).

Situating this contemporary condition within recent history, Italian theorist Paolo Virno (2004) argues that new regimes of post-Fordist production and immaterial labour represent capital's response to the social movements and socio-political crises of the 1960s and 1970s. Rather than resulting in either exclusively liberatory or exploitative outcomes, this transition allowed for capital's survival in the face of profound challenges to it while simultaneously opening new paths for resistance and alternative-building. This paradoxical situation is described by Virno as the 'communism of capital' (111). The consequence of all of this is that even as neoliberal capitalist globalization accelerates dynamics of exploitation, commodification, enclosure, and destruction, the possibilities for the articulation and emergence of new forms of struggle, new terrains of struggle, and new subjectivities in struggle similarly accelerate. Once again, there is nothing inherently or automatically liberatory about this situation; rather, it remains fundamentally ambivalent, ambiguous, and – most importantly – open to radical alternatives.

A New Revolutionary Subjectivity?

Elaborating on the character of immaterial labour, Hardt and Negri (2004) note that communication, cooperation, and network forms are its hallmarks and because of immaterial labour's hegemonic position within the global neoliberal economy, these forms of collaboration and interaction infiltrate other forms of labour as well (66). As a biopolitical force, the impact of immaterial labour also has consequences beyond the economic. As immaterial labour has become constitutive of the social, it has also impacted upon forms of socio-political struggle. As Hardt and Negri (2004) write, not only is contemporary networked struggle increasingly 'biopolitical' in its aims and consequences (evidenced in part by the emphasis upon 'democracy' as both a central characteristic and demand of so many networked popular movements), it also 'does not rely on discipline the same way [as does the military, the factory, even the guerrilla band]: creativity, communication, and self-organized cooperation are its primary values' (83).

In fact, Hardt and Negri (2004) assert that the Zapatista movement represents 'in the clearest possible terms the nature and direction of the postmodern transition of organizational forms' while globalization movements represent the latest stage in the development of movement forms (85–7). This transition and biopolitical focus is significant for several reasons. In contrast to biopower, which stands above society as a transcendent force imposing order, biopolitics is immanent to the social, creating social relations and formations through collaborative labour (ibid., 94–5). Such a conceptualization evokes Deleuze and Guattari's (1987) 'plane of immanence' as well as their assertion that social bodies are nothing more than 'affects and local movements, differential speeds' (260). Creation is not imposed from above, it is not ordered by an outside force; rather, the only truly creative and generative capacity is immediately immanent to the social itself. Furthermore, the subjectivities in struggle emerging from this new terrain are not constituted as a 'class,' a 'people,' or as 'masses' – such concepts belong to regimes of transcendental biopower that imbues them with meaning only from above or outside of the social. As Hardt and Negri argue, the subject that is emerging is that of the 'multitude.'

Hardt and Negri (2004) describe the multitude as 'a set of singularities – and by singularity here we mean a social subject whose difference cannot be reduced to sameness, a difference that remains different ... The multitude is an internally different, multiple social subject whose constitution and action is based not on identity or unity (or, much less, indifference) but on what it has in common' (99–100). The multitude is not a modern socio-political subject, it does not conform to the concepts of a modern political analysis and the notion of sovereignty is completely alien to it because sovereignty implies a transcendent principle residing above the social. The multitude, argue Hardt and Negri, is both political and ontological, political because it is a project (a 'not-yet') and ontological because it is part of humanity ('always-already') and manifested in a refusal of authority and a profound desire for freedom, but above all else, 'the multitude is created in collaborative social interactions' (ibid., 221–2). Communication and collaboration constitute the new socio-political subjectivity of the multitude, and it is in this space that a radical democracy driven by freedom and equality becomes not only viable but central to the political.

As Richard Day describes in *Gramsci Is Dead: Anarchist Currents in the Newest Social Movements* (2005), a politics of affinity based in a 'groundless solidarity' and 'infinite responsibility' characterizes much contemporary radical political action all too often inaccurately subsumed beneath the label 'anti-globalization.' While Day takes issue with Hardt and Negri's concepts of 'Empire' and 'multitude' both for their reductive and monolithic tendencies, the politics of affinity he analyses is a powerful dynamic within the subjectivity of the multitude as I deploy it here. In contrast to a quintessentially modern politics of hegemony rooted in the state, the 'people,' and the seizure of power as the end game of any revolutionary struggle, a politics of affinity is not reducible to a singular terrain of struggle or a privileged historical subject. Instead, a politics of affinity is focused upon building connections across difference without seeking to obscure it. Rather than reducing a multiplicity of identities to a singlular one, the 'groundless solidarity' of a politics of affinity seeks to build links amongst a multitude – or multitudes – of different struggles (18). The 'infinite responsibility' of this politics requires that those who seek to connect their struggles with those of a multiplicity of others always leave themselves open to critique and criticism, particularly from those voices least like one's own (ibid.). A politics of affinity is a politics of the multitude and much like the tendential, emergent nature of the multitude so, too, is a politics of affinity a relational possibility to be struggled for rather than a discrete project to be actualized or a set of principles to be simply taken up.

Dissenting Voices

Of course, the concept of the multitude and the politics and possibilities it is associated with are by no means uncontested potentialities. While rather predictable criticisms of this formulation, particularly as it has been conceived of by scholars such as Hardt and Negri and Virno, have emerged from a more orthodox Marxist camp that sees in this theoretical trajectory a denial of class struggle, the materiality of history, and the privileged role of the proletariat as the revolutionary subject in history, far more serious and substantive critiques have been levelled from other directions as well. In line with the rise to power of several leftist figures in Latin America – from Venezuela's Hugo Chávez to Bolivia's Evo Morales to Luiz Inacio da Silva (Lula) in Brazil – several scholars in the North have also sought to foreground the possibility of 'radical trans-formative nationalisms' (Laxer 2003) and progressive notions of sovereignty (Cockcroft 2006) as among the most significant sites of struggle against the violences generated by global neoliberal capitalism and U.S. imperialism. While these perspectives and the scholars and activists who advance them do not always posit this political vision predicated on state sovereignty and progressive nationalisms against the conceptualization of a politics of the multitude explicitly, the contrast should be obvious.

I will look at the issue of the 'progressive nationalism' approach as it has manifested itself in the Canadian context in the next chapter; however, for my purposes here two central points demand recognition. First, while the rise of 'progressives' to power in Latin America has been the source of much corporate media attention, neoconservative hand-wringing, and financial nervousness in the North and has obviously attracted the attention of U.S. elites and their proxies (as in the case of the defeated coup in Venezuela in 2002), it is by no means clear that these regimes represent the radical challenge they are frequently suggested to be. In almost all of these cases, 'progressive' and sometimes even avowedly 'socialist' regimes have made extensive promises to foreign interests and capital on their way to power. Lula's highly ambivalent record in Brazil is certainly a testament to the fact that regardless of the hope invested in a regime, the terrain of political power in neoliberal times remains precarious. The second point that bears recognition is that even in cases where state power is mobilized in a form that represents a powerful challenge to foreign domination and neoliberal capitalist interests – as is perhaps the case in Chávez's Venezuela and Castro's Cuba – serious questions about the durability of these alternatives, as well as their internal political dynamics, persist. This is certainly not to say that these routes do not represent alternatives to the status quo or that they are fundamentally anti-democratic or inauthentic. Chávez is perhaps the *most* democratically legitimate political leader in the world today having clearly won three consecutive elections declared free and fair by a host of international observers as well having survived a rigorous recall vote in 2004.

Nevertheless, these politics remain committed to notions and practices of social control rooted in 'power-over.' By its very nature, such power requires agencies, institutions, and organs of social control in line with singular, top-down visions of social change and development. It also remains unclear whether the social gains made by these regimes will survive after the powerful and charismatic leaders who helped usher them in have vacated the political stage. In this sense, it might be fair to say that while oppositional, socialist regimes such as those led by Castro and Chávez are necessary, particularly within a geopolitical context that desperately needs alternative models to U.S. hegemony, they are not sufficient in the end to cultivate the kind of radical social and political change lying at the heart of the multitude. Finally, and perhaps most significantly, the possibility for progressive governance in the North in neoliberal times seems much more bleak than it does in the South, but this is a matter to which I turn in greater depth in the next chapter.

Important challenges to the political subjectivity and possibilities of the multitude have also emerged from other critical positions. Philosophically, Malcolm Bull (2005) has taken contemporary valorizations of the notion of the multitude to task for misidentifying the philosophical tradition in which the term is steeped and for misunderstanding the simple fact that, 'from Cicero onwards, it was axiomatic that only when unified into a people could a multitude become a political agent' (38). Within this tradition, as Bull emphasizes, this means that the multitude is not 'an agent of limitless potential'; rather, it is 'always the raw material of the political' (ibid., 38–9). But if the multitude is the 'raw material of the political' (and by 'political' we can be assured that Bull means 'legitimate' political entities associated with the state form), does this mean that it has no liberatory or revolutionary potential by not conceding to its role as mere 'raw material'? Bull sums up his analysis of the contemporary radical theorists of the multitude and the politico-philosophical path walked by them in the following way:

> Seeking a route out of the impasse posed by the global market and its reactive populisms, [the champions of multitude] have retraced the path that led to it. The difficulty comes from starting with the multitude as an aggregation of individuals, and then proceeding to dichotomize the one and the many. Agency is then transformed into a choice between general will or general intellect, state or society. Rather than being an agent of limitless potential, the multitude contracts political possibility to the primitivisms of the security state and the free market. Within contemporary politics, the problem of agency demands a more complex resolution. (ibid., 39)

Bull's critique is certainly relevant, particularly with respect to his insights regarding the philosophical roots of the relationship between the 'multitude' and the 'people.' However, his assertion that on this basis the radical possibilities attributed to the multitude are *necessarily* rendered non-existent is by no means assured. Bull compellingly demonstrates that the philosophical legacy of the 'multitude' is a good deal more complex than it might initially appear in contemporary reformulations of the concept. However, his conviction that deploying the multitude as a revolutionary subjectivity leads to a dichotomous situation represented by either the 'security state' or the 'free market' does no justice to the complexity of the reformulation of the notion of the multitude as a way of thinking beyond politico-philosophical constructs of the state, the nation, and the people. Indeed, it would seem to be inherent to the possibility of the multitude that both as a philosophical concept and as a political tendency it remain mixed, impure, complex, and even contradictory. As with Deleuze and Guattari's war machine or the global immanence described by Buck-Morss, hope for radical possibility – of the capacity to live and be otherwise – ultimately resides in current states of partial incoherence and lack of fixity.

One of the most sophisticated and formidable challenges to the multitude as a revolutionary subjectivity, bridging both philosophical and material concerns, has been articulated by Tim Brennan in his book *Wars of Position: The Cultural Politics of Left and Right* (2006). Brennan takes aim at a range of cultural theory emerging out of the mid-1970s, a period he calls the 'turn,' which he regards as having participated in the banishing of social democratic alternatives from the field of public consideration as well as facilitating a shift from 'belief to being' in politics (ix). As Brennan states unequivocally:

> We are still living under the common sense of this short span of years that might be thought of simply as the 'turn.' Its credos were first launched and are today reinforced in a process of interpretive violence ... In my view, the transitional moment of 1975–1980 is best characterized as the fusing of right and left positions still evident today, above all, in viewing the state as an arena of innate corruption to which no claims for redress can or should be made. (ibid., ix)

Brennan traces the 'turn' to several forces acting in concert: the 'deadening effects of middle-class immigration and entry into the university' of intellectuals directly or indirectly related to formerly colonized peoples and who were identified as 'the oppressed' even though this was often not the case; the 'popularization of right-wing philosophies from interwar Europe' embodying a 'fundamental confusion ... between conservative and radical rejections of capitalism'; and, finally, the 'hyperprofessionalism that put the humanities in competition with a postliterate media and entertainment sector in a climate of privatization' (ibid., ix–x). At a socio-political moment of 'reassessment' and 'fatigue,' these forces were brought into play and, according to Brennan's analysis, paved the way for the theoretical and analytical traditions that would follow. Within this matrix, Brennan identifies theories of the multitude – and Hardt and Negri's theorizations of Empire specifically – as being representative of the deeply problematic post-turn context.

Rather than radicals, Brennan (2006) contends that Hardt and Negri operate on terms of deep complicity with contemporary regimes of power and domination on a global scale. Not only does Brennan accuse Hardt and Negri – along with other 'new Italian' thinkers and theorists interested in 'immaterial labour' – of ignoring the materiality of global neoliberal capitalism, the 'War on Terror,' and the very real existence of U.S. imperial ambition, he also charges them, much more fundamentally, with mistaking complicity for liberation (171–2). In light of this criticism, Brennan asserts, 'the main interest of imperialism for Hardt and Negri lies in the new forms of identity it unleashed across the globe – a view that fits, mutatis mutandis, very comfortably with a mainstream perception that America's global influence has been largely positive' (ibid., 172). Through Brennan's eyes, the work of Hardt and Negri, as well as other associated works, serve to facilitate the denial of imperial realities and to herald neoliberal capitalism as a threshold onto new forms of subjectivity and a terrain of infinite possibility. Yet while Brennan's critiques certainly have merit with respect to theorists like Hardt and Negri (along with others such as Virno and even Dyer-Witheford), whose work can be read as approaching neoliberal capitalism at times ambivalently and accord too much importance to the role of 'post-industrial' or 'immaterial' labour within it, his contention that the 'primary postulate' in their work *Empire* (2000) is that 'liberation is achieved by declaring oneself "autonomous"' (Brennan 2006, 175) is grossly misrepresentative of the complexity and richness of this body of political thought. It is abundantly clear, for instance, in reading *Empire* and their companion work *Multitude* (2004), along with similar works produced by theorists like Deleuze and Guattari, Virno, Dyer-Witheford, Holloway, and Day, that liberation is far from easily achieved and that autonomy is a relationship consisting of much more than its mere declaration. To suggest otherwise is to confuse theory with a blueprint for political action, an act which is disingenuous at best.

In his critique, Brennan rightly identifies the contemporary theorizations of multitude, immaterial labour, and zero-work, among others, as originating in the philosophical work of Deleuze and Guattari, the struggles of the Italian autonomia movements, the radical activism of 1968, as well as within the tradition of anarchist political thought and autonomist Marxism. However, contrary to Brennan's indictment, the connection of these theorizations to these movements and moments hardly invalidate them. Here, as throughout the rest of his work, Brennan manages to build up a straw figure in place of a more critical and substantive analysis of the failures of the politically social democratic and philosophically left Hegelian traditions he contends were undermined by theory after the 'turn.' Social democratic governance, the labour movement, progressive political parties, and theorizations of dialectical materialism were not somehow cunningly subverted by the intellectual sleight-of-hand Brennan rather audaciously attributes to cultural theorists. Rather, in ways which I will develop further in the chapters that follow, these social democratic practices and their associated philosophical roots have been undermined by their fundamental inability to deal with the challenges of neoliberal capitalism, their desire to see the world and liberation through the lens of a politics of power, and, perhaps most disappointingly, the degree to which these institutions and the elites in command of them were more than willing to control, repress, channel, and co-opt dissent from below in the service of gaining 'a seat at the table' with other powerful stakeholders. Nowhere in his account does Brennan even nod in the direction of these histories. Instead, Brennan (2006) simply retreats to a dichotomy of the state versus globalization:

> The enemy of revolutionaries in the neoliberal age is not the state – which in spite of Hardt and Negri's diagnosis, is still an extraordinarily resilient form of command – but the sovereign, freely experimenting, hybrid subjects of corporate utopia against whom the state (or one version of it at any rate) continues to be the last refuge. The Left fights in this space, or it refuses to fight. (204)

The passage above provides some interesting insights into the political vision offered by Brennan and the nature of his critique of concepts like 'multitude' and 'Empire.' In this passage, we are reminded (and I emphasize) that *one* version' of the state offers '*the last refuge*' against the predations of neoliberal capitalism, and it is in this space, and no other, that meaningful struggles are to be carried out. Is the fact that the state 'is still an extraordinarily resilient form of *command*' supposed to inspire hope or does it merely offer the assurance that faced with the domination of neoliberal capitalism we are better off dominated by the state form? Is this not precisely the determinism that Deleuze and Guattari and Holloway warn of in their explorations of the state form? Is this not a tautological invocation of a narrow and pessimistic rationalism that, confronted by the reality of its own failures and unable to marshal an effective alternative to current challenges, merely retreats to that which it knows best? While Brennan's critiques of the excessive valorization of 'immaterial labour,' the interstitial and slippery language, the heroization of the multitude as a revolutionary actor, the lack of acknowledgment of material and imperial realities, and the ambivalence of some of this theory towards neoliberal capitalism as a historical moment are certainly demanding of serious consideration, what is the vision offered in their place? The multitude is nothing, autonomy is collusion, return to the state. Brennan is right to criticize the notion that states are somehow being swept away by globalization, but his assertion that in the state lies humanity's last refuge for liberation simply offers another absolute in its place. It also, more troublingly, offers another example of statements aimed at lighting the way to 'true' revolutionary action while identifying those tendencies that are clearly 'counter-revolutionary.' In the final anlysis, and in spite of what is largely a penetrating and powerful critique, Brennan's only alternative is to return to the discipline of the state form and to seek 'refuge' there, hardly an inspiring or hopeful vision of possibility. As will become clearer as this work unfolds, while critiques like Brennan's hold a great deal of value for activists engaged in radical global justice and anti-capitalist struggles, the political imaginations of those engaged in these movements clearly lie elsewhere.

Historical Currents of the Multitude

The critiques offered by dissenting voices such as James Cockcroft, Gordon Laxer, Malcolm Bull, and Tim Brennan of the political subjectivity of the multitude and its related formulations of immaterial labour, a politics of anti-power, and a politics beyond the state cannot be ignored; however, it cannot be said to have subverted the powerful possibility of these concepts and the glimpses of new socio-political terrains which they provide. Buttressing this assertion are histories testifying to the fact that the phenomena of transnational resonance and the political imagination which I seek to illuminate in this work are by no means entirely new or autonomously constituted. In fact, the powerful and provocative works of historians that recover 'histories from below' (see Federici 2004; Linebaugh 2003; Linebaugh and Rediker 2000; Rediker 2004; Wilson 2003; Zinn 2003) provide an excellent backdrop against which to situate the phenomenon of Zapatismo's transnational resonance and the possibility of the multitude as a revolutionary political subjectivity. Concretely, these accounts often provide opportunities to explore the shifting contours of the multitude as it has manifested itself in a variety of socio-political and cultural contexts. As Peter Linebaugh and Marcus Rediker brilliantly illustrate in *The Many-Headed Hydra: Sailors, Slaves, Commoners, and the Hidden History of the Revolutionary Atlantic* (2000), the circulation and proliferation of powerfully liberatory and revolutionary ideas, and the human beings and social relationships which gave them form, was a central – if all too often hidden or ignored – feature of the rise of capitalism, the colonial enterprise, and the emergence of the modern world system. What is so striking about the circulation of these powerful revolutionary ideas traced by Linebaugh and Rediker is that they were carried throughout the Atlantic world by those whom history has so often forgotten and despised – sailors, slaves, market women, labourers, criminals, pirates, indentured servants, and commoners. Indeed, their account can be read as a history of the multitude.

As Linebaugh and Rediker (2000) write, 'The classically educated architects of the Atlantic economy found in Hercules – the mythical hero of the ancients who achieved immortality by performing twelve labors – a symbol of power and order' (2). In contrast, the unruly multitude, upon whose labour these elites so depended, were despised as a 'many-headed hydra' for the resistance and challenges they offered to these emerging systems of exploitation and accumulation (2–4). The 'many-headed hydra' thus came to embody the revolutionary imaginations and socio-political alternatives of this Atlantic multitude, and the elite struggle to decapitate it was conceived of as a feat, quite literally, of Herculean proportions. But if the hydra was a powerful threat to the interests of the ruling class in the emerging Atlantic world, for Linebaugh and Rediker it represented a 'hypothesis':

> The hydra became a means of exploring multiplicity, movement, and connection, the long waves and planetary currents of humanity. The multiplicity was indicated, as it were, in silhouette in the multitudes who gathered at the market, in the fields, on the piers and the ships, on the plantations, upon the battlefields. The power of numbers was expanded by movement, as the hydra journeyed and voyaged or was banished or dispersed in diaspora, carried by the winds and the waves beyond the boundaries of the nation-state. Sailors, pilots, felons, lovers, translators, musicians, mobile workers of all kinds made new and unexpected connections, which variously appeared to be accidental, contingent, transient, even miraculous. (6)

As Linebaugh and Rediker describe, this motley revolutionary crew was multi-ethnic, comprised of men as well as women, and possessed of revolutionary desires that were profoundly egalitarian, democratic, and liberatory. Long preceding the grand declarations of modern political writers and philosophers, and in fact often serving to inspire them directly, this motley multitude articulated not only ideas but socio-political and economic relationships that aimed not to seize power, build a state or take control of an existing one, or enshrine their struggle in some transcendental concept of 'nationhood' but to build socio-political spaces and practices aimed at reconstituting the commons, levelling hierarchical systems of authority, and building bonds of solidarity unmarked by racism, classism, and even sexism. They did so without elite leadership, without formalized ideological training, without concretized processes directed towards transforming them into 'proper' subjects of revolution. Driven off the commons through the violent and terror-filled process of enclosure and privatization, through experiences of criminalization, exploitation, subjugation, travel, and encounter, this motley multitude brought Atlantean revolutionary imaginations into being that would not die even with the consolidation of the modern nation-state and capitalism at the beginning of the nineteenth century.

The Multitude, Hope, and Uncertainty

In considering what he calls the 'remarkable resonance' of Zapatismo, John Holloway (2002a) argues that this resonance can be traced to the growth of what might be termed 'anti-power.' Put differently, Holloway reminds us that 'our capacity to do is always an interlacing of our activity with the previous or present activity of others' and that it is only when 'the social flow of doing is fractured that power-to is transformed into its opposite, power-over' thus reducing the vast majority of people 'into the done-to, their activity transformed into passivity, their subjectivity into objectivity' (28–9). This is the understanding of power and of the capacity to create, the power-to, that the Zapatistas invoke when they assert: 'We are not a safety valve for the rebellion that could destabilize neoliberalism. It is false that our rebel existence legitimizes Power. Power fears us. That is why it pursues us and fences us in. That is why it jails and kills us. In reality, we are the possibility that can defeat it and make it disappear' (Ejército Zapatista de Liberación Nacional 2001b, 126). The socio-political terrain invoked here is not one in which the seizure of power or the state is primary or even at all desirable, instead it is a space within which we are reminded of the inherent relationality of our existence, an experience which requires a mutual recognition of obligation, responsibility, and dignity if it is to find a way beyond the relations of power which currently overdetermine it.

Upon this terrain, I argue that the 'multitude' is the subjectivity most appropriate to comprehending the transnational resonance of Zapatismo. Once again, this does not mean that the multitude is an already-existing subjectivity, fully constituted in the world and prepared to reconfigure socio-political realities. Rather, I argue that the multitude is a tendency, it is a possibility that needs to be self-consciously imbued with the force of global human agency in order for it to realize itself, a circumstance which to be sure is by no means imminent. And yet it remains a possibility offering a powerful opportunity to begin to build a new kind of radical politics, a politics capable of breaking through the enclosures of terror, war, capital, and the failures of past revolutions into a future marked by hope and uncertainty. The histories that I seek to trace here and the transnational resonance of Zapatismo which I engage in the chapters to come are linked deeply to the possibility of the multitude. The multitude is not merely a contemporary political subjectivity, it has deep historical roots as well. But the project of tracing larger connections over such expanses of time and space is beyond the scope of my current work, for now I merely wish to affirm my awareness that Zapatismo did not create the possibility of a revolutionary project of the multitude above borders and nations, it merely reinvigorated it. But before proceeding to analyse the political imaginations inspired by the transnational resonance of Zapatismo, I turn to some of the more immediate histories of radical political action in Canada and the United States against which this resonance needs to be set.

2 Northern Struggles, Northern Histories

We know we have brothers and sisters in other countries and continents.

We are united by a world order that destroys nations and cultures. Today, Money – the great international criminal – has a name that reflects the incapacity of Power to create new things. Today, we suffer a new world war, a war against all peoples, against humanity, against culture, against history. It is an international war, of Money versus Humanity, carried out by a handful of financial centers, without homeland and without shame. Now, this international terror is called neoliberalism – an international economic order that has already caused more death and destruction than the great world wars. We have become brothers with more poor and more dead.

We are united by dissatisfaction, rebellion, the desire to do something, by non-conformity. History written by Power taught us that we had lost, that cynicism and profit were virtues, that honesty and sacrifice were stupid, that individualism was the new god, that hope was devalued money, without currency in international markets, without buying power, without hope. We did not take in the lesson. We were bad pupils. We did not believe what Power had taught us. We skipped class when they taught conformity and idiocy. We failed modernity. Classmates in rebellion, we discovered and found ourselves brothers.

We are united by the imagination, by creativity, by tomorrow. In the past, we not only met defeat but also found a desire for justice and the dream of being better. We left skepticism hanging from the hook of big capital and discovered that we could believe, that it was worth believing, that we should believe – in ourselves. We learned that many solitudes did not make one great solitude but a collective that found itself united beyond nationality, language, culture, race, and gender.

From 'Flowers, Like Hope, Are Harvested,' Subcomandante
Insurgente Marcos (2001c)

To attempt to synthesize the tremendously diverse and expansive histories of radical political struggle in Canada and the United States –
even limiting such a synthesis to the twentieth century – would be impossible to achieve here. Instead, in what follows I aim to provide a
backdrop against which to set the transnational resonance of Zapatismo
and the attendant political imaginations to which it has given rise. The
histories which I engage here are drawn from radical movements and
moments in the twentieth century in Canada and the United States with
a focus on the period after the Second World War to the present and with
a particular emphasis on the histories of radical political action in the
last twenty years. There are many histories that could be told, but here
I only recount a selection of the ones most relevant for appreciating the
resonance of Zapatismo in Canada and the United States.

The emphasis that the Zapatista struggle has placed upon imagination, hope, creativity, and a conceptual as well as a concrete socio-political revolution is by no means entirely foreign to the history of radical
political action in the north. As Barbara Epstein notes in *Political Protest
and Cultural Revolution* (1991), 'Cultural revolution, the transformation
not just of economic or political structures but of the ideas that govern
social life as a whole, has been a continuing theme in protest politics
in the United States,' and, while it has been 'submerged,' at times it
manifested itself perhaps most powerfully during the movements of the
1960s (21). In his analysis of Canada's left history, Ian McKay (2005)
makes a similar argument, considering the histories of Canadian socialism not simply as attempts at reforming or revolutionizing politico-
economic relationships but as a series of experiments in 'living otherwise.' In what follows, I seek to illuminate the significance of these
northern histories, particularly those directed towards the articulation
of new subjectivities and new socio-political realities, against which the
resonance of Zapatismo is best understood.

Radical Roots, Compromised Legacies

Radical socio-political action and imaginations are by no means the
exclusive province of contemporary political activism. The concepts of
direct action and an expansion of the terrain and subjects of radical
political struggle were not merely products of the 1970s and 1980s direct
action movement nor even of the 1960s and the New Left. As Francesca
Polletta illustrates so compellingly in her work *Freedom Is an Endless
Meeting* (2002), practices of direct action, participatory democracy, and

an expansion of the terrain and subjectivity of struggle owe their existence not only to the politics of cultural revolution in the 1960s, 1970s,
and 1980s but also to the work of pacifists and labour activists in the
early part of the twentieth century (27–8).

In the United States, radical pacifists – many of whom were veterans
of civilian public service camps and jails where men who refused to go
to war confronted the brutal authority of the state – emerged from the
Second World War ready to challenge the more conservative leaders of
their own movement (Epstein 1991, 28). Radical pacifists were key
actors in the civil rights movement, founding the Congress of Racial
Equality (CORE), the Southern Christian Leadership Conference
(SCLC), the Fellowship of Reconciliation (FOR), and training leaders
like Martin Luther King Jr. in non-violent resistance as well as assisting
in the organization of freedom rides through the southern United States
(Epstein 1991, 29; Polletta 2002, 27). Pacifists joined the commitment to
internal democracy with strategies of mass, non-violent direct action
that would become the hallmark of movements in the 1960s. In the 1940s
and 1950s they even articulated many of the concerns of the New Left
by criticizing 'technocracy and orthodox Marxism and championed the
rights of racial minorities' (Polletta 2002, 27).

While the labour movement of the early twentieth century in the
United States was dominated by the conservative and reactionary business unionism of the American Federation of Labor (AFL), an image of
struggle and organizing against which the New Left would rebel, this
was by no means representative of the totality of the labour movement.
In fact, as Polletta (2002) asserts, the 1920s witnessed the proliferation
of 'union education programs, independent labor colleges, and univer-
sity-affiliated summer schools' where 'educators operated on the belief
that a democratic pedagogy could bring about radical social change'
(24). While these programs would not survive hostility from the labour
oligarchs in the AFL, allegations of being hotbeds for 'Communist tendencies,' and sectarian conflicts within the left, they would nevertheless
serve to train and inspire generations of labour, pacifist, and civil rights
activists, fundamentally contributing to the shaping of radical politics
in the United States for decades to come (ibid., 35–6).

In addition to the labour movement, the late 1920s and 1930s bore witness to the significance of the Communist Party as a political force in the
United States. Forwarding a vision of socialist revolution based on the
1928 Communist International's prediction that the crisis of capitalism
was imminent, a prediction seemingly supported by the Great Depres-

sion, the Communist Party's politics called for building revolutionary organizations and refusing to cooperate with liberals and socialists, a militant stance that allowed the party to build organizations of the unemployed, attract blacks and intellectuals, and even to organize unions outside of the AFL with unskilled and semi-skilled workers (Epstein 1991, 24–5). Roosevelt's New Deal undermined much of the social base of this politics, however, and the failure of attempts at social-ist revolution elsewhere ultimately ended up persuading the Comintern to abandon the politics of imminent revolution and to focus on build-ing a popular front and winning democratic reforms (ibid., 25). In the U.S., this shift in position would mean organizing 'basic industry' through the Congress of Industrial Organizations (CIO), 'winning a place for the labor movement in the political process, constructing a welfare system, and gaining legitimacy for the industrial working class in American life' (ibid.). The Communist Party was actually instrumen-tal in terms of 'feeding ideas' to the labour movement and the New Deal, helping to make American society more democratic by 'giving more of its members some social standing and by winning greater acceptance for a definition of American culture as multi-ethnic and mul-tiracial,' but none of these contributions fundamentally challenged the nature of capitalism and the party's accomodationist stance ended up alienating members and allies, ultimately leading to its downfall during the McCarthy era (ibid., 26). This history of organized labour and the Communist Party would prove to be profoundly informative for the ways in which the New Left would construct its politics less than two decades later.

The collapse of the Communist Party, the business unionism of the labour oligarchs of the AFL-CIO, and post-war prosperity had managed to seriously diminish the left by the 1950s. This 'Old Left' was also frac-tured by internal divisions as native-born American radicals and recent immigrants tended to espouse very different perspectives on radical change (Epstein, 1991, 27). Whereas native-born Americans tended to be self-employed, farmers, or skilled workers and shaped the politics and culture of 'Populism, the Knights of Labor, feminism and the larger women's movement, and a wide range of reform movements often infused with a Christian sensibility that shaded into utopianism,' the radical politics of the emerging industrial working class, drawn mainly from recent immigrants, was much more 'oriented to questions of class, more politically pragmatic, grounded in Marxism and related intellec-tual traditions of socialism' (ibid.). This also meant that the radical politics of the new industrial working class tended to be somewhat less experimental than that of native-born radicals and less open to feminism, spirituality, and utopianism (ibid.). These two tendencies did manage to coexist in the Socialist Party, and in places where native-born Americans and immigrants lived and worked together such as on the west coast and in New York City organizations like the Industrial Workers of the World and the Women's Trade Union League, respectively, managed to organize both elements and construct a radical culture combining class focus and socialist thought with feminism and a utopian radicalism (ibid.; see also Buhle and Schulman 2005). In other places, however, the tensions remained and by and large labour was not a part of building a radical leftist politics.

In this context, radical pacifists continued to be an important force in shaping the contours of political struggle (Polletta 2002, 38). In the 1950s, pacifists argued not only for a political utopianism that refused to withdraw from the world but also became increasingly critical of the social structures and cultures that sustained war (Epstein 1991, 28; Polletta 2002, 38). Pacifists organized 'intentional communities' to experiment with new socio-economic forms, but they also formed groups like the Committee for Non-Violent Revolution, the Peacemakers, and the Committee for Non-Violent Action to mobilize against war taxes, the draft, segregation in the prison system, and atomic weapons testing (Polletta 2002, 38). Yet radical pacifists never managed to emerge from political marginality and, despite their influence and success, radical pacifism never formed the core of a lasting peace movement. Under the weight of internal (critiques of religiosity and a willingness to take risks that alienated radical pacifists from the broader public) and external pressures (anti-communist forces and Cold War ideologies), the movement declined (Epstein 1991, 32–3). Its legacy, however, would be significant in shaping the directions of future radical political struggle.

In his reconnaissance of the topography of the history of the Canadian left, Ian McKay (2005) traces five major left formations and alludes to the presence of a contemporary sixth 'post-socialist' formation under construction today (146–7). I will come to this sixth formation shortly, here I seek only to consider the shape, scope, and significance of the first five. Broadly speaking, McKay conceptualizes and periodizes the first five formations as follows: the first formation, 1890–1919, was characterized by the 'applied science of social evolution'; the second, 1917–39, took the shape of revolution aimed at the seizure of power by a movement of the working class under the direction of a vanguard party; the third, 1935–70, was a project of 'national economic and social management' carried out by a 'bureaucratic planning state answerable to parliament'; the fourth, 1965–80, was defined by the presence of 'grassroots liberation movements' aimed at overcoming both 'individual and national alienation'; and the fifth, 1967–90, was a movement for women's liberation from patriarchal domination (ibid., 147). The 'formations' McKay identifies are only useful as the most general of signposts marking the terrain of the left in Canada. Nevertheless, they serve as significant markers allowing for an explicit consideration of the shifting forms, terrain, and context of political action across time and space.

While kernels of socialist thought and action can be traced in Canada to the 1820s, the first significant radical left movements would not emerge until the end of the nineteenth century. Inspired by Herbert Spencer's theories of 'social evolution' – with all its problematic overtones – and a rather teleological reading of Marx, the emergent Canadian socialist left drew upon the U.S.-based Socialist Labor Party for its initial impetus before giving rise to numerous domestic socialist parties and organizations (McKay 2005, 147–50). The late 1800s and early 1900s witnessed the publication of socialist papers such as the *Labor Advocate* and the emergence of the Canadian Socialist League, the Socialist Party of Canada, and the Social Democratic Party of Canada (ibid., 150–2). With an emphasis on education and 'rabble-rousing' rather than parliamentary reform, this formation of the Canadian left represented the materialization of a movement fuelled by the belief that the laws of social evolution would lead to capitalism's demise and the role of the left within this circumstance was to accelerate the pace of this evolution (ibid., 153).

But immutable laws of social evolution did not bring about the downfall of capitalism and, as McKay (2005) analyses, by the 1920s the first formation had given way to the second, one in which the newly and clandestinely formed Communist Party of Canada (CPC) would play a prominent role (155). This period of leftist activism would also bear witness to the committed revolutionary work of the Industrial Workers of the World and the One Big Union movement in Canada, both of which competed with CPC in the 1930s (ibid., 156). Reaching approximately 16,000 members and many more in affiliated organizations such as the the Canadian Labour Defence League, the Women's Labour Leagues, the Young Communist League, the Workers' Sports League, and the Progressive Farmers' Educational League, the CPC positioned itself as the 'central revolutionary agent' aimed not only at a national socio-political and economic transformation but also at an international revolution (ibid., 158–9). In contrast to the social evolutionism of earlier socialisms that rested upon the 'inevitability' of social transformation, the CPC asserted the need for direct – and 'correct' – revolutionary science and action to bring radical change about and in this reformulation the CPC itself would occupy the vanguard (ibid., 160). While the CPC's Marxist-Leninist line, vanguardism, realpolitik, and dogmatism did not appeal broadly to Canadians, it nevertheless exerted considerable influence upon the contours of radical political action in Canada in the early twentieth century.

In the 1930s, new leftist actors emerged in the Canadian context to contest the primacy of the CPC within the left and to forge new paths of political action. Rather than 'social evolution' or 'revolution,' which were hallmarks of the first and second formations identified by McKay (2005), this third formation was marked by an emphasis on 'social planning' (169). Within this formation, the Co-operative Commonwealth Federation (CCF) displaced the CPC as the central leftist agent and with it came a new language, imagination, and repertoire of action directed towards socio-political and economic change (ibid.). As McKay notes, within this formation 'the question of transforming the *existing Canadian state into a socialist state* became the central question of politics' (ibid., 170, emphasis added). While McKay refers to this formation in terms of 'radical planism,' it is also possible to see in this formation a greater acceptance of dominant socio-political and economic realities, an even greater reliance upon 'scientific' methods of social analysis and transformation, and a much greater investment in an explicitly national project. As with the dominant leftist currents in the United States, as the Canadian left sought the power and institutional support necessary to embark upon a project of socialist transformation, it also moved steadily towards a more overtly accommodationist stance with respect to capitalism, the dominant liberal order, and elitist modes of governance and social control.

By no means a monolithic party, the CCF drew leftists of a wide variety of dispositions together during the 1930s and, through the university intellectuals affiliated with the League for Social Reconstruction, articulated a vision of Canada as a planned socialist state (McKay 2005, 171–2). In fact, the first social democratic government in North America was elected in Saskatchewan in 1944 and, in contrast to other social democratic parties, the CCF found its strongest base of support amongst wheat farmers and farm labourers (Warnock 2005, 82). And yet in spite of its initial 'pragmatic radicalism' enshrined in the *Regina Manifesto* and electoral success at the provincial level, by the 1950s the CCF's parliamentary prospects had become bleak (McKay 2005, 172–3). Faced with the oppressive context of the Cold War, the CCF liberalized its platform and, at a party convention in Ottawa in 1961, it merged with the Canadian Federation of Labour and officially transformed itself into the 'liberal leftist' New Democratic Party (NDP) (McKay 2005, 173–4; Warnock 2005, 82). This 'shift' from a commitment to democratic socialism to a more nebulous commitment to social democracy had profound consequences, not only for the party but also for the shape of the organized left in Canada. Stephen McBride (2005) sums up the fundamental nature of this shift in the following way:

> In the 1930s and 1940s, the socialist aspect of the social democratic inheritance [of the CCF] was externally visible and internally legitimate. In the post-war era a process of clarification occurred that identified the CCF, and subsequently the NDP, as parties of moderate social reform whose ideological roots increasingly lay in the liberal, Keynesian and technocratic critique of unregulated capitalism rather than in a socialist critique of capitalism *per se*. (28–9, emphasis in original)

The significance of this shift is much more than a matter of emphasis or 'reform' versus 'revolution'; the CCF was never a 'revolutionary' party. However, as a result of this transition rather than approaching capitalism as a key problem with democratic socialism as its solution, under the Keynesian democratic socialism of the CCF/NDP understandings of 'class' and 'class conflict' became diluted and configured as 'social problems' (McBride 2005, 29). Indeed, the CCF/NDP was 'resolutely Keynesian' as were social democratic parties of Western Europe, despite criticisms that Keynesian reforms did not address the structural inequalities and violences of capitalism (ibid.). Again, this lack of vision and commitment had consequences far beyond narrow issues of the party's electoral success (or lack thereof). While many political and business actors in Canada only adhered to Keynesian policies halfheartedly and primarily out of necessity, many social democrats saw it as ushering in the 'end of ideology' (ibid.). McBride summarizes the implications of this failure of analysis and imagination for the politico-economic landscape by noting that 'the consequences of this history are that renewed economic crisis has been more disruptive for social democracy than for ideologies with right-wing origins, which "rediscovered" ideology and launched an assault on the post-war consensus' (ibid.). This failure on the part of the CCF/NDP and, in fact, of social democratic parties around the world, provided the ideal context for the rise of neoliberal capitalism.

The shift from a committed – albeit pragmatic – democratic socialism to a managerial Keynesian liberalism would indelibly mark the mainstream terrain of political alternative-building from the 1950s onward. Pre-war social democrats sought to 'organize, mobilize and use working-class pressure' in order to bring about 'genuine and far-reaching reforms'; however, competition with more radical actors often resulted in a close connection between an organized base and a reform program, and since 1945 both base and program have atrophied (McBride 2005, 30). As McBride notes, 'one can argue that Keynesianism facilitated a technocratic approach to political processes' (ibid., 31). A naive belief in the durability of the post-war class compromise, a facile conception of Keynesian theory as the solution to capitalism's inherent inequalities, and a cynical drive for electoral success rendered the CCF/NDP an increasingly insignificant political alternative. Outside of election periods, the party's efforts at mobilization declined and, with advances in 'electoral technology' and an increased reliance upon electronic media for campaigning, this decline spread even further. While the 'post-war consensus' was maintained, there were relatively few repercussions; however, once economic crisis set in, the absence of a mobilized and activist base proved fatal (ibid.). Although social democratic parties made attempts to adapt Keynesianism to the new neoliberalized economic conditions, trying to articulate a 'post-Keynesian' approach emphasizing some form of socialization of investment combined with state planning held together by a social contract among trade unions, industry, and the state, the results were predictably fruitless. As should be obvious from even the most cursory of analyses of these half-measures, these 'solutions' often pitted social democratic governments against their own supporters (ibid.).

The history of the CCF/NDP in Canada is instructive on several levels with respect to contemporary considerations of radical political possibility and struggles for meaningful social justice. Certainly the records of social democratic provincial governments, both the NDP and the Parti Québécois, in post-1960s Canada reads like a litany of the failures of the social democratic imagination (see Carroll and Ratner 2005; Grace 2005; Graefe 2005; McBride 2005; Warnock 2005). Perhaps most significantly, the profound failure of the CCF/NDP to offer a viable and inspiring alternative to the predations of neoliberal capitalism and its trappings of democratic ritual speaks much more broadly to the failure of social democrats the world over to meet similar challenges. In his examination of social democracy as a political movement, William Carroll (2005) identifies the key points of this movement and why they have proved to be insufficient to meet neoliberalism's challenges. As a political movement, social democracy is organized 'around labour-based parties and a program of incremental reforms to extend the liberal-democratic idea of citizenship rights into the *social* realm' (9, emphasis in original). Its social democratic vision – or political horizon – is one characterized by the belief in an egalitarian society where 'bourgeois freedoms coexist with and are tempered by social solidarities' (ibid.). In line with this horizon, the cornerstones of social democratic governance are redistribution, democratic economic governance, and social protectionism, with the Keynesian welfare state as the key mechanism historically for the realization of these goals (ibid.).

The problem with this seemingly progressive and benevolent vision is that it misunderstands both capital's capacity for innovation as well as the role of the state in relation to it. As Carroll (2005) argues, the 'power resources model' that many social democrats have adapted, is rife with misdiagnoses and misunderstandings of political and economic realities, including misunderstanding the role of the state as a potentially friendly arbiter on behalf of the working class against capital; misdiagnosing the balance of class power by overestimating labour's resources and underestimating capital's resources; and equating forming a government with controlling the state and buying in to the notion that socialism can be introduced 'by installment' (10). He further emphasizes that, 'although union density, electoral strength and the elaboration of social citizenship are important factors, they become less efficacious when set against capital's increasing mobility and its political organization into neoliberal parties, activist business councils and policy-planning groups' (ibid.). Perhaps most significantly, and most problematically with respect to social democracy's political imagination, there is no evidence from any context that 'gradual social reform' has the capacity to ameliorate let alone challenge capitalism's tendencies 'to generate massive inequality on both national and global scales' (ibid.). Indeed, as the histories of NDP governments across Canada so amply demonstrate, social democrats, confronted by neoliberal realities and elite pressure, have been more than willing to do the dirty work of social, political, and economic cleansing when called upon to do so.

This brief history of the CCF/NDP is particularly relevant and illuminating for two reasons: first, because the emergence and parliamentary successes of the CCF points towards the viability of socialist and deeply democratic imaginaries within the Canadian context; and second, because the eventual transformation of the CCF's 'radical planism' into the NDP's 'liberal leftism' speaks to the robustness of the established liberal-capitalist politico-economic order in the face of accommodationist and reformist challenges. While the CCF is remembered within Canadian national mythology as the party of public health care, its much more radical proposals have not survived in the public memory or in the form of its NDP successor. Participating enthusiastically in a thoroughly modern game of politico-economic social management, the legacy of the CCF/NDP in Canada is one of absorption, cooptation, and ultimately political marginality. Although McKay (2005) stresses the role of the CCF/NDP in 'rewriting' Canadian nationalism shifting it away from a 'decaying empire' to a vision of society emphasizing 'egalitarianism, social equality, and peace' (181), this shift would occur largely in the realm of national mythology rather than concretely shaping policy.

In the decades to follow, this national mythology would allow Canadian elites to embark upon all manner of aggressively neoliberal projects both nationally and internationally in addition to supporting and participating in a variety of neo-imperial and neocolonial adventures, all concealed beneath a cloak of a mythology valourizing Canada's commitment to social justice. Today, one need only look at the situation of Indigenous peoples, single mothers, the growing disparity between rich and poor, homelessness, child poverty, an aggressive foreign policy that sees Canada occupying both Haiti and Afghanistan and forsaking its commitments to the United Nations, and the role of Canadian-based corporations in a slew of humanitarian and ecological catastrophes to verify the hollowness of this mythology. It would be against this history that new and radical political currents associated with the New Left and the global social justice, anti-capitalist, and alter-globalization movements would emerge in the decades to come. Before turning to these newer Canadian histories, I must return to the United States and an exploration of histories of radical political action in the decades following the 1950s.

Northern Histories of the New Left

In the United States, the peace and civil rights struggles of the late 1950s and early 1960s provided much of the impetus for the emergence of the student New Left in the 1960s. A desire to find a new vocabulary of struggle and a new, non-accommodationist direction beyond the perceived narrowness of the Old Left inspired the student activists of the 1960s to experiment with decentralized participatory organization and new forms of peaceful direct action such as sit-ins (Epstein 1991, 44). Taking this point a step further, George Katsiaficas (1987) argues that the New Left was a 'world-historical movement' that not only reacted against the perceived failures of the Old Left but actively sought to reconceptualize radical social struggle and change. Katsiaficas' theorization of the New Left as a 'world-historical movement' of global proportions is by no means unproblematic, particularly given the retroactive nature of this theorization, but given the constraints of time and space and my central points of focus at hand this is an issue to which I cannot now attend. Asserting the properly global dimensions of the New Left as a movement aimed at the redistribution and decentralization of power and resources, Katsiaficas compellingly details the radical shifts in understandings of socio-political action and revolution introduced by the New Left, particularly in places like France and the United States.

Katsiaficas contends the global New Left was marked by five key characteristics: first, an opposition to racial, political, and patriarchal domination as well as economic exploitation; second, expressing a notion of freedom that extended beyond material deprivation to the production of subjectivities; third, forwarding an understanding of democracy that sought to deepen and radicalize it; fourth, promoting an enlarged conceptualization of revolution to emphasize the socio-cultural as well as the politico-economic; and fifth, focusing upon direct action tactics (23–7). While the lived reality of New Left struggles in countries around the world often did not live up to the promise of these principles, the New Left nevertheless provoked radical shifts in the understanding and practice of socio-political action and, as many theorists would contend, actually forced capitalism and its attendant systems of socio-political control on a global scale to drastically innovate in order to maintain force and coherence (see Dyer-Witheford 1999; Hardt and Negri 2004; Katsiaficas 1987; Virno 2004). Of course, these innovations would also simultaneously produce new possibilities for resistance and alternative-building.

In the United States, the sit-ins that swept the south at the beginning of the 1960s ushered in a new kind of politics, one which appealed to a younger generation in both the north and the south, convincing them that 'protest in the service of high ideals, and enacted with love and mutual respect, could be militant, radical – and effective' (Epstein 1991, 48). Out of this new political culture would emerge groups such as the Southern Non-Violent Coordinating Committee (SNCC) and the Students for a Democratic Society (SDS). As Polletta (2002) argues, 'Against the backdrop of the old left whose political paranoia and internecine squabbling seemed to be matched only by their ineffectuality, a movement characterized by radical democracy made good sense' (123). Yet the critiques mobilized by groups like SDS against the Old Left to some extent reflected a McCarthy era-inspired ignorance of the diversity of past struggles as well as the contributions they made to the socio-political context (Epstein 1991, 33). Indeed, the emergence and character of the New Left in the 1960s is a powerful demonstration of the tremendous importance of these histories of struggle upon emergent contours of political action. Reacting to the perceived failures of the Old Left, the New Left gravitated towards issues such as how social life as a whole should be organized and what ideas it should be governed by (ibid., 38). The increasingly obvious gaps between the rhetoric of democracy and the reality of it in the United States, the obvious reluctance of the Democratic Party to support progressive change, and the inflexibility of the ideology of liberalism and the dominant political order to address these fundamental concerns led to an increasing radicalization of the movement and a steady shift toward an explicitly revolutionary stance (ibid., 40–1). In reacting to these histories of compromised politics and the lapsed promises of liberalism, the New Left sought to forge a political subjectivity for itself that would be imminently revolutionary, but in so doing, it simultaneously brought about its own demise.

SNCC and SDS along with other movements of the 1960s would collapse by the end of the decade, a collapse that is often attributed to their turn towards an explicitly revolutionary focus and violence (Epstein 1991, 23). Both Epstein and Katsiaficas counter this prevailing analysis convincingly. In her analysis, Epstein (1991) asserts that it was not the explicitly 'revolutionary' position of the New Left that was a problem; rather, it was the framing of this revolutionary impulse according to largely traditional and economic conceptions of change coupled with the belief that this radical change could be brought about quickly (24). Reaching for 'models most readily available' and which turned out to be 'either outdated or based on foreign experience,' the movements of the late 1960s collapsed not only because of internal divisions and conflicts but also because of their failure to articulate a notion and project of revolution that made sense with regard to the context it was situated within (ibid.). In Katsiaficas' (1987) view, the New Left in the United States collapsed not only because of the abandonment of the mass movement by invaluable members who chose to adopt the tactics identified by Epstein and go underground but also because of government repression, infiltration, and propaganda combined with the system's capacity for reform, cooptation, deflection, and defusion (142–73). Thus the New Left's demise emerged out of a confluence of critical elements, including the inability to understand their own historical situatedness; the misappreciation of the socio-political system's capacity for repression, cooptation, and innovation; and the failure to critically evaluate their own reading of the histories of radical political action against which they set themselves. Of course the left would not simply disappear after the collapse of the movements of the 1960s. As Epstein and Polletta indicate, the direct action movement and a left countercultural movement would keep these histories alive through the 1970s and early 1980s, although without nearly the same profile as their predecessors. Furthermore, as Katsiaficas contends, the New Left would continue to exert significant influence long after its formal demise with respect to both legacies of radical political action as well as the ways in which the challenges it marshalled would force the socio-political and economic system to respond.

In Canada, the 1960s and 1970s also witnessed the emergence of New Left politics and struggles. Characterized by the same radical anti-hierarchical, non-accommodationist, extra-parliamentary spirit as the New Left movement to the south of the border and motivated by the same expansive understanding of the terrain of socio-political struggle, New Left organizations in Canada sought to work past the limitations of the Old Left and articulate a fundamentally new vision of the world. Groups such as the Student Union for Peace Action, the Student Christian Movement, and the Canadian Union of Students represented new forms of struggle in a left formation increasingly driven by youth and by an emphasis on radical and decentralized action (McKay 2005, 184). Significantly, New Left politics in Canada would find its centre in Montreal, Quebec, and this new leftism would emerge alongside of and in relation to the Québécois struggle for independence from the Canadian state (ibid., 186). Fusing international anti-colonial and anti-imperialist struggles with their own nationalist struggle against Canadian anglophone hegemony, embodied most militantly by the Front de Libération du Québec, Québécois leftists explicitly situated themselves as part of a world revolutionary process that was anti-capitalist, anti-imperialist, and radical rather than liberal (ibid., 187–8). In his survey of New Left activism in Quebec and English Canada, John Cleveland (2004) asserts that:

> ... 1960s new left activists recognized the difference between the movements and struggles they led and those led by existing Old Left communist and social democratic parties. The parties and unions of the workers' movement were mostly 'integrated.' The 1960s new left was self-consciously 'outside.' For many new leftists, this was because their own politics were outside socialism. For others, this was because the majority of workers were not (yet) supportive of radical socialism. A new socialism, stressing such ideas as national/racial-minority liberation, anti-authoritarianism and participatory democracy (workers' control) had to be developed to win workers over. By 1968 and after, the second perspective of rethinking the left's project as a new socialism was increasingly predominant in the left wing of contentious movements. (83)

In English Canada, outside of student radicalism, the New Left also influenced members of the New Democratic Party who, in the late 1960s, formed a splinter group within the party known as the Waffle movement (McKay 2005, 188). The Waffle movement sought to connect the party as only one element in a much broader and more radical socialist movement dedicated to fundamental social change rather than aiming at liberal reformism (ibid.). Nevertheless, much as the New Left in the United States, the movement in Quebec and in English Canada largely dissipated by the end of the 1970s. An inability to build a popular base outside of Quebec and the widening cultural and political chasms between the Québécois and the anglophone left eroded the radical potential of the New Left in the north of the Americas and brought about a premature end to dreams of fundamental social transformation (ibid., 191).

Beyond Histories of the 'New' and the 'Old'

The Canadian landscape, as in other contexts around the world, was far from barren even following the decline of New Left struggles of the 1960s. While new social movement (NSM) theory has chosen to depict activism in the post-1968 era as 'immaterially' rather than 'materially' oriented, based on socio-cultural rather than class struggle, directed towards issues of 'quality of life' rather than economic redistribution, and constituted by middle- rather than working-class constituents, critical analysts of contemporary histories of radical political action have forwarded very different interpretations of the legacies of the New Left. As Cleveland (2004) contends:

> New lefts since the 1960s wave have generally not promoted a public, new socialist politics. But this does not mean that there is a coherent New Left politics that is post-socialist and non-socialist, as NSM theory would have it. Rather, new lefts around the world face the task of rethinking the left radical project and rebuilding a new political left. This requires coming to terms with the legacy of previous lefts, including the socialism of the Old Left and the 1960s new left. NSM theory presumes the death of socialism but, ironically, it is the maintaining of the new liberal assumptions of the NSM approach that prevents seeing the centrality of the crisis of the left radical project (and the struggle to build a new one) to explaining the character of new movement left politics from the 1960s to the present day. (83–4)

On what grounds is it convincing to argue that post-1960s activism has not simply been characterized by a shift from socialism to liberalism? Cleveland (2004) outlines three main reasons to believe that much political contention after the explosiveness of the 1960s is marked by 'rethinking' of histories of radical action rather than their rejection: first, capitalism and imperialism continue to be identified as central to the injustices that new movements seek to overcome; second, 'classic left critique-transformation principles,' such as radical equality and direct democracy remain at the core of most proposed alternatives; and third, thinking about radical social change, even when it is posited as rejecting elements of past practice and theory, always occurs – as I have sought to demonstrate – in relation to past struggles, victories, failures, and histories (70). It bears mentioning that Cleveland's attempt to highlight the continuity between past and present left struggles for social change may overstate the degree to which this continuity is manifested, as well as overemphasizing the 'progressive' and 'cumulative' nature of social struggle and its attendant theories. Nevertheless, as the histories I have surveyed in this chapter demonstrate, even at times where the perspectives and practice of radical social struggle have undergone profound reformulation and even involved outright rejections of elements of contemporary and past practice, this process of rethinking and reformulation always occurs in relation to those elements and histories against which it is inevitably set. Even at times when it appears to disappear from view – such as during the 1980s in many parts of North America and Western Europe – the spirit of radicalism continues to operate, generating new possibilities and potentialities underground. From the 1960s onward, this radical spirit would be kept alive in the north of the Americas in large part through the work of radical and socialist feminists and direct action movements.

From the late 1960s to the 1990s, socialist and radical feminism emerged, coalesced, and produced profound effects upon the socio-political landscape, both within and outside of radical movements (McKay 2005, 192–5). Vigorously critiquing patriarchy, liberalism, capitalism, and the failures of New Left organizations and the movement in general to address issues of male power and privilege, radical and socialist feminists in Canada dramatically affected the nature and scope of leftist struggles as well as broader socio-political and economic relationships (ibid., 194–7). Indeed, as I will examine shortly, the feminist movement would prove to be absolutely central to the emergence of the alter-globalization movement in Canada during the late 1980s and early 1990s. Apart from this, as McKay emphasizes, radical and socialist feminists had a profound effect upon a tremendous range of social phenomena from issues of employment equity to the proliferation of women's studies within the academy to the legalization of abortion to the questioning of an expansive range of beliefs and assumptions about the social order and women's roles within it (ibid., 198). In the late 1960s and 1970s, the women's liberation movement exploded with feminist groups, parties, and bookstores proliferating across Canada bringing a radical and militant feminist network to bear upon injustices of the status quo (ibid., 199). In fact, 'women's liberation' from patriarchal domination was a project that also resonated in concert with other liberation movements globally, and in Canada this movement would achieve lasting institutional significance not only due to the scope and strength of the movement itself but also because of its impact upon the trade union movement and the New Democratic Party (ibid., 198). While the liberal-capitalist order and Canadian elites moved to coopt, absorb, and defuse this explosive movement in order to do so, the system was forced to accommodate many of its demands (ibid., 199–200). While the new millennium has borne witness to a significant feminist backlash, not coincidentally operating alongside the rise of neo-conservativism, a hyper-aggressive neoliberalism, and a re-armed and eager militarist imperialism, radical politics and even dominant socio-political and economic relationships in the North have been dramatically reshaped due to the influence of radical and socialist feminism.

As these partial histories of leftist political action in the north of the Americas demonstrate, new left formations and imaginations emerge and respond not only to the challenges and opportunities of the dominant socio-political order but also to what they perceive to be the failures and systemic complicity of their own predecessors and contemporaries. As Barbara Epstein (1991) asserts, movements have often criticized each other without recognizing either their own historical situatedness or the fact that there can be no 'correct revolutionary practice,' given that movements respond to different challenges at different times (22). While socialists, radicals, and other dissidents focused upon education, propagandizing, and grassroots agitation in the first two decades of the 1900s, the 1930s and 1940s would bear witness to an increasing emphasis upon parliamentary involvement, scientific models of social change, and the creation of the welfare state. Arguing that the movements of the 1930s 'can be seen as a baseline for the politics of the postwar era,' establishing the importance of class and the organization of the working class, bringing into focus the relationship between political movements and the state, and in fact through mobilization and struggle leading to the creation of the welfare state, Epstein incisively notes that these dynamics would of course shift over time (ibid.). For movements after the Second World War, the centrality of the working class and the state became increasingly problematic and activists of the New Left turned towards issues such as race, gender, or even a redefinition of the 'working class' (ibid., 23). For radical and socialist feminists of the 1960s and 1970s, patriarchy and women's oppression became central points of struggle deeply interwoven with other liberation movements globally and with the struggle against capitalism and the failures of liberalism more locally. By the late 1970s and early 1980s, the direct action movement moved away from a focus on the state 'both by placing the transformation of culture at the center of political activity and by envisioning a revolution that does not entail seizing state power' (Epstein 1991, 23).

It is against these histories that the contemporary resonance of

Zapatismo and its attendant political imaginations should be considered. As the histories presented here demonstrate, political subjectivities are not self-constituting, nor do they merely emerge out of the political context of the time; rather, they are products of a complex interplay between agency, context, imagination, and (re)readings of the socio-political histories against which they are set.

Neoliberalism, Social Justice, and a Newer History of Struggle

The histories of the Old and New Left are essential with respect to the resonance of Zapatismo in Canada and the United States. Alongside neoliberalism, these are the traditions against which the transnational significance of Zapatismo is set. However, contemporary socio-political challenges are, of course, just as relevant for appreciating the resonance of Zapatismo. The Canadian context is particularly illustrative of this. As Sherry Deveraux Ferguson asserts in her article 'A Cacophony of Voices: Competing for the Future' (2002), there are many challenges that face Canadians at the beginning of the twenty-first century, including a threat to cultural identities by new information and communications technologies; feminist challenges to a system that neglects older and single women and leaves many children in poverty; an aging society; issues concerning social cohesion as the country becomes more racially and ethnically diverse; sovereignty challenges from Quebec and Western Canada; and struggles for Aboriginal self-government (3). These are, of course, challenges perceived from a mainstream, liberal perspective and, if one were to factor in more radical critiques of the neoliberal capitalist order and of the nation-state itself, the list would be considerably longer and much more expansive and challenging. As Ferguson suggests, to deal with these challenges (including the ones not mentioned) requires a 'new paradigm' and yet there are no apparent models for such a paradigm (ibid.). While the Canadian federal government has sought to answer some of the challenges of national identity and social cohesion through such 'cultural' approaches as the *Heritage Minutes* (short films produced for Canadian audiences and delivered via TV, and often preceding feature films in movie theatres) produced by the Historical Foundation in the service of dominant and hegemonic interpretations of Canadian history (see Hodgins 2002), such approaches constitute little more than ideological bandages on an increasingly fractured body politic. Indeed, more recent histories of popular and radical mobilization in Canada are best understood as situated against this evermore riven national context and, in a sense, emerged alongside it.

In Canada, the histories perhaps most significant to the resonance of Zapatismo begin in the mid-1980s. To return to McKay's analysis of the formations of the Canadian left, this period represents the sixth formation of global social justice, anti-capitalist, and alter-globalization movements. Rather than being limited to the Canadian context, however, these histories also help explain the broader resonance of Zapatismo in the North. Central to these histories is the rise of a new phase of capitalist accumulation: neoliberalism. As a new phase of capitalism, neoliberalism emerged in the 1970s as a response to 'the contradictions between democratically governed national states responsive at least partially to citizens' needs and a global economy organized around profit-seeking [transnational corporations] and increasingly stateless financial capital' (Carroll 2005, 11). As Carroll notes, neoliberalism exacerbates and proliferates social divisions and inequalities; thus, rather than signalling the decline of the state, neoliberalism actually increases the need for a 'well-armoured' one (ibid., 12). Of course, the consequences of neoliberalism reach beyond its material implications. As cultural theorist Henry Giroux (2004) asserts:

> Neoliberalism is not simply an economic policy designed to cut government spending, pursue free-trade policies, and free market forces from governmental regulations; it is also a political philosophy and ideology that affects every dimension of social life. Indeed, neoliberalism has heralded a radical economic, political, and experiential shift that now largely defines the citizen as a consumer, disbands the social contract in the interests of privatized considerations, and separates capital from the context of place. (52)

Giroux argues that neoliberalism has effectively generated the conditions for the emergence of 'proto-fascism' in the United States, but surely this potential does not exist in the U.S. alone. This proto-fascism is characterized by a 'cult of traditionalism and reactionary modernism'; the corporatization of society and the privatization and 'diminishing' of public space; a culture of fear combined with 'patriotic correctness designed to bolster a rampant nationalism and a selective popularism'; control of the mass media through government regulation, concentration of corporate ownership, and 'sympathetic media moguls and spokespeople'; the rise of an 'Orwellian version of Newspeak' whose purpose it is to remove the tools of complex and critical reasoning; the collapse of the separation between church and state and the increasing use of religious rhetoric both as a marker for political identity as well as tool for policy formation; and the militarization of public space (Giroux 2004, 17–32). This proto-fascism and the neoliberal policies that have helped give it form and substance are much more than political or economic platforms, rather, they represent a particular kind of imagination in the face of which social democracy and Keynesian management has proven woefully inadequate. We require new imaginations, new sources of hope, if challenges are to be raised and alternatives are to be realized.

In light of this, in what must be considered nothing less than a gross understatement, Carroll (2005) asserts, that 'the neoliberal state offers precious little room for social reform' (13). While the relative class compromise of the post–world war years yielded a brief period of material success for workers in the North (the story is, of course, very different for the world's majorities located outside of these enclaves), the 'hyper-capitalism' that emerged in the 1970s and whose form continues to take on ever more aggressive, invasive, and rapacious contours has effectively undermined the practice and imagination of social democracy (see Ratner 2005, 151–4). In its place stands the 'Third Way,' which – while withdrawing resources from communities, dismantling the welfare state, forcibly evacuating the public sphere in order to prepare it for privatization, and refusing to address the structural inequalities generated by capitalism – speaks in the quiet and soothing language of consensus, individual empowerment, and opportunity.

Of course, neoliberalism has been far from uncontested. In the north of the Americas it is these histories of popular movements attempting to challenge the neoliberal agendas of their respective governments and business elites – and their failures – that provide a compelling backdrop against which to situate the resonance of Zapatismo and the emergence of radical new imaginations of struggle and possibility. In the Canadian context, as Jeffrey M. Ayres (1998) explains, the period between the massive victory of the Progressive Conservative Party in September 1984 and the initiation of formal free trade negotiations between Canada and the United States in December 1985 'represented a watershed in Canadian political history' (21). This period marked the emergence of anti-free trade coalitions and the consolidation of organizations in the anti-free trade movement. Analyst and activist Tony Clarke (1997) has characterized this moment as witnessing the rise of a 'dynamic' and multi-sectoral 'movement of resistance' to the 'corporate agenda' (138). Linked to fears about the loss of sovereignty and identity, the broad nature of the perceived threats presented by the Free Trade Agreement (FTA) facilitated the emergence of a country-wide anti-FTA coalition comprised of both nationalist and popular sectors (Ayres 1998, 23–31). The nationalist sector was represented primarily by the Council of Canadians (COC), while the popular sector was comprised of a diverse range of organizations from church groups to women's organizations to organized labour (ibid., 31). Clarke (1997) asserts that the 'backbone' of 'this broadly-based citizens' movement' has been comprised of labour unions, particularly the Canadian Labour Congress and the Confédération des Syndicats Nationaux in Quebec, while its 'sparkplug' has been 'various social organizations' such as the COC and the National Action Committee on the Status of Women (NAC) as well as the National Farmers' Union, Greenpeace and the Canadian Environment Network, the Ecumenical Coalition for Economic Justice, Oxfam, CUSO, and Inter Pares (138–9). Significantly, the ground had been prepared for the emergence of an anti-FTA coalition by the 1981–2 recession, which had impacted 'popular sector' groups such as churches, unions, women's groups, social agencies, Native peoples, and farmers most severely and led them to begin articulating a counter-discourse on the Canadian economy (Ayres 1998, 32–9). With FTA negotiations looming, the groups that found themselves most vulnerable during the recent recession perceived increasing market liberalization as a threat to their survival cutting across more particular or 'sectoral' interests.

These popular groups not only reacted to the threat of an increasingly liberalized economy, they began to construct new discourses about society and the economy. Rejecting the ideology of neo-conservativism espoused by the Mulroney government in Canada, Reagan in the U.S., and Thatcher in Britain, the popular sector focused on promoting a vision of Canada that included full employment, national self-reliance, and democratizing decision-making processes (Ayres 1998, 39–40). Within this emerging coalition, a particularly significant role was taken up by the National Action Committee on the Status of Women, which gave voice to a radical and resonant critique of the FTA in addition to convincing other groups to move beyond their sectoral interests and focus on coalition-building (ibid., 41–3).

Founded as an autonomous umbrella organization in 1972, NAC united fifteen smaller women's groups across the country, but by 1988 it had grown to include 586 different groups (Macdonald 2002, 157).

NAC's founding members included 'older middle-class groups and newer, more radical groups that originated in student, anti-war and new left activism' (ibid.). While NAC's membership was largely white and middle class at its inception, working-class and leftist women nevertheless maintained a significant, if minority, presence within it, as well as within the broader women's movement. Furthermore, in contrast with the European context where socialism was based primarily in organized labour, Canadian socialism was rooted in broad popular movements, rendering it more receptive to feminist challenges than the more conventional version of Marxism. In line with this, NAC sought to reach beyond class-based notions of solidarity and to build deep links with immigrant, Indigenous, and other women of colour (ibid.).

At the time of its formation in the 1970s, a responsive government and a relatively friendly political opportunity structure encouraged the state-friendly character of the English-Canadian women's movement. The women's movement was also deeply inflected by a nationalist sentiment that arose in the 1960s as a response to fears about U.S. domination. During the 1970s, NAC's liberal, lobby-group approach yielded some considerable successes including the expansion of day care, the inclusion of 'sex' as a prohibited basis of discrimination in human rights provisions, decriminalization of abortion, and equal pay (Macdonald 2002, 157). NAC also paved the way for the inclusion of equality on the basis of sex in the constitution during the 1980s, a victory that was all the more important given the U.S.-based National Organization for Women's (NOW) failure to achieve an Equal Rights Amendment during the same period. In fact, while NOW espoused a strongly mainstream liberal approach and relied upon mechanisms such as court challenges to attempt policy change (often unsuccessfully), NAC adapted to an increasingly hostile political environment by radicalizing its approach through the 1980s (ibid., 162). The inclusion of more 'radical' identities (lesbians, women with disabilities, immigrants, Indigenous) led to NAC's rejection of its earlier corporatist and reformist style, as did the rise to power of the Conservative Party under Brian Mulroney in 1984 (ibid., 158). NOW and the U.S. women's movement remained by and large on the sidelines during debates over the FTA and NAFTA, and the Mexican women's movement – along with much of Mexican civil society – was largely excluded from these debates. In Canada, however, NAC openly and vigorously opposed the Conservatives, their free trade policy, and their deficit-cutting agenda (all fundamental tenets of neoliberal politico-economic dogma) (ibid., 162–4). Due in no small part to NAC's dedicated coalition-building effort, the Coalition Against Free Trade (CAFT), the first anti-FTA coalition in North America, was born in the Toronto office of NAC on 11 December 1984 (Ayres 1998, 43).

However, the cohesion of CAFT was almost immediately threatened by internal tensions. Conflicts emerged primarily between women's and church groups on the one side and labour represented by the Canadian Labour Congress (CLC) on the other (Ayres 1998, 55). Exemplifying the classical corporatist, business unionism approach to labour organizing, the CLC located its interests in the realm of 'social democratic electoralism,' collective bargaining, and 'deference to the hierarchical leadership and vertical decision-making structures of the labour bureaucracy' whereas the 'new politics' of church, women's, and environmental groups in particular sought to develop 'an extraparliamentary stance,' with a focus upon coalition building within the popular sector characterized by a more horizontal, democratic decision-making and organizational structure (ibid., 55–6). At Dialogue '86, the first major gathering of popular sector community groups and labour to discuss free trade, this mounting tension would be resolved largely in favour of the 'new politics' of the popular groups. In the face of the CLC's attempt to impose its own politics and agenda on the larger movement, popular groups and sympathetic labour unions met on an ad hoc basis to share concerns and established a powerful challenge to the CLC leadership in so doing (ibid., 56–9). With the support of key unions such as the Canadian Union of Public Employees and the Canadian Auto Workers, church and women's groups prevailed over CLC attempts at domination and planted 'the seeds of a new, non-hierarchical style of cooperation between labour and the popular sector' (ibid., 59). In the face of attempts to impose hierarchy, rigidity, and a narrow pre-established agenda upon the larger anti-FTA movement, popular groups and sympathetic labour unions found a way to work past their own specific issues and to cultivate a much broader terrain of struggle.

Despite the success of this new politics in building and maintaining a broad coalition against free trade, the movement was about to face challenges that it would not be able to meet effectively. Although in April of 1987 a 'coalition of coalitions' emerged to oppose the FTA calling itself the Pro-Canada Network (PCN), the force of the movement had begun to decline in the face of an aggressive business counter-response and the emergence of rifts and conflicts between affiliated groups both towards the movement as well as around relationships between the movement and political parties (ibid., 107). At the time of the free trade debates,

Canada's federal political spectrum (parties who could claim to represent constituencies throughout Canada, thus essentially excluding federal parties with a regional base like the Quebec nationalist Bloc Québécois), moving roughly and rather loosely from 'left' to 'right,' was represented by the New Democratic Party (NDP), the Liberal Party (LP), and the Progressive Conservative Party (PCP). The conflicts within and challenges to the anti-FTA movement were compounded when, during the 1988 election campaign, the New Democratic Party abandoned its stance against free trade in the final weeks of the campaign even as the Liberal Party opportunistically moved to become more receptive to the PCN, fracturing an important relationship between progressive electoral and extraparliamentary forces (ibid., 110). But the challenges to the anti-free trade movement went much deeper than tactical failures.

The collapse of the relationship between the federal NDP and the PCN was a severe blow to the anti-free trade movement, but its impact would be multiplied by several other significant challenges and failures. First, the movement's inability to overcome regional and national cleavages, and particularly to convince a majority of Québécois to identify with and support a predominately anglophone and explicitly nationalist anti-free trade movement, proved too great a failure from which to recover (Ayres 1998, 111). Second, the aggressive and effective business counter-response seriously eroded the movement's momentum. Third, the movement's strength as an extraparliamentary and popular force was seriously drained as a result of the constraints of participating in an electoral campaign, particularly when the NDP abandoned the movement in the last weeks of the campaign and its capacity for institutional leverage essentially disappeared. Finally, the movement suffered from a waning sense of political efficacy due both to the proliferation of internal divisions and the 'inhospitable environment' of the federal election (ibid., 115). Once again, one of the most significant points of tension to emerge within the movement was between organized labour and other popular actors in the coalition.

While organized labour contributed resources, research, regional offices, experienced activists, and a mobilizeable membership to the coalition, difficulties persisted (Huyer 2004, 51). These tensions emerged in a number of ways, including difficulties in reconciling approaches; mixed views on the part of labour with respect to participating in a coalition; inter-group conflict, especially between women's and environmental groups and labour; differences in structure, decision-making, and leadership styles; concerns about the relationship between labour and the NDP; and issues of 'representation and accountability' (ibid., 49). NAC struggled particularly with labour's patriarchal attitudes and refusal to engage issues through a gendered lens of analysis (ibid., 55; see also Macdonald 2002). In addition to this, resource-rich unions were seen as exercising disproportionate control over the coalition in addition to forcing a particular style of leadership and decision-making on others (ibid., 57). As Huyer summarizes in her analysis of the tensions experienced in the PCN:

> The feminist, environmental, and anti-racist analyses of other groups at times came into conflict with what was seen as a predominately political and economic perspective of labour, further complicated by the situation that many union members, especially auto workers, are now solidly middle class. This problematised the belief that the unions speak for the disenfranchised and marginalized – who, in the Canadian coalition, were more closely tied to the National Action Committee on the Status of Women and anti-poverty groups. (57)

The combination of these elements would lead to another Progressive Conservative victory in the November election as well as a de facto defeat of the domestic 'anti-free trade insurgency' (Ayres 1998, 107–15). While both the PCN and the COC would persist following this defeat (the PCN would be renamed the Action Canada Network, ACN, in 1991), the political environment between 1988 and 1993 would prove decidedly less favourable to mobilization (ibid., 117). Yet even as domestic opportunities closed down, new transnational terrains of struggle and opportunity opened up within the context of the negotiations over the North American Free Trade Agreement (NAFTA).

While domestic political opportunities for mobilization continued to erode as a result of economic globalization, the passage of the FTA, and the state becoming less willing, able, or interested in meeting the demands of the Action Canada Network, new transnational terrains were emerging for activists. Initiatives such as Common Frontiers (CF), the International Citizen's Forum (ICF), Mujer a Mujer (Woman to Woman), and Mujeres en Acción Sindical (Women in Union Action) emerged on this terrain providing a variety of fora and organizations for new forms of transnational political action (Ayres 1998, 123–9). A working group on North American economic integration, Common Frontiers emerged out of a visit in September 1988 by representatives of various social groups to the U.S.–Mexico border to investigate the implications of maquiladoras for Canada under the FTA (ibid., 123). Common Frontiers brought together labour, church, human rights, environmental, and economic justice groups in a 'multi-sectoral network' to research and mobilize around economic and social justice issues of an increasingly integrated continental economy. Common Frontiers also organized regular strategy meetings such as the 'Canada-Mexico Encuentro' held in Mexico City in October 1990, which brought together Canadian and Mexican organizations to discuss the potential implications of NAFTA for Mexican sovereignty, a meeting that led to the formation of the Mexican Action Network on Free Trade (ibid., 123–4). Groups like Common Frontiers provided not only concrete moments of transnational anti-free trade linkage but also marked the shifting contours of continental political action.

The International Citizen's Forum (ICF) held in Zacatecas, Mexico, in October 1991, which coincided with the third meeting of trade ministers negotiating NAFTA, is another example of how the site of political action had begun to shift to a somewhat more transnational terrain. Bringing together more than 300 popular-sector representatives from the U.S., Canada, and Mexico, the ICF endorsed a declaration proposing an alternative to NAFTA for continental development, emphasizing 'development, democracy, self-determination, and the elevation of living standards' (Ayres 1998, 125). In a similar vein, in February 1992, Mujer a Mujer and Mujeres en Acción Sindical brought women's groups together from across North America in the First Trinational Working Women's Conference on Free Trade and Continental Integration in Valle de Bravo, Mexico (ibid., 127). Previous histories of popular political mobilization and struggle had taught Canadian activists important lessons regarding the nature and terrain of political action in an increasingly globalized world, lessons which profoundly shaped the contours of their activism in the period leading up to the implementation of NAFTA.

The period between the Progressive Conservative victory in 1988 and the federal election in 1993 represented a tremendously significant time with respect to the Canadian political terrain. As Ayres (1998) notes, the 1993 federal election in Canada in many ways represented the closure of political opportunities that had 'nurtured and sustained popular sector influence on the Canadian party and parliamentary system' (131–2). The 1993 elections would sweep the federal Liberal Party to power, reduce the Progressive Conservative Party to near oblivion, and consign the federal New Democrats to total marginality (ibid.). The significance of this dramatic electoral shift for social action was that the Liberal Party had moved steadily rightward since 1988, becoming supporters of free trade and the global economy while once-powerful actors such as the Action Canada Network had come to be seen as unimportant as a base of support (ibid., 129). At the provincial level, the early 1990s witnessed electoral victories for the NDP in British Columbia, Saskatchewan, and Ontario, but rather than ushering in progressive social democratic governments, these governments proceeded to enact prototypical neoliberal economic 'reforms' (ibid., 130; see also Carroll and Ratner 2005). Bob Rae's government in Ontario was the most ambitious of all, imposing a 'social contract' on the public sector, ripping up collective agreements, wooing the business sector, and doing tremendous damage to the fabric of the social welfare system (see McBride 2005).

Although these actions produced a harsh backlash against provincial and federal branches of the NDP, combined with the results of the federal election, they would also serve to convince many that the institutional political arena was one increasingly devoid of possibilities. This would be the new political terrain confronting popular and radical movements from the mid-1990s onward. As Ayres (1998) suggests, the North American continental economy helped facilitate shifts in protest strategies adopted by various popular-sector groups across Canada, from state-centred campaigns mobilized around the 'nation' and 'national sovereignty' to 'broader collective campaigns' transcending national sovereignty and borders to focus on 'transnational democracy and popular sovereignty,' a shift whose impetus resided largely in the globalization of the world's economy (135). While Ayres is careful to note that such a transition does not point to an end of traditional national or state-based movements, it does suggest 'an era of greater transnational activity and protest by movements within a context of growing North American continental integration' (ibid.). The nation-state need not be in 'decline' for activists to consider the transnational a vital terrain for political action, particularly when one considers the powerful force of regional and global economic integration.

Of course none of this should be taken as absolute. As Josée Johnston and Gordon Laxer (2003) argue, 'It is possible to have nationally-rooted projects for economic self-determination that also make transnational connections of solidarity with movements in other nations, and that allow for the co-existence of transnational and sub-national identities' (78). In part, this new terrain is inhabited by more familiar and established 'progressive nationalist' movements centred around issues such as 'good governance' and 'empowering civil society' and motivated by critiques of 'corporate capitalism' and the 'hijacking' of the state and liberal democracy – although rarely of capitalism, the state form, and liberalism themselves (see for example Barlow 2005; Barlow and Clarke 2001; Clarke 1997). While these groups and movements have taken up many of the challenges and opportunities of mobilizing in an increasingly globalized and neoliberalized context, they remain wedded to largely liberal, state-centred, softly nationalistic, and social democratic values and visions. Given the histories I have explored in this chapter, there is clearly significant doubt about whether these movements and the terms upon which they operate are capable of addressing the force and dynamics of neoliberalism and its attendant proto-fascism. But this new political terrain is also occupied by movements inspired by much more radical political imaginations and it is to these movements, and the resonance of Zapatismo within them, which I will turn to shortly.

The political histories that I have offered here constitute a partial picture against which to set the resonance of Zapatismo as well as the emergence of contemporary forms of global justice and global anti-capitalist action. As my narrative has detailed, there is no progression in histories of political action – the New Left did not emerge as the next stage in a struggle; rather, it was a response articulated by people who interpreted histories of political action as they understood them, and interpretations – as with all human action – are never perfect or complete. The implications of my analysis here are twofold: first, that alongside of considerations of contemporary context, it is through the engagement of these histories of activism and political action that contemporary socio-political subjectivities emerge; second, neither these histories nor these socio-political subjectivities are ever absolute or complete – they are inspired by perceptions of political opportunities and challenges, by the agency of human actors, by the desire to imagine and begin to build a better world. In considering the possible futures of revolutionary action, Eric Selbin (2003) argues forcefully for the importance of story, narrative, and symbol for understanding not only radical and revolutionary change as it has been envisioned and attempted in the past but also for the ways in which it may do so in the present and future. I share his conviction. Indeed, as I will demonstrate in what follows, it is through a consideration of contemporary histories that it becomes possible to catch glimpses of the political movements of the past and of possible future movements as well.

3 Dreams of Revolution, Myths of Power: Mexican Revolutionary Histories

We are a product of five hundred years of struggle: first, led by insurgents against slavery during the War of Independence with Spain; then to avoid being absorbed by North American imperialism; then to proclaim our constitution and expel the French empire from our soil; later when the people rebelled against Porfirio Diaz's dictatorship, which denied us the just application of the reform laws, and leaders like Villa and Zapata emerged, poor men just like us who have been denied the most elementary preparation so they can use us as cannon fodder and pillage the wealth of our country. They don't care that we have nothing, absolutely nothing, not even a roof over our heads, no land, no work, no health care, no food or education, not the right to freely and democratically elect our political representatives, nor independence from foreigners. There is no peace or justice for ourselves and our children.

But today we say: ENOUGH IS ENOUGH!

From 'The First Declaration of the Lacandón Jungle,' The General Command of the EZLN (Ejército Zapatista de Liberación Nacional 2001c)

Revolution is everywhere in Mexico. Or, more accurately, the mythology of revolution is everywhere in Mexico. The myth and metaphor of revolution is woven through and materialized in a tremendous diversity of socio-political forms. As I asserted in the previous chapter, by myth I am not referring to something untrue or something that is merely a constructed foundational story; rather, in the spirit of the work of Roland Barthes (1972), I understand myth as a kind of interpellating mode of signification or speech, one which participates in the formation of subjects even as it engages them (124). As I noted in chapter 1 with respect to histories of radical political action in Canada and the United States, myth 'calls' to us and our subjectivity is shaped as we respond to it. In Mexico, 'revolution' has become just such a mode of signification and interpellation.

From the art of the great Mexican muralist Diego Rivera, which adorns the halls of the Palacio Nacional and the Palacio de Bellas Artes, to the national monuments honouring the revolution of 1910 and its fallen heroes, to the names of political parties, to the educational curriculum, to the names of subway stations in the Federal District, to the rhetoric of generations of dissidents and insurgents, Mexico is a nation in which the notion of 'revolution' is charged with deep power and profound significance. The trope of revolution continues to resonate powerfully within Mexican nationalism, and it has served as one of the most powerful symbolic tools in the nation-state building project engaged in by Mexican elites since the 1910 revolution. Yet as Mexican anthropologist Claudio Lomnitz (2001) asserts, 'Nationalism is neither an accomplished fact nor an established essence, it is, rather, the moving horizon that actors point to when they need to appeal to the connections between the people and the polity, when they discuss rights and obligations, or try to justify or reject modernization and social change' (xiv–xv). If nationalism is a horizon without fixed essence, however, then the mythology and metaphor of revolution is even more so. The story of revolution in Mexico has been appropriated, rewritten, contested, and continually deployed and redeployed by a tremendous diversity of actors from political and economic elites to the Indigenous insurgents and base communities of the Zapatista Army of National Liberation. What this means of course is that neither nationalism nor revolution are historically transcendent entities; rather, they have been and continue to be deployed in the service of widely divergent social agendas and they themselves continue to be shaped and reshaped by the people who inhabit the territory known as Mexico.

Of course, by contending that 'revolution' has mythological forms and properties in Mexico I do not mean that the Mexican Revolution did not happen or that it is somehow untrue. Instead, I contend that the legacy of the Mexican Revolution of 1910–17 has been and continues to be the object of appropriation and contestation by a multiplicity of actors. These revolutionary histories are deployed by different actors at different times in order to establish the legitimacy of various projects, generate popular consent and support, and, ultimately, to bring certain kinds of subjects into being in the world. They also serve as a vital point of engagement for the emergence of new kinds of political projects and their attendant imaginations.

Revolution is the theme that structures this chapter. It is not my aim to delve into the profound complexity of Mexican revolutionary history, such an endeavour is beyond my purposes here. Rather, this chapter is directed towards situating Zapatismo and the Zapatista movement within the socio-symbolic context of Mexican history, particularly since the Revolution of 1910. I have two purposes in doing this. First, in order to appreciate the processes of transmission, translation, and resonance that have facilitated the transnationalization of Zapatismo, it is necessary to engage the socio-historical and political roots of the Zapatista movement. This is not an attempt to construct a clear lineage for Zapatismo; it is, instead, an effort to conceive of it as what Deleuze and Guattari (1987) would call a 'body without organs,' as a social body which is not simply an organism characterized and constituted by the organization of its organs (in this case its contemporary socio-political organization and its historical roots) but as a 'living body all the more alive and teeming,' because it fundamentally exceeds the sum or organization of its 'parts' (30). This is also not an attempt to understand what Zapatismo 'really is' in order to compare it to how activists in Canada and the United States have 'read it' or 'appropriated it'; rather, this contextualization is necessary both in order to understand the sociocultural and political matrix from which Zapatismo has emerged and upon which it has grounded the articulation of struggle – both in terms of concrete strategies and tactics as well as the production of meaning. As I will demonstrate in this chapter, the emergence of the EZLN and its radical critique of power, a critique which would become one of the central pillars for Zapatismo's resonance transnationally, cannot be separated from the cultural-political-historical matrix of the Mexican revolutionary tradition.

My second purpose is to examine the ways in which Zapatismo has resonated within the Mexican national context. Specifically, I seek to illuminate the socio-symbolic – even 'mythological' – character of Zapatismo that has served as the foundation for its influence on Mexican national consciousness broadly and upon specific sectors of Mexican civil society particularly. In some ways, this chapter is an attempt to take up Daniel Nugent's challenge in his essay 'Northern Intellectuals and the EZLN' (2002) to 'consider ... discourses historically, comparing the ways in which words like "freedom" and "justice" figure in their respective vocabularies, and how they relate to their concrete and changing historical referents, their material and social conditions, their political practices and struggles' (362). In other ways, this chapter is an attempt to explore the complex histories of Zapatismo and revolution more broadly in Mexico and to examine how these histories are implicated in the production of powerful signifying assemblages at times directed towards the creation and maintenance of regimes of paternalistic and hierarchical socio-political control and at others towards the articulation of deeply liberatory political imaginations and practices.

The Roots of Rebellion

Mexican history is rich with local revolts, regional uprisings, national revolution, and counter-revolution. Apart from the drama of these events, they have contributed powerfully – concretely, conceptually, and symbolically – to the shaping of the social and political space within which popular organizing and mobilization has occurred. Following the Spanish invasion of Mesoamerica, Indigenous peoples frequently sought ways to resist Spanish rule, resistance that often took the form of active rebellion (Cockcroft 1998, 35; see also Weinberg 2000). In addition to open and armed rebellion, however, Indigenous peoples also sought to resist Spanish plunder of their lands through the legal channels available through Indian legislation, which 'declared respect for the territorial patrimony of indigenous peoples'. and, while rarely respected, created a precedent which would not soon be forgotten (Warman 1976, 29). Thus, Indigenous peoples contested Spanish incursion through various means, both 'legal' and 'extra-legal,' during the colonial period, an approach which would continue in the independence and revolutionary periods as well.

Popular rebellion was unleashed in Mexico during the Wars of Independence, which began in 1810. But this revolutionary story of struggle against Spain is by no means as simple as a 'Mexican' rejection of Spanish domination. The independence movement was an internally contradictory affair comprised of 'commercial-industrial-agricultural' interests aiming to gain control over the 'bureaucratic pivot' of Mexico City, elements in rebellion against 'centralized officialdom' of the colonial state, and, finally, agents seeking to realize a regime of social justice (Wolf 1969, 7–8). In this final dimension, it was two priests,

Father Miguel Hidalgo and Father José María Morelos, who raised peasant armies in opposition to the abuses and excesses of the colonial state and its masters (Cockcroft 1998, 55). The element of social justice was particularly evident in the leadership of the insurrection by Morelos. On 17 November 1810 Morelos proclaimed an end to discrimination and institutionalized racism (Wolf 1969, 8). Furthermore, Morelos declared an end to slavery and to Indian tribute as well as demanding the return of lands that had been stolen from Indigenous peoples (ibid.). However, as Eric Wolf notes, 'as soon as it became evident that the revolt was also a war of the poor against entrenched privilege, the army, the Church, and the great landowners came to the support of the Spanish Crown and crushed the rebellion' (ibid., 9). Independence would ultimately be won for Mexico from Spain in 1821 by elites seeking to protect their own advantage and wealth in the face of a liberalizing Spanish constitution, prefiguring a liberal/conservative conflict that would reach its climax in the 1860s. The revolutionary struggle for independence mobilized by Hidalgo and Morelos was thus both exploited and ultimately crushed by an opportunistic and self-interested elite bent on satisfying its own desires. This was not the last time this situation would occur.

In Chiapas, this national move for reactionary independence found its echo. Following Mexico's independence from Spain, Chiapas was annexed by Mexico, an event engineered by the Chiapanecan elite to preserve their commercial interests and maintain their domination of Indigenous labour (Benjamin 1996, 11). Following the annexation, it quickly became clear that two primary elite factions were emerging to struggle against each other in the control of land and labour: 'the grandees of the Central Highlands, and the farmers and ranchers of the Central Valley' (ibid., 13). Each of these factions in turn became linked to the struggle that was playing itself out in central Mexico, with the farmers and ranchers of the valleys challenging the power of the heirs of the colonial oligarchy and identifying with liberalism while the established powerholders, including the church, identified with conservatism. In Chiapas, the primary prize at stake was the control and exploitation of the Indigenous population and their labour (ibid., 13–14). With the identification of regional elites with the liberal/conservative polarization of central Mexico, the dynamics of national struggle that would explode in the 1850s and after would have profound resonance in Chiapas as well.

The next chapter in the Mexican revolutionary story would take place in the 1850s. While the dictator Santa Anna had successfully managed to repress, jail, or execute many of his political foes, the challenge posed by liberal leaders such as Benito Juárez with the support of anti-government rebels in Guerrero proved to be too much and Santa Anna ceded power and sailed into exile (Cockcroft 1998, 70–1). While this act of power changing hands by no means signified lasting social peace in Mexico, it did entail some profound consequences. Once in power, the triumphant liberals passed into law what became known as the Liberal Reform (or Reform Laws), abolishing clerical and military special privileges and forbidding any 'corporation' from owning property. While conservatives were enraged by these changes, the abolition of 'corporately held property' affected not only Church lands but peasant ejidos (communally-held and worked land) thus representing a profound challenge to traditional forms of peasant landholding (ibid., 71). However, once again, 'revolutionary' history in Mexico would be written by elite factions rather than popular movements. In this case, it would be the conservatives of Mexico rather than the peasantry who would stage a powerful challenge to the liberal regime through the assistance of direct French military intervention and the imposition of Mexico's new 'emperor,' Austrian Archduke Maximilian, resulting in civil war from 1862 until 1867 (ibid., 72).

In order to finance their war against their conservative opponents and the French invasion, the liberals proceeded to accelerate the pace of land expropriation from its largely Indigenous holders, peasants who often could not 'prove' their ownership (ibid., 72). While the Reform Laws were intended to 'free the individual from traditional fetters,' they succeeded only in introducing new forms of bondage to the lives of people who already faced multiple forms of domination and exploitation (Wolf 1969, 13). In the words of Eric Wolf (1969), 'Freedom for the landowner would mean freedom to acquire more land to add to his already engorged holdings; freedom for the Indian – no longer subject to his community and now lord of his own property – would mean the ability to sell his land, and to join the throng of landless in search of employment' (13). This social struggle, a conflict between liberal and conservative elites, of course had profound consequences for the peoples inhabiting the territory known as Mexico. However, within this unfolding narrative of liberal reform versus conservative privilege, they would figure only as those acted-upon, not as actors in their own right.

In Chiapas, 'progress' and 'modernization' entailed very particular dimensions. Indeed, Indigenous indebted servitude and debt servitude became 'one of the faces of ... "progress" in the 1870s and 1880s' (Benjamin 1996, 28). Ironically, 'revolution' or claims to progressive reform for Chiapanecos would all too often come to signify new and even more pervasive forms of domination and exploitation. The history of revolution and reform in Chiapas, and in Mexico as a whole, is indeed a complicated and ambivalent one. Ultimately, the radical destabilization that would result from this liberal-conservative conflict would culminate in the Mexican Revolution. It is a sad irony that even as liberal and conservative elites sought to consolidate their privilege and power by pillaging the nation's peasantry, the war against the French invaders was fought and won largely by peasants and workers engaged in guerrilla struggle (Cockcroft 1998, 75). This, too, is a circumstance that would not be manifested for the last time.

The Science of Progress and Dreams of Revolution

The liberal victory, however, secured neither peace nor prosperity. What it did do, from the perspective of revolutionary history, was set the stage for the Mexican Revolution in 1910. Made vulnerable by debt, feuding, and internal strife, the liberal 'bourgeois-democratic' state gave way in 1876 to an 'oligarchic-dictatorial' one led by General Porfirio Díaz who would rule the country until the Revolution unseated him in 1911 (Cockcroft 1998, 81). During his thirty-five-year reign, Díaz would pursue the liberal modernization project for Mexico, building industry and elite wealth on the backs of the peasantry and workers and brutally silencing opposition (ibid.). Díaz and his inner circle of advisers came to be known as the 'Científicos' (scientists) due to their claims to be positivist scientists who saw the modernization of Mexico through the obliteration of the Indigenous element and the 'furtherance of "white" control, national or international' (Wolf 1969, 14). Under Díaz's paternalistic control, Juárez's liberal reform became a modernizing 'revolution' that undermined the few remaining bases of social and political autonomy afforded to Indigenous peoples throughout Mexico.

Chiapas, under the 'enlightened caciquismo' (charismatic and coercive leadership) of Porfirian governors such as Emilio Rabasa and his successors, would become 'one of the laboratories of modernization' (Benjamin 1996, 34). In Chiapas, modernization meant many things, including 'building roads and railroads; erecting telegraph and telephone lines; establishing schools; applying scientific methods to farming and industry; and,' most significantly, 'transforming Indians into yeoman farmers, free laborers, and Mexicans' (ibid., 33). Modernization, progress, development, and science thus came to represent the obliteration of all that was 'backward' and, by extension, all that was Indigenous. Under Governor Rabasa's program of agrarian reform known as 'el reparto' and 'el fraccionamiento,' which sought to increase the number of small farmers and property owners in the state in line with liberal ideas of development and progress, the assault on village ejidos was intensified (ibid., 49). Indigenous peoples, now largely land-less, would form the new labour base for the haciendas, which had swallowed up their lands. With the loss of land experienced by Indige-nous communities, forms of labour exploitation proliferated in Chiapas. Indigenous peoples were forced into systems of 'indebted servitude, temporary migrant labor, and slave labor' with those not tied to large estates by debt working as day wage labourers, sharecroppers, or renters (ibid., 89). Despite these conditions, it would not be until the beginning of the twentieth century that Díaz would experience the beginnings of a serious challenge to his dictatorship, a challenge mar-shalled by what would become known as the Precursor Movement of the Mexican Revolution.

The Partido Liberal Mexicano (PLM, Mexican Liberal Party), also known as the Precursor Movement, was officially organized in 1905, but had grown out of hundreds of 'Liberal Clubs' formed at the beginning of the century by 'disgruntled bourgeois liberals and intellectuals from the intermediate classes upset by the regime's authoritarianism and concessions to the clergy' (Cockcroft 1998, 91). PLM anarchist leaders such as Ricardo and Enrique Flores Magón and Antonio Diaz Soto y Gama worked to 'radicalize' the 'pro-democracy anticlericalism' of these Liberal Clubs and moved their demands in a more 'class-based peasant-proletarian direction' (ibid.). In 1906, the PLM officially turned itself into a political-military organization motivated by a radical anti-imperial ideology and strongly in favour of the working classes, peasants, and 'progressive elements of the intermediate classes and the bourgeoisie,' drawing tens of thousands of Mexicans to its cause (ibid.). It is at this point that an anarcho-revolutionary Mexican discourse emerges in opposition to the elite-driven reformist projects of the last century. Within a history of the Mexican revolutionary tradition, the PLM signifies a consolidation of a genuinely popular revolutionary entity. Over the next four years, the PLM would organize strikes and even armed uprisings against the Díaz regime, actions that were ruth-lessly and bloodily put down by the military (ibid., 92). The PLM was the only authentically revolutionary force on the political scene in Mexico as the Porfiriato neared its end in 1910. Although the PLM had succeeded in shaking the legitimacy of the regime, the unseating of the dictator himself (in a refrain typical of this revolutionary history), would fall to another representative of Mexico's elite: Francisco Madero.

While peasants and workers were massacred by the military for demonstrating their opposition to Díaz's regime, northern industrialists were chafing against what they perceived as a regime that had ceased to serve their interests. When Díaz decided to accept the nomination for president himself once again in 1910, the northern bourgeoisie rallied behind the affluent and liberal-minded Francisco Madero as their choice for president (Cockcroft 1998, 95). Revolution became a vehicle – both concretely and symbolically – for these northern elites to ensure that their interests would achieve primacy once again. After escaping from the prison where he had been put by Díaz, Madero fled into exile in the United States and issued his Plan of San Luis Potosí, which called for a general insurrection against the Díaz regime (ibid., 96). Once again, in what seems to be a dominant theme in this revolutionary narrative, Madero would have to rely upon 'the masses' to do the dirty work of bringing the revolution to fruition. Madero would not even lead an army to victory in the war against the Porfiriato; instead, the regime would be toppled by the revolutionary fighters of the PLM and the labourers and peasants of Pancho Villa's and Emiliano Zapata's armies. In order to understand why these marginalized groups would risk rising up in arms against the powerful Porfirian regime and how this mobilization would affect the shape of the post-revolutionary state, it is necessary to turn to a more detailed examination of Emiliano Zapata and his Liberating Army of the South.

'Liberty, Justice, and Law': The Story of Zapata and the Mexican Revolution

Zapata's revolt is a story of community organization and a shared history of struggle and resistance combined with an explosive confluence of forces unleashed in the years following Mexico's independence from Spain (see Galeano 1973, 120–6). This history is particularly significant not simply because Zapata is the namesake of the contemporary Zapatista movement but also because Zapata would become perhaps the single most co-opted figure by the post-revolutionary Mexican regime. Following the liberals' rise to power and their decision to make the destruction of communal landholding national policy in 1856, agrarian

rebels began to accept alliances with radical political actors and ideo-
logues that led to greater participation in national politics (Tutino 1986,
359). Following these associations, 'politicized agrarian insurrections,
demanding a reconstitution of Mexico in the interests of the rural poor,
began in the late 1860s, recurred in the late 1870s, and became the dominant mode of insurrection after 1910' (ibid.). Clearly, the very concept of
'revolution' within the Mexican nation-state and the national imaginary
was – and indeed remains – a profoundly contested one.

Agrarian insurrection exploded in Morelos from the outset of the
Revolution, but in order to appreciate the reasons for this as well as the
lasting impact Zapata and his Liberating Army of the South have had
upon political, institutional, and ideological space in Mexico since then,
it is necessary to understand the roots of the movement itself. Emiliano
Zapata was born in the village of San Miguel Anenecuilco in the state of
Morelos in 1877 (Huizer 1970, 376). Anenecuilco was a largely Indigenous village, which had fought for years against the encroachment of
local haciendas upon their lands, and Emiliano Zapata grew up within
this tradition, often finding himself in conflict with officials and haci-
enda owners in his attempt to fight for community land (ibid.). On 12
September 1909, Zapata was elected head of the village defence committee and, after attempting to recover village lands through legal channels
and failing, began his tenure as head of this committee by retaking communal lands seized by local haciendas and distributing it to the villagers
(ibid., 377). What is interesting about the early history of this great
Mexican revolutionary and the movement he would inspire is that the
original Zapatismo emerged not as a 'revolutionary' struggle directed
towards radical social transformation but as a defensive action taken to
protect peoples and communities under threat from the Reform Laws as
well as relatively new structures of 'progress' and capital accumulation.

As Arturo Warman (1976) notes, 'The first stage, the birth of Zapatismo, was an armed defensive reaction of the peasants in the face of a
set of external aggressions'; it was a rebellion against many specific
causes, 'all of them more or less directly related to the breaking of the
precarious equilibrium between the great capitalist enterprise and the
peasant community' (93). The implementation of the Reform Laws, the
expansion of haciendas, the continuing impoverishment of the rural
population, and 'the rigidly negative reaction of the landholders to
moderate demands' of the peasantry ultimately led to the awakening of
the peasants to the possibility of more militant action (Huizer 1970, 398).
This internal dynamic within Mexican revolutionary history, that of

communities and collectivities forced to take radical action in order to defend themselves from the imposition of an externally imposed oblivion, is one that would repeat itself throughout the rest of the century and, most spectacularly, on 1 January 1994. The northern bourgeoisie spoke grandly but acted ineffectually against the regime of Porfirio Díaz, even as rebellion broke out autonomously amongst peasant groups such as Zapata's. However, as the 'explicit revolutionaries' of the north had included a clause involving demands of an agrarian nature in their Plan of San Luis Potosí, an alliance between an explosive peasantry and the northern bourgeois revolutionaries developed that overthrew Díaz and his regime in less than four months (Warman 1976, 94).

Following Díaz's exile and leading up to the election of the first new president of Mexico in thirty-five years, Madero sought to disarm the various revolutionary groups which had so successfully toppled the Porfiriato. With promises of democracy Madero attempted to pacify the insurgent peasants of Morelos, but as Warman notes, 'they did not want the vote in the first place; they wanted access to the land' (ibid., 96). As campesinos occupied land under the orders of Zapata, they 'entered into direct conflict with the heirs of power' who did not look kindly upon the radical agrarian demands of the Zapatistas (ibid.). Before the dust had even settled from the collapse of Díaz's regime, northern elites were working actively to ensure that the unfolding story of the Revolution would work in their interests and provide the necessary justification for an 'appropriate' post-revolutionary regime. The story itself, however, would not be written so easily. In order to deal with this insurgent and explosive force in the south, the ascendant elite sent General Victoriano Huerta and the 'cream of the federal army' on a punitive expedition. In the face of this challenge, the Zapatistas declared their 'counter-revolution' against Madero's 'revolution' (ibid.). At this point, the Zapatistas truly became an autonomous revolutionary movement, a transition made clear by Zapata's issuing of his Plan de Ayala, a revolutionary program to which I will now turn.

The Plan de Ayala was signed and issued by Zapata in the villa de Ayala on 22 November 1911 in an effort to clarify to the rest of the Mexican nation why the Zapatistas had not yet laid down their arms (Huizer 1970, 382). This struggle over who would appear as the 'authentic revolutionary' in the eyes of the Mexican nation would also find its echo more than eighty years later when the neo-Zapatistas would declare their struggle to be in defence of the true Mexican Revolution rather than the version of it co-opted by elites. Beginning with a complete rejection of Madero as the legitimate chief of the Revolution, the Plan proceeds to lay out the fundamental tenets of Zapatismo. Particularly significant in the Plan are Articles 6, 7, and 8, which directly address the redistribution of land to those who work it as well as the nationalization of lands of those 'landlords, científicos, or bosses who oppose the present plan' (Womack Jr. 1968, 402–3). While remaining committed to Madero's Plan of San Luis Potosí – which called for the dismissal of all incumbent officials at both the local and federal levels, the free election and impartial appointment of new officials and the judicial review of all disputed cases involving rural real estate – the Zapatistas' Plan of Ayala goes much farther in its call for peasants to immediately reclaim lands themselves and to defend them by force of arms, without the need for approval by any higher authority (Warman 1976, 97).

The Zapatistas' Agrarian Law signed on 26 October 1915 was as revolutionary as their Plan of Ayala. While it set out specific limits for various types of agricultural lands, more importantly, it signed into law principles regarding not only the return of land (provided individuals possessed original titles) but also enshrined the 'traditional and historic right which the pueblos, ranchos, and communities of the Republic have of possessing and administering their fields of communal distribution ... and communal use ... in the form which they judge proper' (Womack Jr. 1968, 406). Furthermore, the Agrarian Law provided for the right of all Mexicans to possess enough land to cover the needs of themselves and their families, the rights of sharecroppers to own the land they worked, and decreed the land ceded by the government to communities and individuals as inalienable (ibid., 407–9). These twin decrees exemplified the principles for which the Zapatistas refused to lay down their arms. Simply put, in the face of regimes that had successively worked to rob the rural population of their livelihood and their capacity for autonomy and security, the peasants of Zapata's Liberating Army of the South were no longer willing to wait on the empty promises of elite politicians, landholders, and industrialists.

Of Death, Betrayal, and the Fading of a Dream

Brothers and sisters, we want you to know the truth. And it is like this:
    From the first hour in this long night of our death, our most distant grandfathers say there was someone who gathered up our pain and our oblivion. There was a man who, walking his word from afar to our moun-

tains, came and spoke with the tongue of the true men and women. His walk was and was not from these lands. From the mouths of our dead, from the mouths of the most knowing of our ancient ancestors, his word walked from him to our heart. There was and is, brothers and sisters, he who – being and not being seed from these lands – arrived to the mountain, dying in order to live again, who lived with his heart dying from his walk, a foreigner when he first arrived to the mountain with its nocturnal roof. He was and is a man. His tender word halts and walks in our pain. He is and is not in these lands: Votán Zapata, guardian and heart of the people.

Votán Zapata, light that came from afar and was born here from our land. Votán Zapata, named again forever a man of our people. Votán Zapata, a timid fire who lived our death 501 years. Votán Zapata, the name that changes, the man without a face, the tender light that watches over us. Death was always with us, and with death hope died. Death arrived with Votán Zapata. The name without a name, Votán Zapata looked in Miguel, walked in José María, was Vicente, was named in Benito, flew in a bird, rode in Emiliano, shouted in Francisco, visited Pedro. We lived dying, named without a name in our own lands. Votán Zapata arrived in our lands. Speaking, his word fell into our mouth. He arrived and is here. Votán Zapata, guardian and heart of the people.

From 'Votán-Zapata or Five Hundred Years of History,' the Clandestine Indigenous Revolutionary Committee – General Command of the EZLN (Ejército Zapatista de Liberación Nacional 2001d)

I have related the details of the origins of Zapata's Liberating Army of the South as well as the Zapatistas' refusal to lay down their arms not simply to provide a degree of historical contextualization for the EZLN's uprising more than eight decades later but also to position the contemporary Zapatista struggle within a larger revolutionary narrative. Revolution is a powerful interpellating myth in Mexico and the choice made by urban insurgents and Indigenous organizers in naming their clandestine guerrilla army the 'Zapatista Army of National Liberation' after Emiliano Zapata more than sixty years after his death was a conscious and deliberate one. While some might argue that the invocation of Zapata by the insurgents of the EZLN was merely a propagandistic manoeuvre, it is my contention that this decision was made intentionally to reclaim the history, agency, and power of the Mexican Revolution from national elites and official channels. More than this, however, in reappropriating this revolutionary legacy, the insurgents of the EZLN also brought the force of this revolutionary history to bear on a model of political and economic development that had sought to establish itself as the only possible future. In reclaiming and redeploying this story of revolution, by reinventing Zapata not merely as Emiliano Zapata but as Votán-Zapata, the men, women, and children of the EZLN recreated and reinvigorated a future of possibility. But before I come to this part of the story, we must return to the history of the Mexican Revolution itself.

In 1913, tired of Madero's inability to stabilize the situation and pave the way for entrepreneurial progress, the northern bourgeoisie in collusion with General Huerta and the government of the United States had President Madero assassinated (Warman 1976, 97). The revolutionary forces now split into two distinct camps: 'the reformists,' known as the constitutionalists and led by Venustiano Carranza, 'who fought for changes of a political nature within a legalistic framework'; and 'the agrarians,' led by Emiliano Zapata, 'who demanded the immediate restructuring of the country' (ibid., 98). Ultimately, attempts to reconcile these disjunctures proved fruitless, and while the followers of Emiliano Zapata and Pancho Villa claimed control of the Aguascalientes convention government formed at the end of 1914, the two groups never overcame their mutual distrust to implement reform on a national level (ibid., 99). As for the constitutionalist camp, with military chief Obregón delivering two severe military defeats to the Villistas in 1915 and Carranza receiving diplomatic recognition of his government from the United States in October of the same year, they effectively consolidated their hold on the emergent 'revolutionary' government of Mexico (ibid.). Arturo Warman's (1976) comments on the failure of the Villa-Zapata forces to consolidate an effective revolutionary regime are profoundly significant and speak to a central theme of radical political struggle in Mexico. They also prefigure the story of revolution that the neo-Zapatistas would tell, and use to frame their own political struggle, eighty years later. In Warman's analysis, the failure of Villa and Zapata to consolidate revolutionary power was

> the result, not – as it is frequently presented – of the fear of power ... but of their congruence with a revolution that was being made from below and that still had not triumphed. The capture of the State, ever the enemy of the peasants, was not the Zapatistas' revolutionary objective; it was the consequence of a revolution at the base, in the free and sovereign villages. (100–1)

Despite the convention government's failure to form the revolutionary regime on a national level, the Zapatistas realized their agrarian
vision in Morelos in 1915. Land distribution, village autonomy, nationalization of production, and community-based consensus decision-
making processes were all realized in Zapatista territory (Warman 1976,
102). Ultimately, however, the weight of Carranza's federal army and
the repression they levelled at the populace of Morelos, the inclusion of
elements of agrarian reform in Article 27 of the new constitution of 1917,
and the isolation and deprivation faced by the Zapatistas took their toll
(ibid., 127–32). On 10 April 1919, Emiliano Zapata was lured into an
ambush by constitutionalist forces and assassinated. While the post-
revolutionary regime of Carranza was beginning to consolidate itself,
there remained significant challenges ahead for the new elite regime
seeking to construct a post-revolutionary state in the face of powerfully
radicalized peasants and workers. Not the least of these challenges
would be the writing of a revolutionary history capable of tying the victorious post-revolutionary elites and their fragile state to the very revolutionary dream they had worked so hard to crush.

Institutionalizing the Revolution and a Spark is Lit in Chiapas

There was no revolution in Chiapas. Instead, Chiapas bore witness to
regional and largely inter-elite struggles for power and the control of
Indigenous labour (Benjamin 1996). None of these struggles involved
any degree of popular involvement; rather, to a surprising degree, these
struggles mirrored the elite struggles in Central Mexico over which elite
faction would inherit the benefits of the Revolution. The oppressed
peasants of Chiapas did not rebel, as tight systems of social and economic control as well as ethnic, geographical, and linguistic divisions
and the absence of progressive leadership maintained an enforced passivity (ibid., 96). However, the national and regional political crises generated a fissure in the 'paternalistic, repressive control of the landed elite
over peasant villages and landless workers' and led to the 'accidental
politicization' of the people and the space for their eventual mobilization through structures of political parties, agrarian communities, and
labour unions (ibid.). The spark had been lit by which a new story in
Chiapas would eventually be written.

While there was no revolution in Chiapas, there was guided social
reform under the government of Venustiano Carranza, and when this
was combined with the 'dislocation and disruption of war [it] led to the

beginning of a popular revolutionary climate' (ibid., 132). Under the 'cover of war,' and sometimes even with military protection, the people of Chiapas asserted greater control over their own lives, stopping the payment of rent, seizing livestock and land, and running away from their former employers (ibid.). Thus, while Chiapas had remained relatively quiescent during the national upheavals of 1910–20, the Mexican Revolution had lit a spark of latent social and political unrest in the far south-east of Mexico, a spark that would have profound consequences for the future of the state and the nation.

Mexican revolutionary history is charged with tremendous significance within the national imaginary. This significance is due not only to the defeat of Porfirio Díaz but also to the radicalization and mobilization of the peasantry and the urban working classes. In the years following the assassination of Emiliano Zapata, the post-revolutionary elite would be forced to confront these mobilized masses and find ways of co-opting, accommodating, and repressing them. This process, however, could never be completely successful for the very reason that rural rebellion actually served as one of 'the modes of confirmation and existence' of the Mexican state community (Gilly 1998, 268). In other words, rural rebellion was not only a fundamental factor in bringing the post-revolutionary Mexican state into being, it also served to profoundly influence the nature of the relationship between 'those who govern and those who are governed.' Peasants could not easily be repressed or co-opted because they figured into the constitution of 1917 'with status and specific rights as peasants, not simply as citizens,' a status built upon the expectation of protection by the state in exchange for their obedience to the ruling elite (ibid.). This is perhaps one of the most powerful legacies of Mexican revolutionary history. Even as post-revolutionary elites consolidated their power and that of the Mexican nation-state upon the foundation of a captured revolutionary mythology, this mythology was creating the very conditions for new challenges and possibilities for popular struggle. This relationship and the mutual obligations it implies would have powerful consequences for the state and for peasant mobilization in the years to come.

But while 'peasants' entered into the consolidation of the Mexican state in explicit and particular ways, Indigenous peoples did not. Following the liberal tradition embodied in the Reform Laws, the project of the post-revolutionary Mexican state with respect to Indigenous peoples was embodied by the ideology of 'indigenismo,' which 'involved the assimilation and absorption of the indigenous in the Mexican, and

the "citizenization" of Indians through public education, state protection, and economic development' (Gilly 1998, 278). While the Indigenous past of Mexico was valorized, Indigenous peoples themselves
were consigned to a fate of 'modernization' or oblivion. It was not a
choice they would resign themselves to.

Attempts at co-optation with respect to the peasantry began most
effectively through the mechanism of land distribution. As Arturo Warman (1976) notes, for land distribution to become a mechanism by
which the loyalties of the peasant benefiting from the grant are trans-
ferred to the state, 'it was necessary for the peasant masses to lose the
initiative for the distribution and for that initiative to pass into the
hands of the State through the formalization, the instrumentalization,
of the process of territorial redistribution as a government monopoly'
(141). Article 27 of the 1917 constitution provided for just such a situation. Thus, in this constitutional article, the aspirations of a radicalized
peasantry, the revolutionary agenda of the Zapatistas, and the desires
of a national elite for power would find codification. Article 27 can
therefore be seen as a concretization of the revolutionary mythology in
Mexico.

At the federal level, the post-revolutionary regime of Lázaro Cárdenas (1934–40) worked more than any other to nationalize resources and
to effectively incorporate diverse sectors of the population into the
machinery of the government and, ultimately, to bind them to it. Reading such initiatives as purely attempts at co-optation would be to fundamentally misunderstand the resonance of these acts with respect to
how the Mexican national community was being created and imagined.
As Gilly (1998) notes, 'the nationalization of oil and the (partial) redistribution of land came to be, rather like the living myth of the Mexican
revolution, essential components of the form in which the national community imagined itself and of the ideology comprising Mexican nationalism' (271). Through the appropriation of such figures as Emiliano
Zapata and Pancho Villa, the uneven and elite-controlled redistribution
of land, the formation of 'official' organs of 'sectoral' representation,
and the consolidation of a paternalistic, corporatist state, the post-revolutionary Mexican elite effectively foreclosed on the possibility of radical and popular revolutionary action 'from below.' The mythology of
the Revolution became a powerful ideological weapon in this arsenal.

In Chiapas, the story was not very much different. The formation of
what initially appeared to be powerful confederations of workers and
peasants were incorporated into 'the party of the state,' and the 'flawed

but extensive advance of agrarian reform' led to the virtual immobilization of potentially revolutionary groups (Benjamin 1996, 210). Land reform particularly operated as a divisive force within what might have been a mobilized, unified, and politicized peasantry as it 'restored and strengthened the separate indigenous municipios at the expense of broader Indian or campesino solidarity ... [as] land was distributed within municipios to landowning and landless Indians ... [aggravating] internal community stratification and [discouraging] class-based organization spanning Indian municipios' (ibid.). The formation of ejidos through Article 27 and government initiatives created communities closely tied to the state, as these communities were, and continued to be through the 1980s and early 1990s, 'dependent on the state for credit, material assistance, and amplification of their original land grants' (ibid.). Interestingly, a revolutionary history woven through with powerful demands for autonomy and democracy instead became a mythologizing of the state, its authority, and its benevolence. In Chiapas, the government successfully subverted the organizing capacities and the emergent political consciousness of the peasants and workers and replaced it with a co-optive model of 'official' and 'institutionalized' representation, which served primarily as a source of legitimacy and support for the elite interests of large landowners, plantation owners, and politicians.

Within this political context of the Mexican 'institutionalized' party-state, expression, organization, and mobilization of dissent developed in very specific ways. With Cárdenas's consolidation of the corporatist state, channels for legal organization and expression of demands operated to reinforce the division between sectors (Carr 1992, 81). Furthermore, by laying claim to the 'revolutionary' pedigree of leaders like Hidalgo, Morelos, Zapata, and Villa, the political elite could subvert dissent through appeals to revolutionary nationalist pride. The regime of Miguel Alemán (1946–52) particularly 'embraced a conscious effort to marginalize the forces of the political left within mass movements, the official party, and education' (ibid., 146). Following the emergence of rival and leftist labour organizations from 1947–49, the government responded by replacing independent and combative leaders with 'charros' (corrupt labour bosses) (ibid., 188). When confronted by the teacher, railway, telephone, and metal trades workers insurgencies during the 1950s, the government did not hesitate to respond with force, demonstrating the darker side of the corporatist Mexican regime (ibid., 201–7). Thus, beneath banners of national pride, revolutionary heritage, and unity, the Mexican post-revolutionary state successfully and ruthlessly co-opted, accommodated, and crushed dissent. It would not be until the emergence of a new type of political actor in the 1960s that the regime would begin to show signs of stress and new political openings would emerge.

Openings

During the 1950s and the 1960s, Chiapas experienced an economic boom that would significantly affect the future of political mobilization in the state. With cattle ranching and the production of export crops such as coffee, cacao, sugar cane, and cotton leading the way, private landowners benefited greatly from this explosion (Benjamin 1996, 223–6). For ejidatarios, however, the situation was not equally beneficial. Many of the ejido parcels were too small to support a single family, which forced ejidatarios to work on neighbouring estates or as migrant workers; furthermore, the high population density on these ejidos led to 'soil degradation, severe deforestation, and the near-disappearance of wild game' (ibid., 226). While small landholders constituted nearly half of all landowners, they occupied less than 1 per cent of the land while large landowners holding properties of more than 1,000 hectares and constituting only 2.4 per cent of the landowning population owned nearly 60 per cent of the land (ibid.). A measure of social peace was preserved, for the time being, largely through the employment of socio-economic 'safety valves' such as the continuation and expansion of land reform involving the opening of the Lacandón Jungle to colonization and programs of social and economic improvement organized by the National Indigenist Institute (ibid., 228). However, these initiatives could not stem the emergence in the 1970s of a 'grassroots, widespread, and increasingly organized agrarian struggle' in Chiapas (ibid., 229). It was, quite simply, a diversion of resources which was 'too little, too late.' Against a national backdrop of increasing agitation, militancy, and the inability of the dominant Partido Revolucionario Institucional (PRI, Institutional Revolutionary Party) regime to suppress these manifestations of dissent, the rural poor of Chiapas were moving towards direct confrontation with the elite, their institutions, and their interests.

In the 1960s, students, Christian activists, mass organizations, and guerrilla groups began to emerge as the new militant leftist actors on the political stage in Mexico. Newly radicalized students, inspired by Maoism, Trotskyism, and the Cuban Revolution, situated their demands within the broad context of democracy in Mexico rather than simply being concerned with strictly student-based demands such as the autonomy of university campuses, posing a direct challenge to the institutionalized student organizations set up by the PRI (Carr 1992, 229–30). The radicalization of both Protestant and Catholic activists in Mexico occurred after 1965 due to the inspiration of Vatican II, the 1968 Medellín conference, and liberation theology (ibid.). The hostility from church authorities faced by many of these lay Catholic activists led them 'to break completely with official church structures and to embrace worker and peasant movements' (ibid., 231). In addition to this, the success of the Cuban Revolution and its rapid leftward movement in 1960–1 reconfigured traditional notions of 'Latin American reality that emphasized two-stage theories of revolution in which socialism was indefinitely postponed until capitalism was sufficiently matured' espoused by parties and organizations such as the Mexican Communist Party (ibid., 232). Most importantly, these developments signalled the increasing fragility of both the Mexican state's capacity to simply negotiate or co-opt dissent away and the officialized mythology of the Mexican Revolution and its legacy.

Significantly, the Cuban Revolution inspired in Mexico a new commitment to the route of armed struggle, most notably in Chihuahua and Guerrero (Carr 1992, 233). Even more importantly, the Cuban Revolution put anti-imperialism and 'proletarian internationalism' back on the agenda for the Mexican left, resulting in the formation of the National Liberation Movement (MLN) in 1961. Representing a broad spectrum of interests from existing socialist parties to 'progressives' and 'liberals,' the MLN concerned itself primarily with 'the defence of the Cuban Revolution, a revival of authentic agrarian reform, the struggle to free political prisoners ... and the defence of economic sovereignty and national independence' (ibid.). In this context, new political actors and new political practices were beginning to emerge that would pose new and difficult challenges to the corporatist institutions of the Mexican 'institutional revolutionary' regime.

In the 1970s, mass popular organizations of neighbourhood residents, students, teachers, and poor peasants began to emerge (Carr 1992, 235). In addition to their specificities, these popular movements need to be understood as comprising a more general struggle to constitute 'the people' as political actors outside of the institutionalized spaces of official political representation (Foweraker 1990, 5). By and large, the impact of these movements must be understood not as points of pure opposition to the political system but in relation to it as points of possibility and political space. These new leftist fronts expressed a commitment to shorter-term objectives and local movements rather than identifying with the longer-term or strategic goals of parties and unions (Carr 1992, 236). Furthermore, rather than seeking to form alliances with progressive sectors of the state apparatus or capturing state power, these new movements sought to increase the capacity for autonomy and self-determination of the people who constituted them (ibid.). Thus, a new ideological and structural approach to a politics of dissent and possibility, emphasizing autonomy and democracy, emerged in the 1960s and 1970s in direct opposition to the corporatist structures of the state and the ruling party. Seen from the perspective of a revolutionary Mexican history, this opening also constituted a moment of rupture with respect to the official mythology of revolution.

The student movement of 1968 was a watershed moment in Mexican history. Set in motion by a series of violent, and initially politically insignificant, clashes between students and police in July 1968, the movement escalated to a direct and politically explicit challenge to the PRI and the antidemocratic nature of Mexican society (Carr 1992, 258–9). While the demands of the students were couched in essentially liberal democratic terms, they directly challenged the corporatist structure of the state and the dominance of the political elite, thus taking on 'revolutionary proportions' (ibid., 258). As the mythology of the party-state and its 'authentic' roots in revolution became worn away and exposed as a result of a corporatist system overburdened by multiplying popular claims and increasingly radically democratic demands, the stakes of struggle became even more serious.

The structure of the student mobilization was as fluid as its ideological make-up, with the struggle coordinated by the National Strike Council but made up of largely independent 'struggle committees' with no permanent or centralized leadership and informed by political ideologies ranging from 'revolutionary nationalism and internationalism ... [to] liberal democratic, Marxist, anarchist, and Maoist doctrines' (Carr 1992, 260–4). The movement resisted all forms of co-optation and division and posed a powerful challenge to the corporatist structures of the state and, in doing so, earned its wrath. On 2 October 1968, after occupying the campuses of dissident universities, the army surrounded a large gathering of students and citizens at the Plaza of the Three Cultures in Mexico City and opened fire (ibid., 263). Massive waves of

arrests and violent repression followed the massacre and the movement
was crushed.

Crisis: The Beginning of the End or the End of the Beginning?

Perhaps even more significant than the mobilization and commitment
of the students involved in the 1968 movement were the consequences
it, and the government's brutal response to it, had for the state and for
popular struggle in its aftermath. While the Tlatelolco massacre convinced many of the futility of struggle against the party-state machine,
it convinced others of the necessity of armed struggle leading to a violent but ultimately ruthlessly crushed urban guerrilla struggle from
1968–73 (Carr 1992, 267). What these diverse struggles and the brutal
responses to them did reveal, however, was the illegitimacy of the
nature of the corporatist 'revolutionary' state. No longer could the PRI
lay claim to representing the demands of large sectors of the population,
nor could it claim to be democratic in any meaningful sense and, most
significantly, the government's draconian response to popular mobilization eroded the last vestiges of the revolutionary heritage of the party-
state. For the PRI, the mythology of the Mexican Revolution, once such
an effective mechanism for the consolidation of its power and the very
basis for the legitimacy of the corporatist party-state, was now increasingly seen not only as largely hollow but as a parody of what the state
had in fact become.

While the 'institutional revolution' in Mexico was badly shaken, it
was far from over. The governments of Echeverría (1970–6) and Portillo
(1976–82) attempted to return a sense of legitimacy to the PRI regime
through their respective Democratic Opening and Political Reform Law
initiatives, but they were only partially successful (Carr 1992, 273–80).
This growing political crisis was combined with the financial crisis of
1976–7, during which inflation, foreign debt, high interest rates, and a
balance of payments deficit resulted in a 'drastic austerity program,'
and the direct intervention of the International Monetary Fund created
a radically new economic environment within which the PRI and other
political actors were forced to operate (ibid., 279). Nothing would
challenge the corporatist party-state of the PRI and its revolutionary
mythology as seriously as the reshaped political-economic terrain imposed by this financial restructuring. In 1982, the collapse of oil prices in
addition to tremendous foreign debt led to a full-blown crisis. This crisis

directly challenged the PRI's ability to sustain the corporatist approach, the material basis for their tenuous hold on revolutionary legitimacy, and for the propagation of the 'official' revolutionary mythology. In fact, as Jan Rus, Shannan Mattiace, and Rosalva Aída Hernández Castillo (2003) note, as a result of these mounting crises, in an ironic twist 'the PRI – a party whose existence was tied to state corporatism – itself undertook to dismantle that corporatism and remake itself in the 1980s as the party of structural adjustment and neoliberal economics' (11). In a by-now familiar refrain, the consequences of this neoliberal restructuring were felt immediately by workers and peasants in the form of drastically decreased expenditures on everything from health care and education to guaranteed agricultural prices and subsidies for basic foodstuffs (ibid.). Severe as these economic cuts were for workers and peasants, they would prove even more devastating for the PRI itself – 'without money to grease the wheels, the patron-client system simply ceased to function' (ibid.). Economic liberalization without political democratization would prove to be far too much for the PRI's hollowed-out revolutionary mythology to sustain.

In the face of this neoliberal onslaught, several broad popular fronts and organizations emerged to coordinate a response to drastically declining living conditions. The emergence of these new fronts represented a significant shift in orientation from the workplace to the 'barrio, street, and school, and around struggles over access to land, housing, and urban services such as potable water, roads, and power' (Carr 1992, 281). Then, on 19 September 1985, when a huge earthquake devastated Mexico City and the government and military failed miserably to respond effectively, it was the civilian population that mobilized in a dedicated and well-coordinated rescue and rebuilding effort (Cockcroft 1998, 280). Finally, in 1988, when Cuauhtémoc Cárdenas, son of the populist president of the 1930s, electorally defeated the PRI and their candidate Carlos Salinas de Gortari and then had the presidency stolen from him through widespread 'computer failure' on election night, the PRI's veneer of legitimacy was nearly entirely eroded (ibid., 300). The enormous ramifications of these successive crises and the response of the PRI to them should not be understated. The PRI's power radiated not only from its material, institutional, and coercive capacities but from its appropriation and deployment of a revolutionary mythology.

This revolutionary mythology, as I have sought to demonstrate, not only allowed post-revolutionary elites to lay claim to a revolutionary pedigree and thus to present their interests as identical to the interests of the Mexican people and the nation, but it also articulated the bases and terms upon which the rulers and the ruled were mutually beholden to one another. As Adolfo Gilly (1998) comments, 'If that [social] pact originating in the armed revolution has now been broken, even if only symbolically, the right to take up arms is once again ours' (269). Thus, in the 1980s, with the decline of the PRI hegemony as a result of successive crises rooted in the economic and political spheres and the emergence of new political parties and popular organization, a political opening had been created within which alternative forms of organization and mobilization could emerge. In effect, the history and possibility of revolution was increasingly being reclaimed by popular movements. It is within this context that, in the far south-east of Mexico, the Zapatista Army of National Liberation began to take shape.

Beginning in the 1970s and 1980s, the rural poor of Chiapas, after learning the bitter truth of 'institutional organizing,' increasingly turned to independent labour, agrarian, and community organization. The Zapatista rebellion of 1994 is a direct continuation of this type of organizing as well as an outgrowth of the revolutionary trajectories described throughout this chapter. It is also perhaps the most spectacular example to date of a popular reclamation of Mexican revolutionary history and possibility. Faced with a history of incredible violence, exploitation, co-optation and contempt as well as with the fracturing of the social pact and its official revolutionary mythology, organizing amongst the Indigenous peasants of Chiapas began to take an increasingly militant and independent shape. Perhaps even more significant, however, is the spirit that came to animate organization, militancy, and eventually even open rebellion. As Gilly (1998) notes,

> rebellions present themselves as secular and successive collective acts, material and symbolic, at times very diverse in the immediate motivations apparent to their participants, but whose ultimate content could be found in the will of these communities to persist. The participants resist and rise up in order to persist, because they can persist only by resisting the movement of a world that dissolves and negates their Being. (263–4)

As the material and symbolic base of the PRI's power continued to be eroded, Indigenous communities in Chiapas turned once more to rebellion in order to radically contest the movement of a world which evermore sought to 'dissolve and negate' their being.

Indigenous politicization in Chiapas was assisted by the First Indian

Congress of 1974 sponsored by Bishop Samuel Ruiz, which brought
together Tzotzil, Tzeltal, Tojolabal, and Chol leaders representing more
than 300 communities (Benjamin 1996, 235). Significantly, the well-orga-
nized Indigenous movement that emerged from this congress was
assisted not only by clergy and church workers but also by radical political activists from urban centres who had fled police and army repression or decided that the countryside would be a more fruitful venue for
radical political movement (ibid.). Several political parties and organizations also began grassroots organizing in Chiapas, including Proletarian Line, People United, the Independent Organization of Agricultural
Workers and Peasants–Mexican Communist Party, the Socialist Workers
Party, and a democratic union movement which had emerged among
the state's teachers (Hernández Navarro 1994, 7). During this period,
the Unión de Uniones Ejidales y Grupos Campesinos Solidarios de Chiapas (UU, Union of Ejidal Unions and Peasant Solidarity Groups of Chiapas), the Central Independiente de Obreros Agrícolas y Campesinos
(CIOAC, Independent Central of Agricultural Workers and Peasants),
and the Organización Campesina Emiliano Zapata (OCEZ, Emiliano
Zapata Peasant Organization) emerged in the eastern, northern, and
central areas of the state (Benjamin 1996, 235–6). While facing both private and state-based attempts at repression and co-optation, these independent and combative mobilizations would form the basis for the new
forms of popular contestation of government abuses and elite exploitation and provide the context within which new strategies of struggle
and innovation would begin to emerge.

During the early 1980s, into this matrix of liberation theology, political and physical repression, peasant and worker mobilization, and a
crumbling corporatist pact and its 'official' revolutionary mythology,
cadres from a Che Guevara-inspired urban guerrilla movement arrived
to add the last elements necessary to give rise to the Zapatista Army of
National Liberation. Formed in the north in 1969 by survivors of earlier
guerrilla initiatives, the Fuerzas de Liberación Nacional (FLN, Forces of
National Liberation) had sent new cadres into the highlands of Chiapas
in order to initiate a new front in preparation for the long military and
political national struggle to install a socialist system (Womack Jr. 1999,
36). Indeed, Subcomandante Insurgente Marcos would recount years
later that the EZLN was born on 17 November 1983 in a meeting attended by three Indigenous people and three mestizos, including himself (Harvey 1998, 164). In 1984, along with the first group of guerrillas,
Marcos went to live in the Lacandón Jungle's harsh mountainous ter-

rain, and it is there that the urban and Marxist core of the EZLN came face to face with the Indigenous culture and heritage of Chiapas, a confrontation which would force the former to reconfigure and subordinate itself to the latter (ibid., 165–6). The 'defeat' of Marxist dogma by the cultural and historical force of Indigenous reality in Chiapas allowed the EZLN to expand and to begin recruiting new members from communities.

In the 1980s, the state attempted to respond to the increasingly mobilized and politicized rural poor in Chiapas through various programs designed to ameliorate their suffering. The ground had shifted under the PRI's feet, however, and its mythologized revolutionary mask had fallen away to reveal an increasingly unstable and illegitimate regime. Initiatives such as the World Bank-sponsored $300 million 'Plan Chiapas' and the Programa de Rehabilitación Agraria (PRA, Program of Agrarian Rehabilitation), which operated by compensating estate and plantation owners for lands invaded by peasants, attempted to stem the growing tide of dissent, but they proved insufficient to the task (Harvey 1998, 247). Even as the state attempted to quell popular dissent through mechanisms such as 'Plan Chiapas' and the PRA, the De la Madrid federal government also issued 2,932 certificates of agricultural ineffectability and 4,714 certificates of ranching ineffectability, protecting 'productive' and elite-owned land from reform (ibid., 248). Invasions by independent campesino organizations continued, followed by violent expulsions and repression (ibid., 249). Tensions between strategies of co-optation and outright repression were becoming increasingly obvious, further fuelling independent organizing.

Compounding this already tense situation was the collapse in the international price of coffee, a profound contraction in credit available from the state, and an end to price supports for maize growers that came with an obligation to compete on the international market (Gilly 1998, 290). The 'revolutionary' state embodied by the PRI had essentially given up all pretense of attempting to act as the paternalistic protector of its 'children,' a situation which signalled the fundamental fracturing of the relationships of mutual obligation between the rulers and the ruled established after the Mexican Revolution. This set of initiatives by itself may have provided the basis for a commitment on the part of Indigenous communities in Chiapas to take up arms against state and national elites who had clearly abandoned them to the whims of the 'free market'; however, there still remained several key developments before this would occur.

The first of these was the massive and audacious electoral fraud that robbed Cuauhtémoc Cárdenas of his presidential victory in favour of the PRI candidate Carlos Salinas de Gortari in 1988 – a circumstance regarded throughout Mexico as fundamentally shattering the social pact (Gilly 1998, 291). The second development occurred in 1992 when Patrocinio González Garrido, governor of Chiapas since 1989 and brutal oppressor of popular movements in that state, became Secretary of the Interior (ibid.). As governor, González Garrido was instrumental in cementing ties between the Chiapan oligarchy with the increasingly neoliberal elite outside of Chiapas (particularly those in the Salinas government), but his promotion to Secretary of the Interior would simultaneously accomplish three very different outcomes. First, his promotion signalled the near complete abandonment of the nationalist sector on the part of the state as well as leaving the Salinas government without the skills and experience of the previous Secretary of the Interior who was well-versed both in matters of internal security and effectively combining repression with negotiation. Second, it cemented the ties between the Chiapan oligarchy and the federal government, leaving González Garrido both to prepare Mexico's internal affairs for the implementation of NAFTA and for the upcoming federal election. Third, González Garrido's promotion actually removed from Chiapas a man who had been particularly effective at infiltrating, containing, repressing, and destroying popular movements (ibid., 292). Interestingly, as state socialism was collapsing in Eastern Europe, conditions in Mexico and especially in Chiapas were actually pushing some communities towards an armed uprising that would shake the foundations of the New World Order.

The End of Institutionalized Revolution

Soon after ascending to the presidency, Carlos Salinas (1988–94) attempted to rework the now terminally damaged social pact in the image of a neoliberal model. No longer truly capable of managing a corporatist structure, the Salinas government attempted to '"reform" the political system by converting patron-client into more direct citizen-state relationships' (Rus, Castillo, and Mattiace 2003, 11). This 'reworking' also definitively signalled the state's abandonment of its own mythologized revolutionary tradition as Mexico's elite looked forward to NAFTA as their ticket into the First World. While the Salinas government established the National Solidarity Program 'for small projects of community development and improvement,' and while no state received more money from the Solidarity Program than Chiapas, no single program could have hoped to 'dent the massive poverty and vast income disparity' present there (Harvey 1998, 251). Once again, government intervention in this explosive situation was a case of too little, too late. Combined with the reform of Article 27 of the constitution in 1992, which removed the rights of campesinos to petition for land redistribution and made ejido land open to privatization in order to encourage investment in agriculture, the stage was set for a head-on confrontation between the state, large landowners, and the peasantry.

In this context, a new grassroots peasant organization emerged in the highlands, eastern frontier, and north of Chiapas calling itself the Alianza Nacional Campesina Independiente Emiliano Zapata (ANCIEZ, Emiliano Zapata Independent National Peasant Alliance) (Harvey 1998, 253). Indeed, ANCIEZ was in fact the first public face of the Zapatista Army of National Liberation (Womack Jr. 1999, 39). While claiming member organizations in six central and northern states, it was clearly strongest in Chiapas among the Tzotzil, Tzeltal, and Chol communities and in the highland communities of El Bosque, Larrainzar, Chenalhó, Huixtán, Oxchuc, Tila, and Tumbalá (Harvey 1998, 195). For some time, the need to take up arms had been advocated by people working in the Lacandón Jungle and several communities in the highlands, a position persuasively argued on the basis of 'the explosive combination of unresolved land claims, lack of social services, institutional atrophy, authoritarian political bosses, monstrous deformations in the justice system, and the general lack of democracy' (Hernández Navarro 1994, 8). On 12 October 1992, in commemoration of 500 years of survival and resistance, thousands of Indigenous people flooded the streets of the colonial city of San Cristóbal de las Casas and toppled the statue of the city's conquistador founder Diego de Mazariegos (Gilly 1998, 293–4; see also Hernández 1994). As would later become apparent, this demonstration was a trial run – and the last call for civil, peaceful struggle – prior to the uprising on 1 January 1994. The stage was now fully set for that explosion and for the emergence of the Zapatista Army of National Liberation.

Enough!

Why do we need to be pardoned? What are they going to pardon us for? For not dying of hunger? For not accepting our misery in silence? For not accepting humbly the historic burden of disdain and abandonment? For having risen up in arms when we found all other paths closed? For not heeding the Chiapas penal code, one of the most absurd and repressive in history? For showing the rest of the country and the whole world that human dignity still exists even among the world's poorest peoples? For having made careful preparations before we began our uprising? For bringing guns to battle instead of bows and arrows? For being Mexicans? For being mainly indigenous? For calling on the Mexican people to fight by whatever means possible for what belongs to them? For fighting for liberty, democracy, and justice? For not following the example of previous guerrilla armies? For refusing to surrender? For refusing to sell ourselves out?

Who should ask for pardon, and who can grant it? Those who for many years glutted themselves at a table of plenty while we sat with death so often, we finally stopped fearing it? Those who filled our pockets and our souls with empty promises and words?

Or should we ask pardon from the dead, our dead, who died 'natural' deaths of 'natural causes' like measles, whooping cough, breakbone fever, cholera, typhus, mononucleosis, tetanus, pneumonia, malaria and other lovely gastrointestinal and pulmonary diseases? Our dead, so very dead, so democratically dead from sorrow because no one did anything, because the dead, our dead, went just like that, with no one keeping count, with no one saying, 'ENOUGH!' which would at least have granted some meaning to their deaths, a meaning no one ever sought for them, the dead of all times, who are now dying once again, but now in order to live?

Should we ask for pardon from those who deny us the right and capacity to govern ourselves? From those who don't respect our customs or our culture and who ask us for identification papers and obedience to a law whose existence and moral basis we don't accept? From those who oppress us, torture us, assassinate us, disappear us for the grave 'crime' of wanting a piece of land, not too big and not too small, but just a simple piece of land on which we can grow something to fill our stomachs?

Who should ask for pardon, and who can grant it?

From 'Who Should Ask for Pardon and Who Can Grant It?'
Subcomandante Insurgente Marcos (2001g)

On 1 January 1994 the Zapatista Army of National Liberation seized several towns and hundreds of ranches in Chiapas. Later it would be known that in mid-1992, Zapatista communities had made the decision to go to war 'to coincide with 500 years of resistance' (Harvey 1998, 198). In 'The First Declaration of the Lacandón Jungle,' the Zapatista declaration of war, the General Command of the EZLN states that 'we are a product of five hundred years of struggle,' explicitly narrating a history of struggle not only of Indigenous peoples against Spanish invaders but also of the people of Mexico against invasion, dictatorship, poverty, and repression (Ejército Zapatista de Liberación Nacional 2001c, 13). While asserting their goal to advance on the Mexican capital and depose the federal executive in order to allow 'the people liberated to elect, freely and democratically, their own administrative authorities,' the Zapatistas also outline the central goals of their struggle, namely, 'work, land, housing, food, health care, education, independence, freedom, democracy, justice, and peace' (ibid., 14). These demands evoke not only the concrete concerns of peasants living in the far southeast of Mexico today but also echo the demands of Mexican revolutionaries of the past three hundred years. 'The First Declaration of the Lacandón Jungle' is, in this sense, an explicit reclamation of the Mexican Revolution and the Mexican nation from those who had usurped it.

It is important to realize that, with respect to the prevailing socio-historical conditions on a global scale, the timing of the Zapatista uprising was not particularly auspicious. In interviews and communiqués published since the uprising, Marcos and other Zapatista leaders have repeatedly asserted the divergence between the leadership of the EZLN and the communities on the issue of the potential for armed rebellion. In order to understand the Zapatista movement itself, as well as how it has resonated so profoundly with others (including those far removed from Chiapas), it is essential to appreciate this circumstance and the reasons for this divergence. Gilly's (1998) comments about this fundamental difference in perception surrounding the potentials and timing of armed rebellion bear quoting at length:

> The channels through which communities, on one side, and the leadership of the EZLN (or for that matter any other left-wing organization), on the other, get their perceptions of the surrounding society are not the same; nor are the filters and the codes according to which they are interpreted. This difference, invisible to all in 'normal' times when the capital decision – insurrection – is not in play, comes to light at the moment of making that decision. For that reason, while some see in the 'disappearance of the Soviet Union' a negative factor, others who are distant from that interpretation of an upheaval, regarding which they are not concerned, measure by other methods – against the arc of their own lives – the maturation of conditions for rebellion. (303)

· Thus, in place of a theoretical orthodoxy or a distanced evaluation of larger socio-political forces which could amplify or nullify the rebellion, Indigenous communities in Chiapas relied upon measuring the conditions and necessity for rebellion 'against the arc of their own lives,' a philosophy that would deeply infuse Zapatismo and its resonance transnationally in the years following the uprising.

Communities in the canyons and Lacandón Jungle, formed only decades earlier by Chol, Tzeltal, Tzotzil, and Tojolabal migrants from the highlands, had become products and practitioners of a very different kind of politics than that which was practised in highland communities based on ranks of honour and established channels of privilege and power (Womack Jr. 1999, 18). Separated from the highland context, the new communities developed systems of politics based on the communal assembly and consensus-based decision-making, thus, in this setting the community ruled their authorities and it was the communities who had decided to go to war (ibid., 19). This relationship exemplifies the key Zapatista democratic notion of 'commanding obeying,' as all authority and legitimacy in this case resides in the community and in the assembly rather than in military strongmen or political bosses.

It is vital to note that in calling themselves 'Zapatista,' the insurgents of the EZLN and the civilian base, which comprises the bulk of the movement, have adopted the name of one of the greatest Mexican revolutionary heroes, even though he was neither active nor particularly well known in Chiapas until quite recently (Collier and Quaratiello 1999, 158). In fact, the source of the image and ideology of Zapata in Chiapas must be primarily traced to the 'ideological messages of the Mexican urban left and through those organizers from the left who went out into the Mexican countryside after 1968 to work with the rural population' (Stephen 2002, 150). In the statutes of the Forces of National Liberation, written fourteen years before the Zapatistas of Chiapas would initiate their rebellion, the choice of Emiliano Zapata as the icon for the revolution is attributed to the fact that 'Emiliano Zapata is the hero who best symbolizes the traditions of revolutionary struggle of the Mexican people' (Fuerzas de Liberación Nacional 1980, cited in Stephen 2002, 152). By invoking the man, his image, and his legacy, the Zapatistas are currently engaged in a process not only of engaging the national imaginary and reaffirming the 'Mexicanness' of their movement but also of rearticulating and redeploying Mexican revolutionary mythology.

As I mentioned before, however, the image of Zapata ultimately employed by the EZLN is a hybridized one referred to as 'Votán Zapata.' As Juana Ponce de León (2001) notes, 'For the Mayan Tzeltales, Votán represents the third day in the Tzeltal calendar, and corresponds to "the heart of the people." He is also the first man sent by God to distribute land among the indigenous' (21). Lynn Stephen views this hybrid figure rather instrumentally and argues that it 'provided a focal point for the emerging Zapatista movement when it first consolidated among an isolated multiethnic group of mestizo, Tzeltal, Ch'ol, Tojolabal, and Tzotzil guerrillas and then was exported to surrounding communities through indigenous leaders and political operatives of the EZLN' (2002, 162–4); however, I take a somewhat different view. Stephen's analysis of the initial deployment of this hybrid figure may indeed be correct, but the longer-term processes in which the Zapatistas' use of Zapata and the hybrid figure of Votán Zapata are implicated speak rather to the Zapatistas' use of Votán Zapata as a new kind of orienting story.

In the EZLN's communiqué 'Votán Zapata or Five Hundred Years of History,' which I quoted from at length earlier, the General Command of the EZLN writes, 'The name without a name, Votán Zapata looked in Miguel, walked in José Maria, was Vicente, was named in Benito, flew in a bird, rode in Emiliano, shouted in Francisco, visited Pedro' (Ejército Zapatista de Liberación Nacional 2001d, 20). What is missing in this statement are the last names of these individuals, and if they are inserted they become Miguel Hidalgo, José Maria Morelos, Vicente Guerrero, Benito Juárez, Emiliano Zapata, Francisco Villa, and Pedro Páramo, all revolutionary heroes in Mexico, all inhabited by the spirit of Votán Zapata (Ponce de Léon 2001, 21). I contend what the General Command of the EZLN set out to accomplish in this communiqué and, more generally, through communicative actions aimed at national civil society, is not simply to reclaim Mexican revolutionary history but to tell a new kind of story about rebellion and revolution. In effect, through communicative actions such as this, the Zapatistas set out to reshape the terrain of political struggle and the way in which people positioned themselves upon it. In essence, the Zapatistas did not set out to reclaim history, they set out to reinvigorate a future of possibility through the use of national, and particularly revolutionary, myths.

Rebel Mexico and the National Resonance of Zapatismo

... what was needed was for someone to give a lesson in dignity, and this fell to the most ancient inhabitants of this country that is now called Mex-

ico, but when they were here it did not have a name, that name. It fell to
the lowest citizens of this country to raise their heads, with dignity. And
this should be a lesson for all. We cannot let ourselves be treated this way,
and we have to try and construct a better world, a world truly for everyone, and not only a few, as the current regime does. This is what we want.
We do not want to monopolize the vanguard or say that we are the light,
the only alternative, or stingily claim the qualification of revolutionary for
one or another current. We say, look at what happened. That is what we
had to do.

We have dignity, patriotism and we are demonstrating it. You should
do the same, within your ideology, within your means, within your beliefs, and make your human condition count.

Subcomandante Insurgente Marcos (2002a) speaking in
San Cristóbal de las Casas, Chiapas, on 1 January 1994

In her article 'The New Zapatista Movement: Political Levels, Actors
and Political Discourse in Contemporary Mexico' (1998), Xóchitl Leyva
Solano examines the reasons for which the Zapatista movement has
been able to create ties not only with specific sectors of Mexican civil
society but also with what she refers to as 'México Rebelde.' 'México
Rebelde,' according to Leyva Solano, includes 'traditional parties of the
left and centre-left, cells of clandestine political organisations and
"legal" peasant, indigenous and sector organisations together with non-
governmental organisations and civil associations' (38). The bases for
identification between Zapatismo and México Rebelde include worsen-
ing living conditions for people throughout Mexico; the entrenchment
of ruling party power and privilege; the fragmentation of the organized
left and its electoral defeat through massive fraud in 1988; and, finally,
the 'unanimous rejection of armed struggle as an option to solve the
country's problems' (ibid.). Leyva Solano argues that the Zapatista cry
of '¡Ya Basta!' – 'Enough!' – reverberated so strongly within Mexico
because it came at a particularly delicate time, just as the country was
preparing to enter into the North American Free Trade Agreement with
the U.S. and Canada and to engage in the six-year ritual of PRI presidential succession (ibid.). Significantly, Leyva Solano contends that this
'convergence of different political actors,' which occurred following the
Zapatista uprising, should not be seen either as an accident or as a
peripheral consideration 'since the EZLN discourse had always empha-
sised the necessity of fomenting ties between the various popular strug-

gles that had taken place in Mexico, in "isolated nuclei," over the past five decades' (ibid., 48).

Through their engagement of national and international civil society via their communiqués published and distributed on the Internet; hosting of events such as the Intercontinental Encuentro for Humanity and Against Neoliberalism in the Lacandón Jungle; sending of delegates throughout Mexico to consult with citizens nationally; conducting referenda on the national and international levels regarding the future of the EZLN and support for Indigenous rights; trekking unarmed but masked to Mexico City in the March of Indigenous Dignity in March 2001 in order to press for the fulfillment of the San Andrés Accords; the formation of the Juntas del Buen Gobierno and the birth of the Zapatista Caracoles in August 2003, which have further consolidated the building of Indigenous autonomy in Chiapas; and the dynamic ability of their spokesperson Subcomandante Insurgente Marcos to generate media attention and national and international civilian engagement, the Zapatistas have managed to engage in a dialogue focused on the search for political spaces and alternatives. This dialogue provoked an impassioned and engaged response on the part of diverse sectors of Mexican civil society whose members were already profoundly disillusioned by the corruption, abuses, and failures of an increasingly neoliberal ruling elite whose veneer of 'revolutionary legitimacy' had all but vanished.

Why did Zapatismo resonate among diverse sectors of Mexican society? Why, instead of provoking fear and a desire for militarily enforced 'security' did Mexican and even international civil society reach out to embrace it? In his article 'Chiapas and the Rebellion of the Enchanted World' (1998), Adolfo Gilly explores the bases upon which the resonance of Zapatismo within the Mexican nation occurred. I believe it is of value to review these points of resonance. Gilly considers the 'adoption and protection' of Zapatismo by Mexican civil society to be based upon seven central points, which I will briefly discuss in turn. The first basis of resonance emerged from the nationally transmitted symbolic gesture of columns of armed and masked but clearly Indigenous men and women taking control of the colonial plaza of San Cristóbal de las Casas. This, Gilly argues, evoked 'the historical memory of the country, the memory transmitted in families or studied in school. Indians, those about whom the urban society bore an ancient and unconfessed guilt, had organized themselves and risen up with weapons in their hands,' and 'in a single blow the rebellion had legitimated itself before Mexicans' through these images and their transmission (309). The second basis, related to the first, is that the word 'Zapatismo' instantly explained the rebellion to the nation in 'terms accessible to all'; furthermore, this movement's right to invoke this word and its history, so often co-opted by ruling elites, was demonstrated by the fact that 'entire Indian communities had organized an army' (ibid.). Since the legitimacy of the rebellion had been established, Gilly argues that the third basis of resonance resulted from the state's negotiation with the Zapatistas because, as Gilly explains, 'one doesn't negotiate because one has the right to, but because one has the force to make that right recognized.' This principle is 'rooted in the common culture within which the Mexican state community has sustained itself, above all since the revolution of 1910 and its aftermath, the cardenista reforms' (ibid., 309–10). Situated in relation to these three initial historical, cultural, and political points of reference, the reasons for the 'adoption and protection' of the Zapatistas on the part of Mexican civil society began to crystallize.

The resonance of Zapatismo is not based purely on historical, cultural, and political antecedents, however. As Gilly asserts, the fourth basis of this resonance was established because the demands issued by the Zapatistas in their declaration of war, their invocation of Article 39 of the Mexican constitution, and their call for the removal of Carlos Salinas and his government to allow for free and democratic elections to occur all demonstrated that the Zapatistas did not want to subvert the Mexican state but 'rather to replace the existing political regime and its economic policy with another' (ibid., 310). The Zapatistas did not want to destroy the Mexican state, they wanted to reinvigorate it with a spirit of deep inclusivity and radical democracy. In the fifth instance of this resonance, Gilly explains that the Zapatista movement 'aroused in Mexico an Indian movement independent of the government,' a movement which has since materialized in the form of the National Indigenous Congress (ibid.). Alongside this, Zapatismo and the independent Indigenous movement have stimulated a national debate about the 'Indian question, especially about culture and autonomy,' a moment that Gilly considers to be marked by a 'diversification and democratization of Mexican political culture' that was entirely new and to which other broad sectors of Mexican society could relate (ibid., 310–11). Also linked to the 'Indian question' is the sixth basis for the resonance of Zapatismo. Gilly maintains that the Zapatistas, along with the national Indigenous movement, put the issue of national identity back on the agenda 'during a period when that notion was (once again) the subject of debate,' particularly in light of NAFTA and other globalizing forces (ibid., 311). Once again, the Zapatistas were not calling for an abandonment of the Mexican nation and the identities that were a part of it, instead they called for a direct and explicit consideration of national identity, who it currently excluded, and who it privileged.

Gilly's final point is that the communicative ability of the Zapatistas, their management of modern media, and their profoundly original discourse resonated throughout Mexican society. This discourse, Gilly contends, was so powerful because it was articulated in a language 'of modern images and ancient symbols, [which] does not propose a return to a past either distant or near ... It suggests instead the possibility of a nonexcluding modernity, one that does not destroy history and those who carry it with them but, rather, integrates them into a reality where none are excluded' (ibid., 312). This is a powerful point and connects with the argument I have been trying to advance in this chapter, namely, that the Zapatista movement has worked not merely to reappropriate a stolen revolutionary tradition or to secure state power, but rather that it has sought to tell a new kind of story, one in which forward-looking and diverse – rather than reactionary and singular – dreams of social revolution could be imagined and even lived.

As Gilly convincingly demonstrates, both this set of interwoven factors and the social resonance of Zapatismo to which they have given rise ultimately rests upon the central pillar of the Zapatista movement itself, that is, 'the material, human, and historical substance of this rebellion: the indigenous communities and the Indian leadership of the movement, without which the combination [of factors] would be impossible' (ibid., 312). As for Marcos's role in all of this, Gilly situates it brilliantly in relation to this set of bases of resonance by simply stating that Marcos 'knew enough, first, to comprehend and assimilate that substance [of the Indigenous communities] and, then, how to be the mediator or the guide through which its image is transmitted to urban society' (ibid.; also see Higgins 2000). Through a complex interplay of cultural, historical, and political reference points, a deep rootedness in the Indigenous communities from which it emerged, a communicative approach at once profoundly evocative of Indigenous culture and yet capable of speaking powerfully to diverse audiences, and a political project that challenges relations of power and domination (both long-standing and newly emergent) and seeks to enrich democracy and reinvigorate the Mexican nation, Zapatismo has initiated a powerful resonance on a multiplicity of levels within Mexican civil society.

The making of meaning and connections are central aspects to appreciating the resonance of Zapatismo within Mexico. While the original stated goal of the EZLN was to topple the government of Carlos Salinas, defeat the Mexican military, and establish the space necessary for people to restore democracy, liberty, and justice to their own lives, the seizure of state power or the imposition of a unitary vision was never part of the EZLN's aspirations. In pressing for the opening of democratic spaces within which others could also engage in the pursuit of democracy and social justice in Mexico, the EZLN 'established a cultural strategy that called into question the PRI's hegemony by reinterpreting national symbols and discourses in favor of an alternative transformative project' (Gilbreth and Otero 2001, 9). But it was also more than just a strategy of 'reinterpretation.' Since 1994, the Zapatistas have sought to communicate new kinds of possibilities and experiences not in order to recapture a stolen tradition or history but to make room for a future that has not been foreclosed upon. This approach to political struggle, profoundly informed by an engagement with Mexican revolutionary histories, has also served as a powerful base for the transnational resonance of Zapatismo.

As several observers have remarked, the Zapatista movement has brought unprecedented national attention to the 'Indian Question' in Mexico, raising debate about the conditions of life and the sociopolitical and cultural aspirations of Indigenous peoples living within the Mexican state, and making these issues among the most important with respect to the national political agenda (Aridjis 2002; Gilly 1998; Mattiace 1997; Monsiváis 2002). If this was all the Zapatista movement had accomplished, it would be a tremendously significant outcome in and of itself; however, in addition to this the Zapatistas have also succeeded in galvanizing a broad range of democratic movements in Mexico through new and innovative political projects and encounters. In the words of Luis Hernández Navarro (2002), 'among the most important consequences of the Zapatista movement in our times is that it has stimulated dreams of social change, and resisted the idea that all emancipatory projects must be sacrificed to global integration,' and it did so through 'the symbolic force of the image of armed revolution that still holds sway for many parts of the population' and 'the moral force that indigenous struggles have acquired.' Furthermore, once 'the cult of the rifles' had worn off, what remained and what sustained the Zapatista resonance was the very fact that they continued to articulate and build a new political project (64–5). Once again, this dynamic of struggle to achieve new political spaces and practices would also serve to amplify Zapatismo's resonance transnationally.

This is not to say that the Zapatista struggle has resulted in unqualified democratic gains; on the contrary, several scholars have pointed out that the Zapatista movement has had a range of less glamorous consequences from exacerbating tensions in and between Indigenous communities in Chiapas to actually inhibiting significant pre-existing articulations of community and municipal autonomy (Cal y Mayor 2003; Eber 2003; Gilbreth and Otero 2001; Leyva Solano 2003; Mattiace 2003). Yet the uprising was nevertheless seen by many as 'a bold statement by an oppressed minority against an encroaching global capitalism that threatened the small Mayan farmer and, by extension, any subordinate group unable to shoulder the weight of global competition' (Gilbreth and Otero 2001, 18). Furthermore, what the Zapatistas have proposed is not a return to old social pacts or a simple change of current power-holders for new ones; instead, they have sought to realize 'a social project based on the plurality of the peoples and cultures that make up Mexico and the diversity of their ideals' (Esteva 2003, 248). They have sought to engage in a project of building a world capable of holding many worlds. By challenging ruling elites both through physical acts of creation and resistance as well as through symbolic or cultural acts of communication aimed at the subversion of the sociocultural and historical foundations of power, the Zapatistas have opened new spaces of political struggle and reawakened the possibility of articulating truly democratic and inclusive alternatives. While the historical memory, political traditions, and revolutionary mythology that the Zapatistas have engaged so successfully are undeniably Mexican, the political imagination and the project of Zapatismo that have emerged from this matrix continue to resonate far beyond the borders of Mexico.

4 Echoes and Openings: Resonance

Antonio dreams of owning the land he works on; he dreams that his sweat is paid for with justice and truth; he dreams that there is a school to cure ignorance and medicine to scare away death; he dreams of having electricity in his home and that his table is full; he dreams that his country is free and that this is the result of the people governing themselves; and he dreams that he is at peace with himself and with the world. He dreams that he must fight to obtain this dream, he dreams that there must be death in order to gain life. Antonio dreams, and then he awakens ... Now he knows what to do, and he sees his wife crouching by the fire, hears his son crying. He looks at the sun rising in the east and, smiling, grabs his machete.

The wind picks up, he rises and walks to meet others. Something has told him that his dream is that of many, and he goes to find them.

From 'A Storm and a Prophecy – Chiapas: The Southeast
in Two Winds,' Subcomandante Insurgente Marcos (2001a)

In *The Dialogic Imagination* (1981), Mikhail Bakhtin states that 'every word is directed toward an answer and cannot escape the profound influence of the answering word that it anticipates' (280). If this is so, then what answer did the cry of '¡Ya basta!' – 'Enough!' – which issued from the mouths of the masked guerrillas of the Zapatista Army of National Liberation (EZLN) in the early hours of 1 January 1994 anticipate? What was the nature of the reply that the insurgents and civilian bases of the EZLN hoped to hear? The Zapatistas' first public word, the Zapatista declaration of war, was addressed to the Mexican people in the form of 'The First Declaration from the Lacandón Jungle,' and in addition to explaining the reasons and aims of the uprising, it also spoke directly to the issue of what the Zapatistas hoped for in terms of Mexican society's response:

> To the People of Mexico,
>   We, the men and women, full and free, are conscious that the war that we have declared is our last resort, but also a just one. The dictators are applying an undeclared genocidal war against our people for many years. Therefore we ask for your participation, your decision to support this plan that struggles for work, land, housing, food, health care, education, independence, freedom, democracy, justice and peace. We declare that we will not stop fighting until the basic demands of our people have been met by forming a government of our country that is free and democratic.
>   JOIN THE INSURGENT FORCES OF THE ZAPATISTA NATIONAL LIBERATION ARMY. (Ejército Zapatista de Liberación Nacional 2001c, 15)

While the EZLN declared its intention to advance on Mexico City, overcome the federal army, depose the federal executive and allow for free and democratic elections, the shape of the insurgency would ultimately bear little resemblance to the relatively straightforward revolutionary agenda established in this initial declaration. Even more significantly, although Mexican civil society would indeed respond to the Zapatista uprising, it would not be in the way that the Zapatistas had originally called for. Perhaps even more dramatically, the Zapatista uprising and the cry of '¡Ya basta!' would echo far beyond the borders of Chiapas and even of Mexico, entering into a complex and unanticipated transnational dialogue with a diversity of voices.

The resonance of Zapatismo amongst groups of North American political activists is the phenomenon upon which I focus here. Zapatismo's 'resonance' is not identical to more traditional forms of political solidarity, nor is it simply a facile romanticization of the Other's struggles on the part of northern activists. In using the term 'resonance,' I seek to describe an experience by which people are able to engage with political struggles that have emerged far from the contexts within which they live and work and, more significantly, through which they are able to find those struggles meaningful within their own spaces and places. In this sense, 'resonance' refers neither to the act of 'projecting' a struggle nor to the act of 'receiving' it; rather, it is the non-linear process and experience of making new political connections and new political meanings out of an encounter with another. Significantly, this dynamic of resonance often produces effects that are not at all predictable and, in their most powerful forms, are capable of producing new imaginations, repertoires, and even landscapes of socio-political and cultural struggle. Out of a confluence of encounters and engagements, and within a context conducive to it, resonance can produce profound shifts in the ways in which radical socio-political and cultural change is imagined, pursued, and manifested. It is this complex and densely interwoven set of spaces, relationships, and processes to which the concept of resonance draws analytical attention. It is upon this *lived terrain* that resonance acquires force as a dynamic potentially generative of radical alterity.

The encounters generative of resonance need not be physical; in fact, communications technologies such as DVDs, CDs, and the Internet, as well as a variety of textual forms can, and often do, serve as the 'connective tissue' facilitating resonance. The significance of this concept lies in the fact that it addresses political practices, spaces, and experiences that occur in the absence of direct channels of communication, organizational infrastructure, or even direct experience. Yet resonance is neither random nor is it simply romantic; instead, it testifies to the emergence of new understandings of political action, struggle, and possibility. Amongst the actors involved, it also speaks to a sense of sharing a terrain of struggle – however broadly defined – as well as the recognition of a common threat or subject against which to struggle. Nor does resonance imply a unitary conception of political struggle; rather, it signifies an emergent conceptualization of struggle and possibility that is both context-specific and therefore necessarily and irreducibly diverse and consciously and explicitly recognized as shared and interconnected.

Zapatismo and the Dynamics of Resonance

Before engaging the bases from which the resonance of Zapatismo has emerged amongst North American activists, it is necessary to elaborate briefly on what 'Zapatismo' is and what it is not. Contemporary Zapatismo could be said to have originated out of the encounter between Indigenous communities in the Lacandón Jungle and highlands of Chiapas and the urban and Marxist-inspired revolutionary cadres who arrived in Chiapas in the early 1980s to begin the work of organizing the peasantry for a revolution (see Collier and Quaratiello 1999; Gilly 1998; Harvey 1998; Womack Jr. 1999). By all accounts, however, this encounter did not result in the 'revolutionizing' of the Indigenous communities but rather in the 'defeat' of Marxist dogma at the hands of these Indigenous realities, a defeat which actually allowed for the emergence of the Zapatista struggle itself. Renouncing a teleology of revolution, Zapatismo is instead a project driven by a desire to create a 'world where many worlds fit, where all worlds fit,' a project that by necessity has as its pillars a fundamental rejection of neoliberal capitalism, an equally fundamental commitment to a radically democratic practice, and a foundational belief in the importance of dignity, creativity, and hope.

Does this mean that Zapatismo is a political theory or a designation for a particular type of social struggle? This question is best answered by examining some of the most essential aspects of the Zapatista struggle. As Subcomandante Insurgente Marcos himself has said, 'The EZLN has reached a point where it has been overtaken by Zapatismo' (García Márquez and Pombo 2004, 5). What does this mean? First, it means that Zapatismo is not identical with the EZLN. The EZLN is the Zapatista army that exists to defend the Zapatista communities in Chiapas, and it is an army that is subordinated to the authority of the Zapatista communities themselves. This relationship is formally expressed through the Indigenous Revolutionary Clandestine Committee–General Command (CCRI–CG), which is comprised of civilian Zapatista comandantes who are in turn beholden to the authority of their respective communities, a relationship which exemplifies the Zapatista slogan of 'to lead by obeying.' Secondly, Zapatismo is not a coherent ideology, it is not a codified set of absolute rules or a party line to which one can adhere, and while I have referred to it as a 'political philosophy' in the past, it is also more than this. Marcos has called Zapatismo an 'intuition,' a position elaborated upon by Manuel Callahan (2004b) in the following way: 'Zapatismo is a political strategy, an ethos, a set of commitments claimed by those who claim a political identity' (218–19). Zapatismo thus embodies an approach to politics based on the pursuit of 'democracy, liberty, and justice' for all. What each of these terms mean of course differs, depending upon the space and place within which people find themselves. Even within each specific context, these meanings can never be fixed because such an assertion would be to claim a singular and transcendent truth, a notion that the Zapatistas reject. 'Walking questioning' is the Zapatista slogan that perhaps best embodies this commitment and expresses the belief that if one begins with answers and seeks to impose solutions, systems of power and domination are merely reproduced.

Within Zapatismo, the concepts of autonomy and interconnectedness are constantly at play. Autonomy because dignity is only possible when individuals and communities have both the freedom and responsibility to govern themselves and interconnectedness because a world that does not recognize existence as shared and interdependent is a world pitted against itself, a world doomed to replicate exclusion, division, and violence. The challenge of creating a new world rooted in social relations that are not power relations and that emerge out of the mutual recognition of dignity is something the Zapatistas have undertaken most seriously. This refusal to claim a 'power-over' and simultaneously the affirmation of a 'power-to' create a world rooted in dignity, democracy, justice, and liberty can thus be seen as embodying what Subcomandante Insurgente Marcos means when he calls Zapatismo an 'intuition.' It also forms an essential component of what has facilitated the transnationalization of Zapatismo beyond the borders of Mexico.

The Bases of Resonance

This is who we are.
The Zapatista National Liberation Army.
The voice that arms itself to be heard.
The face that hides itself to be seen.
The name that hides itself to be named.
The red star who calls out to humanity and the world
to be heard, to be seen, to be named.
The tomorrow to be harvested in the past.

Behind our black mask,
Behind our armed voice,
Behind our unnameable name,
Behind us, who you see,
Behind us, we are you.

Behind we are the same simple and ordinary men and women,
who are repeated in all races,
painted in all colors,
speak in all languages,
and live in all places.
The same forgotten men and women.

The same excluded,
The same untolerated,
The same persecuted,
We are you.

Behind us, you are us.
Behind our masks is the face of all excluded women,
Of all the forgotten indigenous,
Of all the persecuted homosexuals,
Of all the despised youth,
Of all the beaten migrants,
Of all those imprisoned for their words and thoughts,
Of all the humiliated workers,
Of all those dead from neglect,
Of all the simple and ordinary men and women,
Who don't count,
Who aren't seen,
Who are nameless,
Who have no tomorrow.

> From 'Opening Remarks at the First Intercontinental Encuentro for
> Humanity and Against Neoliberalism,' the CCRI–General
> Command of the EZLN (Ejército Zapatista de Liberación Nacional 2001a)

Within Mexico, the resonance of the Zapatista struggle amongst other sectors of the population has been thoughtfully analysed and has brought to light the numerous and diverse points of intersection from which this resonance has emerged (Aridjis 2002; Gilbreth and Otero 2001; Gilly 1998; Hernández Navarro 2002; Leyva Solano 1998; Monsiváis 2002). Outside of the Mexican context, however, the reasons for and consequences of the resonance of Zapatismo have remained largely, although by no means entirely, unconsidered. Perhaps not surprisingly, one of the first organizations to appreciate the potential impact of Zapatismo was the RAND Corporation in a report written for the U.S. military entitled *The Zapatista Social Netwar in Mexico* (Arquilla et al. 1998). Defining 'netwar' as 'an emerging mode of conflict (and crime) at societal levels, short of traditional military warfare, in which the protagonists use network forms of organization and related doctrines, strategies, and technologies attuned to the information age,' the RAND Corporation has identified this form of social conflict as one

which involves a 'war of the swarm' in which each group or protago-
nist functions as a 'node' in an 'all-channel' matrix (Arquilla and Ronfeldt 2001, 6–7). Netwar thus involves many 'nodes' working together
without a hierarchical organizational structure – in fact, often with very
little 'structure' at all – and without a 'head' that can be effectively targeted by adversaries. I note this analysis here both to acknowledge the
fact that a corporate-military think tank and policy development institute understood the organizational model of the emerging Zapatista
solidarity network prior to it being broadly understood in more academic analyses as well as to assert that while this organizational contribution is significant (no doubt even more so to RAND's military
employers), it reduces the significance of the resonance of Zapatismo to
an issue of structure and instrumentality. To appreciate why this resonance has occurred and what it means, it is necessary to understand
what this struggle means to North American activists themselves.

In *The New Transnational Activism* (2005), Sidney Tarrow makes the
case for the 'diffusion' of the 'Zapatista solidarity network from Chiapas
to North America' (113–17). Tarrow's analysis contributes importantly
to appreciating how forms of collective action arising out of specific
national 'configurations of conflict spread to other venues' through
processes of relational (small personal networks), non-relational (generalized communication amongst people with few or no social ties), and
mediated (brokered by a third party) diffusion (ibid., 103). Fuelling the
transnational diffusion of collective action, according to Tarrow, are processes of internationalization and communication, processes which
have only accelerated through technological innovation, economic integration, the proliferation of new forms and sources of media, and the
increasing importance of international institutions and their non-state
challengers. Tarrow's analysis is certainly not incorrect in the claims it
makes about the channels and forces that have facilitated the diffusion
of Zapatista solidarity efforts across borders, but in focusing on channels and forces, other significant elements escape its scope.

It is by now a well-worn trope that the transnationalization of the
Zapatistas' struggle cannot be divorced from considerations of 'globalization' and the spread of new communications infrastructure. In fact, it
has been a common tendency for northern analysts of the movement to
focus on the innovative communication strategies of Zapatista spokesperson Subcomandante Insurgente Marcos and the role of the Internet
to such a profound extent that it often overshadows basic realities on
the ground in Chiapas. For example, in 'Rebellion in Chiapas: Insurrec-

tion by Internet and Public Relations,' (1993), Jerry Knudson suggests the following: 'Did the Internet, with instantaneous communication and "the whole world watching," short-circuit ... slaughter in Chiapas? Coupled with the adroit public relations by Subcommander Marcos of the Zapatista National Liberation Army (EZLN), it was as if the conflict was fought on symbolic rather than real terms' (507).

Of course, although Knudson never mentions it explicitly, 'the whole world' was – and is – not watching. Despite a revolution in telecommunications technology, outside of the overdeveloped North, few people have access to telephones in their own homes let alone a TV or the Internet. More importantly, Knudson's article proceeds to recount by now a familiar refrain that 'public relations' was the main weapon of the Zapatista struggle, that Marcos is a master of media manipulation, that the Zapatistas are Internet warriors, and that the uprising of 1 January 1994 was perhaps little more than a carefully managed public relations stunt designed to draw attention. What such a fascination with the tools of communication does is not only obscure the very real conditions of organizing on the ground but it also assumes that the Zapatista struggle – with its very real costs for the people who comprise it – is akin to a postmodern spectacle designed and deployed for the consumption of conscience constituencies and armchair revolutionaries in the North. Absent from this analysis is any kind of explicit acknowledgment that, despite Marcos's use of the media to communicate with a wider world, the technology to which Knudson refers is rare if not entirely absent from the Zapatista base communities themselves, many of which lack running water and electricity let alone have TV and Internet connections. Moreover, analyses such as Knudson's regularly overstate the extent to which international – or 'world' to use Knudson's own term – opinion has mattered to the Zapatistas and their struggle. While it would be inaccurate to ascribe no significance to it at all, had the Zapatistas relied upon the fickle attention of an international public, their movement would have been crushed long ago. Knudson extends this valorization of 'world opinion' mediated through the Internet and other (corporate) information/entertainment channels by ascribing to it the ending of apartheid in South Africa, deposing Ferdinand Marcos of the Philippines in a 'bloodless coup,' ending the genocide in Argentina, and compelling Pinochet and the Sandinistas to honour elections (ibid., 516).

Such an impressive list of accomplishments is only possible when one ignores the realities and histories of struggle on the ground in these places and the committed concrete solidarity efforts of activists internationally. Nowhere in Knudson's analysis do such efforts make an appearance. While one cannot deny the role of the Internet as a vital tool for communication and the dissemination of information (an analysis actually posited in a more sophisticated fashion by the RAND analysts) amongst activist communities and with respect to a broader (and wired) public, communicative tools should not be mistaken for social action. As Arjun Appadurai (1996) has noted with respect to electronic media in a globalizing world, 'part of what the mass media make *possible*, because of the conditions of collective reading, criticism, and pleasure' is the formation of a 'community of sentiment,' a 'group that begins to imagine and feel things together' (8, emphasis added). While media provides the possibility for the dissemination and diffusion of imaginaries of political struggle, it is not a substitute for it.

Of course, not all analyses of the role of media in relation to the transnationalization of the Zapatista struggle are as reductive as Knudson's. Both Harry Cleaver (1998) and Adrienne Russell (2005), for example, offer analyses of the role of media in relation to the transnationalization of the Zapatista struggle that reflect the complexity of this phenomenon. In Russell's case, the point of focus is upon the intersection of the myths that have been constructed in relation to the Zapatista movement and the communicative infrastructure used to deploy and disseminate them. Russell examines the myth of Subcomandante Insurgente Marcos as a universal, 'timeless,' 'uberhuman' figure, the myth of the Indigenous peoples of Chiapas as 'noble warriors' paradoxically 'backward' and 'advanced,' and the myth of the 'neoliberal beast' as central to the constitution of a network identity amongst international supporters of the movement. For his part, Cleaver focuses on the 'Zapatista Effect,' which refers to the 'impetus given to previously disparate groups to mobilize around the rejection of current policies, to rethink institutions and governance, and to develop alternatives to the status quo' (623). This 'Zapatista Effect,' Cleaver contends, is the result of pro-Zapatista mobilization around the world, which has been stimulated by the explosive growth in 'electronic NGO networks' catalyzed by the Zapatista uprising (ibid., 622). While highlighting the profound role electronic communication networks have played in the linking of disparate activist groups both in support of the Zapatista movement and in a project of resistance and alternative-building to neoliberal capitalist globalization, the strength of Cleaver's insights is that they do not reduce issues of mobilization, political innovation, and radical political action to issues of communication, infrastructure, or media.

In *International Zapatismo: The Construction of Solidarity in the Age of Globalization* (2005a), Thomas Olesen considers the international impact of Zapatismo from an analytical position deeply rooted in social movement theory. Olesen's work does make some significant contributions to appreciating the international consequences of the Zapatista movement, and the reasons he identifies as essential to appreciating its international resonance offer important insights. Olesen argues that the international appeal of Zapatismo is based upon six essential features: first, the Zapatistas situated their uprising in globally historical terms in addition to national ones; second, through their analysis and actions, the Zapatistas helped to redefine a 'common enemy' for the left – neoliberal capitalist globalization; third, and connected to the second point, the Zapatista uprising was tied at an early stage both to a criticism of NAFTA and the neoliberal model of development, which had become popular in the 1980s; fourth, the Zapatista uprising signalled for many disillusioned leftists a new hope that history had not ended after all in spite of the supposed global victory of liberal democracy and neoliberal capitalism; fifth, the Zapatistas did not seek to retreat from globalization but to invoke an alternative form of it; sixth, and finally, the Zapatistas did not seem to be rejecting liberal democracy but rather calling for its radicalization (11–13). Olesen also notes that in order to appreciate the global impact of Zapatismo, it is essential to understand the globalized basis upon which it has operated. Globalization in Olesen's formulation is best understood as marked by four central features: first, the development of a 'global consciousness,' which took shape following the Second World War; second, the ascendancy of the neoliberal model of economic restructuring that has taken place since the 1970s; third, the spread of democracy since the 1980s and the end of the cold war; fourth, the invention and expansion of the Internet (ibid., 19). It is upon a globalized terrain marked by these four core features that Olesen argues that Zapatismo has established its significance.

While Olesen does provide some useful insights into the resonance of Zapatismo in his work, particularly with respect to how globalizing processes have facilitated the possibility of transnational resonance, he relies almost exclusively upon the twin analytical tools of framing and cycles of protest to demonstrate the impact of Zapatismo globally. In this way, 'resonance' becomes entirely reducible to the ability of the EZLN and Subcomandante Insurgente Marcos to 'frame' their struggle in a way that spoke to issues touching people in other parts of the world as a result of globalizing processes. These connections have become easier to articulate, in Olesen's analysis, because 'the primary consequence of the end of the Cold War has ... been the globalization of democratic and human rights ideas' (ibid., 46). This assertion, of course, is rather more ideological than informative, and to state that the globalization of democratic and human rights ideas has been the primary consequence of the end of the Cold War at the very least attempts to present a tremendously simplified picture of a much more complex reality.

In Olesen's account, 'frames' of all sorts become the most significant mechanisms within this transnational social movement machine, and it is the ability of certain actors to utilize these frames – latent frames, action frames, master frames, movement frames – that produce resonance and ultimately social action and change. The way in which Olesen describes the operation of these latent and action master frames is instructive with regard to what his analysis adds to a sophisticated appreciation of the resonance of Zapatismo and what it misses:

> A latent master frame is understood as a reservoir of ideas and interpretations providing social actors with a kind of ideational toolbox. In the present context, the ideational complex of democracy and human rights is considered to be the dominant dimension in the latent master frame. An action master frame, in turn, is built on a latent master frame but is elaborated more concretely by particular social movements so as to be directly applicable in the construction of specific movement frames. (Olesen 2005a, 44)

The picture of socio-political action that Olesen presents is one in which actors access 'ideational toolboxes' in pursuit of the achievement of specific goals. Their attempts resonate or not depending on whether or not they manage to access these latent master frames that Olesen and other social movement theorists contend form the background against which claims are judged by the wider public. While the apparent explanatory power of this formulation may appear robust, it achieves its force by 'framing' social struggle itself as a formula that needs to be solved and that requires only the substitution of the specific variables to operate across an infinite variety of contexts.

Elaborating on the 'transnational framing' approach he utilizes to explore the transnational dimensions of Zapatismo, Olesen argues that a 'common social critique tying together physically, socially and culturally distant actors' has been provided by 'some of the economic (neoliberalism) and political (elite democracy) aspects of globalization,' developments which in turn have provided the 'background for transnational grievance perceptions and for the construction of injustice frames' (2005a, 40–1). He notes that 'notions of radical democracy often make up the content of the grievance interpretations constituting a fundamental element of transnational frames' (ibid., 43–4). To be sure, there are many valuable points offered by Olesen in articulating this analysis and, from a social movement theory perspective, this is a rigorous application of the theory's tools and structural approach. However, this structural, hydraulic approach is precisely what my own analysis seeks to move beyond because it only offers a snapshot of a much more complex and dynamic process. As Eric Selbin (2003) argues:

> Approaches overly reliant on the political, the psychological, or the economic are ill equipped, for example, to capture the ways in which Zapata's white horse, Che's beret, Sandino's hat, Ho's pith helmet, bamboo walking stick and wispy beard, or Cabral's knit cap have become symbols freighted with significance and import, consequential in their invocation and deployment, their story – and the part they are made to play in other stories – contested by people from all sides in the struggle to articulate the case for or against revolution.
>
> ... along with the material or structural conditions which commonly guide our investigations, it is imperative to recognize the role played by stories, narratives of popular resistance, rebellion and revolution which have animated and emboldened generations of revolutionaries across time and cultures. (84)

As I have already sought to demonstrate in this work, histories of political action and the complex and conflicted processes involved in the articulation of socio-political subjectivities are vital to the perception of the challenges and opportunities facing political action and radical social change. These dynamics are simply not appreciable within the dominant tradition of social movement theory, even within more sophisticated analyses such as Olesen's. In place of frames, networks, repertoires, opportunity structures, and macro-narratives, focusing upon the phenomenon of resonance compels us to take issues of history, imagination, and context seriously.

How and why has the resonance of Zapatismo manifested itself in activist communities in Canada and the United States? Upon what grounds is it possible to make a claim for a 'transnational resonance' of the Zapatista struggle? Perhaps the most obvious materialization of the resonance of Zapatismo amongst North American activists is in the adoption of the rhetoric of Zapatismo, most frequently expressed through the communiqués of the Zapatista spokesperson Subcomandante Insurgente Marcos. These communiqués have been disseminated not only through the Internet but also through CDs, DVDs, audio and video tapes, as well as through an abundance of published material about the Zapatista movement. But the Zapatista uprising has also taken on a special significance within the contemporary global justice/ anti-capitalist movement. A brief review of some of the literature that has emerged from this 'movement of movements' is all that is necessary to confirm at least the rhetorical impact of Zapatismo and to illuminate some of the bases upon which it is articulated. As Paul Kingsnorth writes in *One No, Many Yeses: A Journey to the Heart of the Global Resistance Movement* (2003), 'The Zapatistas would become the unwitting, but not unwilling, forgers of a truly global insurgency against history's first truly global system' (7). Or, as Manuel Callahan notes in his article 'Zapatismo and the Global Struggle: "A Revolution to Make a Revolution Possible,"' (2004a): 'In many respects the Zapatista uprising is the moment when the movement against globalization found its global audience, and it is perhaps the place where the tactics of that movement began' (12).

The significance of Zapatismo with respect to the global anti-capitalist movement is perhaps most powerfully captured by the editorial collective Notes From Nowhere in *We Are Everywhere: The Irresistible Rise of Global Anticapitalism* (2003). In the first entry of their timeline of global anti-capitalism entitled 'The Restless Margins: Moments of Resistance and Rebellion' the editorial collective writes of 1 January 1994: 'The EZLN ... declares war against Mexico, bringing its inspirational struggle for life and humanity to the forefront of political imaginations across the planet' (31). Elaborating upon the resonance of Zapatismo, Notes From Nowhere proceeds to explain the relationship between Zapatismo and the global anti-capitalist movement as well as to situate it historically:

> Movements of the past are laden with charismatic leaders – Che Guevara, Rosa Luxemburg, Huey Newton, Karl Marx, Emma Goldman, Lenin, Mao Tse-Tung. But whose face can be found in the foreground of today's movement? Ironically, the first face that comes to mind is masked and bears the pseudonym 'Subcomandante Marcos.' This is the spokesperson for the Zapatistas, whose words have profoundly influenced the spirit of the movement. But he, like so much of this movement, thrives on the power

and creativity of paradox, for he speaks of leading by obeying, carrying out the policies of a committee of indigenous campesinos. Note the 'sub'commander, and the anonymity of the mask. He warns that the name Marcos is interchangeable – anyone can put on a ski mask and say 'I am Marcos.' In fact he says that Marcos does not exist, but is simply a window, a bridge, a mediator between worlds. He says that we are all Marcos. Not what one expects from a traditional leader.

It follows that a movement with no leaders organizes horizontally, through networks. And it was the poetic communiqués and powerful stories that trickled from the Zapatista autonomous zones in the Chiapas jungle onto the relatively new medium of the internet which told of their suffering, their struggles, their mythologies, that began to weave an electronic fabric of struggle in the mid-nineties. This web of connections between diverse groups gave birth to a series of face-to-face international gatherings – the Zapatista Encuentros – which soon grew to become the roaring, unstoppable torrent of movements for life and dignity and against capital that are emerging across the world. 'We are the network,' declared the Zapatistas, 'all of us who resist.' (64–5)

In her article 'Rebellion in Chiapas' (2002), Naomi Klein considers what she labels 'the Zapatista effect' by asking, 'what are the ideas that proved so powerful that thousands have taken it on themselves to disseminate them around the world?' She answers: 'They have to do with power – and new ways of imagining it' (219). While Klein discusses the centrality of 'democracy, liberty, and justice' to the Zapatista struggle in addition to their disavowal of the desire to seize state power as fundamental aspects of their global appeal, she also acknowledges some of the less tangible dimensions of Zapatismo's resonance. In concluding her article, Klein notes, 'This is the essence of Zapatismo, and explains much of its appeal: a global call to revolution that tells you not to wait for the revolution, only to start where you stand, to fight with your own weapon' (ibid., 220–1). Perhaps even more significantly, Klein ends by reflecting on the role of Marcos and the Zapatistas within a larger history of political struggle in order to situate their appeal and relevance:

As I listened to Marcos address the crowds in Mexico City, I was struck that he didn't sound like a politician at a rally or a preacher at a pulpit, he sounded like a poet – at the world's largest poetry reading. And it occurred to me then that Marcos actually isn't Martin Luther King Jr.; he is King's very modern progeny, born of a bittersweet marriage of vision and necessity. This masked man who calls himself Marcos is the descendant of King, Che Guevara, Malcolm X, Emiliano Zapata and all the other heroes who preached from pulpits only to be shot down one by one, leaving bodies of followers wandering around blind and disoriented because they had lost their heads. And in their place, the world has a new kind of hero, one who listens more than he speaks, who preaches in riddles not in certainties, a leader who doesn't show his face, who says his mask is really a mirror. And in the Zapatistas we have not one dream of a revolution but a dreaming revolution. 'This is our dream,' writes Marcos, 'the Zapatista paradox – one that takes away sleep. The only dream that is dreamed awake, sleepless. The history that is born and nurtured from below.' (223)

In the same vein as Naomi Klein, Rebecca Solnit, author and U.S.-based activist, offers a telling perspective on Zapatismo and its global significance in her work *Hope in the Dark: Untold Histories, Wild Possibilities* (2004) that also bears quoting at length:

In dazzling proclamations and manifestos, the Zapatistas announced the rise of the fourth world and their radical rejection of neoliberalism. They were never much of a military force, but their intellectual and imaginative power has been staggering ... [The Zapatistas] came not just to enact a specific revolution but to bring a revolution, so to speak, in the nature of revolutions. They critiqued the dynamics of power, previous revolutions, capitalism, colonialism, militarism, sexism, racism, and occasionally Marxism, recognizing the interplay of many forces and agendas in any act, any movement. They were nothing so simple as socialists, and they did not posit the old vision of state socialism as a solution to the problems of neoliberalism. They affirmed women's full and equal rights, refusing to be the revolution that sacrifices or postpones one kind of justice for another. They did not attempt to export their revolution but invited others to find their own local version of it, and from their forests and villages they entered into conversation with the world through encuentros, or encounters – conferences of a sort – communiqués, emissaries, and correspondence. For the rest of us, the Zapatistas came as a surprise and as a demonstration that overnight, the most marginal, overlooked place can become the center of the world.

They were not just demanding change, but embodying it; and in this, they were and are already victorious ... They understood the interplay between physical actions, those carried out with guns, and symbolic actions, those carried out with rods, with images, with art, with communications, and they won through the latter means what they never could have won through their small capacity for violence. (34–5)

I have quoted these passages by Naomi Klein, Notes From Nowhere, and Rebecca Solnit here at length not as a perfect description of the essence of Zapatismo but rather to offer them as particularly eloquent statements of Zapatismo's significance in the eyes of many – but by no means all – U.S. and Canadian activists. The dimensions of the movement that these authors talk about are not wrong, but they do speak to issues that resonate perhaps more strongly within the contexts of U.S. and Canadian-based activists rather than within the reality which the Zapatistas themselves inhabit. Foregrounded in these articulate passages are notions of hope, creativity, human dignity, communication, democracy, and what could be termed an intellectual and political cosmopolitanism. These elements I would argue are most certainly present in Zapatismo, all the more so with respect to the communiqués and communicative actions directed towards supporters transnationally, and they also speak to needs (a powerful rejection of neoliberalism; affirmation of human dignity; peace; autonomy and interconnectedness; the desire to speak and be heard as well as to listen) and means (communicative and symbolic rather than violent action) familiar to people struggling within 'First World' or 'post-industrial' societies like Canada and the United States. Less apparent, but by no means always absent, from this perspective on Zapatismo are the complexities of the Zapatista struggle on the ground in Chiapas, the mundane work of building relations of 'good government' amongst the communities and municipalities in rebellion, and the unavoidable contradictions which occupy the sphere of human action.

It is important to distinguish here between a recognition of the fact that Zapatismo's resonance beyond the borders of Mexico speaks to the contexts and experiences that activists live on a daily basis and the assertion that such resonance is an indication of a facile and selfish romanticization or exploitation of the Zapatista struggle. While scholars have accused northern activists of mistaking the 'trope' of Chiapas for the reality and complexity of struggle, of seeking revolution 'somewhere else' as opposed to confronting issues 'at home,' and of seeing in the Zapatistas a projection of their own desires (see Hellman 2000; Meyer 2002), such criticisms by no means apply to the range of individuals and collectives who have responded to the Zapatista struggle and its attendant political imagination. In considering the resonance of Zapatismo and its consequences, the dangers and failures of imagination and romanticization must be considered, and I will come to this shortly. However, to cynically label the transnational resonance of Zapatismo as selfish or as a mere projection of fantasy is to summarily dismiss a rich, complicated, and powerful phenomenon. In order to begin to understand the implications of Zapatismo's resonance amongst Canadian and U.S. activists, it is first necessary to appreciate the reasons for which these activists found Zapatismo so very compelling.

Beyond the acknowledgment of Zapatismo as a foundational moment or point of reference within the emergent history of the global justice/anti-capitalist movement as it has been related in the literature coming out of the movement, how have political activists living and working in the U.S. and Canada positioned themselves in relation to the Zapatistas? Patrick Reinsborough, a grassroots activist and co-founder of the smartMeme Strategy and Training Project, a collective directed towards 'injecting new ideas into culture' and challenging the system at 'the point of assumption,' described his own experience with Zapatismo to me in the following way:

> I [have been] deeply inspired by the Zapatista movement since 1994 ... because I was so inspired, for me it was a logical step to ... unite Indigenous resistance with earth-centred values ... There's the level of the inspiration and then the model ... looking at it in terms of Zapatismo [and] the importance of autonomy, the importance of people [and] challenging power itself, so instead of looking at ... taking state power finding new openings and new opportunities. I found that very inspiring ...

The dimensions of resonance raised by Patrick are strongly evocative of the passages I quoted earlier, but tellingly for Patrick, as for many of the other activists with whom I spoke, the significance of Zapatismo and its resonance within their own lives and political action extended far beyond a repudiation of a desire to seize power and a commitment to autonomy. For Patrick, the significance of the Zapatista struggle, and ultimately its resonance within his own political commitments, rested not only upon their rhetoric or their inspiration but also upon the clarity of vision, commitment, and innovative strategies they brought to a post–Cold War terrain of struggle:

> The Zapatistas are an incredible model for how to do organizing, how to combine local work ... how to choose your own battlefields, you know,

even having had that brief stint as a military struggle they were very clear right from the beginning ... that their battleground was really being set on their own terms ... They said it was a war of ideas, a war of words, more than a war of guns or bullets ... The phenomenon they created in terms of the importance of networks, the importance of contesting idea space and [pointing out] that the system really is most vulnerable not where a line of riot police might be gathering ... in a military sense, it's most vulnerable at its intellectual underpinnings, that we're fighting a pathological system ... If we can frame the debate and if we can ... decolonize people's imaginations and give them an experience of the potential of what democracy really means, of what really having control over your own life and your community, having actual freedom and autonomy and sustainability what that can mean ... it attacks the system at some of its deepest levels, that has opened up a whole new range of possibilities, and really without the leadership of the Zapatistas there would be no people's globalization movement in the way that there is today.

The revelatory aspects of Zapatismo have been commented on by other scholars, particularly within the Mexican context (Harvey 1998), but they hold particular significance when one considers the fact that the inspiration and tactical lessons of Zapatismo were received so dramatically outside of their originating context.

Rick Rowley and Jacquie Soohen, tactical media activists from Big Noise Films and makers of *Zapatista, This Is What Democracy Looks Like*, and *The Fourth World War*, spoke compellingly about the reasons for the resonance of Zapatismo both personally and more broadly when I interviewed them. Reflecting on her own experience growing up in Canada, Jacquie related the significance of Zapatismo in terms of her own political development in the following way:

I don't come from a political family but ... from a farming family ... For me it was just being part of a single-parent family and having to deal with a lot ... It wasn't a political activism thing it was just the way you live your life ... How do you live every day being poor, being in a really small town, living on welfare? ... A lot of the things that opened my mind initially ... were around women's issues, and working around domestic violence and things like that, but ... there was never a systemic view. Living in Canada for me then was a lot about people telling me what the tools were that I needed to change things, and it all involved ... these very liberal ideas of being able to mediate conflict resolution and things like that ... all inside the system and trying to move along those ladders that were placed [there] for you ... And then through a very bizarre series of circumstances, I ended up in Yugoslavia during the war there, and I was living and working there and still trying to function within this model of conflict resolution, but it didn't work ... Then I ended up coming to the [United] States and finding a whole other series of problems and lived circumstances ... that I couldn't mediate away, especially race, and feeling race in a way that I had never felt before, and so hearing about the Zapatistas ... it became apparent that you just couldn't mediate these things away, that there were things that were systemic, that there were things that you couldn't approach in a liberal sort of way ... [I] had to rediscover a history that belonged to me but that I think was kept from me ... [it was] a history I had to rediscover about people actually standing up and fighting for things, but then how do you approach that and deal with that ... [when] at the same time you're rediscovering this history, you're being forced to feel like everybody's apathetic and that people don't care? Yet you know it's not true, you know that people don't believe what's going on, you know that people are smarter than that but ... that they feel powerless and helpless to change things.

It should come as no surprise that activists' personal experiences served as a particularly significant basis of resonance for Zapatismo. What is particularly significant about this circumstance however is that one of the central consequences of this resonance was not limited to a personal moment of satisfaction or fulfilment but rather facilitated a renewed systemic political analysis as well as reinvigorated hope for the realization of meaningful alternatives outside of the ascendant neoliberal agenda.

When I asked Rick Rowley of Big Noise Tactical about his own history of politicization, he related a story that explicitly connected notions of personal inspiration and hope with the 'invitation' of Zapatismo. Travelling through Central America and Mexico by bus with friends after he finished high school, Rick found himself in Mexico as the situation in Chiapas was on the verge of exploding once more:

In February of 1995 we were riding buses through Chiapas ... right as the military was breaking the cease-fire and 35,000 Mexican troops were invading Chiapas. We were heading north on buses and [when] we arrived in Mexico City, [we] ended up living in the south of the city in the university district, the UNAM, at this amazing moment ... when the country's on fire, there's a civil war in the south, there's movements emerging all over the country. No one in the States had any idea that ... any of this was going on ... I ended up staying for six months in Mexico City and became involved with the Zapatista solidarity movement there, so it was an amazing time to be alive. Every day we'd come down to buy *La Jornada* and read the new communiqués from Marcos that came out. Every weekend there were demonstrations in the Zócalo, sometimes as big as 300 or 500 thousand people and demonstrations unlike anything I'd ever seen in the North ... It was a party, we were dancing, there were huge puppets, it was an entire artistic, cultural, creative [experience] ... It was every aspect of life being caught up in this feeling of change and opening and possibility, so that was amazing. Even more amazing than that was the fact that we won, the demonstrations not just in Mexico City but uprisings throughout the rest of the country stopped the Mexican military from invading and ended the aggression. You know, understanding a little of the history of the region ... that there had been uprisings in the south of Mexico every fifty years for the last 500 years and the response of the Mexican military and the state system [has] always [been] the same ... the state system tries to quietly encircle, contain, and destroy the uprising, so military encirclement is accompanied by media encirclement, so that you never hear a word of the wars in the south. There's an ideological encirclement so that when word leaks out, as it inevitably does, through the cracks in the system people are told well, there might be something violent, horrible, criminal going on in the south, but it has nothing to do with you, it has nothing to do with your life in the city, it's an Indigenous peasant problem and that's it. So when we marched in the centre of Mexico City, in the Zócalo in 1995, we didn't march the way that people like us had marched in the 1970s and the 1980s, saying we're against the war in the south, we support these people down there; we marched and said we are Zapatistas and the war is right here under our feet, that the Zapatistas have survived and won victories against this First World military armed with sticks and their word because they've managed to tell a story about struggle that's an invitation to people to read themselves in as participants and not as observers on the outside.

The importance of people being able to 'read themselves in as participants' in a story of struggle is a cornerstone of the transnationalization of Zapatismo that cannot be ignored. The intentionality of this invitation to struggle together is something that should not be underestimated, either. Alex Halkin from the Chiapas Media Project asserted the centrality of the Zapatistas' capacity to both solicit the participation of others globally in struggle as well as to recognize their own struggle as one among a global multitude:

> I think principally it's because they asked for international civil society to participate with them and I don't know any other Indigenous movements that really up front ... said that, and I think that's a really important distinction. I think also that Mexico, because of its relationship with the United States, its proximity to the United States ... also has a very important place ... certainly in terms of Latin America, and I think that's part of it, but I really believe that it's because in the beginning they just said we want people from all over to come and work with us on this project and that we feel connected to ... other poor people in the world whether they're in Afghanistan or Africa, wherever, that this is the same struggle. They had the savvy to come and say ... we want you to come and we understand our connection to all of you as well.

Of course, connections cannot be forced and simply because the Zapatistas acknowledged their desire to see others join them in a global struggle 'for humanity and against neoliberalism' does not necessarily explain why others actually responded to this call. The persuasiveness of Marcos's communiqués aside, the transnational resonance of Zapatismo required more solid and fundamental bases in order to find more than just a global audience waiting to consume it.

If the Zapatistas had extended an 'invitation' to others to read themselves in as participants in struggle, why was this invitation received and accepted in the first place? To answer this question, issues of historical context become irreducible in their importance. As Patrick Reinsborough related:

> I think there's a very simple analysis people have developed around technology and the rise of the Internet, not to diminish the tools, but tools don't build a house, carpenters use tools to build a house and I think that ... the beauty and the wit and the strategy with which the Zapatistas set the terms of their own conflict and intervened in something much deeper than ... state power in Mexico. They intervened in a global system in a way that was creating new spaces, and I think that certainly someone like myself, much of my political work is sort of like tiny ripple effects from some of the amazing leaps of work that the Zapatistas created. Also the power of poetry, just these incredibly powerful poetic critiques that were happening

in a very systemic way that incorporated all the different pieces, whether you're talking about an economic critique or a political critique or an ecological critique, [and they were] also grounded in a common-sense emotional critique. I think that's something that I've been very attracted to ... in the struggle of the Zapatista movement – other similar resistance movements – trying to figure out how we translate some of that clarity of vision ... how we can help the people who are right now ... caught up in the brainwashing apparatus of consumer culture [understand] ... how can we help translate some of the experience ... [of] the communities that are being massacred and bulldozed and the places that are being destroyed to feed the insatiable appetite of global consumer society? [How can we find] that connection, change the feedback loop so that those messages, those new ideas are able to reach different parts of society? Particularly now in America [where] the affluence ... has been perceived as being the reason that Americans haven't been involved in systemic movements ... A lot of that affluence is actually increasingly becoming mythologized ... we're seeing a mythology of affluence. [In America there are] people without health care, vanishing jobs, [an] increasing propaganda state using weapons of mass deception to convince Americans that they should have troops occupying the world ... It seems like we're in ... a real exciting time, a real crisis and breaking point in the story of global capitalism, and that breaking point is really very articulately and effectively foreshadowed by the Zapatistas ... In the face of what would seem like the most powerful destructive empire ever created, a global empire of corporate control ... the Zapatistas were very effective in reminding us where our real power was; those are the ripple effects that are being felt around the world.

A global systemic analysis framed in the context of a critique that embraced both potent economic and political analyses as well as a profound sense of poetry, imagination, hope, and dignity provided the fuel for the transnational resonance of Zapatismo. Significantly, the dimensions of the Zapatistas' message and the terms upon which it was met by northern activists precluded merely a romanticization of the struggle, although romanticization did and continues to occur. I will address this dimension of resonance shortly.

The notion of a systemic and inclusive analysis of the global terrain of struggle emerging at a moment seemingly defined by the defeat of the insurgent left and state-sponsored socialism is a vital element in appreciating the resonance of Zapatismo. Dave Bleakney, a member of the Canadian Union of Postal Workers and one of the North American activists involved in the formation of Peoples' Global Action articulated this very sentiment to me when I asked him about his initial 'encounter' with Zapatismo and the reasons he felt this movement mattered:

> The first time I heard about it was actually when it happened. It was on the news that night and I'd been feeling pretty down because I thought that the movement in Canada capitulated against FTA. Here people were saying everything is on the line, everything that you have as a people is on the line and yet there was no ... meaningful fight other than a few letters and petitions, and politicians have come to learn that they can live through demonstrations, that it's not a big price to pay anymore. There was a time when a hundred thousand people in the street was a big deal, now it's ... just something else to be managed. So I was pretty distressed by that and when people in Chiapas rose up it gave me real hope, real hope and also an understanding that there was still dignity ... that people [who] had very little in the way of money or capital or standard of living had incredible dignity. I remember Fidel Castro once saying the enemy looks a lot smaller when you're standing on your feet and couldn't help but thinking that, so that was an incredible inspiration to know that struggle ... I mean, I was naively hoping that it would just spread through the Americas like wildfire.

While an insurrectionary struggle did not in fact emerge either in Mexico or in the Americas as a response to Zapatismo, the impact of the Zapatista uprising and its radical challenge to the foreclosure of meaningful alternatives at the hands of neoliberal dogma and hegemony had perhaps even more subversive and significant effects. Rick Rowley from Big Noise Tactical responded this way to a question about the significance and reception of Zapatismo by northern activists:

> In terms of the continent 1993 was a low point for movements in this hemisphere. The resistance movements in Latin America had been successfully destroyed, NAFTA had just been signed, Mexico was already bought and sold basically when NAFTA was signed and the union movement in the States, which had been limping along barely, was smashed ... there was a political horizon in which there was no hope and there were no actors who you could point to or who would give you the least inkling of the possibility of movement – not in the universities, not in the countryside, not in the factories, not in the cities, nowhere. So [when] the Zapatistas did emerge, [they] were a tear in the fabric of the present, they were a crack through

which it was possible for people to ... remember again histories of struggle that they'd been taught to forget or had been worn away by the last couple of decades and to imagine possibilities of struggle and resistance and imagine different worlds that could be built in this world that they ... had not been allowed to imagine. That was the main thing that Zapatismo gave us – it gave the lie to NAFTA and the entire world view it stood for, to the triumphalism of the Washington Consensus and its model of corporate globalization.

In this poetic articulation of Zapatismo's reception and immediate resonance, Rick points particularly to the importance of Zapatismo as a 'tear in the fabric of the present,' a crack through which it became possible for activists in the North to remember, reimagine, and reconnect with both histories and future possibilities of struggle that seemed to have all but disappeared. The centrality of the conceptual break that Zapatismo facilitated in the face of the ascendance of neoliberal capitalism is something that cannot be overstated, and it is reflected in the written histories of the contemporary global justice movement as well as in many of the reflections of the activists with whom I spoke.

The explicit and fundamental recognition of the connectedness of people's struggles on a global scale as well as the diversity and irreducible significance of each of these struggles is a powerful element of Zapatismo's resonance. In many ways, what the Zapatista discourse of radical inclusivity and openness achieves is what Ernesto Laclau and Chantal Mouffe consider in *Hegemony and Socialist Strategy* (1985) as the construction of 'the chains of equivalents' between struggles. Rather than privileging any particular subject position or site of struggle, the Zapatistas explicitly sought to redefine the terrain of political struggle by articulating a vision of socio-political change in which all people's struggles for 'democracy, liberty, and justice' for humanity and against neoliberalism become equally as important as any other. Fiona Jeffries, a scholar, activist, and writer and who had attended the First Intercontinental Encuentro for Humanity and Against Neoliberalism in Chiapas in 1996, reflected upon the inclusivity of Zapatismo and its implications for political action in the following way:

That quote, that amazing quote, 'Marcos is gay in San Francisco and a student without books and a Jew in Poland and a Palestinian in Israel.' That was such a powerful, pluralistic call that was like everybody's got something. There are very few people that are actually benefiting from this situation. We're all being convinced that this is as much as we can expect to benefit and we shouldn't ask for anything more, or we shouldn't fight for anything more, we shouldn't fight for freedom, that we should just exist 'cause it could be a lot worse. So I thought that was amazing, and I think ... that is their strength, their historical subject is not in any singular being; their historical subject is people's desire for freedom ... and justice and dignity ...

Fiona expresses one of the most powerful elements of Zapatismo's resonance here by asserting that the Zapatistas' 'historical subject' is not a particular identity or subject position but rather it is 'people's desire for freedom ... and justice and dignity.' Within such a formulation, it is possible for people participating in a multiplicity of struggles to see themselves as vital participants in a shared struggle without subordinating themselves to it.

Friederike Haberman, a journalist, activist, and one of the people who participated in both the Intercontinental Encuentros and the founding of Peoples' Global Action, also reflected on the importance of the Zapatistas' emphasis on inclusivity and their innovative approach to politics when I asked her about the attraction of Zapatismo beyond the borders of Mexico:

[The Zapatistas] stress not only the meaning of capitalism but also of racism and sexism and all kind[s] of struggles of identity or anti-identity. They always speak of the excluded and always include all struggles ... and don't focus just on capitalism ... and this had been entirely new on the international level. [The Zapatistas] also [exposed the false] contradiction between reformism and revolution [and demonstrated that neither is sufficient] with this saying, 'We don't have to conquer the world, it's enough to recreate it.' We have to start with a new world today in our daily lives, in our social movements, this is exactly what the Zapatistas have done, too. I'm sure it's not perfect what they're doing, but they just started to go on this way ... what they call 'preguntando caminamos,' so while we walk, we are walking questioning. So you can't have a ready-made utopia because this would mean to [impose] your utopia on other people but [it] has to be developed in the struggle. For me this is the most fascinating point, combined of course with the including of all identities ... that they speak of the many worlds that need to fit into the one world ...

Friederike ties many of the key threads and central themes of the Zapatista struggle together here in order to articulate the reasons for which it resonated so powerfully beyond its context of origin. Inclusivity, non-hierarchical organizational and conceptual structures, an expansive vision of the terrain of political struggle as well as the injustices faced by people in other places, and an affirmation of the fact that political struggle is a lived and constantly unfolding process rather than a teleology are among the most powerful themes characterizing Zapatismo's resonance amongst northern activists.

Carleen Pickard, director of the Mexico program at Global Exchange, invoked many of the same themes when I asked her about the resonance of Zapatismo both personally and more broadly in her own experience as an activist and organizer in the United States:

> If I go back to when I was first reading about the Zapatistas, I think the whole mandate of inclusivity seems to me like a big deal. It [facilitated the spread of the movement] around the world and [allowed] people to simply say 'I think all of those things the Zapatistas are calling for are rights as well and I reject the things the Zapatistas reject, too.' Then, if you continue to go through all the eloquent readings, you go, wait a minute! I can be a Zapatista, too! – and that for people was something that really resonated in terms of wanting to be included in something, [because] in their life they were alienated from what was going on in the day-to-day. The thing that fascinated me at the beginning was how you could have a movement that believed so hard in being Mexican yet was so accepting of international support and also saying we all suffer the same things, we suffer them in different ways and we can change them in different ways.

Again, the notion that the Zapatistas managed to extend a bridge to people in different parts of the world and invited them to participate in a genuinely shared struggle is a powerful dimension of the resonance which Carleen describes here. This invitation and sensation of inclusion is even more significant if it is considered in light of the feelings of alienation and profound individualization that have come to characterize life under neoliberalism.

The political example and the concrete manifestation of the building of alternatives at a time in which there supposedly was no alternative is also a pivotal element of Zapatismo's resonance. As Rick Rowley of Big Noise Tactical explained to me during our conversation:

> I think the biggest reason [that Zapatimo found such resonance outside of

Mexico] is because we were all waiting for them, we were waiting to hear a word like this [on] the day that NAFTA became law, at the southern tip of the North American Free Trade Area, at the darkest moment for movements in the Americas ... it was a word we were waiting to hear.

Eric Doherty of Building Bridges, a Canadian organization dedicated to human rights observation in Zapatista communities in Chiapas, also affirmed the notion that the Zapatistas managed to illuminate possibilities and renew hope in a time that had otherwise become quite silent and dark:

I think they played a really important role in being a spark and an inspiration. It may have been a small spark, but it seemed bright because it was quite a dark time. There wasn't that much else out there that was ... looking hopeful.

Jessica Marques, the grass-roots coordinator at Mexico Solidarity Network, focused on the Zapatistas' commitment to political alternative-building as well as their willingness to be accessible and engaged as hallmarks of their resonance outside of Mexico:

What set the Zapatistas apart for me and motivated me was the fact that they didn't try to be a traditional revolutionary movement that's trying to take power or become a political party. That's something new, and I think it's something that people haven't really known how to do. The Zapatistas are still figuring it out ... they don't have it figured out, they're making and they've made mistakes but they're really trying to create a new movement that's not going to replace a bad power structure with a new power structure. So, for example, they haven't been engaged in human rights abuses against the civilian population and, in fact, in areas that they are now more or less controlling even non-Zapatistas are going to the Zapatistas to mediate conflicts, because the way that the Zapatistas are mediating conflicts is significantly better than the way that the Mexican court system has operated locally. So I think there's just a lot of examples of the way that the Zapatistas are creating a new political space but without trying to take power for themselves ... The accessibility of the Zapatistas has allowed people to engage in the movement in ways they couldn't before, just the fact that you can go to Chiapas as an individual on a trip and communicate with Zapatistas and learn about their struggles [has] allowed some of us to be really humbled by the ideologies that we've held, and we've been able to question things and develop completely new ways of thinking.

From these reflections of a diversity of activists engaged in their own political struggles in Canada and the United States, it should be clear that Zapatismo's resonance is a much more complex and powerful phenomenon than critics of northern activists' response to it would admit. This is not to contend that the resonance of Zapatismo amongst activist communities in the United States and Canada is always unproblematic or uniformly beneficial for the Zapatistas or for political struggles in the North. The complexities and ambivalences of Zapatismo's transnational resonance and the possibilities as well as the dangers of the 'political imagination' are something that I will come to shortly. For the moment, however, I wish simply to state that cynical reactions to the transnationalization of the Zapatista struggle and its attendant political imagination are neither particularly useful nor seek to take seriously the consequences and potentials of this phenomenon of resonance. While there has undoubtedly been a romanticization of the Zapatistas and their struggles on the part of some activists and observers outside of Chiapas, such facile romanticism is neither dominant nor is it merely a selfish manifestation of fantasy.

Notions of possibility, hope, dignity, inclusiveness, interconnectedness, transnationalism, renewed political analysis, imagination, and creativity are deeply inscribed in the reflections offered by my research partners with respect to the significance of Zapatismo transnationally. Zapatismo's resonance is intimately and undeniably interwoven with histories that are both personal and socio-political. While many activists had personal experiences in life that prepared them individually for their reception of Zapatismo, equally significant within this dynamic are narratives concerning the larger socio-political context into which Zapatismo entered and became a crack in history, an invitation and an opening to begin dreaming and building something new. In this sense, the northern activists with whom I engaged have not, as some sceptical critics have claimed, appropriated the Zapatista struggle for their own narrow reasons. Neither have these activists 'read' the Zapatista struggle instrumentally or opportunistically. Rather, Zapatismo has resonated for these people and within struggles and movements in the United States and Canada because of an emerging and powerful sense of the necessity of a shared struggle that must be 'as global as capital,' to borrow a well-known phrase from the global justice movement, if it is to be effective.

Beyond a sense of shared struggle, Zapatismo has resonated for political activists in Canada and the United States on the basis of an emergent transnational consciousness, which has been shaped in part by the operation of neoliberal capitalism that has introduced forms of exploitation, insecurity, and violence previously largely unknown in the North. At a moment when neoliberal capitalism had become intimately and explicitly concerned with exerting total control over the production of subjectivities and over the reproduction of life, the Zapatistas reclaimed the struggle for human dignity through their radical and innovative political project and were joined by people all over the world who also rejected the same erasure of their agency and humanity. Rick Rowley from Big Noise Tactical eloquently articulates the connections between Zapatismo's radical and inspiring political imagination and the emergent transnational fabric of struggle for humanity:

Zapatismo's not like an ideology that's easy to lay out. It's not structured like that. It's more like a structure of myth and parables, but so much of it just so clearly articulated something that was in the water already just waiting to be spoken. In the same way that Seattle worked ... we were all waiting, the entire world was waiting for so long for something like that to happen in America, and when it did, it instantly captured everyone's imagination because this is what we were waiting for. Indymedia, which was created right then too, was theoretically possible, technically possible for a while before that happened ... other people had tried it at the last Democratic Convention in Chicago [and] there were other attempts at it [too], but this was a moment we got together [and] it clicked ... the movements were waiting for this to happen ... [Then] at this difficult moment, when the old logic of movements that was based on nationalism ... both state nationalism and inside of that cultural nationalisms ... had been successfully defeated pretty much all over the place – certainly inside the [United] States it had been marginalized and effectively screwed over – this new model of organizing [offered us] something that we had all been looking for ... [and] a bunch of [its] central points hit home ... The first and most important one, I think, was the way they reimagined cross-border solidarity ... especially First World–Third World solidarity ... [it was so different than] the way that movements in the North had organized their solidarity with the South around guilt and said that what connects you to people down there is the connection that exists between the oppressor and

the oppressed ... and that's it, and that [style] created hierarchical structures of authority inside of organizations that did solidarity work in the
States, and so it was a difficult thing to dislodge [that way of organizing].
For example, in Latin American solidarity ... lots of Latino and Chicano
organizers were fighting for a long time against hierarchies of radical
authenticity, which is based on religious proximity to a culture that you
could never quite touch. [For example, some people made statements
like], 'I'm not Indigenous and I would never claim to be Zapatista myself
but, you know, I am Chicana so I'm closer to it than you are.' That's something that the Zapatistas effectively made impossible ... [When] the one
person who could out-trump anyone else's claim to authentic ownership
of the struggle says that, then it's something totally different ... So it's
because we were all waiting for them to say what they had to say and they
were, in many ways, the only people who could say what they said and
have it mean what it meant.

The consequences of this resonance and the potentials and dangers of
imagination and political action are the dimensions of Zapatismo's resonance to which I turn next.

5 Imagining Struggle/Struggling to Imagine: Imagination and Political Action

In our dreams we have seen another world, an honest world, a world decidedly more fair than the one in which we now live. We saw that in this world there was no need for armies; peace, justice and liberty were so common that no one talked about them as far-off concepts, but as things such as bread, birds, air, water, like book and voice. This is how the good things were named in this world. And in this world there was reason and goodwill in the government, and the leaders were clear-thinking people; they ruled by obeying. This world was not a dream from the past, it was not something that came to us from our ancestors. It came from ahead, from the next step we were going to take. And so we started to move forward to attain this dream, make it come and sit down at our tables, light our homes, grow in our cornfields, fill the hearts of our children, wipe our sweat, heal our history. And it was for all. This is what we want. Nothing more, nothing less.

From 'In Our Dreams We Have Seen Another World,'
Subcomandante Insurgente Marcos (2001d)

In his play *Accidental Death of an Anarchist* (2003), Dario Fo paints a farcical yet compelling picture of political scandal not as a subversive spectacle but as a spectacle which actually serves to reinforce existing systems of power and privilege. In Fo's play, based on an actual series of events, the 'accidental death' of an anarchist in police custody and the spectacle of the investigation that follows it allow for a moment of critical reflection on the nature and purpose of spectacle in relation to systems of power. As Fo demonstrates so poignantly, rather than undermining the legitimacy of the system and its human agents who have actually created and enforced the conditions for the imprisonment and subsequent murder of a political dissident, the spectacle of scandal actually serves as a form of collective catharsis ultimately reaffirming our faith in these existing structures of power. Fo shows how spectacle can allow the spectator to condemn the particularities of a given incident while reaffirming her/his faith in the larger system out of which it has emerged. The spectacle is visible, it reinforces the belief that 'the system works' precisely because we believe that in seeing the spectacle we are seeing an aberrant event, an aberrant event which is being exorcised through the workings of the system itself. The event may be 'bad,' as indeed individual actors may be, but the larger socio-political framework is reinforced precisely because the spectacle provides a moment both to view 'deviance' and to see it expunged. Through an engagement with it, the spectacle that Fo describes allows us to imagine our world in particular ways and thus to continue acting in ways that accord with the world as we imagine it to be. The world 'works' because we have seen these spectacles of scandal and we have seen them dealt with, larger systemic issues rarely penetrate this convincing equation.

Yet, if scandal is reaffirming of existing structures of power, what about the idea of counterspectacles, spectacles designed intentionally to disrupt the 'business as usual' of modern, liberal-democratic structures of power? Can these counterspectacles bring about moments of rupture within a given socio-political context or do they also serve to somehow reinforce it? Furthermore, what is the relationship between spectacles, the imagination that inspires them, and the socio-political imaginations to which they in turn give rise? Spectacles do not exist as ends in themselves, they serve to provoke action or reaction, a sentiment, a feeling of possibility, a sense of hope. At their most fundamental level, spectacles are directed towards and built upon imagination, the capacity to think about that which does not currently exist but which might be brought into being. Imagination is not simply a personal, internal, or self-gratifying escape, it can also serve as a powerful and even collective force capable of allowing us to see possibilities beyond the pale of a narrowly defined and increasingly rationalized 'reality.' As Mary Zournazi states in her work *Hope: New Philosophies for Change* (2003), 'Reflections, conversations and dialogues build new social and individual imaginaries – visions of the world that create possibilities for change' (12). What are the possibilities of imagination politically and what are its limitations or dangers for political action? These are the questions which I consider here.

I ask these questions about the spectacle, the imagination, and political action in part because the Zapatistas' flair for the dramatic has been one of their most frequently commented-upon traits in the years since their 1994 uprising (Klein 2002; Ross 2000; Stavans 2002; Weinberg 2000; Womack Jr. 1999). In fact, it has been argued that many of the Zapatistas' initiatives from the Intercontinental Encuentro in Chiapas in 1996 to the March of Indigenous Dignity in 2001 to the uprising of 1 January itself have all been spectacles designed to rally popular support nationally and internationally in order to achieve the goals set out by Marcos and other Zapatista commanders (De la Colina 2002; Meyer 2002; Oppenheimer 2002). In my analysis, this not only misses the point but it also reduces the Zapatista struggle to that of yet another 'special interest group' applying pressure to elites in order to achieve their own ends. Even more cynically, this analysis descends into a view of the Zapatista movement as a mass of poor, gullible Indigenous people being manipulated by a few 'revolutionary' elites.

I argue instead that the Zapatista movement has exerted an imaginative and inspirational force far beyond its material capacity and its 'concrete' victories since 1 January 1994, a force rooted in and animated by a distinctive political imagination that has resonated far beyond the Indigenous communities of the Lacandón Jungle from which Zapatismo initially emerged. I use the term 'political imagination' here in a double sense: first, as a reference to imagination as an integral part of radical political practice; and second, as a term referring to both the impetus and processes involved in envisioning and articulating political projects which have emerged, directly and indirectly, due to the influence of Zapatismo. Thus, political imagination is both an act and a constellation of political projects. Theoretically, this conceptualization of the political imagination shares an affinity with Susan Buck-Morss's use of the 'political imaginary.' Drawing from the work of Russian philosophers Valerii Podoroga and Elena Petrovskaia, Buck-Morss (2000) explains that rather than referring merely to 'the logic of a discourse, or world view,' the political imaginary is a 'topographical concept ... not a political *logic* but a political *landscape*, a concrete visual field in which political actors are positioned' (11–12). Imagination seen in this way is the terrain of possibility. This imaginative terrain – its possibilities, limitations, and even dangers – generated through the encounter between northern activists and Zapatismo is precisely what I explore in this chapter. Imagination is significant here not in and of itself as an escape or release but as a window onto a terrain of new socio-political possibilities and opportunities. This is what in my analysis makes imagination particularly significant: it is one powerful way of accessing realms of possibility that for so many people are foreclosed upon by the realities of their everyday lives.

Imaginations

Now, who will be able to tell us that dreaming is lovely but futile? Now, who will be able to argue that dreams, however many the dreamers, cannot become a reality?

How is joy dreamed in Africa? What marvels walk in the European dream? How many tomorrows does the dream encompass in Asia? To what music does the American dream dance? How does the heart speak that dreams in Oceania?

To whom does it matter how and what we dream here or in any part of the world?

Who are they who dare to let their dreams meet with all the dreams of the world? What is happening in the mountains of the Mexican Southeast that finds an echo and a mirror in the streets of Europe, the suburbs of Asia, the countryside of America, the townships of Africa, and the houses of Oceania? What is it that is happening with the peoples of these five continents who, so we are all told, only encounter each other to compete or make war? Wasn't this turn of the century synonymous with despair, bitterness, and cynicism? From where and how did all these dreams come to La Realidad?

From 'Tomorrow Begins Today,'
Subcomandante Insurgente Marcos (2001f)

I begin this section with the quote above by Subcomandante Marcos from the closing ceremonies of the First Intercontinental Encuentro for Humanity and Against Neoliberalism held in Chiapas in August 1996 because it so powerfully expresses the centrality of dreaming and imagination with respect to political struggle. I begin this section with the quote above also because of its capacity to unsettle, discomfort, and even anger many who would read it, invoking as it does this centrality of the imagination and, for some, perhaps conjuring up images of utopianism, escapism, and the threat of seduction at the hands of the imaginary as opposed to the 'concreteness' of the 'real.' The pages and screens of the mainstream media are filled with admonishments on the part of government officials and industry leaders to those who make up

the 'movement of movements' of global justice and global anti-capitalism to put forward their concrete proposals instead of simply saying
'no' to global neoliberalism (as if this is all these diverse groups are
doing), to accept certain financial and political 'realities,' and to work
with and within existing institutions and dominant organizations to
affect change. However, these peoples' movements have responded not
only with concrete proposals and initiatives but also with powerful and
resounding invocations of hope and imagination. The slogan of the
World Social Forum that 'Another world is possible' is only among the
most obvious and well-known articulations of the centrality of hope,
creativity, and imagination.

Henry Giroux (2004) argues that this is not the dystopian, privatized,
cynical, and individualized 'hope' of neoliberalism, it is an 'educated
hope' embodying an 'oppositional utopianism,' grounded in everyday
experience and motivated by a powerful critique of institutional and
symbolic power (137). As Giroux eloquently asserts, this hope,

> ... makes concrete the possibility for transforming politics into an ethical
> space and public act that confronts the flow of everyday experience and
> the weight of social suffering with the force of individual and collective
> resistance and the unending project of democratic social transformation.
> Emphasizing politics as a pedagogical practice and performative act, edu-
> cated hope accentuates the notion that politics is not only played out on
> the terrain of imagination and desire but is also grounded in relations of
> power mediated through the outcome of situated struggles dedicated to
> creating the conditions and capacities for people to become critically
> engaged political agents. (Ibid., 137)

Giroux's explicit reference to hope and imagination as vital components of radical, and grounded, political struggle is both inspiring and
evocative of the reflections offered by my research partners. The only
element in need of qualification in relation to the phenomenon of the
political imagination which I examine here is Giroux's reference to 'utopianism.' By way of clarifying this point I also seek to address the issue
of why utopias and idealized visions of the possible do not occupy
space in my analysis. While I do not deny the power and significance of
utopian imaginations and aspirations, I contend that the phenomenon
of Zapatismo's resonance, the political imaginations it has provoked
and entered into dialogue with, and the concrete political practices that
have emerged out of them cannot be appropriately characterized as

'utopian.' Rather than signifying a yearning for utopia, literally 'no-place,' the political imaginations I trace here emerge, are situated in, and are inspired by a multitude of places. Connected to the places and spaces in which activists live and work, these imaginations coalesce not out of an idealized nowhere but out of lived everywheres. Rather than seeking something beyond where and what we are, these imaginations and those they inhabit strive to remember, dream, envision, and create situated ways of living and being differently in the time and space we occupy.

One further note on the notion of 'utopia' bears mentioning prior to turning to a more detailed consideration of concepts of hope and imagination. In many ways, utopia is a quintessentially modern concept, an orienting idealized principle born of sweeping visions of progress and development. To some, these fantastic nowheres were dreamscapes of limitless promise, for others they were nightmares, representing the obliteration of their ways of life and, often, their very physical existence. In her work *Dreamworld and Catastrophe: The Passing of Mass Utopia in East and West* (2000), Susan Buck-Morss speaks eloquently to the rise and fall of notions and projects dedicated to realizing utopia. Asserting that 'the construction of mass utopia was the dream of the twentieth century ... the driving ideological force of industrial modernization in both its capitalist and socialist forms,' Buck-Morss details how this dream manifested as 'an immense material power' transforming the natural world and 'investing industrially produced objects and built environments with collective, political desire' (ix). But this utopian project, in both its material and conceptual forms, failed in its promise. Commodities are still feverishly produced, consumed, and marketed the world over and the legitimacy of the state form continues to rest on a conception of 'rule by the people' drawn from received political wisdom 'now several centuries old.' However,

> the mass-democratic myth of industrial modernity – the belief that the industrial reshaping of the world is capable of bringing about the good society by providing material happiness for the masses – has been profoundly challenged by the disintegration of European socialism, the demands of capitalist restructuring, and the most fundamental ecological constraints. In its place, an appeal to differences that splinter the masses into fragments now structures political rhetoric and marketing strategies alike – while mass manipulation continues much as before. Commodities have not ceased to crowd people's private dreamworlds; they still have a

utopian function on a personal level. But the abandonment of the larger social project connects this personal utopianism with political cynicism, because it is no longer thought necessary to guarantee to the collective that which is pursued by the individual. Mass utopia, once considered the logical correlate of personal utopia, is now a rusty idea. It is being discarded by industrial societies along with the earliest factories designed to deliver it. (Ibid., ix–x)

As Buck-Morss so eloquently expresses in this passage, and compellingly demonstrates in the rest of her analysis, modern mass utopias were 'pronounced a failure' in the socialist world even as they were intentionally abandoned in the capitalist one. We need not mourn the passing of these utopias, for in every promise they held a new nightmare of exploitation, extermination, objectification, and domination was born, coloured differentially according to which faction – capitalist or socialist – it belonged. As Buck-Morss (2000) asserts:

The gap between the utopian promise ... and the dystopian actuality ... can indeed generate a force for collective awakening. This is the moment of disenchantment – of recognizing the dream *as* a dream. But a political awakening demands more. It requires the rescue of the collective desires to which the socialist dream gave expression, before they sink into the unconscious as forgotten. (209)

Rather than despairing at the decline of the dream of utopia, we need to collectively recognize – and seek to reclaim – the spaces and capacities of radical imagination and hope their passing has left room to explore.

How can we understand radical invocations of imagination and hope in a political context that is effectively post-utopian? Does an explicit theoretical and practical consideration of concepts such as imagination and hope allow for new and significant conceptualizations of political spaces and practices? I contend that it does. In countries that have benefited most from neoliberal globalization, imagination and hope have become new terrains for capitalist commodification. As Giroux (2004) contends, in these places, 'market relations now become synonymous with a market society, freedom is reduced to a market strategy and citizenship is either narrowed to the demands of the marketplace or becomes utterly privatized. The upshot is that it has become easier to imagine the end of the world than the end of capitalism' (125). Popular myths produced and distributed by corporate media-makers from newspapers to blockbuster films promote a conception of the world in which justice is only possible through exceptional individual action and that we are hopelessly naive if we express a desire for a world that embodies principles such as meaningful democracy, justice, and liberty.

In this vein, Mary Zournazi (2003) asks, 'Where is hope when compassion, empathy and dignity are synonymous with self-gratification – getting what you want at the expense of others, whether in the workplace, in our relationships or "across the board?"' (14). 'The search for happiness,' in First World or 'post-industrial' nations like Canada and the United States, 'becomes a search for emotional security based on economic success, and our personal dreams are part of the drive to get more out of life – more success, more money, more hope' (ibid., 15). But when these relations are marked by insecurity and an ever-present sense of crisis, 'success' and even 'hope' come to mean protection from anyone who might threaten our sense of comfort (ibid.). In order to find a way beyond individualized, commodified, and mutually destructive and unsustainable relationships, a capacity for collective critical imagination needs to be reclaimed.

The activists with whom I spoke offered a variety of perspectives on the significance of imagination in relation to political action and the search for new social and political spaces. In addition to reflecting on the role of imagination with respect to political action, many of my research partners also spoke articulately about its potentials and limitations. This is my attempt to synthesize this complex, amorphous, and potent dynamic. I will come to these reflections shortly, but first, through an engagement with an eclectic but powerful diversity of theorists, I turn to a consideration of the role of imagination with respect to the production and reproduction of society and subjectivities as well as imagination's relation to political action and political change.

The Biopolitics of Imagination, or, Why Imagination Matters

What is the significance, if any, of imagination as a socio-political force today? In *Modernity at Large* (1996), Arjun Appadurai argues forcefully for the recognition of the imagination as a 'constitutive feature of modern subjectivity' (3). In doing so, he engages the changing role of the imagination as it is linked to the developing dynamics of globalization. For Appadurai, imagination has over the last few decades become 'a collective, social fact' resulting in 'the basis of the plurality of imagined worlds,' a development which in itself is due to transformations in electronic media and mass migrations (ibid., 5). In many ways, Appadurai's argument is quite radical in that he posits not only that imagination is increasingly significant today but that the consequences of these shifts are 'new resources and new disciplines for the construction of imagined selves and imagined worlds' (ibid., 3). Appadurai bases his argument on three essential distinctions: first, that imagination 'has broken out of the special expressive space of art, myth, and ritual and has now become a part of the quotidian mental work of ordinary people in many societies' (ibid., 6); second, Appadurai distinguishes between imagination and fantasy, contending that while fantasy carries with it an individualistic and transitory connotation 'the imagination, especially when collective, can become the fuel for action' (ibid., 7); third, Appadurai emphasizes the distinction between the individual and collective sense of the imagination, arguing that 'part of what the mass media make possible, because of the conditions of collective reading, criticism, and pleasure' is the formation of a 'community of sentiment,' a 'group that begins to imagine and feel things together' (ibid., 8). In this sense, Appadurai argues that mass electronic media and mass migrations not only enhance the agency of individual actors but also provide the basis for the construction of 'diasporic public spheres,' the first manifestations of a truly 'postnational political order' (ibid., 21–2; see also Buck-Morss 2000, 277).

Appadurai (1996) conceptualizes a new role for the imagination in our contemporary moment, a role in which the imagination has become nothing less than 'a social practice' (31). Indeed, he contends that 'the imagination is now central to all forms of agency, is itself a social fact, and is the key component of the new global order (ibid.). Rather than rendering imagination as merely a vehicle for escapism or individual self-gratification, Appadurai instead implicates it directly in the possibility for social change and for the articulation of new social subjectivities. But upon what basis is this possible? In answer to this question, theorists Michael Hardt and Antonio Negri (2004) take up human creative capacity and imagination as central social forces and primary points of analytical focus. Hardt and Negri explore the significance and power of these human creative capacities through an exploration of the connections between contemporary regimes of 'immaterial labour,' 'post-industrial production,' and subjectivity. 'Immaterial labour' for Hardt and Negri refers to 'labour that produces immaterial products, such as information, knowledges, ideas, images, relationships, and affects' (65), a description which clearly speaks to the dominant economic sectors of advanced capitalist countries. Hardt and Negri argue that 'the qualities and characteristics of immaterial production' are actually transforming other forms of labour and, in fact, society as a whole (ibid.). This situation yields several consequences, but with respect to my focus here upon imagination, social reproduction, and the articulation of subjectivities, Hardt and Negri assert that 'the production of ideas, knowledges, and affects, for example, does not merely create means by which society is formed and maintained; such immaterial labour also directly produces social relationships' (ibid., 66). Such labour thus is no longer simply concerned with the economic but rather expands to 'become immediately a social, cultural, and political force,' a transition which, according to Hardt and Negri, ultimately signifies that 'in philosophical terms, the production involved here is the production of subjectivity, the creation and reproduction of new subjectivities in society' (ibid.). Imagination in this sense is a 'biopolitical' force, a force which is 'immanent to society' and which 'creates social relationships and forms through collaborative forms of labor' (ibid., 94–5). Much like Appadurai, Hardt and Negri see in the imagination, and, more importantly, in regimes of immaterial labour the potential for people to not merely reshape relations of power and domination but also to remake the fabric of life itself. Of course, imagination as a biopolitical force does not therefore mean it is a necessarily liberating force.

While Appadurai views transnational flows of images as a powerful resource for the enrichment of human agency and even liberation, this rather laudatory analysis of mass mediated images and communication is by no means uncontested. In *The Society of the Spectacle* (1994), Guy Debord takes the concept of the spectacle as his point of focus and examines the relationship between mass mediated spectacles and capitalism. Although Debord's arguments refer directly to a phase of capitalist accumulation that many would argue has passed, his reflections upon the nature and consequences of a society whose social fabric and interactions are mediated by spectacle are still very much relevant today. Beginning with the assertion that 'the whole life of those societies in which modern conditions of production prevail presents itself as an immense accumulation of spectacles,' he argues that social reality has become dominated by 'representation' rather than 'directly lived' experience (12). The spectacle that dominates lived reality in these societies is not a collection of particular images; rather, it is 'a social relationship between people that is mediated by images,' a social relation consisting fundamentally of separation (ibid., 12). The spectacle, Debord explains, is neither a 'deliberate distortion of the visual world' nor is it a 'product of the technology of the mass dissemination of images,' it is a world view materialized and imbued with presence and force (ibid., 12–13). Furthermore, Debord explains that regardless of its specific form – news, advertising, entertainment, propaganda – 'the spectacle epitomizes the prevailing model of social life'; thus, the spectacle provides both the content and the structure of lived reality (ibid., 13). In place of intersubjective social relations among people within a consciously constituted community, the spectacle imposes its ideological content upon individuals through the images it conveys, mediating all social relations and reshaping lived reality in its own image.

While Appadurai acknowledges that issues of access, history, politics, mobility, and freedom are implicated in this newly invigorated global landscape of the imagination, he does not truly engage them or their consequences – his focus is the role of the imagination and the liberatory potential it possesses. Additionally, he does not truly engage the issue of differentials of power and control over the 'flows' and '-scapes' that characterize the terrain upon which his vision of a 'postnational political order' is built. Debord's view of societies constituted through spectacles is considerably more critical. Significantly, the spectacle in Debord's view is differentiated according to the developmental stage of society. Whereas in bureaucratic capitalism the spectacle is unified to allow for a more strictly regimented control of society, in modern capitalism the spectacle becomes diffuse to allow for the furthering of the desire of people for the abundant commodity (Debord 1994, 41–2). In line with this, today one might say that the spectacle has become not simply diffuse but ubiquitous, and is no longer restricted to representation; rather, it has become indistinguishable from the 'lived reality' of many, particularly with respect to those segments of society most deeply implicated in a 'post-industrial' transition. Those most deeply enmeshed in a social-technological fabric and whose labour focuses on the production of images, information, knowledge, and even affects (through such diverse avenues as advertising or technologically driven simulations of reality) may even experience the spectacle in ways as immediate as daily life. Even outside of these groups, the spectacle of such contemporary forces as neoliberal capitalism, liberal democracy, and even the 'War on Terror' has achieved a global projection previously undreamt of, in part as a consequence of the 'flows' and '-scapes' that Appadurai views as resources for agency, imagination, and hope.

Yet the spectacle as Debord conceptualizes it should be seen not only in its most obvious forms of propaganda, advertisements, popular media, and celebrity but also in terms of the fundamentally limiting power of the spectacle to determine acceptable ways of thinking and being in the world. This is the true power of the spectacle and of its direct relationship to the imagination. It is also where the notion of the spectacle coincides, as the inverse, of Appadurai's liberatory conception of the imagination as well as with Hardt and Negri's conceptualization of biopower and the biopolitical as subjectifying forces of determination and possibility, respectively (see also Foucault 2003). Debord (1994) argues that even our notions of time and historicity are implicated in the processes that animate the spectacle. Irreversible time is the time of the commodity, a time that dispenses with lived experience and memory and replaces it with production (105). Space is similarly commodified and controlled within capitalist society, a control that extends not only to the factory and the workplace – if these locations are even truly singularly relevant anymore in a world shaped by regimes of flexible production and financial speculation – but also to 'halls of culture, tourist resorts and housing developments' designed to ensure the appearance of a 'pseudo-community' while reasserting the isolation of the individual (ibid., 121–2). Indeed, autonomist Marxists argue that contemporary forms of neoliberal capitalism and regimes of immaterial labour under it turn society itself into a factory – or into a prison. This conceptualization of space, time, and subjectivity under the sway of the dystopian political imaginary of global neoliberal capitalism resonates strongly with Giroux's analysis of the rise of 'proto-fascism' and Buck-Morss's exploration of the passing of mass utopias and the yolking of the collective imagination to projects of control, consumption, and cynicism. 'Separation,' Debord (1994) writes, 'is the alpha and omega of the spectacle' (20). Over all of this, the spectacle maintains the ideological unity of an alienated environment, ensuring that the images, symbols, values, and modes of interaction remain within the dictates of the capitalist system. The spectacle is a form of biopower, it looms above the social, applying transcendental principles and ordering social life and the subjectivities that inhabit it. Biopolitics is the possibility that life can be made and remade by subjects themselves; it defies the transcendental force of the biopower of the spectacle; it represents the reclamation of human creative capacity and of our collective imagination.

Imagining Possibilities

Without exception, the activists whom I engaged during the course of this project all affirmed the significance of imagination with respect to the search for new socio-political spaces and practices. Of course, beyond this affirmation, the role and potential of imagination was both complex and complicated. Before proceeding to explore some of the complexities of what I have termed the 'political imagination,' I would first like to offer two comments that express the centrality of imagination to political action and to socio-political change. One of my research partners who had visited Chiapas as a member of a Mexico Solidarity Network delegation, worked as an intern for MSN, and was deeply involved in grass-roots activism in her own community reflected on the significance of imagination in the following way:

> I think everybody has imagination, I think even if you strictly adhere to ... some kind of formulaic way of living your life or having a political system then you still have imagination that brings you to the place where you understand what you think that might look like. But I also think that imagination is a pretty revolutionary force in terms of resistance, like a creative life is a revolutionary life in a world where creativity is totally undermined and undervalued, and it's also essential for imagining anything other than what we do live in.

Rebeka Tabobondung, Indigenous activist and filmmaker, picked up on many of the same themes during our conversation in the winter of 2004 with regard to the foundational character of the imagination:

> I think [imagination] has everything; it is so huge and powerful because I think in this way that if we can imagine something ... an image or a new reality then in that kind of strange way we're making it real ... As a Native person ... [I know Native peoples have] lost so much of our oral history ... just from that immediate separation ... or disconnection from residential schools ... But the elders will say just because that's lost there's other ways it will come, it can come in dreams, you dream those ceremonies again ... And ... I think for a lot of people who I see kind of as warriors now, a lot of artists, writers, [who are] creating stories ... [have the] imagination [that] has the potential to show that there's different ways of relating to the world [and] it's people, [an] infinite [number] of ways, Western society is only one ... so, we need imagination I think for any kind of change.

The notion that imagination is a foundational, constitutive, and essential force is clearly reflected in both these comments, and I note it here in order to establish one of the central pillars of the analysis that follows. The capacity to create – and the necessity of being able to envision that which does not exist in order to do so – are dynamics that run deeply within the phenomenon of imagination. Nevertheless, imagination as a creative and inspiring force does not mean that it is one which is unequivocally liberatory or empowering. The character of imagination and its relationship to political action and the search for new socio-political spaces and practices is ambivalent and by no means predetermined, but before considering this, it is first necessary to examine the role of imagination with respect to the articulation of political alternatives.

During our conversation in the winter of 2004, Eric Doherty of Building Bridges, an organization that trains and accredits human rights observers who work in Zapatista communities in Chiapas, Mexico, offered a compelling perspective on the role of imagination in relation to social and political change. Eric situated imagination in relation to political developments over the last twenty-five years as well as its broader significance today:

> To me one of the things that's really holding people back from making positive social change ... and, historically, has been for a very long time, is that we went from a situation where there were only two alternatives being presented to people – capitalism and authoritarian socialism – to post-1990 [and no alternatives]. Well, actually, Margaret Thatcher said it in the 1980s, 'There is no alternative.' There [was] nothing to be imagined [in the 1990s], and to me it's essential that it doesn't matter how bad things are ... if there's nothing imagined out there for the future that's better, [then] the only logical thing to do is to enjoy whatever pleasures there are in this society, in this life and ignore it. And to me, it's just essential that there be something that's imagined, some kind of a future ... that's one of the things that's quite good that's happened is that in the past a lot of the alternatives were spelled out in ... extremely concrete terms, whereas now, that kind of thinking has faded; that's now the discourse ... of the neoliberal powers, that there is no alternative ... whereas what's being talked about by the Zapatistas and by a large number of other people is that we can do better than this, and we have to, but we're going to work it out as we go along, we're going to ... form the future as we struggle for it. To me that's essential, because ... without the possibility of a better future there's no logic to struggle, there's no logic to it at all other than as sort of as a release.

Eric's comment speaks to two particular and essential issues relating to the imagination. First, he posits the significance of imagination in relation to a world that neoliberal ideology tried to posit as closed and bereft of alternatives. Second, he discusses the imagination in relation to leftist political projects of the past, which sought to assert a teleology of revolution. Instead, Eric affirms the importance of the unclosed nature of both the imagination and the world.

These two points are fundamental to the significance of imagination within political action, and I will address each in turn. With respect to the foreclosure of possibilities or alternatives by neoliberal ideology, the analysis offered by Theodor Adorno and Max Horkheimer (1972) of the violence woven through Western civilization as a result of the Enlightenment is particularly illuminating. Starting from the position that 'the program of the Enlightenment was the disenchantment of the world; the dissolution of myths and the substitution of knowledge for fancy,' Adorno and Horkheimer proceed to illuminate the profound violence inherent in such a project, both in terms of humanity's relationship to the world as well as our relationship to one another (3). Within this context, notions of imagination and hope are indeed implicated, albeit indirectly. By de-mythologizing the world, the Enlightenment as a project allows the human mind to exert dominance over 'a disenchanted nature' as the world and all that is in it are rendered not only fundamentally 'knowable' but profoundly objectified (ibid., 4). Adorno and Horkheimer posit that the Enlightenment asserts its authority and capacity to know the world in order to escape from a profound fear of the 'outside,' of the unknown. The result of this is not only a powerful compulsion to categorize and impose identification on the world, to render it 'knowable,' but also to establish a hierarchy of ways of knowing about the world. In this schema, positivism, objectivity, and rationality are all conceived of as central pillars of 'enlightened' thought – all too often without explicit consideration or acknowledgment of the fact that these ways of knowing are themselves products of human agency situated in specific socio-historical and cultural contexts. The question of how we as human beings perceive our perception (on what terms and with what consequences) of our worlds is left to scientific disciplines, thus allowing the legacy of the Enlightenment project embodied as it is in the dominant institutions of Western civilization to continually auto-justify itself. Neoliberal capitalism and its agents rest heavily upon the 'rationality' of the Enlightenment tradition and, within this hierarchy of ways of knowing and living, conceptual foreclosure of alternatives and possibilities becomes institutionalized.

Adorno and Horkheimer (1972) deepen their critique of the Enlightenment by reflecting upon the nature of knowledge in the positivist tradition. The process of abstraction, a central tool of the Enlightenment, is a primary tool of subjugation as it necessarily presupposes a fundamental 'distance between subject and object' (13). Furthermore, with its emphasis upon the validity embodied by repetition and the 'laws' and 'truth' that it conveys, the Enlightenment project and the positivist world view thus empty the world of actors and replaces them with objects locked in endless cycles of law-bound repetition. The 'law of the market' and the 'rationality' of neoliberal economics is only one manifestation of this impulse. Adorno and Horkheimer posit that the conceptual domination of the world implicit in the Enlightenment extends equally to the individuals who learn 'order and subordination in the subjection of the world, soon wholly [equate] truth with the regulative thought without whose fixed distinctions universal truth cannot exist' (ibid., 14). Thus, the world comprehended on the basis of the Enlightenment is one in which domination is both conceptually and actually inherent, a world in which the outcomes are always predetermined (ibid., 24). This forms the basis for an industrialized, commodified, and class-differentiated society within which people are alienated not only from each other and their work but also from themselves (ibid., 32). Today, this triumph is manifested through the ruthless logics of capital accumulation, biological determinism, the commodification of all forms of life, and the degradation and instrumentalization of imagination, creativity, and hope.

The imagined and materialized violence that marks global neoliberal capitalism and the political orders that support it were also reflected upon by Manuel Rozental, Colombian political exile, member of the Canada-Colombia Solidarity Campaign, and physician, in our conversation during the winter of 2003. With respect to the importance of imagination in relation to political action and socio-political change, Manuel remarked:

I think that it's the key in the political, it's the essential component, but what one understands by imagination is different and that's the key ... See, we human beings are by nature, as strange as it may sound, creators of history, this is what we do different from a tree or a cow, we make history, so ... that transforms into both a right and a responsibility, an obligation, we have to create history. Now the sources, the inspiration for us to become involved in creating history and the expressions are all related to imagination, we have to imagine what history should be like, what our lives should be like, what everybody else's lives should be like and, in fact, the main thrust of communication between human beings ... is precisely a shared imagination. So, we're alive precisely for that; we're alive to develop an image of what life should be and then to name it collectively, to give it words, and to give it actions, and then that thing turns around in circles. The more we see the more we imagine, the more we imagine the more we act, the more we act the more we see again and imagine and act, and the more we relate to each other through that and political passion is actually the outcome of the passion to achieve something from imagining. Politics are actually the act of sharing imagination, and without that what sense would there be? ... What actually happened to Marcos, as he said, [is that he] was defeated, he came with an ideology, [a] Western [leftist] ideology, to create an insurrectionary army, and he was defeated by the imaginations of Indigenous people who actually taught him to imagine, and then [in] his words, what he names is actually the imagination of a collective.

Imagination as a creative, communicative, and foundational act is eloquently expressed in Manuel's comment. As he asserts when referring to Marcos, imagination is not merely an individual act, it is a collective potential and expression, it is the way in which as human beings we are able to envision and build possible futures.

But in relation to this conception of the imagination and our obligation as human beings to create history, Manuel also spoke about contemporary socio-political and economic dynamics born of a very different spirit. Drawing upon his experiences working in solidarity with Indigenous communities in Cauca, Colombia, Manuel reflected upon the nature and consequences of the project currently inspiring the contemporary geopolitical order:

We see life in danger, life is what matters, not Cauca, not our territory, it's life. Now we do see signs of danger, natural disasters, the heating of the planet, earthquakes – these things are happening, the earth is speaking, it's being hurt badly, it's about to be killed, it's a wounded animal and it's dying. That's our first and greatest concern, and we feel that risk is the outcome of a death project that has been evolving for centuries. It's got one expression in capitalism, but it's not the only one and it's based on, in their words, *ser para tener*, 'to be is to accumulate' ... and those are minorities...that have this kind of mentality but they have accumulated an enormous amount of power to move the planet with that intention. Now they have written history, a history that corresponds to that spirit, *ser para tener*; so, they have written a history that begins by exploring, then exploits, then excludes because it doesn't give everybody the wealth it produces, and then exterminates; it has to kill not only what it doesn't need but also the outcome of its exploitation is destruction, and that's history. Now that history has extended to the entire planet and those sects that run this *ser para tener* process have power and interest over the whole planet, that's the difference from previous history; now we can reach every corner of life, so they can end up destroying everything that there is. Now that death project expresses itself in territories like Cauca or other Indigenous territories; in fact, they were being fenced-out by a combination of three strategies: an ... economic-political strategy that is called structural adjustment today (it changes names), the propaganda or ideologic strategy that actually tries to take over this territory of our imagination, and the war strategy or, more accurately, a terror strategy because [since] they're a minority they have to contain the majority [by using] violence. Those three combined [strategies] establish fences throughout the world to [attack] nature and labour everywhere, production processes and nature everywhere, that's the death project ... Now, we also realize it's not happening to us only but to others as well, so then the life project begins by realizing that nobody will be able to resist on their own, we have to resist together, and every resistance depends on the others.

The vision Manuel expresses here of a project animated by the spirit of 'to be is to accumulate' echoes Eric's comments regarding the neoliberal assertion that 'there is no alternative' as well as Horkheimer and Adorno's analysis of the violence of the Enlightenment and its legacy. With respect to imagination and politics, the collective vision that Manuel conveys and that has emerged from a collective experience of Indigenous struggle in Cauca, Colombia, articulates possibilities beyond the 'death project' which humanity, the earth, and the life that shares it now faces.

But if the 'death project' is the foreclosure of imagination, hope, and life, what possibilities can be envisioned beyond it? Using the metaphor of a net, Manuel articulated a conceptualization of political struggle based on interconnectedness and autonomy, a political formation animated not by *ser para tener* (to be in order to have) but rather *tener para ser* (to have in order to be). Manuel's reflection upon a politics capable of finding a way beyond living in order to accumulate speaks to the strategic capacities imagination possesses:

> So, what do we foresee as a life project? We foresee a net that is moved by the opposite of what this history has been, it's not *ser para tener*, it's *tener para ser* [to have in order to be]. We will generate wealth, we will accumulate wealth, it is necessary but it's got a meaning and a purpose to it and it is ... life. So the protection of life, the attainment of justice, and the consolidation of autonomies, a network [of] ... autonomies, that's what life should be in the future. How do people see ... the life project and the end result of the life project? ... If you look at a person, that person has a liver, the liver is very different from the brain and is completely different from the heart or from blood or from different organs. Now, we're all glad to have a liver there ... but we're also glad to know that the liver does different things from the brain ... and the whole thing is part of the human being that's me and I naturally walk with all these things together, I depend on them, they're me, and I don't even have to be conscious of them ... the whole planet whose life is at risk is exactly that way. History, the way we've written it so far, makes the liver huge, the brain shrinks and threatens to destroy the whole organism ... The life project is [a] struggle to live [autonomously in ways] that are different from each other, that need each other to survive, and if history eventually becomes a living weave ... then there will be life on this planet. That resistance project, joining different places has started, it won't stop. So, to do this whole thing, imagination is the tool ... it is the way by which the people within their own collectives, in their own houses, with their own friends, everywhere, are being affected – [we are being affected] by the same bug. What in the world is it that we want? How should we see it? How do we construct it jointly? And imagining that even if you don't find the words, it's the kind of politics that we need, too. In every sense, politics is imagination and we see it happening ... it's gonna have problems, we will fall back into vanity and try to win an election. Power for myself ... Marcos said, 'the greatest mistake committed by the Zapatistas ... [was] putting Marcos [in] the limelight; it was wrong ... and he acknowledged that it was wrong. As long as we have the questions we might change things, the problem so far is that we move around with answers, and it's very very dangerous.

Drawing from the experiences of Indigenous struggle in Cauca, Colombia, as well as in Chiapas, Mexico, Manuel conveys a powerful vision of political action and human connection rooted in an understanding of imagination that far exceeds narrow escapism. In this articulation, imagination becomes the means through which collective struggle can not only become possible but also profoundly transformative. Through the capacity of imagination, human beings are able to reclaim a sense of possibility denied through the commodification and enclosure propagated by capitalism and the 'death project' it has advanced. Instead of isolated individuals looking for self-gratification and escape, we become subjects engaged in a collective struggle to build interconnected and dignified worlds. In short, we become capable of making a different kind of history.

In *Modern Social Imaginaries* (2004), Charles Taylor discusses what he describes as the 'social imaginary' and its role in shaping the dynamics and contours of human action. Taylor's work is not only part of a renewed scholarly interest in issues such as the imagination, hope, creativity, and possibility, it also intersects importantly with the relationship between imagination and political action as I have examined it so far. Taylor's position is that 'the social imaginary is not a set of ideas; rather, it is what enables, through making sense of, the practices of a society' (2). While Taylor considers 'theory' to be the possession of only a few in society, the 'social imaginary' is broadly shared and understood – albeit implicitly. The 'social imaginary' differs from theory on the basis of three essential points. First, the social imaginary is focused upon 'the way ordinary people "imagine" their social surroundings,' and these imaginings are not expressed in theoretical terms but are conveyed in 'images, stories, and legends' (ibid., 23). Second, Taylor argues that while theory tends to be the possession of a small and elite minority in society, the social imaginary is shared by 'large groups of people, if not the whole society' (ibid.). Third and finally, the social imaginary is distinct from theory by virtue of the fact that it 'is that common understanding that makes possible common practices and a widely shared sense of legitimacy' (ibid.). Significantly, Taylor rejects the false dichotomy between ideas and material factors in the shaping of human action. Rather than attributing constitutive force to either of these elements at the expense of the other, he asserts that 'what we see in human history is ranges of human practices that are both at once, that is, material practices carried out by human beings in space and time, and very often coercively maintained, and at the same time, self-conceptions, modes of understanding' (ibid., 31). Scholars engaged in questions of subjectivity, the imagination, and the constitution of social orders like Appadurai, Buck-Morss, Debord, Giroux, and Hardt and Negri would surely agree with such an assessment. Social formations and actions thus become sites and practices that are simultaneously material and imagined. The importance of Taylor's work for my current analysis is that he points precisely to what he calls the 'social imaginary' as a site of power, not merely as a space of ideological legitimation. While I would argue that Taylor separates what he calls 'theory' from the 'social imagination' too quickly, differentiating between them according to which social class they correspond and the explicitness of the terms in which they are expressed, he also does an excellent job of illuminating the elusive character of imagination in the social context as well as its flexibility, malleability, and constitutive force.

During our conversation in the winter of 2004, Patrick Reinsborough of the smartMeme Strategy and Training Project spoke of his own evaluation of the significance of imagination and its relationship to the social in ways that connect to analyses of imagination as a constitutive force. Equally importantly, Patrick's comments speak to the ambiguous role of imagination, particularly with respect to its 'colonization' or 'commodification' within the neoliberal capitalist order:

[Imagination is] essential to me. [It's] probably the most important tool in the social change toolbox because everybody knows that corporations are out for their own interests ... The Enron and the WorldCom scandals here are ... not exactly treated like [a] big news flash [that] corporations are corrupt and are out for themselves. It's almost like everybody knows that, and so ... in some ways trying to change the world and trying to be involved in activism is almost as crazy and unhip as the corporations. I think that from many people's experience, it's a pretty reasonable [thing] to say, 'Well ... it's obvious the world's fucked up, am I going to spend my life trying to change it and get a good beating at the hands of the cops, endless meetings, and be caught up in anguish and turmoil, or I can at least have the comfort of my own cynicism and knowing that I know the world's fucked up but not having to challenge myself to imagine something different.' I think that to date the symptom that we have is the lack of imagination, the siphoning off of creative resources ... that whole part of our lives, particularly that part of our culture, our collective imagination has been ruthlessly colonized and commodified. The storytellers of our society now are Disney and Twentieth Century Fox and Miramax, and ... there's very little space for imagination that hasn't been seized, and I think that's because of the recognition that that is the central activity of human culture – we can make bigger, better widgets, we can make smaller and smaller microchips, we can do all these things. But you know, if people don't have answers to those fundamental questions about why, then the whole system falls apart. Americans are a deeply libertarian people and very committed to their mythology of revolution and freedom, and it's amazing how that cultural space has been completely neutralized, and completely redirected into preserving the status quo. For me, that whole range of tactics that we can talk about and try to change the way that people think about the system and think about the culture, that is the realm of imagination.

Patrick's comment speaks powerfully to the notion that the imagination in a social context is not merely something to be 'mobilized' but rather is something that is always at work and which can function to inspire reactionary tendencies just as easily as democratic and liberatory ones. The challenge thus becomes finding ways of liberating imagination from the enclosures imposed upon it by neoliberal capitalism and by various political projects directed towards protecting existing structures of privilege and power.

As reflected upon by Eric, Manuel, and Patrick, the imagination is a force that can animate a variety of existing projects, and yet it is also absolutely essential in respect to the capacity to envision social and political alternatives as well. In conversation with Mary Zournazi (2003), Chantal Mouffe and Ernesto Laclau offer insights about the imagination and political possibility that connect productively with the reflections offered by my research partners. In this conversation, Mouffe and Laclau build on the theorizations perhaps most fully expressed in their influential work *Hegemony and Socialist Strategy* (1985) but speak more directly to issues of imagination and political action in the contemporary context. Arguing for a conceptualization of the 'social imaginary,' which does not require some transcendental point of reference or foreclose upon the character or end result of radically democratic struggle, Chantal Mouffe expands on the role of a new imaginary by stating, 'What we need in this new socialist imaginary we are thinking about is the mobilisation of passion in a different way, different from right-wing populism. And that is the very condition of possibility – that an alternative is going to be imagined to the present neo-liberal system. If there is no possibility that things could be different, then one is not going to be able to oppose globalisation' (Zournazi 2003, 135). The insights offered by Mouffe and Laclau are particularly significant in light of the fact that they explicitly characterize the terrain of struggle as a hegemonic one rather than a 'reasoned' or 'moral' one. Asserting that 'it is all a question of mobilising the affect towards hope instead of fear,' Mouffe argues that what the Left has not been able to understand politically is that 'a hegemonic struggle is not a matter of a rational and moral argument' (ibid., 145). Using the example of racism, Mouffe observes that while the Left broadly has tended to see racism as a 'moral disease' and has tried to combat it on this level, the failure of this approach is that it does not recognize that racist identities emerge precisely from 'specific economic and social conditions ... So you can only fight against racism by constructing other forms of identities' (ibid., 146). The logic and language of hegemony mobilized here is, I believe, inherently problematic for reasons I have already addressed that relate to political struggles aimed at achieving 'power-over' people rather than liberating their autonomous and cooperative 'power-to.' Nevertheless, Mouffe's emphasis upon the construction of new identities and the imagination of alternatives intersect significantly with my analysis of the political imagination as a terrain of possibility essential to radical social change. The struggle for new social and political spaces and practices is thus one which must be intimately concerned with issues of subjectivity and imagination, one which seeks to articulate new ways of being in and relating to the world.

Echoing these insights into the relationship between identities, socio-economic conditions, and the foreclosure of possibility, Patrick Reinsborough explicitly connected the enclosure and commodification of the imagination to political apathy and an institutionalized sense of hopelessness, helplessness, and cynicism. Discussing the conditions that allow for the propagation of relations of domination, particularly the capacities of neoliberal capitalism and elite representative democracy to materialize and reinforce a popular sense of profound cynicism towards alternatives, Patrick stated:

I've gone from [thinking about] ... the imagination proactively to now just imagination defensively ... I don't know if it's our first or our last step to decolonize our revolutionary imaginations but if we can't imagine something different, we certainly can't start moving towards it, we can't start enacting it and that is the place that I'm most terrified [of] ... that we'll lose. The business of staying alive in modern capitalism is just so much hard work. I think so many social change movements are just struggling to do the nuts and bolts essential work of the organizing and responding defensively to attacks on their communities that I'm afraid that ... we're not leaving enough space to actually create the kind of new revolutionary stories that will allow us to actually make this jump and make the ecological U-turn that needs to happen.

It is perhaps axiomatic to note that if one cannot imagine alternatives, it becomes impossible to move towards them; nevertheless, the contours of the challenge posed by neoliberal capitalism with respect to our collective capacity to contemplate possibilities and to begin to build alternatives seem particularly stark here.

Fiona Jeffries, cultural writer, academic, and activist, reflected on many of the same issues during our conversation in the winter of 2004 in Vancouver, British Columbia, when I asked her about the relationship between imagination and political action. Fiona explored the ambivalence of imagination in a context characterized by the voracious expansion of neoliberal capitalism:

> Yes, [imagination is] important and, yes, imagination plays a major role, but ... there's no perfect articulation of a problem that's going to grab people's imagination and make people go with it 'cause it's not just about imagination, it's about the circumstances of people's lives ... I think that's one of the things that neoliberalism has done so successfully – this serious frontal assault on the imagination. Well, I mean neoliberalism as the outer limit of commodity fetishism and citizenship through consumption ... as an ethos ... all your sense of imagination and self is externalized into this act of drawing things around you that make you a member, that include you, implicitly and explicitly.

Thus, imagination cannot be taken as an uncompromised force for progressive political change, particularly within a context shaped by the logics of neoliberal capitalism. As Henry Giroux (2004) forcefully argues, under conditions of suffering, inequality, and structural violence generated by neoliberalism, imagination can just as easily be put to work upon a political landscape of proto-fascism. It is therefore not a matter of simply 'liberating the imagination' or creating spaces within which it is possible to 'imagine alternatives' precisely because of the fact that imagination in a social context is always at work, but it is at work according to specific socio-political conditions and dynamics.

Dave Bleakney of the Canadian Union of Postal Workers and a North American activist involved in Peoples' Global Action also reaffirmed both the necessity and challenges of rediscovering a 'revolutionary imagination' during our conversation in the winter of 2004:

... if imagination doesn't just become trite or silly, [its importance is] huge ... I think we're at a moment now in our history where institutions don't have a lot of credibility and even though people will still go out and vote, if you ask them they'll go, 'Well, it doesn't really matter' or 'They're all corrupt' or '[They're] all in it for the money' or 'What can you do?' What can you do? I think some history would have to be a part of it, I think a people without a history is a people without a memory. But I would say in the age of spectacle that probably creativity more than anything is what will feed the change ... and I don't know what that is, but I know that turning things around rather than playing into them [is] a good start.

As evidenced by these comments, the connection between powerful political action and the imagination is a fundamental one. However, it is also clearly not simply a matter of affirming this relationship and then discovering the key to revolutionary political change. One of the central questions lurking behind the affirmation of the centrality of imagination with respect to the search for new political spaces and practices is where does the inspiration for a radical political imagination reside? In a world where the imagination is only one among many terrains that capitalism seeks to colonize and commodify, where might we find sources of inspiration that might allow us to think about possibilities beyond the enclosures and alienation of neoliberal capitalism? In essence, this is a question of where hope can be found in a world that equates hope with the desire and drive towards self-gratification.

The 'source' of hope and its potential for radical social change is an issue that serves as the central animating force in Ernst Bloch's three-volume work *The Principle of Hope* (1986). Articulating a theoretical perspective perhaps best described as 'Utopian Marxism' to critique bourgeois society as well as to illuminate the concept of hope at the core of the search for a 'better life,' Bloch's intention is to deal directly not with what already has come to pass but rather with the anticipation of what is in the process of becoming (12). Hope, in this sense, is not mere emotion but 'more essentially ... a directing act of the cognitive kind' manifested as a 'forward dream' of a distinctly utopian character (ibid.). Essential to Bloch's inquiry into the capacity for hope and the pursuit of a directing and anticipatory cognition – what I might name a 'political imagination' – is the concept he describes as the 'Not-Yet,' that which has not yet come to pass and as such is still open to revolutionary formation. Fundamental to this is Bloch's assertion that being cannot be conceived as either closed or static and that the concept of being needs to be understood not only in terms of its 'Where From' but equally in terms of a 'tendential, still unclosed Where To' (ibid., 18). For Bloch, the revolutionary and utopian potential of hope lies in the fact that the essential characteristic of the 'being' of the world rests not upon what it is or what it has been but rather upon what it might become. Thus, no situation, no matter how apparently hopeless or grim, is devoid of hope or denied the possibility of change.

But aside from the unclosed nature of the social order, where does the hope on which Bloch focuses so greatly reside and, more significantly, from where do hopeful visions of a new social order emerge? Bloch (1986) situates the 'space of receptivity of the New and production of the New' in the realm of the unconscious or, more appropriately, in the realm of the 'Not-Yet-Conscious' (116). Significantly, while the Not-Yet-Conscious is the space of incubation for the 'Not-Yet-Become' in the world, this 'Novum' cannot manifest itself or even be articulated by the subject in whom it resides without the presence of the appropriate socio-historical conditions (ibid., 124–30). This is a point of critical importance because it implies that the conditions that allow for not only the success of a radical refashioning of the 'being' of the world but the very expression of it are dependent upon circumstances outside of any actor's control. The question thus arises: If the socio-economic and historical conditions of reality determine the possibility of thinking and realizing a better world, how can such a circumstance come to pass? The answer that Bloch posits is that many existing works, whether they be works of art, literature, architecture, or political ideals, contain a latent utopian element that extends beyond their connection to the existing relations of domination and ruling ideologies from which they directly emerged (ibid., 164).

Despite this, Bloch nevertheless continues to assert the notion that there is a trajectory of being, not merely that the nature of being remains fundamentally unclosed. It is this notion of tendency that continues to pose a rather troubling problematic within Bloch's work, precisely because it implies that the 'Where-To' of our reality is imbued with an essential and pre-existing direction, a direction to be realized given the 'ripeness' of externally existing conditions (ibid., 202–3). For Bloch it is capitalism – and its destructive, exploitative, and alienating nature – that serves as the inspiring force behind this 'Where-To.' It is capitalism that creates both the possibility and the impetus to realize an alternative to itself. Ultimately, despite Bloch's invocation of the imagination and hope, he nevertheless ends up retreating to a position rooted in Marxist teleology and thus evades the truly radical implications of his own the-orizations. The emergent implication that Bloch cannot face might be stated as follows: imagination, while drawing from existing socio-his-torical conditions, by its very nature exceeds attempts to enclose it and thus provides the grounds upon which to begin to articulate previously unconsidered possibilities – possibilities which are, to be sure, often ridiculous, radical, absurd, and perhaps even profoundly liberatory.

In spite of Bloch's reductive Marxist teleology and his utopian orien-tation, his analysis does point to the irreducible significance of the con-nection between the material and the imaginary. This material-imaginary connection is also one of the points that unifies the diverse work of Appadurai, Buck-Morss, Debord, Hardt and Negri, and Taylor. Cornelius Castoriadis also addresses this issue in his work 'Power, Pol-itics, Autonomy' (1991). In this work, Castoriadis argues that, in order for individual autonomy to be consolidated, a 'reflective and delibera-tive instance' must be generated of 'social imaginary significations and their possible grounding' (163). While this critical and questioning instance will free the radical imagination of individuals and open spaces of socio-political possibility, the responsibility for opening this foundational instance rests solely upon the 'radical imaginary of the anonymous collectivity,' a phenomenon which, in turn, is constrained by the limitations inherent in what Castoriadis refers to as the 'nature of the socio-historical' (ibid., 165–71). If the socio-historical conditions are not 'right,' then imagination, and by extension the emancipatory polit-ical projects for which it is the foundation, remains individualized and essentially politically inert. To be fair, I find the analyses offered by Appadurai, Debord, Hardt and Negri, and Taylor to be much more sophisticated and nuanced with respect to their consideration of the connection between the material, the socio-historical, and the imagina-tion. However, I also believe that the connections between these ele-ments operate on levels aside from considerations of the conditions necessary to realize a radical political imagination in the first place. To be meaningful and generative of political possibility and action, imagi-nation must also be rooted in the realities and conditions that shape people's lives.

During our conversation in the spring of 2004, John Clarke, founding member and grass-roots organizer for the Ontario Coalition Against Poverty (OCAP), articulated the essential connections between a grounded political imagination and meaningful and inspiring political action:

I think the role of creativity is a really important one because the events that have captured imagination haven't just been militant or haven't just been bold mobilizing people, they've actually inspired people and some-times even made them laugh. [It gives you] a sense that you're doing something really important, that you're somehow putting your finger on something and you're at the same time challenging something fundamen-tal. You can think of all kinds of examples drawn from explosive struggles and sometimes even drawn from non-violent resistance ... the Salt March of Gandhi, for example ... such a symbol of British colonialism was high-lighted and it captured imaginations in a way that was so enormous. [Or], the On To Ottawa Trek, to take an example from here, the notion that ... the federal government wouldn't deal with this resistance on the West Coast so [people having to use] a mode of transportation [they] had no choice but to [use], but doing it on a mass basis created a crisis for the govern-ment and a wave of popular support for the homeless. I'd be loathe to use the modest examples of some of OCAP's work ... to compare to those kinds of events but we, too, in our own way have tried to take up actions ... that capture imaginations, highlight injustice and give people a sense that they're actually sticking it to the other side and making them squeal.

The connection between a radical political imagination and a political position that is rooted in the contexts which it seeks to engage is an essential element of John's comment here. Imagination by itself yields nothing, it is only when it is connected to lived experience and rooted in an explicit and self-conscious political subjectivity that it becomes powerful.

Mac Scott, a member of OCAP and its executive committee, elabo-rated on the significance of a meaningful and grounded approach to political imagination and creativity:

You need to do two things with tactics, you need tactics that won't totally alienate whatever constituency you're organizing in ... but you also need stuff that's beyond the pale ... stuff that inspires people, that creates almost a symbol. I think if you look at some of the best actions in poor people's organizations over the last ten years you'll see stuff that relates directly to issues in the community. An example is the Queen Elizabeth action six years ago in Montreal ... where we went in and we took all the food out of the buffet and brought it out on the streets and fed people, that wasn't really going to feed people beyond ... the hundred people who were there and the street people who were around for more than one meal, but what it did do was it created a symbol of people directly taking back what they need, and it broke down an important boundary ... by saying this food's there every day and it can be taken, and it also directly confronted ... the group of people who are responsible for what's going on. I think to really inspire people tactics need to be confrontational and they need to be creative but they don't need to be ... from way out of there ... It's hard to bring in new tactics, it's hard to bring in creative stuff, it's hard to figure out that balance between doing something that's creative and exciting and still won't just alienate people but ... when we just keep doing the same tactics, which don't even visibly accomplish anything, we just turn people off ... [for example, using] the same march and chant and speechify kind of thing ... people get bored easy ... people are really smart and want something that's going to involve them, that's going to interest them. They don't want to just do the same crap again and again.

Mac's reflections on the role of imagination within political action point directly to the necessity of inspiring people and giving them a collective sense of power through an approach that emphasizes the necessity of linking imagination and action to experiences and contexts that serve as the bedrock for their everyday existence. This is not an imagination 'out there'; rather, it is a political imagination that emerges through a dynamic and interconnected understanding of political struggle grounded in the experiences that make up people's lives.

Mike DesRoches, a grass-roots organizer with OCAP, perhaps articulated the connection between imagination, political action, and lived reality best. I quote him at length here precisely because he speaks eloquently to the centrality of a meaningful political imagination within powerful political struggle:

[Imagination is] definitely something that's important, but it's not just being imaginative or being creative, ... it's capturing imagination and pursuing a political course that creates excitement and that creates [an] atmosphere of expectation and an atmosphere that people want to become a part of. When I think of creativity and imaginative actions I don't think of artistic things or street theatre or anything like that ... that stuff can work occasionally, but you can incorporate creativity and imagination in the most militant actions. It's just a matter of thinking a bit outside the box and being prepared to respond to attacks ... with counterattacks that make sense ... Some of the most famous OCAP actions have been along these lines ... When the welfare cuts in Ontario first came in in 1995, there was an

OCAP action where the minister of finance, David Tabuchi, had said 'If people don't have enough to buy groceries, they can negotiate with the grocer,' so there was an action where OCAP went to a grocery store and ... filled up cart after cart with food and essentially shut the store down in trying to negotiate a 21.6 per cent discount on all the food, which was the amount of the welfare cut ... That's something that captures the imagination. Or when news broke in Ontario that Toronto had reached a point where there were 2,000 evictions every month ... the response to that was not to do a rally or a demonstration or a press conference, but it was to do an eviction, to go to the finance minister's office, Jim Flaherty at that time, and throw his furniture out on the street ... and act like the sheriff ... Another amazing example is the question of squats and why OCAP continually goes back to the tactic of taking over abandoned buildings ... It's something that is just an incredibly pure form of action ... OCAP has the capacity now to get together five, six hundred people and march on a building that's boarded up, right in the middle of one of the poorest neighbourhoods in Canada ... there's lots of buildings in this neighbourhood where we could go around at night and see people who sleep in the doorways of abandoned buildings, and then when you go to that building and you rip the boards down and say everyone can go sleep inside it's something that people kinda can't fail to get ... It's an incredibly clear indication of what's twisted and fucked up with our system, the fact that people sleep and freeze to death outside of buildings that are sitting empty. It's things like that that might not necessarily be considered creative or imaginative actions but that are actions that are able to immediately capture people's imaginations ... If there's any truth that I know about political organizing [it's] that people don't come out to political events if they feel like it's a routine type of thing or if it doesn't make sense to people, if people don't see how it affects their lives and how the act of coming out is going to make a difference to them.

Mike's comment both reaffirms the significance of imagination as a fundamental tool for reshaping people's understandings of the world and the possibilities therein as well as explicitly positioning the imagination within the realm of lived experience. The 'socio-historical' is immanent here, not in the form of distanced theoretical conditions for revolution but in an intimate understanding of the conditions of life of OCAP's constituency and of their demands. With this as a foundational reference point, imagination becomes a powerful energizing force for political action.

The concrete dimensions of the political imagination were also evoked by Jacquie Soohen and Rick Rowley of Big Noise Tactical during our conversation in the fall of 2004. Linking imagination to transgression and thus to the capacity to contest hegemony and create new spaces and practices beyond the dominant order, Jacquie and Rick spoke persuasively about the power of a political imagination that is inseparable from the struggle to find new ways of being in the world. Drawing upon the resurgence of popular and autonomous struggle in Argentina, Rick spoke about the powerful connections between political struggle, imagination, and the making of new political subjectivities:

Movements there have been forced to reimagine struggle outside of the space of the factory and outside of the logic of the state, and so there are hundreds and thousands of different responses to the system and there are thousands of different proposals for the future of their people and their country ... I mean they're all wildly different, from new currencies being created by the poor in the city to land occupations out in the country to factories being occupied and put back to work ... to the piqueteros building unions of unemployed workers ... So, there's not a movement that can be taken down now by killing 30,000 people, what you have instead is a network of autonomous experiences, of experiences of autonomy ... you [build] massive popular uprisings and demonstrations that completely rewrite the streets of the city ... When you march with even just 30,000 people down a street and the police tell you to go home and you don't go, when fear breaks in that way and you refuse to allow yourself to be controlled by authority like that, then the world changes ... I think it's hard to talk about it in terms of imagination because it's not limited to that ... Every police officer means something else to you, every street means something else, it is something else in your world, you've rewritten the meaning of the world you walk through and so you have a network of these experiences that extends throughout every aspect of your life ... [If] you're working in a bread collective, you go and sell it with some currency that your neighbours have printed up to circulate in your community and ... you go watch films in the squatted buildings downtown, that produces political subjectivities that are outside of the system ... I'm interested in movements now that are autonomist rather than nationalist, that aren't imagining seizing state power and replacing it with something else, with a whole other system, that don't have a ten-point program for the development of their country but instead [its members] are saying 'Okay ... part of my life has been colonized by capital, many of my relationships with the world around me are mediated through money and through different fucked up oppressive relationships, but there are parts of me and there are parts of my life that are outside of that, and there are things that I really love and there are people who I love and who love me, I have real relationships that are true ... I do things in the day that aren't wired into this capitalist logic, this logic of empire, and these things can be extended, these relations, these spaces in my life that are outside of capital can be extended, enlarged.' Bit by bit we retake our lifeworld without imagining that there's some space outside of the system ... we're not becoming hippies and going up in the mountains and saying, 'Oh we'll just grow our organic beans here ... we can pretend like the rest of the world doesn't exist.' That's not a revolutionary position to take either, that's making yourself irrelevant to the rest of the world, but ... saying I can't disown this world, I was born into this language, this network, this system [is] in a way ... a battle of the imagination.

Significantly, Jacquie added to Rick's expansive analysis with a powerful statement about the location of this imagination, stating that 'it doesn't exist ... as an ideal or something you work towards or something outside of how you're living ... rewriting the world that you're in right now and ... not imagining anything outside of it, living.' The political imagination is not an escape, it is not something 'out there'; rather, it is an intimate part of recreating the world in which people struggle and, simultaneously, the means through which new subjectivities are constituted.

Kevin McKay, grass-roots activist and president of the Skydragon Community Development Co-operative in Hamilton, Ontario, summarized the connection between imagination, creativity, political action, and possibilities for different kinds of futures when we spoke during the spring of 2004. Reflecting upon his experiences in Quebec City in 2001 during the FTAA protests, Kevin noted:

Those are the little moments to live the revolution in real time, you create it, you create those spaces, you say ... right here and right now this is already transformed, this is what it'll be like ... and that's exciting 'cause it gets people pumped. Like in Quebec City, where at this crazy cast-off artists' space ... they had set up the free kitchen and there's artists performing and people painting – it's like ... yeah, this is what it'll be like! Everyone had that feeling [and] yes, of course, the police had to bulldoze that ... 'cause it was probably the most threatening thing there [laughs] ... that was the real scary shit going on, right? It's people waking up to that idea of 'oh yeah, wait a second, we can live like this' ... and life can be meaningful and exuberant and fun, and you can flip off the assholes in power ... that's important stuff.

As Appadurai contends, imagination can indeed be the fuel for action, particularly an imagination that is shared collectively. The spaces and practices that Kevin discusses here are manifestations as well of the bio-political force of political imagination, the materialization of a desire and a will to live in ways not condoned by neoliberal ideology or the narrow rationalities of advanced capitalism. Imagination, in this sense, is not separate from human experience or divorced from political action, it does not stand above lived reality; rather, it is woven through experience, struggle, and reality, and constitutes the not-yet formed terrain of possibility.

In this chapter, I have sought to examine the connections between imagination, political action, and the production of both subjectivities and the social itself. Drawing on a variety of theorists as well as the reflections offered by my research partners I have attempted to sketch the contours of the 'political imagination' and of the possibilities it offers for radical socio-political change. In so doing, I have linked the political imagination to Hardt and Negri's conceptualization of 'biopolitics' and the constitution of new kinds of subjectivities. As my research partners expressed so eloquently, imagination is neither a trivial dimension of political action nor is it the most significant aspect of it. Instead, imagination as a biopolitical force is something that is woven through political struggle and the lived realities within which it is, of course, situated.

Offering concluding thoughts on the passing of modern utopias and the relationship between emerging collective political imaginaries and radical socio-political possibility, Susan Buck-Morss (2000) states:

From the Wall of China to the Berlin Wall, the political principle of geographical isolation belongs to an earlier human epoch. That the new era will be better is in no way guaranteed. It depends on the power structures in which people desire and dream, and on the cultural meanings they give to the changed situation. The end of the Cold War has done more than rearrange the old spatial cartographies of East and West and the old historico-temporal cartographies of advanced and backward. It has also given space for new imaginings to occupy and cultivate the semantic field leveled by the shattering of the Cold War discourse.

As long as the old structures of power remain intact, such imaginings will be dreamworlds, nothing more. They will be capable of producing phantasmagoric deceptions as well as critical illumination. But they are a cause for hope. Their democratic, political promise would appear to be greatest when they do not presume the collectivity that will receive them. Rather than shoring up existing group identities, they need to create new ones ... (277–8)

In this sense, imagination's location, if it is to be powerful and politically productive, is indistinguishable from newly emerging spaces and practices of radical political action. Neither the material nor the conceptual are privileged here. In fact, this dichotomy itself becomes nonsensical. Not only does the political imagination draw from specific contexts and speak to the needs and demands of the people who inhabit them, it also serves to reshape how subjectivity itself is experienced within these spaces, thus creating the opportunity for new and previously unconsidered socio-political possibilities to emerge. It is only through the grounding of imagination in practice and space that meaningful and powerful political alternatives begin to take shape. In this way, imagination, much like life itself, is something that cannot merely be thought about; rather, it must be lived.

6 New Horizons: Resonance and Political Action

But what next?

A new number in the useless enumeration of the numerous international orders?

A new scheme for calming and easing the anguish of having no solution?

A global program for world revolution?

A utopian theory so that it can maintain a prudent distance from the reality that anguishes us?

A scheme that assures each of us a portion, a task, a title, and no work?

The echo goes, a reflected image of the possible and forgotten: the possibility and necessity of speaking and listening; not an echo that fades away, or a force that decreases after reaching its apogee.

Let it be an echo that breaks barriers and re-echoes.

Let it be an echo of our own smallness, of the local and particular, which reverberates in an echo of our own greatness, the intercontinental and galactic.

An echo that recognizes the existence of the other and does not overpower or attempt to silence it.

An echo that takes its place and speaks in its own voice, yet speaks the voice of the other.

An echo that reproduces its own sound, yet opens itself to the sound of the other.

An echo of this rebel voice transforming itself and renewing itself in other voices.

An echo that turns itself into many voices, into a network of voices that, before Power's deafness, opts to speak to itself, knowing itself to be one and many, acknowledging itself to be equal in its desire to listen and be listened to, recognizing itself as diverse in the tones and levels of voices forming it.

From 'Tomorrow Begins Today: Closing Remarks at the First Intercontinental Encuentro for Humanity and Against Neoliberalism,' Subcomandante Insurgente Marcos (2001f)

In their politico-philosophical work *A Thousand Plateaus: Capitalism and Schizophrenia* (1987), Gilles Deleuze and Felix Guattari introduce the concept of the 'rhizome' and relate it to socio-political realities. Literally speaking, the rhizome is a tuber or bulb possessing both roots and shoots, but it is also a new way of thinking about socio-political realities, particularly when counterposed to the image of the tree or the root. While the tree grows according to a structured, predictable, and relatively fixed pattern, the rhizome is composed of 'directions in motion' (21). As Deleuze and Guattari explain:

Unlike trees or their roots, the rhizome connects any point to any other point, and its traits are not necessarily linked to traits of the same nature; it brings into play very different regimes of signs, and even nonsign states. The rhizome is reducible neither to the One nor the multiple. It is not the One that becomes Two or even directly three, four, five, etc. It is not a multiple derived from the One, or to which One is added ($n + 1$). It is composed not of units but of dimensions, or rather directions in motion. It has neither beginning nor end, but always a middle (*milieu*) from which it grows and which it overspills. It constitutes linear multiplicities with n dimensions having neither subject nor object, which can be laid out on a plane of consistency, and from which the One is always subtracted ($n - 1$). When a multiplicity of this kind changes dimensions, it necessarily changes its nature as well, undergoes a metamorphosis. (ibid., 21, emphasis in original)

The rhizome is thus not a 'structure' in any conventional way. It eludes definition and essential identity precisely because it changes its nature as the dimensions or directions in motion that comprise it shift, are added to, or are subtracted from. I invoke Deleuze and Guattari's notion of the rhizome here in order to posit it as the most effective and accurate way of comprehending the nature of transnational resonance and its consequences. Resonance is powerful because it is not predictable, it does not operate according to pre-established paths or links although it may utilize them. In other words, the transnational resonance of Zapatismo has no singular identity, cause, or effect; rather, its nature changes as points are connected to other points. The effects of resonance can only be revealed by examining the histories of political action to which they give rise and the emergent tendencies they reveal. An analysis of some of these rhizomatic histories of resonance is the task that I undertake in this chapter.

The rhizome is not a conceptual phenomenon familiar to social movement theory, the field of social science which has dealt with the kinds of questions I engage here. Much more common to this social scientific terrain are analytical and explanatory tools and models focusing upon issues of resource mobilization (McCarthy and Zald 1979), political opportunity structures (Cloward and Piven 1977), cycles of protest (Brand 1990; Tarrow 1998), framing (Benford and Snow 1992), biography and oppositional consciousness (Goodwin, Jasper, and Polletta 2001; Jasper 1997; Mansbridge and Morris 2001), and networks (Arquilla et al. 1998; Keck and Sikkink 1998). Most recently, social movement theorists have turned their attention towards a greater focus on culture and contentious politics (McAdam, Tarrow, and Tilly 2001; Meyer and Tarrow 1998; Whittier 2002), the 'dialogic' aspects of social movements (Steinberg 2002), analytical 'border-crossing,' which pays attention to culture, identity, and politics (Meyer, Whittier, and Robnett 2002), and transnational action (Bandy and Smith 2004; Olesen 2005a, b; Tarrow 2005). Despite the excellence of much of this scholarship, however, the frameworks within which many of these analytical perspectives are situated are fundamentally structural, rationalist, and instrumental. Inevitably, these analyses produce perspectives on social movements, politics, and socio-cultural change that resemble rigid cause-and-effect formulas. Laws of repetition and predictability come to replace a commitment to appreciating the dynamic and often unpredictable nature of the interaction between culture, politics, action, lived realities and the people who inhabit them.

In opposition to this rigid, narrowly rationalist, and formulaic approach, I draw on the rhizome and all the complexities it suggests. The rhizome is not a diagram and it gives us no easy tools for understanding social movements or radical political action. What the rhizome does is assert the profound and unfixed complexity of social realities; it reminds us that the world is not composed of discrete identities but rather is constituted by the connections between these elements. Thus, socio-political analysis ceases to be a process of interrogating identity, institutions, or any other fixed form and instead becomes a matter of understanding socio-political space as continually reproduced by connection and interaction. As Deleuze and Guattari (1987) remind us, the social is not unitary, it is not the One; rather, the social is multiple, it is comprised of dimensions, not stark and immutable lines. The social, and the political, are spaces, spaces constituted by directions in motion. If we are to understand how the socio-political is constituted, we must then look not for 'frames' or 'cycles,' individuals or institutions; instead, we must look for the connections that bring the social and the political into being, for the communicative acts that articulate the realities which we inhabit.

In this work thus far, I have attempted to trace the contours of the Zapatista 'political imagination,' the reasons for its resonance amongst activists living and working in Canada and the United States, and the possibilities offered for reconceptualizing political action according to the resonance of the transnationalized political imagination of Zapatismo. In this chapter and the one that follows, I seek to provide an analysis of how these dynamics have been materialized through the work of activists on the ground. In so doing, I deploy the notion of rhizomatic histories in order to explore the significance of the resonance of Zapatismo in a transnational terrain of political action. While I argue that Zapatismo has indeed found a profound resonance outside of the Indigenous communities of Chiapas, this resonance is by no means an uncomplicated phenomenon. Indeed, ambivalence and contradiction characterize many of the consequences of this resonance, particularly with respect to the consequences of this resonance for the Zapatistas themselves. In some cases, the resonance achieved by Zapatismo transnationally has led only to a self-gratifying romanticization of Other movements, to efforts to encapsulate or control the struggles of others, or simply to a fleeting interest in political alternatives failing to produce any tangible results at all. However, none of this should be seen as diminishing the significance of the transnational political imagination of Zapatismo or its impact upon political action in the North. The intent here is rather to provide an analysis of both the successes of this resonance as well as a moment of reflection and critique with regard to some of the problematic dynamics and consequences of this resonance.

Zapatismo and the Rhizomatic Histories of Transnational Resonance

> While the Power has done all within its power to erase us from the map of actual history, you have taken the word and the streets (the asphalt ones and the media ones) in order to remind us, and in passing the Mexican government, that we are not alone.
>
> We know little of your struggles. The bridge your generosity has extended to us in order to hear the world of the indigenous Zapatistas has only begun its return flight. With surprise and admiration we begin to recognize your collective histories of rebellion and resistance, your struggles against racism, against patriarchy, against religious intolerance, against xenophobia, against militarization, against ecological destructions, against fascism, against segregation, against moral hypocrisy, against exclusion, against the war, against hunger, against the lack of housing, against great capital, against authoritarianism, against dictatorship, against the politics of economic liberalization, against poverty, against robbery, against corruption, against discrimination, against stupidity, against the lie, against ignorance, against slavery, against injustice, against oblivion, against neoliberalism, for humanity ...
>
> And for humanity and against neoliberalism is what announces the new encounter of rebellions and resistance which appear this year. Then and there, we will have learned more from you and from all the pieces, disperse as yet, of the crystal which dignity preserves even within the best men and women of humanity.
>
> So here, taking advantage of the trip, we want to send our thanks for turning to look at us and for the hand which you extend to us so we will not fall once again into oblivion. Some time ago we sent you a flower. Today we send you a little cloud of rain from here, so that you may water that flower, as you should, by dancing.
>
> Vale. Health and may the joy of rebellion continue to fill the streets of all the continents.
>
> From 'To the Solidarity Committees of the Zapatista Struggle in All the World,' Subcomandante Insurgente Marcos (2004f)

A multitude of groups arose in the aftermath of the 1 January uprising in order to provide traditional forms of political solidarity. However, in the years since 1994, a diversity of projects, collectives, and organizations have emerged that have responded to Zapatismo in ways that have been entirely unpredictable. While news of the uprising was initially transmitted by pre-existing human rights and Latin American solidarity networks (see Arquilla et al. 1998), the response to the Zapatistas and their struggle would quickly overflow the confines of these existing structures and patterns of political solidarity. Jessica Marques, grass-roots coordinator for the Mexico Solidarity Network reflected on precisely this point during our conversation in February 2004:

> I think there's two things that have happened over the past few years that are important to understand in the U.S. with regard to the Zapatistas. First of all, the Zapatista movement is so unique that I think it has actually mobilized a lot of people to work on international human rights issues and trade issues that would not otherwise have been working on it ... Originally the groups that responded most quickly to the situation were groups that were already established as solidarity human rights groups, but it's also mobilized a whole new population of people that see the Zapatistas as having a kind of legitimacy that other movements, other revolutionary movements, haven't necessarily had, and that's really because of a political legitimacy that the Zapatistas have maintained in Chiapas and in Mexico and internationally. They haven't fallen into the trap that a lot of other movements have fallen into ... of using the civilian population and having a strong military force that's fighting the government ... The uprising really only lasted twelve days and while they've been under attack by the government they have not really engaged in violence, but ... recognizing they're not a pacifist movement, this hasn't ... been a long drawn out bloody battle; they have really wanted to discuss with civil society how to move forward and that's something significantly different. They're also making a lot of attempts that other movements like this haven't made towards democracy, towards women's rights issues, so they have a lot of legitimacy that other groups haven't had, and that's helped build a campaign that I've never seen around any other kind of movement like this.

Acknowledging the unpredictability of Zapatismo's resonance amongst people in the United States and Canada is an essential first step in beginning to appreciate the consequences of this resonance. Equally important is the recognition that acknowledging unpredictability is not the same as asserting an entirely random or accidental nature with respect to this resonance. In this chapter, I look specifically at the dynamics of resonance and their consequences as they have been manifested amongst activists in the United States and Canada who are active in what might be considered more 'traditional' solidaristic political activities. These activities range from human rights observation in communities under threat in Chiapas, to facilitating fair trade marketing in the north of products produced by Zapatista cooperatives, to coordinating solidarity delegations comprised primarily of northern activists to communities in struggle in Chiapas. In the next chapter I consider the consequences of the transnational resonance of Zapatismo amongst collectives and organizations operating in more 'experimental' political and cultural fields. Before proceeding in this analysis, however, recent developments in the shape of the Zapatista struggle both nationally and globally require brief examination.

In July 2005, after declaring a General Red Alert in Chiapas and a period of internal deliberation, the Clandestine Revolutionary Indigenous Committee-General Command (CCRI-CG) of the EZLN issued a series of communiqués culminating in the 'Sixth Declaration of the Lacandón Jungle.' This newest declaration outlines an ambitious political project for the next stage in the Zapatistas' struggle, both nationally and globally. Maintaining its commitment to non-violent political action and reaffirming its subordination to the will of the Indigenous communities comprising its base of support as well as its commitment to support and defend these communities, the General Command of the EZLN articulates a distinct set of plans at the global and national levels. Globally, it outlines three general goals: first, 'We will forge new relationships of mutual respect and support with persons and organizations who are resisting and struggling against neoliberalism and for humanity'; second, 'As far as we are able, we will send material aid such as food and handicrafts for those brothers and sisters who are struggling all over the world,' in this regard, the General Command identifies Cuba, Bolivia, and Ecuador as specific destinations for material aid; third, 'To all of those who are resisting throughout the world, we say there must be other intercontinental encuentros held, even if just one other' (Ejército Zapatista de Liberación Nacional 2005). These goals are articulated in the spirit of the Zapatistas' 'simple word sent out to the noble hearts of those simple and humble people who resist and rebel against injustices all over the world' (ibid.). The explicit reinvigoration of communication and interaction with 'global civil society,' while tentative and preliminary, is nevertheless a significant gesture aimed at renewing the global fabric of struggle and alternative-building. The ways in which the global multitude respond to it will of course determine just how significant this gesture will be.

At the national level, the General Command outlines four goals for the next stage of struggle.

1 We will 'continue fighting for the Indian peoples of Mexico, but now not just for them and not with only them, but for all the exploited and dispossessed of Mexico, with all of them and all over the country. And when we say all the exploited of Mexico, we are also talking about the brothers and sisters who have had to go to the United States in search of work in order to survive.'

2 We 'are going to go to listen to, and talk directly with, without intermediaries or mediation, the simple and humble of the Mexican people, and, according to what we hear and learn, we are going to go about building, along with those people who, like us, are humble and simple, a national program of struggle, but a program which will be clearly of the left, or anti-capitalist, or anti-neoliberal, or for justice, democracy and liberty for the Mexican people.'

3 'We are going to try to build, or rebuild, another way of doing politics, one which once again has the spirit of serving others, without material interests, with sacrifice, with dedication, with honesty, which keeps its word, whose only payment is the satisfaction of duty performed, or like the militants of the left did before, when they were not stopped by blows, jail or death, let alone by dollar bills.'

4 We are 'going to go about raising a struggle in order to demand that we make a new Constitution, new laws which take into account the demands of the Mexican people, which are: housing, land, work, food, health, education, information, culture, independence, democracy, justice, liberty and peace. A new Constitution which recognizes the rights and liberties of the people, and which defends the weak in the face of the powerful.' (ibid.)

The General Command describes this project as one which seeks to build a non-electoral, broadly based alternative to 'neoliberal destruction,' an alternative that is 'from below and·for below' (ibid.). The construction of a new kind of politics that is non-violent, non-electoral, broadly based, anti-neoliberal and anti-capitalist, and yet is nevertheless explicitly directed towards the defence of national sovereignty and concerned with the articulation of a new constitution characterizes the national – and dominant – dimension of the 'Sixth Declaration of the Lacandón Jungle.' Concluding the declaration, the General Command reaffirms both the global and national dimensions of this new stage of the Zapatista struggle:

> In the world, we are going to join together more with the resistance struggles against neoliberalism and for humanity.
>
> And we are going to support, even if it's but little, those struggles.
>
> And we are going to exchange, with mutual respect, experiences, histories, ideas, dreams.
>
> In Mexico, we are going to travel all over the country, through the ruins left by the neoliberal wars and through those resistances which, entrenched, are flourishing in those ruins.
>
> We are going to seek, and to find, those who love these lands and these skies even as much as we do.
>
> We are going to seek, from La Realidad to Tijuana, those who want to organize, struggle and build what may perhaps be the last hope this Nation – which has been going on at least since the time when an eagle alighted on a nopal in order to devour a snake – has of not dying.
>
> We are going for democracy, liberty and justice for those of us who have been denied it.
>
> We are going with another politics, for a program of the left and for a new Constitution. (ibid.)

The Sixth Declaration can be read as establishing the parameters within which the Zapatistas envision their emerging political direction. It can also be read as an invitation, a provocation, to others who, without identifying as 'Zapatista,' desire a new kind of social and political practice. While this declaration was issued after I completed work with my research partners, its spirit, goals, and suggestions should nevertheless be kept in mind as I proceed with the analysis of the rhizomatic histories of the transnational resonance of Zapatismo.

Networking Solidarity: The Resonance of Zapatismo and the Mexico Solidarity Network

The transnational resonance of Zapatismo has provoked a tremendous variety of responses on the part of activists in the United States and Canada. Three organizations that have responded to Zapatismo in what might be considered more traditional solidaristic fashions are the Mexico Solidarity Network (MSN), Global Exchange (GX), and Building Bridges (BB). Here I consider the histories of the emergence and activities of each of these organizations, with particular respect to their engagement with Zapatismo. In so doing, I draw on both organizational histories in support of my analysis as well as interviews with key organizers in these organizations.

The Mexico Solidarity Network is an example of a network of organizations that has responded to Zapatismo in extensive and committed ways. During our conversation in the winter of 2004, Jessica Marques, grass-roots coordinator at MSN's San Francisco office, explained the history of MSN's connection with Zapatismo:

> We were founded in 1998 after a massacre that occurred in December of 1997 in the community of Acteal, and we were founded by a group of organizations that were concerned at the time about the role that the U.S. was playing in the conflict, this was several years after the Zapatista uprising which began in 1994 ... So, at the time, we were very focused on the Zapatista issues and we were interested as an organization in mobilizing support for the Zapatistas ... We raised humanitarian aid but our main focus was on political education in the United States, and ... that has focused around raising awareness about the impact that U.S. military aid and training has on human rights in Mexico, especially with relation to the Zapatista conflict and the impact that trade agreements have on Mexico and that international trade in general has, because ... the Zapatistas specifically critiqued NAFTA in their reasoning ... for beginning their uprising and they began their uprising symbolically on the first day that NAFTA came into effect. So, we focus a lot on trade issues and since 1998 we've expanded a lot. We now work on labour issues, especially supporting labour struggles in companies in Mexico that are owned by U.S. businesspeople and we mobilize around globalization issues in the United States. We've worked on a number of the major protests, we work with the immigrant rights movement in the U.S., we have a seat on the steering committee of the National Commission for Dignity and Amnesty for Undocumented Workers. On a day-to-day basis what we do [is] we organize speaking tours for Mexican activists to come to the United States and speak ... to communities across the country in schools, in churches, in community groups about the situation in Mexico with the goal of mobilizing them to take some action, whether it's opposing some type of legislation, raising money, or purchasing fair trade products, but with the goal of tak-

ing action at the end of the tour. We also organize delegations to Mexico for U.S. activists and educators and teachers and congressional staff people, to learn about what's going on in Mexico firsthand and also to take action. Then we do a lot of public speaking and coordinating in the U.S. between the groups that are working on Mexico issues ... We have a really loose infrastructure; staff-wise we have three staff people, so we're very small but our network is made up of loosely about ninety groups, there are probably about thirty groups that are very active within the network and then we have a grass-roots, what we call a steering committee, which is basically a board of directors that's made up of some of the most active groups that help us guide the political aspects of our work ... Most of the work is done by the local groups ... When we coordinate a speaking tour [we] work with twenty different groups in ten different cities, and we will coordinate bringing the person to the U.S., organizing the travel, but the local events are all coordinated by the local groups.

MSN has undoubtedly been one of the most important coordinating structures within North America with respect to Zapatista-related solidarity. Focusing on popular education as well as political action, MSN has actively sought to build links between people in struggle on both sides of the U.S.-Mexico border and to provide concrete resources to the Zapatista communities in resistance.

Since its formation in 1998, MSN has organized more than thirty delegations to Mexico involving students, teachers, labour organizers, activists, religious leaders, members of the United States Congress, and congressional aides. The involvement of members of congress and their aides has also meant that MSN has not avoided engaging government and other official decision-makers and powerholders (Mexico Solidarity Network, 'History,' n.d.). Furthermore, as Jessica notes, while MSN began as a network specifically concerned with the Zapatista movement and issues of militarization and U.S.-backing of repression in Mexico, its mandate has since expanded considerably. MSN operates at the domestic and international level, acting on a number of different issues. MSN has served as the U.S. coordinator for the Alliance for Responsible Trade (ART), 'a national network of labour, family-farm, religious, women's, environmental, development and research organizations that promotes equitable and sustainable trade and development' and opposes the Free Trade Area of the Americas. Through ART, itself a member of the Hemispheric Social Alliance, MSN has been active in coordinating grass-roots opposition to the FTAA, engaging in the research and proposal of alternatives to it, and disseminating relevant information through public outreach campaigns (ibid.).

The Mexico Solidarity Network has also been involved in a leading capacity with the National Coalition for Amnesty and Dignity for Undocumented Workers, the Latin American Solidarity Conference, and the International ANSWER (Act Now to Stop War and End Racism) Coalition, the largest grass-roots anti-war coalition organizing against the war in Iraq and Afghanistan (ibid.). Furthermore, MSN has worked closely with groups like the Coalition of Immokalee Workers (CIW), a coalition of migrant farm workers in Florida, helping to coordinate their successful national boycott of Taco Bell, and with the Latino Union in Chicago, which organizes day labourers in 'struggles to win worker centers around the city' (ibid.). MSN has provided logistical and resource-related support to the National Coalition for Amnesty and Dignity for Undocumented Workers and the Latino Union in Chicago, while playing a significant role in the Coalition of Immokalee Workers' struggle against Taco Bell by organizing speaking tours, popular workshops, and assisting in the organization of a cross-country 'Truth Tour' in 2002, which focused on exposing Taco Bell's exploitation of immigrant labour (ibid.). The boycott and campaign were ultimately so successful that Taco Bell agreed to pay workers a penny more per pound of Florida tomatoes and to work with the CIW to improve working conditions for migrant workers (Coalition of Immokalee Workers 2005). MSN has expanded its interests radically since its foundation in 1998 in response to the Acteal Massacre in Chiapas, Mexico to include a much broader focus on issues of trade, militarism, human rights, migrant workers, articulating a political position that seeks to draw links between phenomena systemically, though not always obviously, connected.

Yet even with this greatly expanded focus, Zapatista solidarity continues to be a prominent feature of the Mexico Solidarity Network's activities. In addition to coordinating solidarity delegations to the Zapatista communities in Chiapas, MSN also organizes speaking tours of Mexican activists through the United States and Canada in a consciousness-raising effort, and it has worked on actively facilitating the emergence of alternative economic projects in Zapatista communities by connecting community cooperatives producing artisanry and coffee with interns in the United States who then set up tables displaying cooperative-produced goods in public places (Mexico Solidarity Network, 'Alternative Economy Program,' n.d.). According to MSN, interns act as the link between producers and consumers, 'revealing the human face behind production' (ibid.). There are no 'set prices' for the cooperative-produced goods but interns may accept 'donations,' a dynamic meant to foster 'a genuine link between consumers and producers based on knowledge and mutual respect' (ibid.).

Beyond this, the Zapatista Juntas of Good Government have also asked that MSN support 'the three pillars of Zapatismo: education, health care and collective development' (Mexico Solidarity Network, 'Zapatista Solidarity,' n.d.). In this respect as well, MSN operates primarily by generating resource-based support for these pillars. The Zapatista education program works by training Indigenous education promoters who teach primary school in their own native languages as well as in Spanish. This is supported by MSN, which accredits U.S.-based students in order for them to attend the international language schools also run by these promoters. In support of the community-run Zapatista local and regional clinics, MSN collects donated medicines to be sent to the largest of the clinics located in the Caracol of Oventik (ibid.). Finally, MSN supports Zapatista cooperative development primarily in the ways outlined above but they also encourage those interested in contributing to this initiative further by 'hosting a Fair Trade tour, becoming an Alternative Economy Intern, or ordering a package of fair trade crafts from the MSN to distribute in your community' (ibid.).

MSN's programs are strongly directed towards providing resources to Zapatista communities in struggle, most often by collecting resources in the North and sending them South. However, in spite of the impressive activities of the MSN and the very important work it has done since 1998, MSN's 'alternative economy' emphasis – while explicitly situated as an alternative to capitalism – is often difficult to differentiate from more familiar capitalistic dynamics. Despite references to the ways in which the process allows for connections and relationships to be developed between consumers and producers through events like Fair Trade tours, the relationship nevertheless remains limited to the identities of 'consumers' and 'producers.' While these dynamics and identities are indeed undoubtedly more humane under fair trade regimes, these regimes in and of themselves do not fundamentally challenge underlying issues of political, social, and economic inequality, nor do they necessarily foster long-term or meaningful connections between those who consume and those who produce.

Despite these other points of emphasis, one of the most enduring demonstrations of the resonance of Zapatismo transnationally – and one which also serves to highlight some of the more problematic dimensions of this resonance – has been the coordination of solidarity delegations to Chiapas by organizations such as the Mexico Solidarity Network and the reality tours coordinated by Global Exchange. These delegations, comprised of people from Canada and the United States but also from other parts of the world, provide an international presence in Zapatista communities and are often described by delegates and organizers as serving to concretize the connections between the Zapatistas and their international supporters. These delegations are undoubtedly important and relevant experiences – particularly for northerners who travel south to the Zapatista communities for the week-long delegations – but they cannot be approached unproblematically as manifestations of political action that are without complication or contradiction.

During our conversation in the winter of 2004, Carrie Sienkowska, an anti-poverty activist living and working in southern Ontario and a Zapatista supporter, described her experience travelling to the Zapatista Caracol of Oventik for the tenth anniversary of the Zapatista uprising as a member of a Mexico Solidarity Network delegation. The issues she highlights here speak to the resonance of Zapatismo transnationally, particularly with regard to the ways in which activists in the North have responded to the Zapatistas' attempt to reconfigure the nature of 'solidarity' on a global scale:

There were [about 200] people from ... Australia, Greece, Norway, France, Argentina, Guatemala, U.S., Canada [in Oventik for the anniversary of the uprising] ... so it was pretty amazing ... You talk about international solidarity, but to be in one building where you can actually see international solidarity, even though nothing's actually going on at that moment, that's still an act of solidarity and that was probably the biggest thing that the Zapatistas taught us ... Before we left as a delegation we struggled with what it means to do solidarity work, we had big discussions around that ... and about the privilege we own by being able to step in and out of the movement at our own convenience ... but the junta totally answered that for us and they [said] ... solidarity work doesn't mean you have to live down here with us 'cause, one, we don't want you living down here with us, and two, that's just such a limited idea of what it means to do solidarity work ... Solidarity work is going home and telling people about us, solidarity work is going home and writing magazine and newspaper articles, solidarity work is donating money to our clinic, so that's one of the most amazing things that I came across ... If you give money to the medical clinic or to the elementary schools – because everything's autonomous ... they fund everything themselves – that's not seen as charity, that's seen as solidarity, whereas when I used to work at the women's shelter ... if someone called you and said, 'I have a box of stuff for you' and they came and they dropped it off and I opened it up and it was a box of shit ... things that were totally useless, I had to take that box and say thank you. [But] there it's like, 'We don't want your shit.' Working in non-profit organizations, it was just easy to see that same act be totally transformed as something that's empowering rather than something that minimizes or diminishes your position in society.

By actively inviting internationals to come to their communities and to talk with them, the Zapatistas have managed to reconfigure what 'political solidarity' means not only to amplify their own struggle but also to connect it to that of others globally. As I will discuss shortly, these delegations are by no means free of ambivalences, but they are powerful manifestations of how the Zapatistas have managed to exercise control over the nature and extent of their contact with international civil society and, to a large extent, to provide concrete lessons in dignity and resistance that cannot help but infiltrate the lives and perspectives of the activists who participate in delegations such as this.

Another of my research partners who had travelled to Zapatista communities in Chiapas as a member of a Mexico Solidarity Network delegation and then proceeded to work as an intern with MSN also reflected upon the complexities of the delegation experience and how it had affected her own political commitments. As she expresses here, the delegation was not an uncomplicated experience and in many ways it challenged many of the preconceptions northern activists harbour with respect to the Zapatista movement. Yet rather than producing a cynical response or undermining her commitment to political action in solidarity with the Zapatistas, this experience actually fortified her desire to continue with it and to connect it to issues at home:

I think [the MSN delegation to Chiapas] was really inspiring, but it was also disillusioning in the sense that ... there's a certain romanticism about the Zapatistas and certainly about Marcos and the women's movement within the Zapatistas, and I think going down there ... was a reality check ... it's not glossy at all ... and it is idealistic in the sense that you have to maintain a certain idealism in order to persist, but the struggles that they're engaging in are really ... everyday struggles ... All those different conflicts to this larger conflict that they're engaging in against the state and against the Plan Puebla-Panama ... it made it so much more complex for me and ... it fortified my commitment certainly to doing organizing work around Chiapas and especially with the women's cooperatives ... I see that as a persistent goal for myself ... in order to support the communities, I think one of the fundamental things is to be able to build a market for fair trade products here and whether it's coffee, which is what the men are mostly involved in in terms of maintaining autonomy for the Indigenous people there, or the women doing the weaving, it's still promoting fair trade and promoting awareness about globalization and how we in Canada or in the States affect those areas. So there's a lot of opportunities for different work to be done, and then I'm interested in pursuing it for my master's research as well, so ... it's gone a long way for me I think. But it's exciting, too; it's constantly engaging me because it is so all-encompassing ... there's a lot of different things that I could focus my energy on.

Travelling as a member of a MSN delegation to Chiapas in August 2004, both the MSN's connections with groups working on the ground in Chiapas as well as their commitment to supporting the Zapatista communities themselves were clear to me. MSN works to support Zapatista communities and their struggle not only by coordinating speaking tours in the U.S., bringing people from the communities to the U.S. to tell their own stories, but also by providing financial support to the autonomous communities by assisting in the marketing of fair trade goods internationally. As an international presence and a facilitator of economic alternatives, the MSN plays an important role in supporting the Zapatista struggle. Furthermore, the delegations allow for northern activists to come into direct contact with the Zapatistas themselves. During the one-week delegations, northern activists actually visit Zapatista communities in resistance and hear from people in the communities about their struggles, yet despite the significance of such encounters for activists, the direct benefits of these meetings for the Zapatistas themselves is uncertain. While the need for an 'international presence' is routinely affirmed, the tangible benefits of such a presence are ambiguous at best. Furthermore, in my own experience, the line between solidarity delegations and what has come to be called 'Zapatourism' is extremely unclear. Where does solidarity end and self-gratification begin? The marketing of Zapatismo, in everything from fair

trade goods to the store at the Zapatista Caracol of Oventik to the ubiquitous Zapatista dolls in the streets of San Cristóbal de las Casas – many
of them made by non-Zapatistas – is a dimension to this resonance and
to the economic and political strategies that have emerged from it,
which is profoundly ambivalent.

Significantly, the Mexico Solidarity Network has been among the first
organizations to respond to the invitations issued by the Zapatistas in
the 'Sixth Declaration of the Lacandón Jungle.' In a communiqué written in a style and structure mirroring that of the Zapatista declaration,
MSN addresses 'U.S. civil society' in order to solicit responses to their
parallel declaration and, ultimately, to deliver the signed statement to
the Zapatistas in the second week of August 2005 (Mexico Solidarity
Network, MSN Response to the Sixth Declaration of the Selva Lacandona, 2005). The statement, addressed, to the 'children, seniors, women
and men of the Zapatista National Liberation Army' from 'members of
civil society in the United States' begins, mirroring the Zapatista declaration, with a statement of 'Who we are':

> We are workers and unemployed, we are immigrants (the vast majority)
> and indigenous, we are people of many races and ethnic groups, we are
> citizens and undocumented, we are gay, straight, bi, and trans-gender, we
> live on both sides of prison walls, we are urban and rural, and some of us
> have no place to call home, we are youth, seniors and all ages between.

> We are not the ruling class. We are not the Democrats or the Republicans.
> We are not the transnational corporations.

> We are members of civil society living in the United States. And we are fed
> up with living in a country that kills and exploits our neighbors in other
> countries as well as workers and immigrants in our own country.

The statement proceeds by following the sections in the Zapatista declaration, 'How we see the world,' 'Where we are now,' 'What we want
to do,' and, finally, 'What we promise in solidarity.' I will not examine
each of these sections in detail but for the purposes of my analysis I
focus on specific elements of this statement, using them as explicit
political – albeit rhetorical – manifestations of a history of resonance.

MSN articulates their struggle in broad and poetic terms (although
employing terms and a style perhaps drawn too closely from Zapatista
discourse), and I quote from this section at length in order to both illu-

minate the parallels as well as to allow the rhetorical dimensions of resonance expressed by MSN here to speak for themselves:

> We struggle against the transnational corporations that exploit workers,
> especially women, in sweatshops in every corner of the world. We strug-
> gle against the wars in Iraq and Afghanistan, and U.S. military presence in
> every corner of the world. We struggle against a corrupt political system
> that represents the interests of the wealthy few at the expense of everyone
> else. We struggle against political parties that compete every two years so
> they can lead by obeying their corporate masters. We struggle against the
> wanton destruction of the environment for the profit of a few. We struggle
> against discrimination and repression and inequality. We struggle against
> police brutality in our communities. We struggle against jobs that pay less
> every day, and against unemployment. We struggle against an unjust sys-
> tem that sends large numbers of our youth-in particular youth of color-to
> spend years in prison instead of in universities. And we struggle against
> the bad leaders in this country who make the United States a dreadful
> neighbor and who are the principle proponents of neoliberal capitalism.
>
> We struggle for genuine democracy and globalization from below in
> which everyone has a voice-a world in which all worlds fit. We struggle
> for health care and social security and good education. We struggle for
> control of our lives, and we struggle so that we can live in a country of
> which we can be proud every day.
>
> We also struggle within our movement for better representation of those
> most oppressed by racism, sexism, heterosexism, ageism and classism. We
> sometimes struggle to listen to one another and to not speak for one
> another. And we recognize that we still have a long way to go before we
> achieve equality and unity within our movements.
>
> We see the world in very much the same way as our Zapatista sisters and
> brothers and our hearts have been made larger by their
> struggle. (MSN Response 2005)

The impact of Zapatismo is expressed powerfully here, and MSN elab-
orates further upon it as the statement unfolds. In writing 'We share
the Zapatista vision of building a new world' and acknowledging the
desire for 'something different,' MSN members affirm that they 'want
to build that "something different" by permanently mobilizing civil

society to take power away from politicians, parties and corporations' with the goal of building 'a genuine democracy by involving everyone on a permanent basis in decision-making' (ibid.). While much of this can be read as merely a rhetorical/political manoeuvre in support of the Zapatistas on the part of Mexico Solidarity Network with little concreteness to it, this statement needs to be seen nevertheless as an explicit and firm expression of support as well as a powerful illustration of the resonance of the political discourse of Zapatismo and, I would argue, its attendant political imagination upon the way in which political struggle is being conceived of by organizations like MSN.

In somewhat more concrete terms, the MSN concludes its statement by offering several promises in solidarity. These promises include hosting Zapatista representatives and offering access to public venues so that they can communicate with a wider public; distributing Zapatista cooperative-produced goods and returning all proceeds to the communities; contributing medicines and even doctors to the Zapatista clinics and supplies to the Zapatista schools; offering a 'series of exchanges between activists in the United States and Zapatista communities' in order to collectively develop strategies 'to confront neoliberal capitalism'; standing in solidarity with the people of Cuba and offering to contribute aid and assisting in its transport; volunteering to host an intercontinental encuentro in the United States; and, finally, the members assert, 'We offer our hands in friendship, our minds in solidarity, and our hearts in struggle, and we commit to stand with the Zapatistas as this new strategic moment unfolds' (ibid.). This is a powerful statement of support and solidarity expressed by MSN, and it provides an excellent illustration of the bases upon which this transnational resonance occurs as well as the political possibilities it offers.

Yet such expressions of resonance are rarely unproblematic. In fact, on 2 August 2005, Schools for Chiapas issued an open letter to Tom Hansen and the MSN regarding their statement (Schools for Chiapas 2005). In it, Schools for Chiapas raises several important criticisms of the MSN's statement that allude to criticisms of some dynamics of the transnational resonance of Zapatismo voiced by some of my research partners and to which I will turn shortly. In the letter, Peter Brown of Schools for Chiapas points to MSN's statement written on behalf of 'members of civil society in the United States':

We also believe that no one organization has the knowledge or ability to accurately portray, with one centralized response, the nature of the many groups and individuals within the U.S. who are involved in the global struggle for justice, democracy and dignity. In other words, we strongly believe that no one organization should try to speak or coordinate on behalf of our entire country.

Additionally and perhaps more importantly, it seems to us that the Sixth Declaration is too subtle, too complex and too important a document for the 'sign-on,' petition-like response you propose. We are glad that the MSN wishes to respond to the EZLN; and we are sure that hundreds of other organizations and individuals will also want to send their own sincere and honest responses to the Zapatistas. The fact that each response will arrive in its own way and speak with its own voice will strengthen the message and maximize the collective creativity. We believe that whatever strength can be mustered from within the United States will flow from the enormous and untapped rebellious diversity which exists within our nation.

This open letter offers a view of some of the more problematic dimensions of the transnational resonance of Zapatismo, particularly when it comes to organizing and concretizing the consequences of this resonance. While the generation of systemic critiques and even movements may indeed be necessary as some of my research partners so eloquently express in their own work (see, for example, Patrick Reinsborough 2004), the dynamics of building these movements is one torn between autonomy and some form of centralization. While MSN's statement and Schools for Chiapas' open letter need to be taken only as a moment in a much larger dialogue, which may indeed resolve itself in new and innovative ways, such tensions point to some of the dangers inhabiting the terrain of transnational political action.

Building 'People-to-People Ties': The Resonance of Zapatismo and Global Exchange

A decade older than the Mexico Solidarity Network, Global Exchange (GX) was founded in 1988. A self-described 'international human rights organization dedicated to promoting political, social and environmental justice globally,' GX focuses on the achievement of four main goals: first, 'to educate the U.S. public about critical global issues'; second, 'to promote respect for the rights outlined in the Universal Declaration of Human Rights'; third, 'to encourage both the U.S. government and private institutions to support policies that promote democratic and sustainable development'; and fourth, 'to link people in our own country and people in the global South who are working for political, social and environmental justice' (Global Exchange, 'Program Summary,' n.d.). Unlike more traditional notions of human rights, the vision of human rights advanced by GX emphasizes the connection between political, civil, social, and economic rights as essential to the realization of human security (Mark 2001). Fundamental to this vision is the centrality of democracy in all aspects of social life, including the realm of economic decision-making (ibid.). Global Exchange is therefore directed towards creating the conditions whereby human dignity can be realized through the cultivation of democratic relations throughout the socio-economic and political order. The meaning and scope of these terms and the nature of the tools used to pursue them, however, need to be considered before accepting this self-definition as an inherently liberatory project.

In order to meet its stated objectives, GX has five main program areas. The first is 'political and civil rights campaigns,' an area divided into 'campaigns to monitor and report on human rights and elections in conflict areas, and to support pro-democracy movements in those countries' and 'campaigns to improve relations between the U.S. and countries with whom we have been in conflict' (Global Exchange, Program Summary, n.d.). The second program area is comprised of 'social and economic rights campaigns,' which is divided into 'campaigns to encourage U.S. corporations to respect the rights of workers, honor local communities and protect the environment'; 'campaigns against the unjust and undemocratic policies of the World Trade Organization, World Bank and International Monetary Fund'; and, finally, 'campaigns to promote humane, environmentally-sensitive economic alternatives, including fair trade, and an alternative green economy.' The third program area of GX is its 'fair trade campaign,' which, as GX describes it, 'helps to build economic justice from the bottom-up' through selling fair trade goods through two 'alternative trade centers' in San Francisco as well as via an online store. The fair trade campaign also aims at educating 'first-world consumers about the social and environmental implications of their spending, and about the importance of building a more just global economy.' The fourth dimension of GX's program areas is its 'reality tours,' which are envisioned as vehicles for providing 'people from the U.S. with an understanding of a country's internal dynamics through socially responsible travel.' Destinations for these tours include Afghanistan, Colombia, Cuba, Haiti, South Africa, Mexico, Palestine, Israel, and Vietnam, with these tours being configured explicitly 'as human rights delegations that observe and report on events in areas of conflict, and as election monitoring delegations.' The fifth and final area is a 'public education program,' which produces a variety of material through its online store, 'organizes educational events and workshops,' and 'works with the media to increase coverage of international issues from a grassroots, citizens' perspective,' as well as bringing speakers from around the world to the United States to help 'educate people on pressing global issues' (ibid.). These goals and program areas are certainly comprehensive and ambitious and they fall in line in many ways with those expressed by the Mexico Solidarity Network, with whom GX shares an office in San Francisco. These objectives, however, are by no means necessarily radical and in many ways are subject to several of the criticisms levelled at liberal democratic, consumer-oriented 'alternatives.'

After the Zapatista uprising on 1 January 1994, Global Exchange responded quickly as Carleen Pickard, director of the Mexico Program at Global Exchange, explained to me during our conversation in the winter of 2004:

[In] mid-1994, Global Exchange first went down to Chiapas ... in a sort of emergency response moment to see what was going on and to try to figure out if there was a need for an international presence ... When we got there, we certainly felt that it was important that there were international groups there and that, although the whole world was responding to the uprising ... to make sure that that didn't go away and to make sure that the area just wasn't totally dropped ... We initially helped a local group in Chiapas facilitate for human rights observers to go out into the communities and participate as peace campers or just as observers in communities ... We did establish an office and we did act as kind of a receiving place for international people to come to and get an explanation of what was going on ... almost like a mediator trying to figure out what skills they had ... could they be observers or could they act in other places better to help the groups on the ground? Through the first couple of years a lot of it was just fairly responsive, trying to figure out exactly where groups could fit in at that time on the ground in Chiapas ... There were also local organizations springing up left, right, and centre ... trying to respond to the focus on the area but also just also increasing needs ... In 1997/1998, [we] came into a position where we could start to write reports, we'd been around long enough and we had ... trust in the communities to be able to go out and see and write some reports, so we did some reports on militarization ... Around 2000, when the presidential election happened in Mexico and the power changed, a lot of different groups were able to shift into this ... proactive mode instead of this reactive mode ... We found ourselves able to be more active in terms of taking people down to Mexico ... being able to have campaigns around some of the issues that were happening. Specifically, some of the stuff that we did was to look at how militarization and deforestation was negatively impacting certain areas in Chiapas.

Global Exchange functioned as an international presence on the ground in Chiapas, a receiving space for internationals coming to offer their skills and support, a facilitator for reality tours encouraging connection and popular education, and an important coordinator for campaigns outside of Mexico. GX's Chiapas program functioned by focusing on six essential elements: (1) 'accompaniment' – providing an international presence in threatened areas, including coordinating the International Peace Camps and supporting Mexican human rights activists; (2) 'information dissemination' at the international level about Chiapas; (3) organizing 'international delegations' in an effort to 'provide participants with a broader understanding of the situation in Chiapas and generate support for local initiatives for social change'; (4) 'support for Mexican NGOs,' including technical and translation aid; (5) running a 'Resource Center' for international visitors to provide them with background information on the situation in Chiapas; and (6) running campaigns in collaboration with Mexican organizations in order to generate national and international pressure to achieve campaign-specific ends (Global Exchange, 'Global Exchange in Chiapas,' n.d.). However, these significant contributions would soon be challenged by realities at home, and Global Exchange would find its role shifting in relation to the Zapatista struggle, a situation not unfamiliar within the sphere of international solidarity action.

New socio-political and economic realities would force Global Exchange to alter the nature of its engagement with the Zapatista struggle. As Carleen explained:

Real life kicked in in 2001, 2002, and unfortunately Global Exchange lost a lot of money for its Mexico work, so while we had an office in Mexico City and in Chiapas until the beginning of last year, we don't have either of those offices right now, so the majority of our Mexico work ... comes out of the San Francisco office, which is the first time for us around Mexico stuff that we've had to do that. Normally we've just had people as eyes and ears on the ground [and] we've been able to find out what's going on, so [it's] just a process of rethinking the way we do some of the work. We still do delegations down to Chiapas and a couple of different areas now, Oaxaca and other areas, we do some speaking tours, and [we are] looking at how can we be talking about trade agreements and about trade policy and about things that ... [we] can engage the U.S. public in specifically.

Changing fiscal and political realities in the United States following 2001, partly due to the 'War on Terror,' and partly due to the fact that U.S. foreign policy was beginning to target new locations that required attention, organizations such as Global Exchange were forced to reevaluate their Zapatista-related activities and even reconfigure the nature of the work they were doing in that regard. This does not point to a 'failure' of the resonance of Zapatismo; rather, it suggests that the capacities of different actors to respond to it are constrained by specific considerations and contexts, depending on how they articulate their own position and role in relation to larger struggles for global justice. Nevertheless, as compared with its impact on an organization like the Mexico Solidarity Network, the long-term consequences of the resonance of Zapatismo within an organization like Global Exchange seem significantly weaker. While GX has recently worked to rebuild its Chiapas program, offering several reality tours to the state, its much broader geographical emphasis and its pre-existing commitments to a human rights-dominated agenda appear to have left few spaces available for a more radical manifestation of Zapatismo's transnational resonance within its own organization.

Human Rights Action across Borders: The Resonance of Zapatismo and Building Bridges

Again, in what might be considered a more 'traditional' response to the resonance of Zapatismo, Building Bridges, located in Vancouver, British Columbia, offers solidarity to the Zapatista struggle through a commitment to human rights observer training. As Maryann Abbs, a founding member of Building Bridges, explained to me during our conversation in March 2004:

Building Bridges actually started in about 1998. It started in Victoria ... earlier than that and then a few of us started a group here in Vancouver in

1998 ... The people who were involved in starting it were ... really interested in the Zapatistas [and] finding a way to support the Zapatistas. This kind of observer project seemed to be something that people were asking for and ... [was] the concrete thing to do ... We'd read a lot of stuff around the Zapatistas, like how the Zapatistas use alternative media, so it really connected with alternative media projects that we were doing, and also, when we started Building Bridges, we wanted to have it ... also connected to Indigenous solidarity [work] that people were doing in BC ... We wanted to always maintain [the] connection that it was a project where people are working in solidarity ... the importance of that for us was that people understand and participate in Indigenous solidarity here as well, as part of the project ... Lots of us in Building Bridges are popular educators, so one of our guiding threads is that there be a focus on Indigenous solidarity locally. In our first training we made sure that some of the facilitators were from local Indigenous groups to try to encourage that connection and ... from time to time we think of different ways to do that ... We've tried to have a small project working with the people at Skwelkwek'welt ... BC's different than the rest of the provinces in Canada because it's unceeded native territory, there weren't any treaties here, so we work with a group in this area called Skwelkwek'welt which is fighting a ski resort development ... We've done a couple of joint projects and joint trainings to try and get people to go up there when they're having actions, that's one of the ways we try to manifest that ... and [we] also try to actively recruit Indigenous youth to go to Chiapas.

Focusing on human rights issues and making connections between Indigenous issues in Chiapas and at home in British Columbia, Building Bridges represents an amalgamation of approaches and commitments to solidarity work as a result of Zapatismo's resonance. Significantly, Building Bridges' commitment to articulating the connections between contexts across socio-political space is a dimension to this project that encourages the materialization and grounding of the resonance of Zapatismo in local spaces as well.

Eric Doherty, co-founder of Building Bridges in Vancouver, related the inspiration and history behind the formation of the group during our conversation in the winter of 2004. Eric's history highlights the very explicit human rights-centred approach of Building Bridges as well as the much more pragmatic nature of Zapatismo's resonance for him and Maryann Abbs:

My partner and I were in Chiapas ... I actually don't remember exactly what year it was ... and there was already human rights observers going down there. We didn't have time to actually do that and met up with an observer that had had a ... bad experience, who basically wasn't prepared [and got involved in a] situation ... that was actually quite dangerous not only for himself but for the people of the community. So I had ... gone through a training with Project Accompaniment, which is a group that send[s] accompaniers down to help bring Guatemalan refugees back from Mexico to Guatemala and then stay with them in the communities ... so, it basically just came together that there was a need for a similar training program for human rights observers [in Chiapas]. So ... what we did [was] we adapted the training program and made it more participatory, putting less pressure on the facilitators, and we designed ... a project around just doing training for observers and supporting them when they head down to Chiapas ... What we're doing [now] is training people and giving them letters of introduction to go to the human rights centres ... The problem that we identified is that the groups in Chiapas don't have the resources to be training people thoroughly, but also it's the wrong time to be doing it. If somebody's spent all their money, got all their hopes up, comes down there and then if they were to go through an extensive training program there and decide well this is not for me ... [then it's a waste for everyone involved].

The primary goal of Building Bridges is thus not even human rights observation but rather the training of volunteer human rights observers for work in Chiapas. This is clearly a markedly different manifestation of the resonance of Zapatismo than expressed by Mexico Solidarity Network and even diverges significantly from the much more explicitly political and broadly based human rights focus expressed by Global Exchange.

During our conversation, Eric elaborated on the specific orientation of Building Bridges, the role that it serves, and the possibilities offered by this kind of activism for making conceptual and critical connections between socio-political and economic issues in the North as well as the South. Reflecting upon Building Bridges' mandate, Eric noted:

Officially our group is very careful to keep a human rights focus and also to keep our relationship clear. Our [direct] relationship ... is with human rights groups in Mexico ... Individual human rights observers obviously

end up being in direct contact with the Zapatistas, but our group's relationship is one that focuses on the Fray Bartholomew Centre for Human
Rights, which is the Catholic Diocese human rights group and then Enlace
Civil and specifically their human rights program ... We actually approach
the Zapatista struggle ... through that lens of human rights because that is
our role that we've taken on. For observers, while they're down there, it's
very important that they keep that focus and not lose that ... We always
connect Indigenous rights in Chiapas to Indigenous rights here in Canada
... We've made some effort to do human rights work here with Indigenous
people, that hasn't gone that far ... largely because the people that we've
been working with, their energies are stretched very thin and the places
that they want us in only allow certain kinds of activities that we haven't
been doing very much of ... We've sent a few people up to do court observ-
ing with the people from the Skwelkwek'welt Protection Centre, that's the
area around [the] Sun Peaks ski development ... and to me it's an interesting issue because it does cross those boundaries. We're dealing with very
similar issues there and here ... There you've got a large transnational corporation trying to expand onto Indigenous land without permission, without any negotiation ... just because they've got the provincial government
onside, they've got the police onside ... Fifteen years from now a court case
may reverse that and make them pay a few million dollars in compensa-
tion, but it's too late for the people there, and then ... in Chiapas you've got
situations where they've got ... the Montes Azules biosphere reserve,
which is a sad little joke of a patch of rainforest ... that's being set aside for
high-priced tourists and bioprospecting.

Again, what is interesting about Building Bridges is not only its commitment to operating in a strict capacity as human rights observers and
not as political activists but also its commitment to making connections
and practising solidarity with respect to Indigenous struggles 'at home'
in British Columbia. In this sense, the 'lens' of human rights becomes a
way to approach political issues through a different discourse that
allows for certain kinds of claims to be made and specific issues to be
raised. It also serves to foreground an internationalized human rights
discourse that is perhaps more moralistically persuasive than other
types of explicitly political discourses.

While reports from volunteer human rights observers trained and
accredited by Building Bridges are available on their website (www.
vcn.bc.ca/building/bbwho.htm), the long-term commitments of people who have gone through the training and worked as human rights

observers is somewhat more difficult to evaluate. When I asked Eric about the commitments engaged in by human rights observers upon their return to Canada, his response was hopeful but vague:

> It's quite mixed ... there's some people who come back and do quite a lot of work, but it's not directly through our group. They become very inspired about the whole situation and ... branch out into doing other things with the broad movement ... but not specifically promoting our group ... But what we've found is that an awful lot of people when they do this are at periods in their lives when they're not staying in Vancouver, we have an awful lot of people ... who do the training, go down to Chiapas, and quite shortly after are off doing something else somewhere else, in Latin America or Asia or wherever ... It would be good if we had more people who stuck with the group to do the work, but on the other hand, I don't think that's a barrier because a lot of these people are going off and doing work that I consider to be part of the movement.

In a similar vein, Maryann Abbs noted that upon their return, human rights observers were

> expected to do ... some educational work, it could be writing articles, it could be doing presentations to groups ... We did a delegation to Guerrero in Mexico and some people have a video project coming from that, so ... it could be whatever, but people have to do some educational work [and] it can take different forms.

Human rights observation in situations as potentially volatile as the 'conflict zone' of Chiapas requires a level of commitment not everyone is ready to offer. The volunteers of Building Bridges engage in important work from a position that allows for a particular – and often morally effective – perspective to be taken with regard to the Zapatista struggle and the challenges it faces. However, Building Bridges is a small organization and trains a relatively small number of volunteers, only a portion of whom will actually undertake the role as human rights observer and even fewer of whom actually put that experience into practice once they have returned home. Of course, all these outcomes are difficult to measure without a comprehensive exploration of the people who have been members of Building Bridges and their political activities, and such an analysis is beyond the scope of my current project. Despite its size and some of its more ambiguous outcomes,

Building Bridges represents an effective, grounded model of an organization that has responded to the resonance of Zapatismo in ways that have sought to be useful to both the Zapatistas and to the communities within which these activists live and work.

The 'Cinderella Syndrome' and the Dark Side of Resonance

> And so make an effort and put yourself in our place: entire years preparing ourselves for firing weapons, and it so happens that it's words which have to be fired. When it's said like that, and now that I read what I just wrote, it seems as if it was almost natural, like one of those syllogisms they teach in high school. But believe me, at that time nothing was easy. We struggled a lot ... and we continue to do so. But it so happens that a guerrero doesn't forget what he learns, and, as I explained earlier, we learned to listen and to speak. And so then history, as someone I don't know said, grew tired of moving and repeated itself, and we were once again like we were in the beginning. Learning.
>
> And we learned, for example, that we were different, and that there were many who were different than ourselves, but there were also differences among they themselves. Or, almost immediately after the bombs ('they weren't bombs, but rockets,' those connected intellectuals – the ones who criticize the press when it talks of 'bombing indigenous communities' – will then hasten to clarify), a multiplicity fell on top of us that made us think, not a few times, that it would have been better, effectively, if they had torn us to shreds.
>
> From 'A Death Has Been Decided,'
> Subcomandante Insurgente Marcos (2004a)

In *Activists beyond Borders: Advocacy Networks in International Politics* (1998), Margaret Keck and Kathryn Sikkink analyse the formation and operation of what they refer to as 'transnational advocacy networks,' which are comprised 'of those relevant actors working internationally on an issue, who are bound together by shared values, a common discourse, and dense exchanges of information and services' (2). The phenomenon of resonance and its consequences is by no means a transnational advocacy network as Keck and Sikkink describe it, but some of the contours of this phenomenon connect importantly with the emergence of these networks. Of course, many of the organizations I engage here would indeed fall into the category of 'transnational advocacy networks' – both Global Exchange and Mexico Solidarity Network could be described in this way. In their work, Keck and Sikkink argue that transnational advocacy networks have depended upon the creation of 'a new kind of global public' which emerged as a result of the cultural legacy of the 1960s (ibid., 14). Similarly, the phenomenon of resonance that I engage here is most certainly linked to developments in 'global civil society' since the 1960s as well as to other globalizing processes such as the acceleration of communication capacities. I note this connection not to posit it as a defining feature of the transnational resonance of Zapatismo but rather to situate it in relation to another observation that Keck and Sikkink make, namely, that one of the challenges to the 'novelty and significance' of transnational advocacy networks is whether these networks have resulted in transnational linkages or in cultural imperialism (ibid., 39). While globalizing processes and the emergence of a 'new kind of global public' are factors of indisputable importance with respect to the resonance of Zapatismo transnationally, these factors are not exempt from issues such as power inequalities, differential access to resources, or the capacity on the part of people living in 'developed' nations to step in and out of the struggle of Others. Such differentials can impact upon the nature and dimensions of transnational political action to a profound degree.

As Jackie Smith and Joe Bandy (2004) note, one of the most significant barriers to building organizations across national borders is power differentials which take different forms in transnational organizations as opposed to national ones (8). Again, while the transnational resonance of Zapatismo is certainly not an organization in any sense, this resonance is often concretized and manifested through organizational forms and the issue of power differentials is no less of a contentious issue. For many northern activists, the Zapatistas have become icons in a global anti-capitalist struggle and they have inspired a wide variety of political perspectives and engagements. Yet the Zapatistas are not merely icons, they are a living people in struggle, and the distance between the lived reality of the Zapatistas and the transnationalized imagination of Zapatismo can be expansive indeed. Zapatismo's resonance has by no means led to unqualified successes in the North, nor has it necessarily always benefited the Zapatistas themselves. In fact, at times this resonance seems to have reproduced dangerous and damaging power relationships, stereotypes, and modes of political action embodying tendencies towards appropriation, co-optation, and romanticization.

In the communiqué entitled 'A Death Has Been Decided,' issued in July 2003, Subcomandante Insurgente Marcos explains the 'death' of the Zapatista Aguascalientes – centres for encounter and dialogue with national and international civil society – in preparation for a new phase of the struggle towards autonomy. In this communiqué Marcos also explicitly addresses the complex, and at times problematic, relationship between the Zapatistas and civil society. I quote from it here at length in order to give voice to the Zapatista perspective prior to discussing what my research partners had to say with respect to this issue:

I told you that we tried to learn from our encuentros with national and international civil society. But we also expected them to learn. The zap-atista movement arose, among other things, in demand of respect. And it so happened that we didn't always receive respect. And it's not that they insulted us. Or at least not intentionally. But, for us, pity is an affront, and charity is a slap in the face. Because, parallel with the emergence and oper-ation of those spaces of encuentro that were the 'Aguascalientes,' some sectors of civil society have maintained what we call 'the Cinderella syn-drome.'

I'm taking out of the chest of memories right now some excerpts from a letter I wrote more than 9 years ago: *'We are not reproaching you for anything (to those from civil society who came to the communities), we know that you are risking much to come and see us and to bring aid to the civilians on this side. It is not our needs which bring us pain, it's seeing in others what others don't see, the same abandonment of liberty and democracy, the same lack of justice. (...) From what our people received in benefit in this war, I saved an example of 'humanitar-ian aid' for the chiapaneco indigenous, which arrived a few weeks ago: a pink sti-letto heel, imported, size 6½ ... without its mate. I always carry it in my backpack in order to remind myself, in the midst of interviews, photo reports and attractive sexual propositions, what we are to the country after the first of January: a Cin-derella. (...) These good people who, sincerely, send us a pink stiletto heel, size 6½, imported, without its mate ... thinking that, poor as we are, we'll accept anything, charity and alms. How can we tell all those good people that no, we no longer want to continue living Mexico's shame. In that part that has to be prettied up so it doesn't make the rest look ugly. No, we don't want to go on living like that.'*

That was in April of 1994. Then we thought it was a question of time that the people were going to understand that the zapatista indigenous were dignified, and they weren't looking for alms, but for respect. The other pink heel never arrived, and the pair remained incomplete, and piling up in the 'Aguascalientes' were useless computers, expired medicines, extrav-agant (for us) clothes, which couldn't even be used for plays ('senas,' they call them here) and, yes, shoes without their mate. And things like that continue to arrive, as if those people were saying: 'Poor little things, they're very needy. I'm sure anything would do for them, and this is in my way.'

And that's not all. There is a more sophisticated charity. It's the one that a few NGOs and international agencies practice. It consists, broadly speaking, in their deciding what the communities need, and, without even consulting them, imposing not just specific projects, but also the times and means of their implementation. Imagine the desperation of a community that needs drinkable water and they're saddled with a library. The one that requires a school for the children, and they give them a course on herbs. (Subcomandante Insurgente Marcos 2004a, 598–9)

Clearly, resonance is a complex and, at times, deeply problematic phenomenon, particularly when it is considered in light of the power relations and long-standing tendencies of northern activists, NGOs, development agencies, church and solidarity groups to impose their vision of 'development' and 'progress' upon southern struggles.

Manuel Rozental, physician and Colombian activist with the Canada Colombia Solidarity Campaign, reflected on many of the same dimensions expressed by Marcos in 'A Death Has Been Decided' during our conversation in December 2003. Linking issues of power differentials to the character of North–South solidarity, Manuel spoke powerfully about what he perceived as the failures of the northern response to Zapatismo:

It's fair and it's useful to get inspiration, there's nothing negative about this. It's actually very positive; it's also good to learn from processes like this. In fact, the relationship has been extraordinary ... much of the survival of the Zapatistas is related to this kind of connection, but I went to Chiapas through a Canadian that helped us get there, which is an exception, but the fact that that is an exception points at a mistake in the solidarity process from the North. If it's ... relatively easy for an activist from the North, or not even an activist, I mean a sensible, sensitive person to get there, why is it not obvious to someone from Canada that they could actually use some of their resources to get somebody from the South into Chiapas or to get people from Chiapas into the South somewhere else? That does reflect some selfishness within a political discourse of solidarity, to me it seems obvious [that] there has been pressure from Colombia to get people from Cauca to go to Chiapas, I mean this is a match, they have to know about each other. It's like Bolivia has to know about Cauca and Chiapas, it's obvious, but how to get them together? ... [So a Canadian solidarity activist] got some funding for a meeting, environmental stuff in Oaxaca, as an excuse to get somebody from Cauca into Mexico, 'cause of course you can't go to Chiapas as a Colombian, you won't get a visa, especially if you're a Native guy and you go to see the Zapatistas ... So [this Canadian activist got us] invited to that and when [we get] to Huatulco then we take a bus and go over there [to] see them and then finally the contact is made but the resources are scarce. It was difficult, we had no money to eat or a place to stay, [and] what do we see first when we get to San Cristóbal? What one of the Zapatistas calls Zapatour, thousands of tourists that stand in the plaza and shout for the Zapatistas with expensive cameras, this is a holiday that provides meaning for the many in the North that feel themselves progressive ... But you don't see any Indigenous people or people from popular movements and organizations ... You see greed, another kind of greed, but it's greed, too.

Manuel's criticism of the northern response to Zapatismo highlights a number of issues which I believe are deeply implicated in the phenomenon of Zapatismo's transnational resonance. As Manuel notes, while people holding U.S. and Canadian passports and with much greater access to resources are able to travel relatively easily to Chiapas, Indigenous peoples, particularly those in the South, have found themselves unable to even connect directly with the Zapatistas. The problems alluded to here, however, run deeper than anything so simple as a zerosum game of the 'rich North' having access and opportunity while the 'poor South' is forever denied it.

Two of the elements most frequently used by the Mexico Solidarity Network, Global Exchange, and Building Bridges are the mobility of northern activists and their (relatively) privileged positions as citizens of wealthy and politically powerful nations. When MSN, Global Exchange, or Building Bridges issue press releases detailing human rights abuses in Mexico or calling for an end to military aid and intervention in Mexico by the U.S. military, they are effective to the extent that they are able to execute what Keck and Sikkink (1998) call 'the boomerang effect.' The 'boomerang effect' is a tool of transnational advocacy networks and operates when a state refuses to address the demands of organizations within it, these organizations then activate the network whose members pressure their own governments and perhaps third-party organizations, which then in turn put pressure on the target state (18). The boomerang effect is effective and has proven to be so precisely because it relies upon the fundamental inequality of nation-states and, by extension, their citizens. When MSN or Global Exchange organizes a delegation or reality tour to Chiapas, they do so not only at considerable expense to those travelling as members of such expeditions (Global Exchange charges U.S.$750.00 for a one-week reality tour to Chiapas, not including airfare; MSN charges U.S.$500.00 for a one-week delegation, not including airfare or meals) but also on the basis of two fundamental geopolitical 'realities': the first is that of the access to other parts of the world given by a U.S. or Canadian passport and the attendant rights and securities that come with that claim to citizenship; the second is that it is valuable for these people to travel in this way to places like Chiapas in the first place. But why is it valuable and what does it yield?

During our conversation, Manuel Rozental drew compelling links, drawing on his own extensive experience in international political activism and solidarity work, between issues of romanticism, inspiration, self-gratification, and the solidarity processes as they have developed from the North towards the South. To a certain degree, his commentary intersects with my question about the value of transnational solidarity activism, but it should not be seen as an indictment of the activities engaged in by groups like Global Exchange, Mexico Solidarity Network, or Building Bridges. Rather, Manuel's comments, and those of activists that follow, illuminate the problematic and conflicted dimensions of the phenomenon of resonance and their manifestation in particular forms of transnational action. In this regard, Manuel drew an explicit and significant connection between globalizing processes, international solidarity, and global capitalism:

> If the Zapatistas had their own embassy here and ran it themselves, would it disappear now? No, it would be stronger today, so the main reason behind it falling apart is that it isn't run by these groups and the main reason explaining that is that solidarity is an extension of globalization ... Capital takes away your land, your food, your resources, your income, your house, your employment ... through different forms of exploitation, because it takes away nature and labour, those are the two things it wants. When you're left without nature and when you as labour are owned by capital, then it gives you a blanket, 'cause you must be cold, [and] that blanket is international solidarity, it comes out and says you're a victim, you need help. [But] when you say, particularly to the human rights groups or the churches, I don't want to be a fucking victim, that's not the

deal, what I want to do is run my own solidarity, don't help me, I've been helping you for years by struggling against the same creature that is destroying us, so don't treat me with indignity as someone who deserves charity, treat me with respect as somebody who can run his or her own affairs, then immediately the door is shut.

The links that Manuel draws between neoliberal capitalist globalization and international solidarity in many ways closely resembles the formulation offered by Michael Hardt and Antonio Negri in *Empire* (2000) with respect to the role of NGOs and other representative groups in 'the pyramid of the global constitution' (309–14). Hardt and Negri by no means group all NGOs into the same category, nor do they assert that they all serve the interests of capital, but what they do argue is that NGOs who claim to 'represent the least among us, those who cannot represent themselves' are directly involved in the formation and articulation of the 'needs of life itself,' they operate on the terrain of biopower (ibid., 313–14). What this means of course is that these NGOs come to define not only legitimate needs and demands, they come to define the quality and nature of life itself. Rather than opening up venues for directly democratic engagement, they channel the struggles of a tremendous diversity of people in ways that reinforce rather than contest the consolidation of Empire. In Hardt and Negri's vocabulary, these organizations are directed towards constituting 'the People' as a unitary entity rather than giving space to 'the multitude' in all its diversity.
    None of this, of course, precludes the facilitation of connections between groups in the South by northern sympathizers. Neither does this analysis invalidate these delegations or the larger phenomenon of northern activists travelling south to express their solidarity with popular movements there. However, what it does point to is a fundamental asymmetry in the dynamics of power, a dynamic that is not limited to political problems or the repercussions faced by activists in different countries for engaging in political activism but which extends to the forms which activism takes and the ends it is directed towards. The most significant outcome of the political activism of reality tours and delegations cannot be to create long-lasting connections between individuals in the North and the South or even individuals in the North and communities in the South. Such connections rarely emerge within the space of a week and if they do they are not in general durable. Neither are volunteer human rights observers meant to build these kinds of links. Similarly, Fair Trade and other economic development initiatives

supported through commercial ventures in the North, despite rhetoric to the contrary, rarely generate non-commodified ties between people. It is not a revolutionary action to buy Fair Trade coffee or weavings, nor should it should be seen to be so. Rather, these moments of encounter are only politically effective if they are seen as vehicles for the mobilza- tion of a northern constituency. In general however, the principles according to which this mobilization is supposed to occur are ambigu- ous at best.

What do people do when they return from delegations, reality tours, and even human rights observation? While there exist a plethora of written reports, articles, general accounts, and presentations issued by well-meaning northern activists upon their return from these delega- tions their impact to a large extent relies upon their capacity to dissem- inate their work and to offer something that can galvanize public attention. But is information the problem? If the aim is to 'tell the truth' and confront the powerful with it, then what effect is this information having on powerholders and decision-makers? Clearly, these initiatives are not capable of coalescing a popular, mass movement – if all it took to mobilize people was presenting them with 'the truth' or compelling evi- dence to the contrary of official narratives, large-scale, sustained mobi- lizations against systems of power and domination would have long since taken place. If the goal is simply to mitigate the worst symptoms of systems of power that find their centres in the West, is this activism significantly different from lobby politics aimed at winning concessions while supporting the overarching system itself? If this is not the goal, then what need is being fulfilled by this variety of activism?

Allegations of a self-centred desire for fulfillment have too often been directed unfairly against northern activists who seek to connect with struggles in other parts of the world. As I have sought to demonstrate, the impetus for the formation of connections with other people in struggle is by no means reducible to self-gratification. Yet it would be dishonest not to acknowledge that the dynamics of resonance and its consequences are, at times, coloured by northern desires for escape, ful- fillment, and meaning. During our conversation in the winter of 2004, Rebeka Tabobondung, Indigenous independent media-maker and an activist involved in the planning committee for the Third Intercontinen- tal Encuentro for Humanity and Against Neoliberalism, spoke directly to issues of fulfillment in relation to contemporary activism. Linking political solidarity to a general sense of the disenchantment of the world within Western society, Rebeka challenged the basis upon which non-Indigenous peoples have articulated their solidarity with other, and particularly Indigenous, struggles:

> I think that people are increasingly becoming more and more unsatisfied by Western society ... And you see that in something that's ... linked to solidarity with Indigenous peoples or this romanticism of the Zapatistas, kind of like New Ageism ... [P]eople being unsatisfied with Western institutions, belief systems, systems in general, and ... looking towards Indigenous peoples for hope, for fulfillment, spiritually or inspirationally ... This is something that the Third Encounter talked about ... to non-Native people who were part of it ... don't come here to help Native people, don't come here just to help us but when we understand what capitalism is doing to people and to the planet ... then, in fact, our struggles are your struggles, so people can take ownership over that. I think that the Zapatistas were trying to appeal to that as well ... this has been happening forever, now it's just happening to everybody ... so there could be solidarity, people felt welcome to give their solidarity in an authentic way ... The Zapatistas actively invited [people] to come [to their territory in Chiapas] ... It's their invitation, so it was authentic in that sense, too, they were invited to be there to document and to be an international presence ... So, this could continue and the Zapatistas needed them to do that, otherwise they would have been massacred ... [but] I think ... that fulfilled in this weird way whatever that void was or giving [these activists] inspiration in a shallow way as well ... But at the end of the day, [many of these international solidarity activists] didn't go and look at their own backyards, and at the end of the day where are the Zapatistas today?

The desire to find inspiration 'somewhere else,' particularly in a non-Western tradition, on the part of many northern activists is powerfully expressed by Rebeka here. But of course while the romanticization of an Other struggle may temporarily fill certain voids, it has very real consequences for the people who are the objects of such romanticism.

This is not to say that the delegations organized by Mexico Solidarity Network or the reality tours organized by Global Exchange, much less the human rights observation work conducted by volunteers with Building Bridges, are reducible to a facile and self-centred desire for personal fulfillment on the part of the activists who engage in them. But it does bear mentioning that the Zapatistas have not survived either through the attention generated by these delegations or the financial support received from them. The Zapatistas have persisted since 1994 in their struggle for justice, liberty, and democracy in Mexico and the world precisely because they have built a mass movement rooted in the communities from which it comes and dedicated to the fulfillment of the objectives identified by that same constituency. While northern activists have done invaluable work in terms of emergency interventions at particularly dangerous or sensitive times, it would be a gross overstatement to assert that northern activists have walked the same path as the Zapatistas or that their own activism has been able to generate the same kind of rooted, mass movements in the North. Organizations like Mexico Solidarity Network and Global Exchange are much more akin to the transnational advocacy networks described by Keck and Sikkink (1998) than to social movements – to understand them otherwise is to misunderstand their capacity to generate change as well as their strengths and limitations.

Romanticization and idealization were twin tendencies that were noted frequently by my research partners as particularly dangerous dimensions of the northern engagement with Zapatismo. Jessica Marques of the Mexico Solidarity Network also expressed the belief that amongst people in Canada and the United States who are drawn to the Zapatista movement there exists a strong tendency to 'idealize the movement.' Once again, this idealization seems to assume there is no distance between the lived reality of the Zapatistas in Chiapas and the content of their communiqués and their other communicative actions. In this sense, the mediated connection so many people in the North have with the Zapatista movement – whether that mediation occurs through the work of organizations involved in transnational advocacy networks, Internet, video, DVDs, or textual sources – actually serves to reinforce the idealization rather than challenging it. As Jessica noted in this regard:

I think there's definitely a tendency to idealize the movement and a lot of people, I've found, on their first trip to Chiapas are kind of surprised to find that the Zapatistas are a people who are struggling to create the society that they talk about and they want. For example ... the Mayan people are a society that is very in touch with nature ... [they have] within their religion a sensitivity towards nature and yet you'll see people kick a dog in a community and sometimes people from the U.S. are just shocked by that because we treat dogs as ... children in this country, and they can't really get it through their head that that exists ... Or there's a lot of ideas about women's rights issues, for example. The Zapatistas have a revolutionary law for women ... Marcos actually said that the uprising that began in 1994 was the second Zapatista uprising and that the first was within the movement related to women's rights; however, that doesn't mean that there's equality across the board in the communities, there are still a lot of power struggles for women's rights within the communities. Sometimes, when I've talked to Zapatista women ... when they articulate what the Zapatista movement has done for women ... [they say], 'Our husbands beat us less now that they don't drink' ... so there is definite improvement and they are definitely articulating that ... It's meant something good but it doesn't mean that there's no abuse of women, they're still struggling with that. So I think that there definitely is a problem when people from the U.S. or from other countries ... [or even] from Mexico City [and] different parts of Mexico ... idealize this movement and think that [the Zapatistas] have things figured out and are.kind of shocked to find out that they are still struggling with those issues.

Being confronted by the incongruity between the lived reality in the Zapatista communities and its transnationalized manifestations is not of course a necessarily negative or damaging occurrence. But when people react to this incongruity out of a sense of betrayal or profound disappointment at the shattering of their illusions, the consequences for the Zapatistas themselves – and others like them – can be damaging indeed.

Romanticism and idealization are dynamics often accompanying resonance that can be dangerous and damaging but are also often ambivalent in their consequences. Carleen Pickard of Global Exchange echoed Jessica's sentiments, while placing greater emphasis on the ambivalence of these dynamics, when she reflected upon her own perceptions of romanticism and idealization with regard to some of the participants in GX's reality tours:

[I have worked with] both sending people from the U.S. and some other countries [to Mexico] but also receiving people on the ground in Chiapas who get there and they're ... so excited 'cause they're going to meet Marcos and they're going to see Zapatistas, and then ... at the end of the ten days when they haven't seen anybody [wearing masks] and you ... have a conversation [with them] and they say they're kind of disappointed [and] you say, 'But all you saw was Zapatistas ... they're everywhere.' When [people from other places get] on the ground, I think people still have a good time and I think they still do get a lot of understanding that they couldn't have got if they hadn't been there ... So, when I hear people talk up here or when people ... call and they ... say they want to sign up and be a Zapatista or talk about the readings or talk about Marcos ... I encourage [them] to go there [because] I think if you've got somebody thinking and if something's resonating with people then generally [that's a good thing].

Romanticism, idealization, and the excitement and desire to participate in these encounters are by no means unequivocally negative forces. Yet the tension always exists in such circumstances that the 'disappointments' of the much more complex realities of daily life and struggle will yield not to a commitment to engage these complexities but rather to disillusionment and a desire to retreat from the experience – and the people who inhabit it – which generated it. In many ways, managing this tension and complexity is the job of tour and delegation leaders and, more broadly, of organizations like MSN and GX in order to channel the energies generated by these encounters in ways which promote political engagement and socio-political change rather than retreat.

Of course, as a point of initial attraction, romanticism can fulfill a certain strategic role in terms of attracting the gaze of others that would otherwise have been focused elsewhere. As Carrie Sienkowska, an anti-poverty activist working in Ontario, Zapatista supporter, and member of a Mexico Solidarity Network delegation to Chiapas, related during our conversation in the winter of 2004, romanticism can indeed be a tactical tool in a larger struggle:

I think [Subcomandante Marcos] has totally exploited the fact that he knows that northerners are gonna totally ... romanticize the Zapatistas, and I think they've used that as a marketing tool ... like the fact that Marcos has been in fashion magazines doing photo shoots and the fact that he's a sex icon in Mexico ... certainly says something about the intentional romanticism of the Zapatistas in order to gain support. In some ways it's like ... exploit as much as you can and ... if you're gonna get people to follow the Zapatista movement just based on romanticism alone then alright, whatever brings international pressure brings international pressure 'cause ... as far as their community activities go that's their own thing that they look after and someone in Canada being totally fascinated or infatuated with the Zapatistas isn't going to affect what's going on at the community level for them, so at least it puts pressure on the Mexican government ... to know that eyes are watching. But the romanticism, it's hard not to fall there ... 'cause we all felt ourselves, the whole delegation felt themselves falling to the romanticism thing and it was hard to pull away from that ... There's such a fine line between just being in total awe rather than just romanticism. Maybe it was just that we were in awe ... all of us identified as some sort of socialist and to be somewhere where people actually are ... executing their socialist principles is a pretty powerful thing to be witness to.

Carrie's assertion that romanticism can be used strategically is indeed a significant point, and it would be hard to dismiss the notion that to a certain extent the Zapatistas have made excellent use of Subcomandante Insurgente Marcos in this regard. Romanticism is certainly undeniable when one considers the fascination on the part of northern activists with the discourse and imagery of the EZLN and with Marcos in particular, a fascination reflected in some of the quotes I drew upon previously in this work from literature that has emerged from the global justice/anti-capitalist movement.

Yet there are undeniable dangers to romanticism, particularly for those who are its objects, but also for the projects that emerge out of it. As Stephan Dobson, member of the Canadian Union of Public Employees, academic, and a member of the planning committee for the Third Intercontinental Encuentro for Humanity and Against Neoliberalism, noted:

I've seen [romanticization] in action ... It's a problem of sustainability ... People find out that ... it's not real or that they're dealing with the image rather than the really existing conditions ... 'cause from my perspective, while you're imagining a better world how do you actualize it? ... Again I fall back to the concrete instances. There's a new book out called *Parecon* ... [about] participatory economics ... here [Michael Albert] is presenting an economic model to replace different capitalist systems with participatory economic trade bodies, and I'm reading this book and I'm thinking, I fought like hell for three years for a tuition freeze for better funding, let alone a tuition roll back ... and all that kind of shit, and my joke is the first collective agreement we got an extra tooth cleaned out of it and there was the tuition money and so on ... like the kind of struggle just to get that extra tooth cleaned and this guy's talking about replacing the IMF peacefully. How do you do that? Who do I vote for? Where do I send the coffee and the fire barrels? My frustration with that kind of imagination way up here [is it] ... strikes me as dogmatic idealism.

Stephan's comment about seeing romanticism as a problem of sustainability and the consequences of a 'dogmatic idealism' seem irreducibly pertinent to the transnational resonance of Zapatismo. The romantic image not only cannot be betrayed, it must also be continually reinvented or boredom ensues. Does this then not begin to border on a desire to be 'entertained' or 'stimulated' by movements and struggles which, for the people who live them, are often quite literally about issues of life and death? As Rebeka asked, where are the Zapatistas today? While they continue their struggle for autonomy and for a world 'for humanity and against neoliberalism' in Chiapas, international solidarity has faded considerably, particularly since the elections of 2000. Expanding upon this, Stephan noted:

> ... but it's always the revolution's elsewhere ... Nicaragua was really the one when I was an undergraduate ... here it is, opportunity, it's happening, you have to be a part of it, you have to mobilize because it's the leading edge, it's something new and it takes on all of the hopes and dreams and the aspirations and ambitions ... But perhaps what I'm trying to get at with one of the things with the Third Encounter that always was falling out of sight was that those struggles [are] directly here, so while you have ... all this wonderful solidarity going on with Zapatistas ... you've [also] got a thousand Patricia Pats moving in on Oka ... No justice on stolen land.

This comment eloquently expresses one of the darkest contradictions of the resonance of Zapatismo: as the Zapatistas have sought to remind us, struggles for humanity, for a world in which many worlds fit, are occurring everywhere. Yet it would be difficult to contend that solidarity has been manifested towards the struggles of Indigenous peoples in Canada to anything approaching the same degree to which solidarity has been expressed for the Zapatistas. If the Fourth World War is also here, why are our own terrains of struggle apparently so barren?

Political struggle always entails cost, what form that cost takes is often a result of where the actors engaging in struggle are situated. The danger of romanticism, idealization, and an uncritical desire to participate in larger struggles for social change is that these costs – particularly for less privileged others – are often not perceived. Alex Halkin, director of the Chiapas Media Project, expressed important concerns during our conversation in the fall of 2004 with regard to how some northern activists position other struggles, and particularly the struggles of Indigenous peoples, within the broader context of the global justice/anti-capitalist movement. Particularly at issue here is the notion that activists from the North do not have a developed or sophisticated appreciation of what the 'real costs' are for these Others in struggle:

> Because I'm not really involved in on-the-ground anti-globalization organizing in the United States ... I don't really know what the discourse is other than in the most general way, but I do think that there is this tendency to broadly say 'Indigenous peoples' without really understanding what's going on and, in fact, without any knowledge of the real resistance that's going on in Indigenous communities in Latin America ... That's why I think ... certainly video is such an important tool because these communities are documenting their resistance to petroleum exploitation, to logging, to all kinds of stuff, but nobody in the U.S. ever sees it ... I think there's this tendency to idealize stuff and not really be informed about it and what the costs are ... The Indigenous struggle may be on the forefront, but in terms of what's really going on there I just think people don't have a fucking clue ... [about] how many people have died and really what the cost has been to these people ... Not to say that everybody needs to get on the bus and go down to Ecuador, but it's very complex ... there's no black and white ... That's the other thing with the Zapatistas that I've encountered is that people [think] 'Zapatistas are good and the government is bad,' and it's very black and white and there's no kind of grey area, you know? The PRIistas are bad, Zapatistas are good, *punto*, and there's much more grey area, there's much more in between than there is the good and the bad, but again that's the idealization, that's the romanticism, that's the simplification of something that's actually very, very complex.

When romanticism or idealization or even a lack of appreciation for the nuances of life 'on the ground' in 'other places' comes to characterize the dimensions that resonance takes amongst activists in Canada or the U.S., resonance ceases to expand the horizons of political possibility and instead begins to collapse them. The consequence of this can lead to disillusionment, disinterest, or cynicism on the part of northern activists when they are confronted by the less-than-ideal realities and people behind the icons but for these Others themselves, this lack of appreciation of the complexities and the costs involved in these struggles can actually compromise the viability of these movements themselves and put the lives of the people who comprise them in danger.

The issue of appreciating the costs involved in struggle is not limited to northern activists appreciating the costs and risks involved in the struggles of Others, however. As Stephan Dobson asserted:

Seattle to my mind has become one of these icons ... you get people coming back and [talking] about how wonderful it is, and ... Quebec City is going to be as big as Seattle and this that and the other thing. My experience in Quebec City ... was five days of sheer hell. It was politically confusing ... the fighting that was going on in the unions ... the Quebec Federation of Labour had claimed ownership, it's their city and [they said], 'The march is going over here and you people are from outside and you're not going to take people up the hill, to the barricades, you are not going to do that,' and there was a lot of really intense arguments about that ... When the march was veering off, some of the CUPE people were saying, 'This way to the hill,' and we were being pushed and shoved around by the Quebec Federation of Labour marshals ... and then there's ... the added complica- tions that ... you've got these fifty-year-old overweight guys who are being directed up the hill by the radicals, they don't even have a fucking ban- dana ... There's a health and safety issue here, these people are going to go up, the barricades are coming down in places and you're going to march the trade unionists up there ... you aren't prepared, you don't have gog- gles, you don't have first aid training, it's a health and safety issue, and ... the police there were in absolute chaos, they couldn't keep up with it, there weren't enough cops, and the army ... What do you actually do in those kinds of situations? ... I get frustrated, I was going to the Canadian Feder- ation of Students march around Queen's Park for tuition freezes and the anarchist components within the organizing groups [were] demanding direct action and all this kind of good stuff ... [they were shouting] the rev- olution begins at the second lane in the road, take over the second lane. The whole shitty structure will come tumbling down, but the constant attacking [of] the trade unionists as being conservative [is disturbing] ... there isn't an appreciation of what is actually involved [and] there's no willingness to learn the risks, either.

As Stephan notes here, there are also risks and costs involved for peo- ple struggling in the North, particularly when considered from a per- spective that takes into account the widely divergent backgrounds and commitments of these people. As noted by Peter Brown and Schools for Chiapas in their open letter to Tom Hansen and the Mexico Solidarity Network, which I quoted from earlier in this chapter, to try to subsume a wide array of experiences, subject positions, political commitments, desires, life histories, and community and cultural backgrounds beneath any overarching banner, or to hold everyone to the same 'rev- olutionary' standard is of little political value in the long run, because it is an attempt to impose a unity upon diversity without actually attempting to cultivate a meaningful basis for unity to begin with. In this case, a romanticization of 'struggle' or 'revolution' – or to mistake an icon for reality – actually degrades and debases the differences between people, assuming a unitary subject in struggle that is willing to do anything in order to fulfil the goal of radical social change. Without a much more sophisticated and nuanced appreciation of the differences between and amongst groups of people engaged in a wide variety of socio-political struggle in Canada and the United States political action becomes reduced once more to a single vision of 'legitimate' action and power is reproduced. Moreover, in the context of the transnational resonance of Zapatismo, the very insistence on the part of the Zapatistas for an appreciation of a multitude of forms, tactics, and agendas of struggle is in fact disregarded.

Justin Podur is a *Znet* (www.zmag.org/weluser.htm) commentator and developer responsible for *ZNet's* South Asia, Africa, and Race Watch pages as well as the Colombia and Chiapas Crisis pages, a member of the Canada Colombia Solidarity Campaign, and a self-described 'camp follower' of the Ontario Coalition Against Poverty. He articulated precisely this dimension of the transnational resonance of Zapatismo during our conversation in the winter of 2004. Describing the impact of Zapatismo upon activist circles in Canada and the United States, Justin noted that in fetishizing Zapatismo, all too often activists had drawn the wrong lessons from the Zapatistas and in so doing had done greater damage to the very struggle the Zapatistas are themselves a part of:

> There are really cynical people who will say that they're a fashion, a fad ... I think [the Zapatistas have resonated amongst northern activists] sometimes for the wrong reasons, too ... I think a lot of people who could have helped, and should have helped, and could and should continue to help a movement in a place like Venezuela [haven't] because they ... can't handle the idea that Chávez tried to take power in a coup in 1992 ... [But] they didn't have a problem with the Zapatistas doing the same in 1994, that's not even on the spectrum ... The Zapatistas, they don't want to take power, they're Indigenous, they want to transform the way that power's exercised, but Chávez is after power ... we can't support something like that, that's old style Marxism ... It's crazy, and it's crazy because the target ... of the U.S. foreign policies ... of the economic policies, of the militarism, is the populations of these countries, the population of Mexico, the Indigenous

population of Chiapas ... exactly the same way as is the population in Venezuela – they're the obstacle in people's plans to exploit the resources of
the region and to exploit the labour of the people ... Because of these
fetishes I think people don't see that, and I think in that sense, the fad
about Zapatismo has been really destructive because there are other
groups, there are other processes, and nobody cares about them, because
they don't understand why the Zapatistas are important and why the Zapatistas are not important·... Long before 9/11 ... in the anti-globalization
work people were doing ... there were a lot of debates about violence and
[whether] it makes sense to use violence ... and the debates were really
superficial ... The non-violence people would say, 'We want to be non-violent like Gandhi,' and the violence people said, 'We want to be violent like
the Zapatistas,' and it was just the stupidest thing in the world because the
non-violence people didn't know a damn thing about Gandhi and the violence people didn't know a thing about the Zapatistas ... I really wish that
people would see [the Zapatista struggle] in that context, as one piece of a
struggle that's going on all over the world but ... all over the continent
especially.

The failure on the part of some activists to actually see the Zapatistas not
as the 'highest point' of a revolutionary trajectory but rather as a movement among many other movements engaged in a struggle against global neoliberal capitalism is perhaps one of the problematic dimensions
of the transnational resonance of Zapatismo. As Justin points out here,
the valorization of their 'revolutionary model' or, even worse, a facile
romanticization of their tactics and structure in fact works directly
against what the Zapatistas have worked so hard to do since their public
emergence on 1 January 1994: connect themselves and others to a larger
fabric of struggle in which no one stands above anyone else and to
explicitly reject the notion that there is only one path to revolutionary
change.

In this chapter, I have sought to illuminate some of the specific rhizomatic histories of the transnational resonance of Zapatismo through
an analysis of the histories of key activists and organizers with the Mexico Solidarity Network, Global Exchange, and Building Bridges. In so
doing, I have aimed to provide an exploration of some of the more 'traditional' manifestations of the transnational resonance of Zapatismo. I
have also in the chapter sought to provide an examination of some of the
most problematic dimensions of this transnational resonance through
an engagement with a number of my research partners from both inside

and outside of this more 'traditional' sphere of political activism. What should be clear from my analysis is that the consequences of Zapatismo's transnational resonance are powerful but uneven. Resonance and its consequences, as the rhizomatic histories which I have engaged here demonstrate, are often deeply linked to dynamics of romanticism and idealization and cannot be divorced from issues of power and privilege. For transnational resonance and the attendant political imaginations that it generates to function as powerful bases for the articulation of alternative political, economic, and social projects, a deep and systemic critique needs to be engaged in by activists and sympathetic academics with regard to the nature, goals, and impetus of transnational political action. This is precisely what I have sought to contribute to in this chapter.

None of the comments or critiques presented here should be taken as delegitimizing or undermining the important and inspiring work engaged in by organizations like Mexico Solidarity Network, Global Exchange, or Building Bridges. Rather, a critical evaluation of the transnational resonance of Zapatismo and the forms of transnational political action that it has given rise to is necessary in order to augment and enhance the already significant work engaged in by organizations such as these. Indeed, this chapter is inspired by the Zapatistas' insistence that while we walk – while we struggle – we do so always questioning. In what follows, I move into the less traditional, more 'experimental' political terrains generated by Zapatismo's transnational resonance in the North in order to explore the rhizomatic histories and forms of struggle and alternative-building that inhabit them and the emergent political tendencies and possibilities they offer.

7 New Terrains: Mapping Emerging Possibilities in a Transnational Field of Action

What am I saying to you? That the world is wide and far away? That only what happens to us is important? That what happens in other parts of Mexico, of Latin America and of the world doesn't interest us, that we shouldn't involve ourselves in the national or international, and that we should shut ourselves away (and deceive ourselves), thinking that we can achieve, by ourselves, what our relatives died for? That we shouldn't pay any attention to all the signs which are telling us that the only way we can survive is by doing what we are going to do? That we should refuse the listening and words of those who have never denied us either one? That we should respect and help those same politicians who denied us a dignified resolution of the war? That, before coming out, we have to pass a test in order to see whether what we have constructed here over the last 12 years of war is of sufficient merit?

We told you in the Sixth Declaration that new generations have entered into the struggle. And they are not only new, they also have other experiences, other histories. We did not tell you in the Sixth, but I'm telling you now: they are better than us, the ones who started the EZLN and began the uprising. They see further, their step is more firm, they are more open, they are better prepared, they are more intelligent, more determined, more aware.

What the Sixth presents is not an 'imported' product, written by a group of wise men in a sterile laboratory and then introduced into a social group. The Sixth comes out of what we are now and of where we are. That is why those first parts appeared, because what we are proposing cannot be understood without understanding what our experience and organization was before, that is, our history. And when I say 'our history' I am not speaking just of the EZLN, I am also including all those men and women

of Mexico, of Latin America and of the World who have been with us ...
even if we have not seen them and they are in their worlds, their struggles,
their experiences, their histories.

The zapatista struggle is a little hut, one more little house, perhaps the
most humble and simplest among those which are being raised, with identical or greater hardships and efforts, in this street which is called 'Mexico.'
We who reside in this little house identify with the band which peoples the
entire barrio of below which is called 'Latin America,' and we hope to contribute something to making the great City which is called the 'World'
habitable. If this is bad, attribute it to all those men and women who,
struggling in their houses, barrios, cities – in their worlds – took a place
among us. Not above, not below, but with us.

From 'A Penguin in the Selva Lacandona Part 2,'
Subcomandante Insurgente Marcos (2005)

Zapatismo's resonance has been complex and unpredictable and to
limit its evaluation to the enumeration of the still-existing explicit Zapatista solidarity groups would be to grossly misunderstand the nature
and extent of Zapatismo's resonance. Indeed, the most compelling
manifestations of Zapatismo's transnational resonance and the political
imaginations to which it has given rise have yet to be extensively analysed. I argue that it is among the most rhizomatic manifestations of
Zapatismo's resonance – among those collectives, networks, and coalitions that are least explicitly and obviously linked to Zapatista solidarity work – that the truly powerful dimensions of resonance and its
political possibilities are manifested. In this chapter, I consider new
forms of political action and struggle that have emerged as a result of –
or, in one case, preceded but strongly parallel to – the transnational resonance of Zapatismo and have cultivated new and challenging political
imaginations. The specific forms of struggle that I consider here are
diverse, from transnational anti-capitalist networks to a militant grass-
roots coalition to a radical filmmaking collective. Yet all these specific
manifestations of struggle and alternative-building embody radical
desires not simply to resist but to build meaningful, sustainable alternatives to the world shaped by neoliberal capitalism. I argue here that
these forms of struggle and alternative-building represent an emergent
possibility, a tendency, connected strongly to the transnational resonance of Zapatismo and its attendant political imaginations, to realize
new terrains of socio-political action and to live new political subjectiv-

ities. This possibility is not without its challenges and it is by no means assured of being brought into being, yet it is a powerful and inspiring current running through the forms of struggle that I explore here.

Encountering Global Anti-Capitalist Action: The Resonance of Zapatismo and Peoples' Global Action

On 27 July 1996, over 3,000 activists from more than forty countries converged on Zapatista territory in rebellion in Chiapas, Mexico, to attend the Zapatista-convoked 'First Intercontinental Encuentro for Humanity and Against Neoliberalism' (Notes From Nowhere 2003, 34). In the words of Paul Kingsnorth (2003), 'The Encuentro sent Zapatismo global. The 3,000 delegates returned to their countries with new ideas, new ways of thinking about the future, and above all, new links' (37). As Fiona Jeffries, activist, writer, academic, and participant in the First Intercontinental Encuentro noted during our conversation in Vancouver in the winter of 2004:

> The Encuentro was just the most amazing experience politically ... that level of organization totally outside of the state and this amazing mobilization of people from around the world who organized this event, and the people I met there [were] just so inspiring and [so was] the level of debate, the level of discussion about politics ... We really felt actually that some big change was going to happen ... people from everywhere talking about this world as it is in so many different ways and on so many different levels and this incredible inclusion ... this level of pluralism that I've never experienced before on the Left ... So, then we came back here and we started [an] organizing process what we were calling an 'International of Hope' ... because at the end [of the Encuentro] the Zapatistas said, 'Okay, this is what we need you to do. We need solidarity, but because we're in a crisis, what's real solidarity for us is to go back to where you are and organize around anti-neoliberal stuff ... We're doing our thing here, you gotta do your thing here, we all gotta do our thing and hopefully that will coalesce in powerful ways.' So there was a commitment [and the Zapatistas] actually asked people to forward formal commitments, and so we did ... There [were] some people from Vancouver, Toronto, and Montreal, so we organized a big conference ... we organized several things.

The model and inspiration of the Zapatista Encuentro in 1996 provided the spark for people from all over the world who then went home and tried to infuse their own spaces and practices with the same joy of rebellion and hope for another world.

At the end of the first Encuentro, the General Command of the EZLN issued the 'Second Declaration of La Realidad for Humanity and Against Neoliberalism,' calling for the creation of a 'collective network of all our particular struggles and resistances, an intercontinental network of resistance against neoliberalism, an intercontinental network of resistance for humanity' (Ejército Zapatista de Liberación Nacional 2001b, 125). Specifying that this network would not be 'an organizing structure,' that it would have 'no central head or decision maker,' 'no central command or hierarchies,' the EZLN called for the formation of a network that would provide channels of communication and support for the diverse struggles 'for humanity and against neoliberalism' around the world (ibid.). Peoples' Global Action (PGA) would be the network emerging from this call, but it would not emerge yet. In the 'Second Declaration of La Realidad for Humanity and Against Neoliberalism,' the Zapatistas also called for a second Encuentro to be held, this time on another continent. The Second Intercontinental Encuentro for Humanity and Against Neoliberalism was held one year after the first, this time in Spain, drawing 3,000 activists from fifty countries (Flood 2003, 74). It would be at the Second Encuentro that the idea for PGA would be born out of a 'need to create something more tangible than the encuentros' (Notes from Nowhere 2003, 96). PGA's 'official' birth occurred at a meeting in Geneva in February 1998 with 300 activists from seventy-one countries present (Kingsnorth 2003, 73). As Olivier de Marcellus (2001), one of the participants involved in the founding meetings of PGA, explains:

PGA is an offshoot of the international Zapatista movement, founded in a meeting that prolonged the Second Encuentro in southern Spain, and drawing a lot of its European support from people who also support the Zapatistas. There is also a certain ideological and organizational resemblance, both being rather unorthodox, eclectic networks attempting to stimulate radical opposition worldwide. The principle difference is that PGA aims beyond debate and exchange to propose action campaigns against neoliberalism, worldwide. (105)

Friederike Haberman, journalist, activist, and participant at both Intercontinental Encuentros as well as the founding of Peoples' Global Action, elaborated on the birth of PGA during our conversation in the winter of 2004. As Friederike asserts, Zapatismo's resonance had a profound impact upon activists from around the world who were looking for new ways to contest the ascendance of global neoliberal capitalism:

> After the Second [Zapatista-inspired] intercontinental meeting in Spain [in August 1997], some movements ... stayed for another week and decided to put into reality the Second Declaration of La Realidad, which is saying ... let's do global networks without hierarchies, without [a] centre ... So the first conference of Peoples' Global Action took place in February 1998 with more than 400 delegates from more than seventy countries ... At this first conference, you could see the resonances of the Zapatistas ... you had different working groups of excluded people, like women or farmers, and on the other side you had people trying to network on more regional levels ... The [PGA] Hallmarks [reflect] the Zapatista policies as well, because you have the call for direct action and the rejection of lobbying and the embracing of people in their diversity, and you have the Hallmark on horizontality [and] this is particular to what the Zapatistas are saying. The Frente Zapatista [FZLN, Zapatista Front of National Liberation] had been part of the very first provisional conveners committee of PGA [but withdrew afterward] ... I've been to Mexico to speak with [the FZLN] about this [and] my impression was that [they withdrew from active participation because] they wanted to focus more on Mexico and the process there ... So, they withdrew after half a year or something ... I think the connection [between PGA and Zapatismo] in the spirit is still there but on the one side, there's been this process of withdrawal from an active participation and, on the other side, Peoples' Global Action is quite inactive at the moment ... but in Europe, for example, we're going to have another European conference, and it looks like it [will] become quite big and the groups that are attracted by this conference are still in this political spirit, they're not all calling themselves Zapatistas, of course, but [they] still [share] the same political spirit, so in this respect there's still a connection.

Since its founding in February 1998, Peoples' Global Action has been one of the most important networks for coordination and communication amongst groups and individuals committed to anti-capitalist action. PGA has been involved in coordinating Global Days of Action against the WTO, G8, and the World Bank as well as a variety of conferences, caravans, and workshops around the world (Peoples' Global Action, 'Brief History of PGA,' n.d.; see also Wood 2004). As Friederike asserts here, the connection between PGA and Zapatismo is powerful, indeed. While the connections now exist more in spirit than through direct links, it is clear that without the resonance of Zapatismo and the model of organizing the Zapatistas have offered the people's globalization movement would look radically different today. Furthermore, while Friederike makes mention of the current state of relative inactivity of PGA, it should be noted that since our conversation, PGA held an Intercontinental Conference in 2005 in Haridwar, Uttaranchal, North India; new PGA infopoints have opened in New York City and Montreal; and Global Days of Action have coalesced in response to G8 meetings in Gleneagles, Scotland (in 2005) and Heiligendamm, Germany (in 2007).

Very clear in its role as a network of coordination rather than an organization, PGA has brought diverse groups and struggles together in a spirit of explicit anti-capitalism. PGA has no membership, it represents no one and no one is charged with representing it; it is a network comprised of diverse organizations and has minimal central organizing structures with its conferences serving as the primary collective decision-making mechanisms (Peoples' Global Action, 'Peoples' Global Action Organisational Principles,' n.d.). The overall success and sustainability of PGA is rooted in a constant de-centralization of power and continual rearticulation of collective identity (Wood 2004). PGA's Manifesto and Hallmarks are 'living documents,' subject to revision at each gathering, and facilitating the continual reinvention of collective identity while PGA's commitment to decentralizing power and decision-making to the most immediate and immanent level (with regions responsible for deciding upon convenors and infopoints) has provided mechanisms for challenging power hierarchies (ibid.). PGA's Hallmarks reflect its radically democratic, confrontational, and explicitly anti-capitalist spirit. As I have already noted, the Hallmarks, just like PGA's Manifesto, are subject to revision at PGA gatherings and have in fact undergone changes at both the Bangalore and Cochabamba Conferences (Peoples' Global Action, 'Hallmarks of Peoples' Global Action,' n.d.). The Hallmarks as they are currently constituted are as follows:

1 A very clear rejection of capitalism, imperialism and feudalism, and all trade agreements, institutions and governments that promote destructive globalisation.
2 We reject all forms and systems of domination and discrimination including, but not limited to, patriarchy, racism and religious funda-

mentalism of all creeds. We embrace the full dignity of all human beings.

3 A confrontational attitude, since we do not think that lobbying can have a major impact in such biased and undemocratic organisations, in which transnational capital is the only real policy-maker.

4 A call to direct action and civil disobedience, support for social movements' struggles, advocating forms of resistance which maximise respect for life and oppressed people's rights, as well as the construction of local alternatives to global capitalism.

5 An organisational philosophy based on decentralisation and autonomy. (Peoples' Global Action, 'Peoples' Global Action in a Nutshell,' n.d.)

While PGA has and continues to face serious challenges in terms of serving as a transnational coordinating network of anti-capitalist action, these mechanisms have allowed it not only to survive but also to coordinate an impressive list of actions. Again, de Marcellus (2001) explains what lies at the root of this success:

> PGA has aroused amazing enthusiasm in very diverse quarters around the world, no doubt because (following the lead of the Zapatistas) it attracted many who had been waiting for such an inclusive but radical anti-capitalist appeal. Co-ordinating neither parties nor NGOs, but autonomous, grassroots movements, PGA has opened a new political space that could give an international projection and a larger political significance to the struggles of these movements. There has been a real 'circulation of struggles': the Indians inspiring the Genevans or Britons, who in turn inspire young Americans to do even better ... a process of mutual discovery that started with the second Zapatista-inspired Encuentro in Spain, when Reclaim the Streets and other activists of continental Europe, for example, discovered each other. (113–14)

Dave Bleakney is a member of the Canadian Union of Postal Workers (CUPW) and another activist involved in the founding of Peoples' Global Action and its manifestation in North America. CUPW actually served as the regional convenor for Peoples' Global Action in North America from 1998–9, a role taken over by the Montreal-based Anti-Capitalist Convergence (CLAC) after 1999. During our conversation in the winter of 2004, Dave expressed the profound value of the lessons offered by Zapatismo to Canadian and US activists since 1994. For

Dave, the resonance of Zapatismo conveyed powerful lessons regarding the character and contours of struggle as well as challenging dominant liberal notions of how politics is done and what other possibilities might look like:

> Over the 1990s ... that struggle and others have taught me that we have more to learn from movements like that than they have from us. We thought we've seen all this and that we're the epitome ... we're the best as it gets, the highest standard of living; we're civilized, we're decent, we're caring Canadians, we have bilingualism ... whereas the analysis was a lot deeper in places like Ecuador and Bolivia and Chiapas about exactly what the North is about ... [We] need to learn from the South as opposed to [believing that] we have the answers ... that's a real struggle and it gets disheartening sometimes because I think it's a real hard one to cross over. I know within the labour movement ... people call it solidarity, but in fact you look at it [and] it's like charity ... We're actually learning and joining movements that already exist, and [in] the belly of the beast ... [in] the rich nations, particularly North America and Japan, those movements haven't taken hold ... labour movements have come to maintain the order ... If you look at global bodies, like the WTO, there's a constant clamour to get a seat at the table, as if somehow being present at your own execution ... surrounded by executioners ... is [an] achievement ... and, of course, if I were the capitalist I'd say, 'sure, let them come in,' which is what they're now doing – the World Bank and the IMF are now saying, 'Oh yeah, we need to dialogue,' where before they were saying 'Fuck you.' Because they're trying to co-opt a movement, they're trying to peel off the labour movement and other NGOs from those movements like the [Zapatista] movement ... So, I think it's a really crucial juncture because, let's face it, the unions in Canada are going to be a lot more excited about going to Geneva to meet with the WTO than they are going to [be living] off rice and beans in Chiapas for three weeks and not have any running water, so it's a real problem, but it's clear to me that ... the greatest lessons to be learned are from the Zapatistas but also the piqueteros in Argentina who occupy factories and the MST who occupy land in Brazil ... Another thing that the Zapatistas teach us is to be resourceful and self-reliant, to not think that there's somebody that's going to take care of us ... I think the Zapatistas open up a whole other area of relations around the importance of honesty, that you don't need to spin anything.

The concept of the Zapatistas as teachers to political movements and activists in the North is an interesting and provocative one. As Dave notes, ever since the fall of the Berlin Wall and the proclamation of 'the end of history,' political elites have heralded liberal democracy as the pinnacle of political expression. What the Zapatistas have accomplished is a powerful questioning of that conclusion as well as a complete delegitimization of the notion that 'there is no alternative.' Significantly, Dave elaborated on the lessons offered by Zapatismo by tying it and its resonance to the renewed 'naming' of neoliberal capitalism as something to be struggled against in the North. This is certainly significant given PGA's stance not merely as an 'anti-neoliberal' network of coordination and struggle but also an explicitly 'anti-capitalist' one.

The notion that the Zapatistas contributed to the emergence of a global justice/anti-capitalist movement has of course been commented on extensively, as has their specific identification of neoliberal capitalism as a threat to humanity globally, but Dave's reflections provide an intimate recounting of the impact this 'naming' has had upon the consolidation of networks of struggles against capitalism since the late 1990s:

I think [capitalism became nameable in the North] effectively between 1998 and 2000, sometime in there, somewhere around Seattle. In fact, when I was in Prague for the IMF meeting in 2000, [some PGA comrades and I] were saying what a difference [we had noticed because] two years ago nobody was saying the word 'capitalism' and now you [could] open a newspaper and actually see the word, and that was a result of the mobilizations ... The discourse had shifted, because [now] when people came and said 'What are you out here for?' you wouldn't just say 'I'm out here to stop the building of big dams' or 'I'm out here to stop racism,' people were [now] saying, 'The system is corrupt, the system is exploiting people and is destroying the environment and the system is jailing people.' So it became not just one issue ... and no matter what your issue was, whether it was a workers' issue or an environmental issue, you could bring it back to the system of profit called capitalism, and really, that period between 1998 and 2000 was when it shifted, particularly around 1999 and after Seattle ... [The Zapatistas absolutely had a role in this] ... the Zapatistas have helped us to question the nature of things, the norms that we've just come to accept without laying out some kind of dogma ... I think in many ways the Zapatistas have put a mirror up to us, and whether that happened by accident or was clearly constructed, the fact is the mirror is up and the questions are [being] asked.

The notion that the Zapatistas have 'put a mirror up to us' is highly evocative, indeed. Rather than the resonance of Zapatismo merely being another example of a distant and facile fascination with revolutionary struggle in the south, for many activists the Zapatistas actually provided not just a moment of inspiration but one of serious reflection as well. The deliberateness and seriousness of their approach to politics and struggle has unquestionably infiltrated the political discourses of the global justice/anti-capitalist movement and has inflected radical political struggle with a new kind of ethics that is explicitly 'for humanity and against neoliberalism.'

The revelatory and self-reflexive impulse that Zapatismo injected into radical politics in the North was commented upon by several of my research partners involved in a variety of struggles. The notion that Zapatismo facilitated the articulation of connections not only between forms of domination but also between possible paths towards a new world is a central element of this revelatory moment as well. As Fiona Jeffries, activist, writer, academic, and participant in the first Intercontinental Encuentro in Chiapas commented, the resonance of Zapatismo wove its way through a variety of struggles in Canada and the United States:

> On a lot of levels, on the level of understanding these places as colonial places and that colonial relations still exist and that is what is built on, I think understanding neoliberalism ... as a system of enclosure ... the new enclosures, and not just something that's [a] natural passage or development, somehow [is important] and I think the anti-state politics of the Zapatistas is really important, really important .... not wanting to seize power, and the importance of concepts like dignity and radical democracy. I mean what can the Left not learn from that? .

The assertion of the relevance of a diversity of projects bound together by a commitment to decentralizing power, radical democratic practice, a militantly anti-capitalist stance, to not one vision of revolution but many, all without being subsumed beneath one single overarching politico-ideological framework is a powerful product of Zapatismo's transnational resonance amongst northern activists. In the words of Mexican scholar Gustavo Esteva (2003), the 'one no' directed at global neoliberal capitalism and its politico-military apparatuses and 'many yeses' representing the many alternatives being envisioned and articulated by people everywhere is the conceptual thread that has served to connect Zapatismo to an emerging global multitude. Fiona Jeffries elaborated on this point during our conversation:

> I think it's interesting that it's not even necessarily that people are conscious of the connection between [us and] the Zapatistas ... 'No One is Illegal,' for instance ... the first time I saw that slogan was at the [First Intercontinental] Encuentro ... or the emphasis on the discourse of dignity that I think is very strong in the World Social Forum discourse but that's also very strong in the Indigenous movements [and] in the Americas in general, too ... [It's] a demand for a recognition of existence or personage ... you are an active subject in the world ... that's what the term dignity implies ... [it's] not something that's given, either. We're not demanding human rights and we're not demanding [that] you give us this or you concede this to us; we are asserting our humanity and our ... personage.

'Personage' and 'dignity' are place-holders here for a diversity of alternative socio-political visions rooted in irreducible diversity and mutual recognition and respect. In this sense, Zapatismo transnationally has functioned to liberate the terrain of the possible from the hegemony of any single dominating conception of 'revolution' or 'struggle'; it has renewed a spirit of agency that resides in humanity itself rather than in the projects, institutions, or systems which are always only the products of this creative capacity.

Friederike Haberman, activist, participant in both Zapatistas-inspired Encuentros, and active in Peoples' Global Action, also picked up on the revelatory significance of the resonance of Zapatismo as well as the tangible lessons Zapatismo has offered to movements elsewhere to seek new ways of contesting neoliberal capitalism and developing new strategies in order to begin to build new political spaces and practices that do not reproduce the hierarchies and violences of past regimes:

> A new language is important because it's easily accessible and it's able to bridge between more theoretical discourse and a discourse everybody understands. This is another very interesting point for me because Marcos is saying this came out of a clash between the smaller group of left-wing intellectuals who came into the jungle and tried to explain to the Indigenous about imperialism and the Indigenous said, 'Well what are you talking about?' ... [The discourse of Zapatismo] is what [has been] born out of [the clash of these traditions] ... Speaking of identities, this is interesting in

the person of Subcomandante Marcos because he speaks of 'us,' of 'us Indigenous,' but of course he's not Indigenous ... and it's not by [accident] that it's him who is the speaker because he can reach the people of his identity, he has been born [into], he has been educated in [the white middle class], but still he shifted his identity so he's not just a middle-class white guy ... For me, this is a good example of how politics can become fruitful, because when you're working for a better world, you're always in danger to know it better for others, to rescue with good intentions brown people or whoever and [Marcos's] history, his person shows quite well how this is affecting him as well and his subject position ... [The Zapatistas make it clear that] you can't copy a tactic or a way to do it, but what you can have are these resonances and to [take action] in a different way, and in your own way [that is] inspired by the Zapatistas [and also] to do it in a self-organized way, not to expect anything from the state, not to do any lobby politics ... not to do it in a violent way [either] ... because they haven't done this for ten years now.

As Friederike expresses here, one of the most compelling dimensions of the resonance of Zapatismo is the way in which it has directly engaged issues of subjectivity, power, and authority. As the history of the Zapatistas and the figure of Subcomandante Insurgente Marcos himself demonstrate, a world capable of holding many worlds cannot be built out of the imposition of the truth upon the lowly masses. Additionally, rather than seeking emancipation from a global system of exploitation and violence, the transnationalization of Zapatismo has instead conveyed the notion that it is possible to build a new world today and to do it in a collective and self-organized fashion without seeking concessions from power.

Fighting to Win: The Resonance of Zapatismo and the Ontario Coalition against Poverty

Peoples' Global Action emerged directly out of the Zapatista Encuentros to take on its own shape and direction after its formation in 1998. PGA represents one powerful example of a non-traditional manifestation of the transnational resonance of Zapatismo, however, there are organizations which have strong parallels with the Zapatistas and whose members recognize strong points of resonance without sharing direct generative ties to Zapatismo. The Ontario Coalition Against Poverty (OCAP) is one such organization (see Vance 2001). Militantly anti-capitalist, dedicated to non-hierarchical, radically democratic grass-roots organizing and action, OCAP is an organization that has weathered some of the most neoliberal moments in Canadian history, suffering both police and government repression, and yet has nevertheless managed to win amazing and inspirational victories for poor people's struggles in the North. OCAP's emergence precedes the Zapatista uprising by half a decade and there is no direct tie or genealogical link between the two, but they figure into this analysis both because of the militant, non-hierarchical, democratic, and grass-roots nature of their movements as well as because of the fact that OCAP's own organizers and activists explicitly attest to the parallels between their struggle and that of the Zapatistas. In light of this, OCAP represents a dimension of resonance that Chris Vance (2001) describes as an emerging 'Zapatismo in the north' predicated on a 'revolutionary coming-together of indigenous and other laborers' (66). As Vance asserts, while the consequences of this potentially revolutionary resonance are still in formation, 'ongoing anti-neoliberal struggles are bridging previously competing sectors of labor, and to succeed, this need only ground itself more deeply alongside the persistent indigenous promise to reclaim land from colonial capital' (ibid.).

As I have illustrated in this work, there exist an abundance of groups focused on social change and solidarity work in the United States and Canada that have explicitly drawn their inspiration for social action from the Zapatista struggle. Many of these groups have come and gone, leaving little more than unmaintained websites as the electronic fossils of their existence. Others continue to exist with little or no public impact. But if resonance has no larger impact, what is its relevance? As Justin Podur, *Znet* contributor and OCAP supporter, articulated provocatively during our conversation:

But are you going to have an effect? 'Cause we're going to be judged by our political effect ... not by how nice an event we have or even how gloriously we refuse to accept something that's happened anyway ... I go to the mass mobilizations, I write about them, I do first aid at them if that becomes necessary, but I feel like ... it's the punctuation at the end of a sentence, but we don't have a sentence ... It's not an either/or thing, but ... if we would take 10 or 20 or 30 per cent of the energy that's going into that and allocate it into trying to figure out what organizations we need to build in order to affect the political situation in the country or internationally, [imagine what we could accomplish] ... How many Canadians, even those that would go to a protest ... know what Canada did in Haiti ... and if [we] do know – and we're supposed to be Canadians and we're sup- posed to have some influence on Canadian foreign policy – are we willing to do what it takes to have an influence? ... These are some of the things that I wish these 'by any means necessary' people [would consider] ... Would that mean writing a letter to the editor or reading something, or coming to understand something, or talking to somebody? ... How are you going to translate all that militancy, which is the only source of power that people are going to actually have, into changes? And could I get 50 per cent of activists to accept that? ... [If] the trajectory is not protest, protest, protest, the state falls, and we build autonomous communities, what is the trajectory? Is the trajectory going to be some kind of reform ... are we going to win control, are we going to have a political party, are we going to try to take control of unions again? All these things are virtually taboo subjects ... but to me that means a lack of seriousness on some level because you're ruling things out that could actually make changes, save lives ... It's fine if you've thought it through and you've ruled it out ... I've thought through and ruled out the idea that I'm going to write for the *Globe and Mail*, it's just not going to happen ... But have I ruled out the idea that we could take control of city council in Toronto? I haven't. I can't necessarily say out of hand that that would be a bad thing if we could do it.

Justin's point is both compelling and troubling. What is the trajectory of struggle that needs to occur in the North in order to realize radical social change? What does 'radical social change' even mean in this con- text? Obviously there is no shortage of activists, intellectuals, and aca- demics who have articulated possible answers to these questions, and yet terrains of struggle in the North seem oddly bereft of passionate direction. Often lamenting this, many cast their eyes southward to places where movements seem much more inspired by meaning and direction, to places where 'revolution' does not seem like a cliché. And yet, in so doing, we ignore the fruitful terrains of struggle here and the movements which inhabit them.

I contend that, while far from perfect, OCAP represents a model of organizing and militant grass-roots anti-capitalist action that in many ways best embodies the grounded application of the principles inspir- ing Zapatismo in the North. Of course, OCAP precedes the Zapatista uprising, but as I have already noted, my point here is not to establish a genealogical linkage or to assert the same dynamics of Zapatismo's res- onance with respect to OCAP as I did with regard to Peoples' Global

Action. Rather, my intention here is to explore how histories of radical political action in Ontario overlap significantly with the themes embodied by the histories of radical political action in the South. In addition, I wish to illuminate here how grounded, grass-roots, community-based groups like OCAP are nevertheless self-consciously articulating themselves as political subjects inhabiting a terrain of transnational political action, a terrain which has begun to emerge evermore distinctly since 1 January 1994.

OCAP's roots lie in a struggle around welfare reform in Ontario in the late 1980s. As John Clarke, an organizer and OCAP founding member, recalled during our conversation in the spring of 2004:

> The union of unemployed workers [in London, Ontario] ... that I was part of was working jointly in the late 1980s with the Toronto Union of Unemployed Workers on a campaign to raise welfare rates by 25 per cent ... The Liberal government of the day [under Premier David] Peterson, commissioned a study that recommended not quite a 25 per cent increase but some very substantial rate increases which were about 10 per cent or 21 per cent, depending on the category of the recipient and a number of other, at least in the short term, quite progressive changes, and so the two unions of unemployed workers met with a series of other social organizations, local anti-poverty committees, some trade unions, some church-based organizations, and the representative of the NDP caucus at Queen's Park, and we agreed upon a plan to put together a three-pronged march on the Ontario legislature. So, that came together in the spring of 1989 and people marched from Windsor, Sudbury, and Ottawa in a fourteen-day period on the legislature, it was a highly successful march, got a huge amount of attention, drew out a crowd of about 4,000 people at Queen's Park, with rallies of several hundred people in various cities along the way. That kind of a crowd on an issue of poverty was pretty unprecedented since at least the 1930s, I would think, and so that led the following year to the formation of OCAP, although of course immediately things changed dramatically, the NDP got itself elected so its appetite for leading the fight against poverty went down fairly considerably.

While the mobilization leading to OCAP's formation was successful in forcing a welfare rate increase of 9 per cent out of the Liberal government, the political opportunities for social action seemed set to open much more widely as a provincial election was called (Clarke 2001). As John Clarke noted during our conversation, the election ended up sweeping the Liberals out of office, an event which OCAP was involved in working to bring about as they followed David Peterson's campaign around the province challenging 'the fiction that the Liberals had been a "caring" regime and to expose the growing poverty crisis in Ontario by targeting the Government's re-election bid' (ibid., n.p.). Little did anyone know that the New Democratic government which came to power under Premier Bob Rae would initiate an attack on the social welfare system, unions, and vulnerable groups in a thoroughly neoliberal mode (see McBride 2005).

While OCAP continued to mobilize during the Rae government's years in office, it was during Mike Harris's Conservative Party's 'Commonsense Revolution,' beginning in 1995 – a full-fledged neoliberal onslaught – that OCAP's struggle would take on the dimensions it still has today. Immediately after Harris's election, OCAP sought to press other progressive movements into a larger, collective struggle against the Conservative government and their neoliberal agenda, culminating in the 'Ontario Days of Action' in which the Ontario Federation of Labour (OFL) initiated a series of strikes and protests (Clarke 2001). While the Days of Action were disruptive, despite agitation by groups like OCAP, the OFL refused to escalate them 'to challenge the ability of the Tories to govern' and these actions never extended beyond Toronto (ibid.). Following the end of the Days of Action, and what they perceived as a retreat from a confrontational and militant approach to the Harris government on the part of progressive forces in Ontario, OCAP turned to focus on 'Direct Action Casework,' supporting welfare claimants, picketing agencies and employers introducing 'workfare,' taking over abandoned buildings to turn them into housing for the homeless, and fighting the criminalization of the city's poor and homeless (ibid.). Casework continues to be a major element of OCAP's work today and is seen by activists and organizers involved with the group as instrumental not only to building support for larger actions but as essential to fighting for people's ability to live a dignified life, empowering poor communities, and challenging the day-to-day violence exercised by the neoliberal capitalist order.

Casework, however, is not the only defining feature of OCAP's militancy and commitment to direct action. On 15 June 2000, OCAP moved to revitalize a 'movement of generalized resistance,' leading a march of homeless people and supporters to the provincial legislature to demand that the government meet with their delegation and address their grievances. Instead of a meeting, the government responded to OCAP by mobilizing riot police, a provocation to which OCAP replied by fighting back, resulting in what became popularly known as the 'Queen's Park Riot' (Clarke 2001). Out of this 'riot' and the revitalized militancy amongst some progressive and sympathetic organizations in the province came the Ontario Common Front, an initiative aimed at a campaign of economic disruption across the province as well as the consolidation of a network of radical anti-poverty groups across the province (ibid.). Recently, OCAP celebrated its fifteenth year in existence, an existence marked by continuing militant efforts to work with and within poor communities in order to build possibilities for lives lived with dignity. Indeed, OCAP's 'Raise the Rates' campaign to raise social assistance rates by 40 per cent won a major victory in 2005 by providing thousands of people with access to the 'Special Diet Supplement,' setting up free clinics so that people without access to family doctors could get the necessary documentation to access this fund, and then defending their access to it when the municipal government threatened to illegally block it. While the Government of Ontario amended legislation to restrict access to the Special Diet Fund in 2006, OCAP has continued to defend access to it and to advance its fight to 'Raise the Rates' in Ontario.

But OCAP's history of grass-roots, militant struggle against waves of neoliberal governance is only a small part of the parallels that exist between a poor people's movement in the North and a movement like that of the Zapatistas in the South. The convergences that I argue are in fact most significant reside in the ways in which these movements position themselves with regard to structures of power as well as the agendas they pursue. These parallels are illuminated by the way in which OCAP articulates its own history:

> OCAP has shown that a poor people's movement can shake those in power and contribute to the building of decisive social struggle. As a militant, anti-capitalist organization, we reject the notion that we have any common set of interests with those who hold economic and political power. We also reject the rituals of token protest that confine movements to the level of futile moral arguments. We fight to win and are part of a growing force in society that is ready to organize on just that basis. (Clarke 2001, n.p.)

Of course, these convergences also extend beyond mere rhetoric. In this sense, OCAP's internal organizational dynamics and its relationship to other anti-poverty groups is significant. Mac Scott, an OCAP activist and an elected member of OCAP's executive, described some of the organizational dynamics between OCAP and other groups as well as the historical basis for them during our conversation in the spring of 2004:

> We were formed at the end of ... a caravan across Ontario that converged on Toronto in 1989 around poverty issues and they decided that they would meet again in a year, and in 1990 they decided to form the Ontario Coalition Against Poverty ... Originally we were a coalition of member groups in cities across Ontario and Toronto [and] actually had what was called a direct action committee which was the Toronto section, but increasingly over time – and I think it's just the nature of large grass-roots organizations – we became much more of what we are now, which is a federation and OCAP's become the Toronto group and [we] have sister groups in many other cities and we operate together ... in a very loose kind of federated structure, which in my experience tends to be the most sustainable way to do large-scale organizing anyways ... Historically, we had really good ties to unions and we actually used to get a lot of our funding from unions, and part of that is due to people within the group having a really good idea that we needed to be ... connected to other movements to avoid becoming isolated and easily crushed, and now I think we really push the envelope a lot, which leads to us really almost coming into clashes sometimes with our traditional backers in the unions, but we still manage not to become completely isolated, and I think that's really important because if you look historically at radical groups coming out of really disenfranchised constituencies when they become isolated they get crushed ...

OCAP's commitment to autonomy and interconnectedness reflects a recognition of political necessity, a belief that issues of poverty are systemic rather than individual or local, and a deep affirmation of the understanding that only by building movements will social change occur. OCAP's 'organizational philosophy' – to assign a very structural term to something which has clearly emerged much more organically – is also very much predicated on the belief that it is only through direct, militant action that true social change is possible.

This attitude towards social change and struggle is itself a product of OCAP's organizational history, particularly during its early years. Of course, the positions actors adopt with respect to systems of power and the myths that underlie them are critical in determining the direction, sustainability, and relevance of any social movement or organization. Groups may seek institutional access and popular influence and be co-opted, others may seek a more radical line and find no receptive audience or constituency. The Zapatistas are an excellent illustration of this difficult path and the choices that can make or break movements. I would argue that OCAP offers similar illustrations in a northern context. Deciding when, where, and how to compromise is never an easy decision for groups struggling for social change, but when the principles upon which struggle is based are clear and compromises are made not for the sake of institutional influence or power these decisions can be made intelligently and tactically. In OCAP's case, broader alliances can only be possible if principles of autonomy are intact, otherwise, such alliances must only be occasional tactical encounters. Mike DesRoches, an activist and organizer with OCAP, related the following to me during our conversation in the spring of 2004:

> When OCAP first started, it came out of the labour movement ... The precursor to OCAP was the Union of Unemployed Workers, which was very much affiliated with the labour movement and saw itself as being part of the labour movement, and that was the whole idea ... OCAP was funded by OPSEU [Ontario Public Service Employees Union] and the CAW [Canadian Auto Workers] for years and years and years ... [but] that funding has fallen away and the funding is an easy way to get a grasp on that type of support ... OPSEU was one of the biggest funders for OCAP and when [the provincial government started to use] OPSEU members as welfare cops to track down welfare fraud people and criminalize them, send them to jail ... OCAP took this up as a campaign and as a question, and OPSEU said, 'Well listen, you've got to back off ... this campaign is attacking OPSEU members,' [and] OPSEU cut the funding. The CAW years later attempted to get OCAP to agree never to do any home visits and go to the homes of anybody and OCAP refused to do that, the funding still remained, but when an eviction took place at Jim Flaherty's constituency office in Whitby and his office was trashed ... [the] $20,000 dollars a year that OCAP got consistently for years and years was cut off immediately, and then again when OCAP did an immigration action where we went and leafleted and drew connections to the fact that Air Canada profits off of deportations, the CAW said, 'These are CAW workers so you can't say this,' and cut off almost all ties with us entirely for a long time. So, it is certainly a question but also I think it's important to recognize that ... in the same way that the debates in the anti-globalization movement were primarily founded on a really

bullshit idea, I think the question in terms of OCAP is also founded on this idea that if you toe the line they will support you and I don't think it's true ... Certainly in Quebec City, for instance, there [were] a lot of trade unionists who put themselves on the line, who went to the fence ... but in terms of the trade union bureaucracy they were completely fucked and ... it's the same thing on a local level ... The labour bureaucracy is one that is not going to support you, they have their own narrow ends, they have their own agenda, they're very entrenched within the system, they're very locked into ... ruling-class agendas and trying to compromise with them for any purpose has to be made on a tactical choice to gain some advantage for yourself, and [it] can't be done in terms of trying to build a broad alliance with them 'cause there's no broad alliance to be had ... it's not in the cards. I don't think it was ever in the cards for the anti-globalization movement, either, because the entire strength of the anti-globalization movement came from its independence and its sense of decentralization and vibrancy, and that's exactly what the mainstream left is against, whether it be trying to get you in the NDP or trying to get you into the labour council or trying to get you into the International Socialist Organization, or whatever ... it's all about exerting a hierarchical control over movements and it's never going to lead to any type of real resistance. So ... OCAP has been isolated, but at the same time our stance has been that if the labour bureaucracy cuts you off that doesn't cut you off from trade unionists in general ... A huge number of people who are involved in trade union struggles are very critical, independent thinking people and don't just follow the lead of the president of the labour council, and as the funding to OCAP from major labour organizations has been cut, individuals have increased their donations, and we have more money coming in now ... than we ever have in the history of the organization. It's gone from a point where in the late 1990s OCAP was a 100 per cent funded by unions to a point now where ... with the exception of CUPE 3903 ... it's entirely insignificant, it's an entirely insignificant amount.

Autonomy and interconnectedness are primary concerns for OCAP – much as they are for the Zapatistas – and their organizational and mobilizing principles are deeply inflected by these principles. While their confrontational and radical approach has at times led to isolation from more mainstream sources of support such as the labour movement, OCAP remains dedicated to responding to the needs of its constituency and the tactics and strategies they identify as relevant rather than to the dictates of larger organizing structures or principles. There are perhaps trade-offs involved here and OCAP has often run the risk of being demonized in the mainstream press and isolated from political and financial supporters. Such isolation can lead to repression and even annihilation, but their continued existence and success testifies to the fact that this strategy has proven to be a powerful source of cohesion and inspiration for their struggle.

OCAP's terrain of struggle also reflects certain parallels with Zapatismo. Not only is OCAP committed to a grass-roots model of action and organizing, but it has also firmly rejected the idea that capitalist relations are 'reformeable,' and while many of their campaigns focus on winning immediate relief for people living below the poverty line, their organizers and activists are clear that this should not be taken as an indication of a position favouring 'reform' over 'revolution.' As Mike DesRoches expressed to me during our conversation, such reform/revolution dichotomies need to be cast aside in favour of a much more comprehensive vision of what the ultimate aim of struggle needs to be:

I think it's something that people set themselves up into falsely ... it's a false dichotomy ... If you're actually going to build a revolutionary organization and you're actually going to fight for revolutionary goals, fighting for smaller goals is not something that you have to figure out how you're gonna convince people not to do ... It's an essential part of fighting for revolutionary goals ... The Zapatistas talked about building a global movement of change and talked about having a worldwide revolution, but the focus of their activity was in defending the communities of Chiapas, and OCAP sometimes uses more revolutionary rhetoric than at other times, we have different demands at different times ... In the fall of 2001, we had a campaign that was essentially to unseat the provincial government ... not because we think that the Liberal Party's going to be better but because attacking this government is a way of building a movement that will exercise power over society and in society ... At the time that we were running that campaign, if someone came to us and said 'I'm getting cut off welfare' the answer wasn't 'Don't worry, we're going to overthrow the provincial government.' The answer was 'Where's you're worker, let's go' ... Dealing with those types of concrete things is how people learn to fight together and it's what makes communities stronger for the bigger fights ... I think the question of reform versus revolution is not a question ... any revolutionary organization that isn't capable of defending the people involved in that movement is going to fail. You have to be able to defend what people have and you have to be able to fight for the best that you can get for people, at the same time as you push towards bigger goals ... It ties right into the question of exercising power, and OCAP certainly is a long way from being able to exercise a tremendous amount of power, but at the same time ... in small ways, we are able to exercise power and we are able to put up blocks whereby the governments know that they can't cross that without a confrontation, without a fight ... A balance of power is not having seven or eight NDP MPPs in Queen's Park who can speak out against policies as they're rammed down people's throats; a balance of power is where you create a situation where the government realizes that it can't just cut a thousand people off welfare because a thousand people, ten thousand people, will be ready to defend those thousand people [or that it] can't just ram down anti-tenant legislation because people are prepared to defend themselves and defend their neighbours ... Creating those types of barriers [that] governments can't move past is the beginning of exercising power, and the Zapatistas have exercised power in Chiapas because they have drawn a line whereby the federal government is unable to exercise any type of control at all ... over a huge section of their country ... That whole concept also started off in smaller ways ... and exists in other places in smaller ways ... I'm hopeful that in North America in the next ten years, it will become impossible for governments to implement certain agendas because it simply will not be tolerated.

Without overstating the case, Mike's reflections on OCAP's position with respect to struggle and social change mirror significant elements of Zapatismo. By fighting for people's daily and basic needs, organizers and activists in OCAP see their struggle as one that creates conditions for the possibility of the realization of much broader, more militant, and more radical struggles. The consolidation of community autonomy in Chiapas can also be seen in a similar light. Rather than seeing these choices as 'reformist' or as an attempt to back-peddle from more radical demands, OCAP and the Zapatistas offer models of community action that aims to empower people, to teach them to struggle together, to defend them from systemic attacks, to reject the co-optation of elite-dominated political venues, and to build communities of resistance and pro-active rather than merely defensive struggle.

The avowedly anti-electoral stance adopted by OCAP also bears a strong resemblance to that of the Zapatistas. Indeed, the reasons both movements offer for having rejected this route are strikingly similar. OCAP's refusal to 'make deals' with powerholders in return for special considerations embodies a deeply held belief in the need to challenge systems of power rather than those who hold positions within those systems. In this sense, OCAP advocates a politics beyond the state without slipping into a facile or escapist utopianism. As John Clarke expressed during our conversation:

> The ability that [power holders] have to proceed with the neoliberal agenda with tactical shifts is considerable ... and their ability to deceive people is also enormous ... The standard model seems to be to go through this period of having a real hard right blood-and-guts vicious government that takes no prisoners and then go through a phase of bringing in a sort of a slightly kinder, gentler (but mainly in words) regime that talks about consensus and third ways ... and intersperse those kinds of hard shock periods with nurturing the belief that things could be a bit different ... and then back to another round of the hard attack ... That has considerable durability, and their control mechanisms are enormous, but I think it would be wrong to underestimate the degree to which that process is falling short of really deceiving people ... We should remember that the turnout in the last [provincial] election was historically low and that trend is worsening, and it's not just an Ontario phenomenon. In the United States the voter turnout has declined and declined and declined, but in Ontario it's reaching crisis levels ... I'm not saying that everybody that fails to turnout in an election does so through some thought-out position of rejecting electoral politics, but at the same time the growth of that constituency of non-voters shows that more and more people are just believing whoever you vote in gives you more of the same, and who can really argue with that position? It's so palpably true. So, first of all, I think the extent to which they're in control of the population shouldn't be overstated, but the second thing is that Chiapas in 1994 was a bit of a watershed ... [and] what's continued to emerge with set backs, with ebbs and flows, with 9/11 creating huge problems along the way ... [is] a conscious opposition that really names the enemy, sees itself increasingly as part of a global movement, rejects the antics of futile protest, and looks for ways to actually fight against this capitalist neoliberal agenda and turn it back ... That is emerging in some of the First World countries and you see it here in Toronto with OCAP's work, and you see it with many other organizations ... and you see it, of course, in some of the explosive movements in the oppressed countries that have been absolutely devastating in their importance. You see it in the clear and growing resistance to the ANC in South Africa; you see everywhere that people are continuing to work on building an opposition that can't be bought, that isn't bureaucratized, and doesn't come to

the table and have discussions – when the labour leaders and the NGOs sit down and have these discussions with the enemy they share a repugnance and a hatred and a dread of that movement. So, I mean, I think it's there, and it's time is coming ... in the sense that neoliberalism isn't a fad or isn't a phase for the corporations and the governments. It's about the kind of future that they're trying to build and there's no room anymore for anything approaching ... the post-war settlement of limited concessions and relative compromise. That's all going out the window and the model is more and more economic and social austerity, but also physical repression, and that's going to be the model that we're going to be confronting, and that's going to get masses of people enormously angry. When you have even modestly sized organizations on the ground that have a body of experience in that kind of explosive context, the potential for decisive social resistance and even ultimately social revolution ... is enormous.

As John asserts here, OCAP is an organization which seeks to participate in a collective effort to cultivate conditions for powerful social resistance and, ultimately, to realize radical social change. The manner in which this change is envisioned is not one that involves the seizure of institutions that are seen as crumbling and largely bereft of popular legitimacy. Instead, organizations must exist that do not seek to siphon off energy from popular movements or to discipline the 'unruly masses' but rather that serve to facilitate the creative and effective channelling of popular outrage into radical social change. This is not to take the perspectives offered by the activists and organizers in OCAP with respect to the possible dimensions of future struggle at face value; it is, however, to offer these perspectives as compelling insights and histories into the dimensions of grass-roots anti-capitalist struggle voiced by those intimately involved with it on a daily basis.

The histories of OCAP's organizing and mobilizing in poor communities in Toronto, Ontario, provides an excellent window onto the ways in which northern activists are working to cultivate new and radical political subjectivities and forms of struggle upon political terrains that are far from fully formed. The significance of these histories is compounded by the fact that not only are there self-identified parallels between groups like OCAP and the Zapatistas but that activists and organizers involved with OCAP self-consciously position themselves as elements of a larger terrain of transnational struggle. While these positionings may only be the reflections of activists as opposed to concrete evidence of processes of interchange and connection, they nevertheless point to an emerging political consciousness and subjectivity that seeks to locate itself both in and beyond its immediate location. As Mac Scott of OCAP noted:

> There are grass-roots groups doing really creative bottom-up kind of stuff all over ... In New York you've got DRUM (Desis Rising Up and Moving), a whole community that you don't even have as much here of people of colour, immigrant organizations working together under a common banner of 'Third World within' to fight for really revolutionary change. Also in New York there's the CAAAV, the Committee Against Anti-Asian Violence ... You have grass-roots movements like the Zapatistas in Chiapas, the MST [Brazil's Landless Workers Movement] and the different landless movements in different parts of South America; there's a really amazing Korean immigrant workers movement now in South Korea ... there's amazing stuff happening in India, remnants of the Communist Party there turning away from there and doing really amazing stuff, or ... the Narmada Dam movement there which is coming directly out of communities ... there are movements all over the place. Hawaii's got Indigenous movements ... you've got grass-roots workers movements in the state of Florida organizing against the anti-union laws down there which require a vote every year to keep a union shop ... we're all over, I just think we're scattered ... The state is particularly well-armed right now, especially in the form of the United States, the global disparities are getting more and more [extreme], and I think it's really hard for grass-roots movements to communicate across the globe and organize together ... The PGA's actually done an amazing job of trying to overcome that in a really democratic, grass-roots way over the last eight to nine years ... but even still, it's tough ... None of us have any money, we can't fly people around like the big NGOs ... but there's groups like OCAP, even more radical than OCAP, all over the place and even more in touch with their constituencies. I think we do really well – there's groups better than us, and there's groups worse than us, and there's lots of groups similar to us all over. Like that book says, we're everywhere.

As significant as the list of movements that Mac provides here is, even more significant is the conscious articulation of a global terrain of political struggle expressed here. While this by no means signifies an imminent transnational – let alone global – revolutionary movement against capital, such articulations do point to a growing awareness of the interconnectedness and relevance of a multitude of others in struggle who do not necessarily walk beneath the same banners, desire identical goals, or employ the same means. It is the tendency towards a radically multiple political subjectivity that can be anti-capitalist without being unified that is provocative here.

Mike DesRoches reflected even more explicitly upon the nature of this emerging and explicit global consciousness amongst movements which, while scattered, nevertheless are engaged in amplifying their struggles through communication and interconnection in ways that appear to mark new perspectives on political action and possibility:

> In terms of the anti-globalization movement, I definitely have talked about the problems that it had in North America, but ... people talk about it being dead now and don't look at the sort of opportunities that it's presented to us right now ... OCAP is in regular correspondence with a migrants union in South Korea, homeless encampments in the south of Japan, the anti-eviction campaigns in South Africa [and various] European movements, and there's things like the Peoples' Global Action network, which is a bit weak in North America but has facilitated people communicating from around the world ... OCAP is somewhat easily isolated in Toronto 'cause there's very few organizations that would support the type of work that OCAP does, but OCAP is a fairly small organization that exists in the context of Toronto, of Canada, but there's links made with the MST. We met with Stedile from the MST last year and the fact is that [there are] movements [and] organizations that [share] the approach of the Zapatistas, the approach of OCAP. Radical, militant organizations that are actively defending communities around the world exist in every country, in every major city, and just the fact that those organizations and movements are talking to each other and learning from each other is something that didn't exist before ... The fact that these global movements are communicating with each other and coordinating with each other and building trust and ... gaining inspiration from each other [means the] movements are much better suited now and much stronger in terms of supporting each other and in terms of coordinating with each other than they have been since the 1960s when there was ... a more coordinated international student movement ... That's another thing that people need to remember, the possibilities and capabilities are greater now and that every round of fight that we go through we're constantly getting stronger, even as it may visibly seem that we're getting weaker ... there's always steps forward that are taking place.

Once again, Mike's comment does not speak to an accomplished fact, it does not describe a revolutionary movement or subjectivity that is fully present; rather, it alludes to a rhizomatic history of connection that is occurring on a partially visible terrain of transnational action that is being brought into being by a multitude of diverse struggles and movements and that was initially given shape by the resonance of Zapatismo transnationally. Whether this tendency, this possibility will yield subjectivities and terrains of action capable of fomenting radical sociopolitical and economic change on a transnational scale will depend on the collective effort of people in struggle to do more than simply imagine it or to conceive of it but to actually begin to build it.

Tissues of Communication and a Tear in the Fabric of the Present: The Resonance of Zapatismo and Big Noise Tactical

Both Peoples' Global Action and the Ontario Coalition Against Poverty represent compelling and complex instances of Zapatismo's transnational resonance. On different terrains, both PGA and OCAP have worked to build powerful and militant manifestations of anti-capitalist struggle. In PGA's case this project emerged out of the resonance of Zapatismo and the Zapatista-inspired Encuentros; in OCAP's case this project is grounded in community-based organizing and struggle that connected with Zapatismo through the histories of individual activists and the increasing interconnectedness of OCAP to other anti-capitalist struggles globally. But in addition to these examples of anti-capitalist networking and mobilizing, the transnational resonance of Zapatismo has also had considerable and unanticipated effects at the intersection of culture and politics, producing other rhizomatic histories. Big Noise Tactical, a radical filmmaking collective based in New York City, is perhaps one of the most interesting examples of the unanticipated consequences of the resonance of Zapatismo. Big Noise produced *Zapatista*, their first film, in 1998. This would be followed by a number of other feature documentaries, including *This Is What Democracy Looks Like* (2000) and *The Fourth World War* (2003), in addition to a host of 'tactical media' pieces produced in collaboration with other artists/activists focusing on a diverse set of events and issues relating to the global anti-capitalist/global justice movement. Big Noise Tactical was also a part of the first Independent Media Center video team at the WTO protests in Seattle in 1999, providing unprecedented independent media coverage of the 'Battle of Seattle.' The members of Big Noise Tactical, very explicitly, do not situate themselves as 'documentary-makers,' 'artists,' or 'filmmakers'; indeed, as they assert:

We are not filmmakers producing and distributing our work. We are rebels, crystallizating radical community and weaving a network of skin and images, of dreams and bone, of solidarity and connection against the isolation, alienation and cynicism of capitalist decomposition.

We are tactical because our media is a part of movements, imbedded in a history of struggle. Tactical because we are provisional, plural, polyvocal. Tactical because it would be the worst kind of arrogance to believe that our media had some ahistorical power to change the world – its only life is inside of movements – and they will hang our images on the walls of their banks if our movements do not tear their banks down. (Big Noise Tactical, 'About Us,' n.d.)

This radical perspective inspires the powerful films of Big Noise Tactical. These pieces seek not to simply document events but to participate in the formation of new subjectivities, new ways of understanding the worlds that make up the world, and to facilitate the emergence of new possibilities of connection and of struggle.

The origins of Big Noise Tactical are intimately connected to Zapatismo. As I have already related earlier in this work, Rick Rowley, one of the founding members of this collective, found himself in Mexico in 1995, just as the Zapatista uprising was once more shaking the country and the world. The uprising and what it represented constituted a moment of radical change for Rick. Reflecting upon the connections between this and the formation of Big Noise Tactical, Rick explained during our conversation in September 2004:

So, we all accepted that invitation to become Zapatistas and we returned to the United States as Zapatistas ... looking for what that might mean in the North and trying to learn from their example of struggle, you know take it seriously, not just as an inspiration but to learn from their tactics and their strategy. So one of the things that was most resonant to us at that moment was ... the famous Zapatista line 'Our word is our weapon,' armed with our word and sticks against this machine, we're winning, and so we thought about what our word would look like in the North ... and we didn't think that communiqués and children's stories and poems in the left-wing papers in the States was the move that would make sense. We thought video made sense as a language that could circulate ... could move through these circuits of American culture ... None of us had ever held video cameras before [or] had any film training but we got credit cards and we bought cameras and went down and started to shoot *Zapatista*, and so that was the beginning of Big Noise, that was the beginning of the work that followed, the work that I've done since then. We've never thought of ourselves as filmmakers but as Zapatistas looking for forms of struggle that make sense in the North.

Rick and others at Big Noise Films have found ways to not simply 'import' Zapatismo to the U.S. but also to find in its resonance meaning for struggles here. Through Zapatismo's resonance, Big Noise Tactical has engaged in the innovative process of interpreting and materializing this resonance in ways that are capable of moving powerfully and dynamically through the 'circuits of American culture.'

But why film? What precisely does the medium of film and the image provide access to, particularly in 'First World' countries like Canada and the United States? Patrick Reinsborough of the smartMeme Strategy and Training Project – an initiative not affiliated with Big Noise but whose project to intervene in capitalism 'at the point of assumption' makes for clear parallels here – spoke to the necessity of 'symbolic' and 'mythological' struggle in our conversation during the winter of 2004:

> Around much of the world and in many marginalized communities in the United States ... coercion is maintained through physical brutality, whether it's the nightsticks of police or the brutality of the paycheque and the factory, but for many people in the United States the coercion that keeps them in line with the system is less about physical brutality and more of an ideological coercion, a mythological coercion.

The coercion exercised by corporate news and entertainment media, educational curricula increasingly tailored to meet the needs of capital, and the neoliberal dogma continually repeated by government and the right wing, 'market-oriented' think tanks produce 'control mythologies' that effectively constrain people's ability to even imagine how the world might look different (Reinsborough 2004). In order to combat these mythologies, people must be convinced that they have the power to act in the world in ways not directed solely towards narrow self-gratification through consumption. Rick Rowley elaborated on this point when he described the principle behind Big Noise Tactical and their use of film as a medium capable of reminding people of their own collective capacity to act powerfully and purposefully:

> We began with the understanding that no one needs to be convinced that the world's fucked up ... No one needs to be convinced that they're living

a less than human existence and that there's terrible violent things happening that they're probably complicit and implicated in, that their government is doing terrible things, that the media is lying to them and that they don't really like the police ... Nobody needs to be convinced of any of these things. What people do need to be convinced of is that they have the power to take control of their own lives, they have the power to change it ... The system can produce victim films ... the CBC can fund a film whose message about Chiapas is 'Oh these poor Indigenous are getting cut up down there and ... somehow vaguely it's your fault.' The CBC can do that. The television news in the States can show you starving kids in Africa ... and can even make you feel guilty about it, but what they will not do is tell stories of people who are successfully challenging the system and are building new worlds in this world. So, that's what all of our films do ... we don't make films about suffering or about victims, we make films about powerful groups of people who are successfully transforming this world and that are invitations for everyone to become part of these things.

The story of Big Noise Tactical is a powerful rhizomatic history of Zapatismo's resonance, even more so because the films of Big Noise have circulated widely both within and outside of global anti-capitalist and global justice struggles, creating powerful rhizomatic connections between people, movements, and political imaginations. In essence, the films of Big Noise Tactical have become dynamic vehicles for the dissemination of radical political imaginations globally; they are the weapons and tools for shattering the ideological encirclement generated by the spectacle-making machines at the service of global elites.

Jacquie Soohen of Big Noise Tactical reflected upon the resonance of Zapatismo and its consequences for herself and for her involvement in Big Noise during our conversation in the fall of 2004. Building upon Rick's comments about the search for weapons that would make sense within struggles in the North, Jacquie elaborated upon the connections between politics, culture, and media and their intersection with Zapatismo from the vantage point of her own experience:

So, [I was] hearing about the Zapatistas and it began to leak through ... I first met Rick and a few of the other people from Big Noise, they'd just come back from one shoot in Mexico, and hearing about it and just being amazed that you could take that inspiration, the idea of victory, the idea of standing up for something and fighting and winning and then also hearing it through stories ... You knew that the demos didn't work, you knew that it had to be something else; it had to be something, and it had to be something about taking possession, beyond identity politics, and taking possession of a history that was both your own and expanded beyond your identity boundaries that were clearly marked for you inside a world of individualistic capitalism ... So then I went down for the second half of that shoot and again hadn't even thought about making films, that's not what I'd ever trained to do or even thought about doing, but when we had *Zapatista* that was the thing ... We started thinking about this and imagining this, how is our word our weapon? It was when we finally started screening the film that it began to make sense ... as a weapon and became something that we decided to keep doing as long as it made sense, because [we would] go places and [we] weren't talking to people who had, for the most part, ever even heard of Zapatismo or, for the most part, weren't politically active. It wasn't like they were audiences of activists; they were people who came because Rage [Against the Machine] was in the film or different musical groups, or because it was sexy in the way that it was presented or something like that, [but then] people were so moved by it ... [and] we came to realize that it was the weapon that we could use and something we could give over to a larger movement ... I think we realize more and more that it's obvious no film is going to change anything and ... we say this over and over again ... it's arrogant to believe that any film or any piece of work like that is ever going to change things by itself 'cause that's not how it functions. All of these things function inside of movements ... [When] that film came out, we were working in tune with a whole bunch of people who were being inspired by the Zapatistas because it was so different and new and because it was a victory that was something that people were winning, and it was so anachronistic, supposedly ... We came to realize that we had to start working inside a movement ... and then things exploded from there in terms of how we saw the movements take on the different parts of Zapatismo but also become something different [in] their own local places and [we] felt [that] build-up of movements that has gone on.

These eloquent reflections offered by Rick and Jacquie of Big Noise Tactical illuminate some of the most interesting contours of the rhizomatic resonance of Zapatismo. While many NGOs or solidarity groups have either disappeared or turned their attention to other issues in the years since the uprising, Zapatismo has also inspired activists to search for new ways of practising politics in their own spaces. The Zapatista use of stories as a means of communicating alternative realities and possibilities is something that has found powerful resonance both within and outside of Mexico, and it is something that activists and even the broader public working and living in so-called post-industrial societies such as Canada and the U.S. can relate to intimately. Even as neoliberal capitalism and the political and economic elites benefiting from it have increasingly turned to their own myth-making apparatuses to suppress dissent and to maintain their ideological encirclement, those looking to create alternative political spaces and practices have similarly rediscovered the importance of culture, stories, and myths and have used them not only as weapons of resistance but as tools for creation.

Focusing explicitly upon the guiding socio-cultural stories of our time as well as the grounded and tangible action necessary to materialize their effects marks a profound shift in the terrain of political action from analyses emphasising relations of production, historical teleologies, or social evolutionary schema. Jacquie Soohen articulated the shift in the dimensions and nature of political action over the past several decades and in relation to the impact of Zapatismo upon it when she noted:

> So much of the activism in the 1970s and the 1980s and this whole idea of solidarity activism was [that] if you just show the truth then that will overcome something and ... it's about speaking truth to power, but ... I think we're entering a whole different time. The Zapatistas made it clear, too, that it wasn't just about this media blockade, it wasn't just about the information not getting out there, it was about this ideological encirclement and how do you break that? So in the same way the films are not about speaking truth to power in that way ... especially *The Fourth World War*, ... it's about creating myths inside this movement and connecting connections and connectivities, like a connection-making machine ... between these different movements and also speaking in a way that shows our humanity and the world that we want things that are all beautiful and that create our own language. So we started to create our own language in different ways and touch people in different ways as opposed to taking the language of the powerful and using it to just show information, because if there's anything we've learned, and we learn more everyday ... it's not just about the information, especially now, it's about how it's interpreted and used and how people are made to feel connected or disconnected from it.

As Jacquie makes clear here, the issue is not one of not enough information, nor is it about getting 'the right' information; rather, what is at issue is the way that meaning is made and this is not merely an individual matter, it is systemic. Indeed, Jacquie's notion of Big Noise Tactical's films operating as a 'connection-making machine' is evocative of the rhizomatic histories of Zapatismo's transnational resonance. The power of Big Noise Tactical's work, as with Zapatismo's resonance transnationally, is not in its subversive content precisely but rather resides in the fact that these phenomena are directed towards the cultivation of new stories, new fabrics of communication that are capable of cultivating new political terrains and subjectivities. This does not mean that such possibilities are bound to be automatically emancipatory or that they will be unconflicted, but it does point to the presence of new opportunities for political action.

As Jacquie asserts, Big Noise Tactical's work is also informed by particular attitudes towards information and its role in social change. Jacquie notes that 'if there's anything we've learned, and we learn more everyday ... it's not just about the information, especially now, it's about how it's interpreted and used and how people are made to feel connected or disconnected from it.' This is particularly true for 'First World' countries whose societies are marked by 'post-industrial' developments in information technology. The issue, of course, is not about 'getting the facts straight' or 'speaking the truth' – much less about the amount of 'information' – but rather about how this information is interpreted. Rick Rowley elaborated on this point in a way that illuminates not only this dynamic but also the relationship between it and the resonance of Zapatismo:

> It's the difference between giving facts and telling the truth. The best example that I've ever heard is the Rodney King trial ... there's many levels of truth, the deep truth is that the LAPD is racist and they go out and they kill black men when they want to ... The truth of that moment is that they went and they beat some defenseless guy within an inch of his life. The facts that were presented in the courtroom were still frames, one-thirtieth of a second, pulled out of context, showed over, those are facts ... that's the image that was recorded on that magnetic tape; they didn't mess with it, they didn't lie with PhotoShop or anything ... they didn't not give the facts, they used facts to lie. The truth is not something that is just in the facts and in the information, the truth is something that has to be fought for, it's something that has to be defended ... so when the Zapatistas say 'named are we now we cannot die,' they're saying we've conquered a place in reality, we exist now because our movement has made a name for us that circulates, that our name echoes in the rocks, our name resonates inside of movements all

over the world, and so we've conquered those realities and we exist. It's not a war of information, it's a war of dreams and images that ... animate information, make that information true, or make it a lie.

What makes information true or not true? It is no more or less than the dreams that inhabit it and that make it so. The radical right in the United States has not convinced the citizens of that country to support their agenda through a wealth of rigorously analysed information or 'objective' and 'empirical' evidence; they have succeeded in gaining power because they have presented a story that is, for the time being, more compelling than those of their opponents. The fact that their mainstream opponents tell much the same story, of course, does not help contest this dominance. Approaching radical political struggle from this direction makes the importance of stories and the need to establish and defend political possibilities, opportunities, and meaning all the more vital.

Big Noise Tactical's film *The Fourth World War,* a name which is an explicit reference to the concept of the Fourth World War first articulated by Subcomandante Insurgente Marcos and the Zapatistas (see Subcomandante Insurgente Marcos 2002b), is a film about the power of people acting collectively to change their worlds. It is also very clearly not a film that aims to 'tell the truth' or to 'give information,' but one that seeks to tell an entirely new kind of story. Beginning at the moment of 'capitalist decomposition,' in Rick Rowley's words, *The Fourth World War* traces the global circulation of anti-capitalist and radically democratic struggles 'for humanity and against neoliberalism.' It is also a profound example of the materialization of a transnational political imagination deeply inspired by Zapatismo that aims not to reproduce Zapatismo but to tell the histories of an emerging global movement that is self-consciously global and yet everywhere takes on its own unique contours. In this sense, the film and the relationships it conveys and helps cultivate (between political possibilities, between struggles, between the filmmakers and audiences, within audiences, etc.) become a mechanism for communication and the proliferation of radical possibilities. As Rick Rowley explained during our conversation:

Films don't change the world, movements of people do, and our films succeed or fail inasmuch ... as they participate in movements that successfully challenge this system ... On one level we [are] a tissue for communication across geographic, political, cultural distance; we're a tissue through which it is possible for rebellious and revolutionary images to circulate, for models and tactics to circulate ... but we're [also] part of a process that movements are already undertaking ... It was amazing in these last couple of years to work on *The Fourth World War* and to see the degree to which movements are already in communication with one another and are self-consciously articulating themselves as global. I mean the piqueteros in Argentina, you can't talk to them about their struggle without having them talk to you about Chiapas, and in South Africa ... in the headquarters for the anti-eviction campaign in Cape Town, they have pictures of piquetero road blockades in Argentina on their walls, and in Korea, they're looking closely and have been studying movements in South and Central America and Africa for a really long time to look for models of struggle against neoliberalism that they could adapt to their location ... We're run through by each other's examples and we're given strength and hope by each other's examples of victory ... One of the things I think that movements here now, in the States especially now, need to remember is that we're a global movement and we're a historical movement, that ... we're tied to people outside of our borders and to moments outside of our time. It might look really bleak in the States right now, the political landscape there, but our movement has just overthrown a couple of governments in Bolivia and is ... still keeping the street hot in Argentina and has defended Chávez against two CIA coups ... We're part of something much bigger than any state that's locked down like that, so I mean one of our most important roles is to remind people, over and over again, to fight against what I think ... is the primary or most disempowering aspect of capitalist culture and the way that capitalist culture reproduces itself, which is producing the feeling in each and every person that they're alone, that they're an isolated consumer who's capable of winning victories [but] only alone ... [on your own] you can get yourself a good education, get yourself a good job, raise yourself out of poverty ... The arc that *The Fourth World War* takes is that it begins at this moment of capitalist decomposition where everyone's alone ... it begins in the moment after war dissolves every form of human connection that you have and tries to bring the audience to a point at the end where Marcos ends the film saying, 'You will no longer be you, now you are us.' I mean you're part of a global movement of people and you're connected to human beings all over the planet in a way that is deeper than the connection that exists between a consumer and a producer, between an oppressor and the oppressed, or between a victim and a criminal ... When those kinds of connections of solidarity are successfully articulated, things can change.

Across arbitrary political borders, across geographic space and time, across cultural distance, the resonance of Zapatismo and the radical images of Big Noise Tactical have begun to build bridges of understanding, connection, and political practice. Beyond this, these experiences and this consciousness are beginning to materialize the possibility for the articulation of a new political terrain and a new political practice rooted in a mutual recognition of dignity and humanity, an affirmation of diversity, and the reclamation of the capacity to build a world capable of holding many worlds precisely because we are the only subjects truly capable of bringing it into being.

During our conversation, Rick Rowley offered a particularly penetrating analysis of the resonance of Zapatismo transnationally and of its symbolic and even mythological functions both inside and outside of Mexico. Rick's interpretation speaks strongly to the influence of Zapatismo upon Big Noise Tactical and its approach to radical political action, but it also provides a compelling analogy with which to appreciate the power of resonance and its attendant political imaginations:

Zapatismo's gone through stages ... It began as a guerrilla, like any other guerrilla ... a couple of decades ago ... and then it became an army sometime before 1994, and then it appeared to the world as an army, no longer as a guerrilla, but it always, from the moment of its appearance, had two different parallel functions ... On the ground, inside Chiapas, it's an army that represents a territory and is defending a territory and a people, and it has political structures there that ... are something like a state, you know, a good state, a *buen gobierno*, not a *mal gobierno* ... and [the Zapatistas] have development programs that are cool and nice and not part of global capital, and they have an education and health system and they have a network and an army. Outside of Chiapas, in the context of Mexico, [Zapatismo] functions as a guerrilla because it isn't an army that's trying to take over the country ... it's a guerrilla that is always a provocation ... I would say the difference between a guerrilla and an army is that an army represents a real on the ground ... When it functions best, it is a transparent servant of an already formed people, a people who is self-consciously articulating its name as a people; it represents the real. The guerrilla is a tear in the fabric of the real, a guerrilla is speaking for a people who do not yet exist ... When Che first theorized the guerrilla ... there were moments, Che said, when revolution [was] objectively impossible by Marxist standards [because] there's no class that is organized as a class, there's no nation that has articulated itself as a nation, there's people who are decomposed individuals who do not yet have any imagination of themselves as connected or as people who have any kind of power. So, in that moment ... the guerrilla's function is to create the possibility of there being an army; it's to create the possibility of there being a class or a nation, so the guerrilla emerges to crystallize a people out of the late stage of capitalist decomposition. In the rest of Mexico and the rest of the world, that's how Zapatismo functions ... it's a guerrilla outside of Chiapas, it's a tear in the present through which we need to be able to allow ourselves to imagine a kind of collectivity against the isolation and alienation of capital and to imagine a kind of power.

The guerrilla of Zapatismo is a provocation, a transgression. Upon a transnational and even global terrain it offers a glimpse of that which is not yet constituted or fully formed but which is a tendency, a possibility. Rick's assertion that outside of Chiapas, Zapatismo is a 'tear in the fabric of the real,' one that allows us 'to imagine ... a kind of collectivity against the isolation and alienation of capital and to imagine a kind of power,' also alludes to the deeply intertwined relationship between imagination and resonance that I have sought to trace throughout this work. Significantly, Rick's analysis also makes explicit the distinction between Zapatismo 'on the ground' in Chiapas and a transnationalized Zapatismo, a distinction which is not always apparent in the discourse of the activists with whom I worked. As I have argued, while these expressions of Zapatismo should not be seen either as a binary of authentic/inauthentic or strictly segregated from one another, Rick's analysis does illustrate the differential manner in which Zapatismo operates across geographical, socio-cultural, and political space. Most significantly, this reflection points to the possibility not only of imagining new terrains of political action, new histories of struggle through which to live new subjectivities, but most importantly to the recovery of the human creative and generative force that has been appropriated and encapsulated by the ideological encirclement and control mythologies of neoliberal capitalism.

In this chapter I have explored what I consider to be some of the most experimental, untraditional, and provocative histories of the transnational resonance of Zapatismo. The histories presented here mark terrains that diverge considerably from those explored in the preceding chapter, in many ways, they mark the most rhizomatic manifestations of the transnational resonance of Zapatismo. By engaging the histories of Peoples' Global Action, the Ontario Coalition Against Poverty, and Big

Noise Tactical, I have sought to provide an illumination of new terrains of radical struggle, the subjectivities who inhabit them, and the imaginations that inspire them. In no way is this analysis meant to be comprehensive; indeed, there are a multiplicity of groups that have interpreted the transnational resonance of Zapatismo in new and challenging ways that exceeded the scope of my present project. However, in engaging in this analysis, I have sought to explicitly demonstrate that the most powerful and potentially fruitful manifestations of the transnational resonance of Zapatismo lie well beyond the horizon of traditional solidarity activism or even what Keck and Sikkink (1998) have called 'transnational advocacy networks.' These manifestations of resonance are so powerful precisely because they transgress the bounds of transnational activism as it has traditionally been envisioned and practised. Rather than working according to more familiar solidaristic models – an activism which is, of course, useful and important in its own right – these groups have attempted to interpret the resonance of Zapatismo according to their own contexts and struggles. They have attempted to adapt the most powerful lessons of Zapatismo to their own terrains and, in so doing, have created the possibility for the emergence of new terrains, subjectivities, and imaginations of political action.

What will become of these possibilities remains to be seen, none of them are in any way fully formed or immediately present, but the boundaries have been transgressed and the opportunities exist for them to be realized. All that truly remains is for them to be collectively fought for. As Jacquie Soohen of Big Noise remarked, 'It's not a factual thing to say the movement started in Chiapas on January 1st, 1994; it's a position to take ... When we locate our history there, when we locate our beginnings and our roots there, we're locating this movement in a space that is functioning as a guerrilla in a space of imagination, in a space of possibility.' The space of the imagination and of the possible is what Zapatismo has reinvigorated and the resonance it has generated amongst activists in Canada and the United States is something that carries with it responsibility as much as it does a promise. Choices and decisions, as much as hope and possibility, carry with them obligations; as Rick Rowley of Big Noise affirmed, 'Beginnings and endings are always tactical decisions. They're dates you choose and they're not justified by what happened before, they're justified by the actions you take later, so it's not enough just to say, you have to fight to make it true that a new world began the 1st of January 1994.'

Conclusion: Globalizing Hope

That is what this is all about. It is war. A war against humanity. The globalization of those who are above us is nothing more than a global machine that feeds on blood and defecates in dollars.

In the complex equation that turns death into money, there is a group of humans who command a very low price in the global slaughterhouse. We are the indigenous, the young, the women, the children, the elderly, the homosexuals, the migrants, all those who are different.

That is to say, the immense majority of humanity.

This is a world war of the powerful who want to turn the planet into a private club that reserves the right to refuse admission. The exclusive luxury zone where they meet is a microcosm of their project for the planet, a complex of hotels, restaurants, and recreation zones protected by armies and police forces.

All of us are given the option of being inside this zone, but only as servants. Or we can remain outside of the world, outside of life. But we have no reason to obey and accept this choice between living as servants or dying. We can build a new path, one where living means life with dignity and freedom. To build this alternative is possible and necessary. It is necessary because on it depends the future of humanity.

This future is up for grabs in every corner of each of the five continents. This alternative is possible because around the world people know that liberty is a word which is often used as an excuse for cynicism.

Brothers and sisters, there is dissent over the projects of globalization all over the world. Those above, who globalize conformism, cynicism, stupidity, war, destruction and death. And those below who globalize rebellion, hope, creativity, intelligence, imagination, life, memory, and the construction of a world that we can all fit in, a world with democracy, liberty and justice.

From 'The Death Train of the WTO,'
Subcomandante Insurgente Marcos (2004c)

In August 2004, one year after the birth of the Zapatista Caracoles, Subcomandante Insurgente Marcos issued a series of communiqués entitled 'Reading a Video' that detailed the successes and failures of the Zapatista struggle. In the third part of this series entitled 'Three Shoulders,' Marcos notes that 'the contemporary history of the Zapatista indigenous communities also has its founding legend: those who inhabit these lands now have three shoulders. To the two shoulders that the usual human beings have, the zapatistas have added a third: that of the national and international "civil societies."' This 'third shoulder,' writes Marcos, has been an integral element of the Zapatista struggle, providing the movement in Chiapas with invaluable support and doing so not on the basis of charity but on the basis of a shared commitment. As Marcos (2004e) explains:

We believe that we have been fortunate. From its beginnings, our movement has had the support and kindness of hundreds of thousands of persons on the five continents. This kindness and this support has not been withdrawn, even in the face of personal limitations, of distances, of differences of culture and language, borders and passports, of differences in political concepts, of the obstacles put up by the federal and state governments, the military checkpoints, harassment and attacks, of the threats and attacks by paramilitary groups, of our mistrust, our lack of understanding of the other, of our clumsiness.

No, in spite of all of that (and of many other things which everyone knows) the 'civil societies' of Mexico and the world have worked because of, for and with us.

And they have done so not out of charity, nor out of pity, nor out of political fashion, nor out of a desire for publicity, but because they have, in one way or another, embraced a cause which is still, for us, great: the building of a world where all worlds fit, a world, that is, which carries the hearts of everyone. (n.p.)

Here Marcos reflects on what this shoulder of civil society has meant to the Zapatistas in their struggle on the ground in Chiapas. In this work,

I have attempted to demonstrate what the Zapatistas have meant to political activists in Canada and the United States. Beyond 'meaning,' I have sought to explore the resonance of Zapatismo transnationally through an exploration of the rhizomatic histories its resonance has produced in the North. If anything should emerge from this analysis, it should be that 'resonance' is a much more complex and dynamic process than it might initially appear. However, it is my hope that this analysis contributes much more than simply an awareness of the complexity of this phenomenon.

The Fourth World War and the Political Imagination of Zapatismo

Today, according to the Zapatistas, the time and space which we occupy is that of 'the Fourth World War.' While the Third World War – more commonly known as the 'Cold War' – ended with the collapse of the Soviet Union and the ascendancy of neoliberal capitalism, the Fourth World War marks a time and space when global neoliberal capitalism has ushered in 'a new world war,' a war against humanity (Subcomandante Insurgente Marcos 2004b, 257). The socio-political challenge today is therefore not a proposition positing capitalism against communism, it is rather one of a geopolitical system and its arsenal of agents, armies, and weapons – economic, political, social, cultural, military, intellectual, etc. – versus the vast majority of humanity. Although the majorities continue to be marginalized, repressed, and exploited, they also actively seek to build alternatives to this system. This is not a uniform or homogeneous struggle, neither is it one which is engaged in by a discrete or distinct group of people. There is no 'correct' revolutionary line, although there are of course dangers, challenges, and pitfalls everywhere. It is a struggle marked by uncertainty, just as it is one marked by hope. It is a struggle that is being joined by people all over the world seeking to affirm their autonomy and interconnectedness and their will to live in a world capable of holding many worlds.

The politico-temporal notion of the Fourth World War provides a powerful example of what the nature of the transnationalized political imagination of Zapatismo rests upon. As I have endeavoured to demonstrate throughout this work, the subject addressed by the Zapatistas, particularly outside the borders of Chiapas, is not any unitary figure, it is rather humanity in all its radical diversity; it is a multitude. The particular manifestations of the transnational resonance of Zapatismo realize themselves in each place differently, producing a multiplicity of rhizomatic histories that, to be effective, must take on the most pressing contours of the struggle against the Fourth World War faced in that place while remaining open and interconnected to the struggles of others. Through a tremendous array of actions – ranging from the uprising of 1 January 1994, to the Intercontinental Encuentro for Humanity and Against Neoliberalism in 1996, to the March of Indigenous Dignity in 2001, to the building of Zapatista territory in rebellion and the consolidation of the Caracoles in 2003 – the Zapatistas have worked to engage and facilitate a newly emergent terrain of political struggle. In so doing, they have also engaged and facilitated the emergence of new kinds of political subjectivities capable of inhabiting this new terrain. But perhaps most significantly of all, what makes these processes and engagements so compelling and important is that they have been joined by people from all over the world.

The transnational resonance of Zapatismo amongst activists in Canada and the United States is, as I have already asserted, a complex and multifaceted phenomenon. It speaks not only to the 'allure' of the Zapatistas themselves but also to the conditions and dynamics at work in the spaces and places which activists themselves inhabit. This is what makes each history of resonance unique. There are obviously distances between Zapatismo as it has been transnationalized and Zapatismo as it is lived on the ground in Chiapas. At the core of many speculative analyses of this 'distance' lie assumptions about the significance of Subcomandante Insurgente Marcos with respect to the larger movement. For some, Marcos is a savvy, cynical, egomaniacal manipulator, using and abusing the poor Indigenous peoples of Chiapas for his own political ambitions (see for example De la Colina 2002; Meyer 2002; Oppenheimer 2002). For others, Marcos is a critical communicator for the Zapatistas, a bridge between Indigenous and non-Indigenous worlds as well as between the grounded struggle of Zapatismo in Chiapas and struggles against neoliberalism and capitalism around the world (see for example Gilly 1998; Higgins 2000). Most recently, renewed speculation has been generated by Marcos's role as 'Delegate Zero' in the 'Other Campaign,' which paralleled the Mexican presidential campaign in 2006, seeking to build a broad-based non-electoral alternative 'from below.' Even some sympathetic observers of the movement read the Red Alert called by the EZLN and the Other Campaign in 2006 as signs of a growing rift between 'civil Zapatismo' and the 'political-military structure,' represented by Marcos (see Ross 2006). Others have characterized such speculation as just that and, drawing upon their experience supporting the Zapatista struggle, have convincingly demonstrated the continuing grass-roots, radically democratic character of the Zapatista movement (see Ross and Giordano 2006; see also Tenuto-Sanchez 2006).

Marcos's role as a communicator and strategist has been undeniably important to the Zapatista movement, particularly so in its transnational manifestations; however, over the years, critics of the movement have frequently sought to overemphasize Marcos's significance and downplay the agency of the movement's support bases and Indigenous leaders. The mainstream media outside of Mexico has also participated in the cult of personality surrounding Marcos, regularly misidenitfying him as *the leader* of the Zapatista movement and, implicitly and explicitly, equating the Zapatista struggle with Marcos's hypothesized personal political ambitions. Nevertheless, outside of these ideologically inspired controversies, one thing remains clear: according to the vast weight of analysis and documentation provided by people with knowledge of the context and of the movement itself, the Zapatista movement, its political trajectory, its goals and tactics, and its successes and failures have always rested with the women, men, and children who make up the movement and without whom no struggle – and certainly no political imagination or resonance – could exist.

Transnationally, Zapatismo is of course mediated by a variety of actors and mechanisms, Subcomandante Insurgente Marcos and his writings certainly central among them. Zapatismo is transmitted through communiqués reproduced in print and on the Internet; it is conveyed via DVDs and video and audio tapes; it is reflected upon – and often packaged – by journalists, 'reported back' by activists, and analysed by academics in a wealth of published material. The experience of Zapatista reality in Chiapas is also engaged by 'Zapatouristas' and solidarity activists travelling to Chiapas, either independently or as members of delegations organized by a host of organizations. None of these channels is 'neutral' in any sense and none is free from issues of romanticism, appropriation, misinterpretation, privilege, and power. Equally, the transnationalization of Zapatismo is not cynically reducible to any of the criticisms that arise from these issues. These histories of resonance are complex and need to be understood in their complexity if the opportunities they offer are to have any hope of becoming more than just possibilities and tendencies scattered across a transnational terrain of action.

At a time when the Left on a global scale found itself largely without direction and was confronted seemingly on all sides by the ascendancy of neoliberal capitalism, the Zapatistas provided a striking example of resistance and possibility. More than this, however, they reinvigorated a focus upon the connection between the political and the imagination; they renewed a belief in possibility, in hope, in the capacity for people to collectively imagine and construct a new kind of world. The discourse of Zapatismo, marked by a profound emphasis on concepts like democracy, dignity, justice, and liberty, challenged not only the narrow rationalizations of neoliberal dogma but also traditional ideas of 'revolution.' Accordingly – and inescapably – Zapatismo's resonance transnationally has had the greatest impact not necessarily upon the processes of political struggle in the North but on the way that political struggle is envisioned and imagined. Issues of consciousness are central here, and this is the space within which I have situated my own analytical engagement.

Throughout this work, I have examined the bases, mechanisms, and consequences of the transnational resonance of Zapatismo as well as the rhizomatic histories that have emerged from it. Resonance is not simply a romanticization of Other struggles, it emerges from the capacity of people to be able to not simply adopt the struggles of Others but to connect with them, to make sense of them in ways that are not divorced from the contexts within which they live and work. In this way, the transnational resonance of Zapatismo says as much about the socio-political contexts within which activists situate themselves as it does about Zapatismo itself. In Canada and the United States, recent years have seen a dramatic and steady decline in rates of voter participation as well as a growing cynicism on the part of large sectors of the population towards the political system. As official political channels and institutions increasingly come to be seen as the province of professionalized and elite 'representatives,' questions concerning alternatives to liberal representative democracy have acquired greater significance. These questions take on even greater significance in the face of often disappointing histories of radical political action in the North. In contrast to the alienation generated by these political structures, the deeply and radically democratic spirit of Zapatismo has served to remind people that there are paths to forge other than the ones offered to us by powerholders.

Furthermore, in a world consumed by the 'War on Terror' and run through by an increasing sense of global insecurity on political, economic, social, cultural, and ecological levels, Zapatismo has offered not a program for change, not a colour-coded map for revolutionary struggle, not another vanguard bent on showing people 'the way,' but has affirmed the capacity of people collectively to work together in order to build a future in which we are all able to fit. Hope, creativity, dignity, and a will to listen as well as to speak are the hallmarks of this political imagination. These principles have broken the ideological and mythical encirclement of neoliberal capitalism and the cynicism which it has so effectively generated in order to maintain control and to convince people that there is no alternative. The World Social Forum assertion that 'another world is possible' is only possible itself because of movements like that of the Zapatistas, who have repeatedly demonstrated that not only is another world possible, it is necessary if we are to live in dignified, autonomous, and interconnected ways.

Yet such resonance also demonstrates the 'double movement' of Zapatismo. In many ways, the transnationalized political imagination of Zapatismo is quite different from Zapatismo as it operates on the ground in Chiapas. This is not to contend that one manifestation is 'authentic' while the other is 'inauthentic'; rather, it is to say that the experience of Zapatismo is intimately connected to the contexts within which it is received. While Zapatismo in Chiapas has grown out of communities which have built and lived resistance for more than two decades now and is therefore expressive of a political practice and conceptualization that has emerged organically from these communities themselves, Zapatismo transnationally has been received, translated, and achieved resonance in markedly different ways. Zapatismo in Chiapas is constituted and lived by communities in resistance. Zapatismo transnationally – and particularly in Canada and the United States – has instead found resonance within people who have 'defected' from the system. This makes for markedly different histories of struggle. While Zapatismo in Chiapas may be thought of as a praxis, in Canada and the United States it might instead be conceived of as a principle of hope. In this way, it is an orienting and directing principle, akin to what Ernst Bloch would call a 'not-yet.'

Zapatismo, the Rhizome, and the Multitude

While the Zapatista communities and the EZLN have been the primary practitioners of Zapatismo on the ground in Chiapas and have directed this practice both towards building autonomy in the far southeast of Mexico and participating in a national struggle for 'democracy, justice, and liberty' for all Mexicans, 'transnationalized' Zapatismo has been conveyed via a variety of mechanisms and mediums and has been directed not towards building national struggles but rather towards building a global network of people joined in struggle 'for humanity and against neoliberalism.' The writings of Subcomandante Insurgente Marcos have played an absolutely central role in this 'transnational-ized' Zapatismo, as have information technologies such as DVDs and the Internet and the solidarity organizations that distribute information, provide the infrastructure for the circulation of Zapatismo transnationally, and even physically facilitate the connection between the Zapatistas and international supporters. This does mean that the character of transnational Zapatismo is somewhat different from the character of Zapatismo on the ground in Chiapas. It also means that while Zapatismo has acquired a special significance with respect to the global justice/global anti-capitalist movement, it has not always been unequivocally beneficial for the Zapatistas themselves.

As I have argued throughout this work, the resonance of Zapatismo transnationally is best understood as rhizomatic in nature. Zapatismo has inspired a tremendous diversity of political activism in the North, ranging from direct and relatively traditional solidarity actions to global anti-capitalist networks such as Peoples' Global Action to radical filmmaking collectives like Big Noise Tactical. It has also generated a wide array of political analyses on issues of 'power,' 'democracy,' 'autonomy,' 'justice,' 'liberty,' and 'dignity.' This work itself is a consequence of the rhizomatic resonance of Zapatismo. This means that the character and direction of this resonance, as well as its long-term consequences, are much more ambiguous than any simple cause-and-effect equation would allow us to predict. What is clear, however, is that this transnational resonance has inspired and provoked activists in Canada and the United States to think about political action differently and it has actually participated in the reshaping of the terrain of political struggle and the subjectivities which inhabit it. Denying the existence of a privileged place as 'historical subjects,' the Zapatistas forcefully reoriented conceptions of political struggle away from teleologies, or essentialized and reified identities, or a debilitating and politically ineffectual relativism, and instead focused upon expanding the political horizon of the possible. Zapatismo has sought to bring both memory and dream back into the political, and it has sought to invigorate a common struggle that must be lived in unique ways. As many of my research partners affirmed, without the Zapatista uprising and the wide-ranging influence of Zapatismo, the terrain of the global justice and global anti-capitalist struggle would look radically different today. In fact, I argue that the Zapatistas and their transnational resonance have actually taken part in the process of bringing what might be properly conceived of as a global multitude into being – a process that is far from complete today, to be sure, but which is nevertheless occurring more and more frequently as people consciously articulate and build their struggles in an interconnected and self-consciously globalized way.

Three Shoulders

If national and international civil society have functioned as a 'third shoulder' for the Zapatistas, then the Zapatistas have at least done as much for collectivities of activists in Canada and the United States. To say that the terrain of political struggle would look different today were it not for the Zapatista uprising is a fantastic understatement. Aside from the adoption of the rhetoric, iconography, and artefacts of the Zapatista struggle, the infusion of a deeply creative and inclusive sense of hope into radical politics since 1994 owes its presence in no small part to the resonance of Zapatismo. More than this, the reaffirmation that people's creative capacities are primary and the encapsulation, enclosure, and commodification practised by neoliberal capitalism on a global scale is parasitical – and not just something to be 'resisted' or 'overthrown' – is also a powerful feature of the Zapatistas' effect on radical political action in the North. And while the global justice/global anti-capitalist movement has apparently lost much of its strength in the years following 11 September 2001 and in the face of the temporally and spatially unlimited 'War on Terror,' as of this writing there are moves throughout the North and the South to reinvigorate the processes not only of resistance but also of alternative-building once again. Both Peoples' Global Action and the Social Forum process are entering phases of renewed activity and expansive mobilization, and grass-roots movements from all over the world are developing evermore fruitful and supportive links with one another. In Chiapas, the Zapatistas continue to consolidate autonomy and to build a reality marked by 'democracy, justice, and liberty.' This process has undergone yet another shift with the issuing of the 'Sixth Declaration of the Lacandón Jungle' and the initiation of a renewed stage of struggle at both the national and global level. These are processes not without their contradictions, but they are also moves that mark the opening of new and hopeful political horizons. While the economic-political machinery of neoliberal capitalism remains powerful, its power bears the marks of vast insecurity and ever-growing cynicism directed at it by large sectors of the populace. In Latin America, popular movements are unseating neoliberal and repressive governments, taking back productive capacity for people's needs as opposed to those of capital, and provoking a considerable degree of concern in Washington, DC.

None of this should be taken as a victory. Without popular mobilizations in the North, changing the socio-political and economic landscapes regionally let alone globally is difficult if not impossible to imagine. If the resonance of Zapatismo transnationally is to have any significant long-term effects, they will reside not only in a conceptual reformulation of power, democracy, and justice but also in the generation of truly popular and powerful people's movements – movements aimed not at narrowly protectionist or nationalist goals but at the possibility of bringing a new world into being, a world made of multiple worlds and marked by a deeply and directly democratic spirit that is rooted in the mutual recognition of dignity and a collective will to 'walk questioning.' Concretely, these northern movements will have to address serious issues of power and privilege as well as a rather dark history of romanticism, abandonment, and appropriation in order to engage in a politics of mutual struggle with those already fighting in other places. Issues of resource redistribution and the provision of a communicative infrastructure will also have to be seriously engaged in by northern activists if our struggles here are to meet the challenges they face and to join with others. The possibility and promise of the multitude is out there and others have already started to forge paths towards it – what will we do to meet them? This, then, is the greatest challenge and the greatest promise of the transnational resonance of Zapatismo: not to conquer the world but to make it anew. It is against the possibility and obligation of building a world in which many worlds fit that our success and the success of Zapatismo's transnationally resonant political imagination will ultimately be measured.

References

Adorno, Theodor, and Max Horkheimer. 1972. 'The Concept of Enlighten-ment.' In *Dialectic of Enlightenment*. Translated by John Cumming. New York: Herder and Herder.

Appadurai, Arjun. 1996. *Modernity at Large: Cultural Dimensions of Globalization*. Minneapolis: University of Minnesota Press.

Aridjis, Homero. 2002. 'Indian Is Beautiful.' In *The Zapatista Reader*, edited by Tom Hayden. New York: Thunder's Mouth Press.

Arquilla, John, and David Ronfeldt, eds. 2001. *Networks and Netwars: The Future of Terror, Crime, and Militancy*. Santa Monica: RAND.

Arquilla, John, Graham Fuller, Melissa Fuller, and David Ronfeldt. 1998. *The Zapatista Social Netwar in Mexico*. Santa Monica: RAND.

Ayres, Jeffrey M. 1998. *Defying Conventional Wisdom: Political Movements and Popular Contention against North American Free Trade*. Toronto: University of Toronto Press.

Bakhtin, Mikhail Mikhailovich. 1981. *The Dialogic Imagination*. Edited by Michael Holquist. Translated by Caryl Emerson and Michael Holquist. Austin: University of Texas Press.

Bandy, Joe, and Jackie Smith, eds. 2004. *Coalitions Across Borders: Transnational Protest and the Neoliberal Order*. Lanham: Rowman and Littlefield.

Barlow, Maude. 2005. *Too Close for Comfort: Canada's Future within Fortress America*. Toronto: McClelland and Stewart.

Barlow, Maude, and Tony Clarke. 2001. *Global Showdown: How the New Activists Are Fighting Global Corporate Rule*. Toronto: Stoddart.

Barthes, Roland. 1972. *Mythologies*. New York: Hill and Wang.

Benford, Robert, and David Snow. 1992. 'Master Frames and Cycles of Protest.' In *Frontiers in Social Movement Theory*, edited by Aldon Morris and Carol McClurg Mueller. New Haven, CT: Yale University Press.

Benjamin, Thomas. 1996. *A Rich Land, A Poor People: Politics and Society in Modern Chiapas*. Albuquerque: University of New Mexico.

Big Noise Tactical. n.d. 'About Us.' Accessed 4 August 2005 from www .bignoisefilms.com/about.htm.

Bloch, Ernst. 1986. *The Principle of Hope*. 3 volumes. Translated by Neville Plaice, Stephen Plaice, and Paul Knight. Oxford: Basil Blackwell.

Brand, K. 1990. 'Cyclical Aspects of New Social Movements.' In *Challenging the Political Order: New Political and Social Movements in Western Democracies*, edited by R.J. Dalton and M. Kuechler. New York: Oxford University Press.

Brennan, Tim. 2006. *Wars of Position: The Cultural Politics of Left and Right*. New York: Columbia University Press.

Buck-Morss, Susan. 2000. *Dreamworld and Catastrophe: The Passing of Mass Utopia in East and West*. Cambridge: MIT Press.

– 2003. *Thinking Past Terror: Islamism and Critical Theory on the Left*. New York: Verso.

Buhle, Paul, and Nicole Schulman, eds. 2005. *Wobblies! A Graphic History of the Industrial Workers of the World*. New York: Verso.

Bull, Malcolm. 2005. 'The Limits of Multitude.' *New Left Review* 35: 19–39.

Cal y Mayor, Araceli Burguete. 2003. 'The de Facto Autonomous Process: New Jurisdictions and Parallel Governments in Rebellion.' In *Mayan Lives, Mayan Utopias: The Indigenous Peoples of Chiapas and the Zapatista Rebellion*, edited by Jan Rus, Rosalva Aída Hernández Castillo, and Shannan L. Mattiace. Translated by Carlos Pérez. Toronto: Rowman and Littlefield.

Callahan, Manuel. 2004a. 'Zapatismo and Global Struggle: "A Revolution to Make a Revolution Possible."' In *Confronting Capitalism: Dispatches from a Global Movement*, edited by Eddie Yuen, Daniel Burton-Rose, and George Katsiaficas. Brooklyn: Soft Skull Press.

– 2004b. 'Zapatismo Beyond Chiapas.' In *Globalize Liberation: How to Uproot the System and Build a Better World*, edited by David Solnit. San Francisco: City Lights Books.

Carr, Barry. 1992. *Marxism and Communism in Twentieth-Century Mexico*. Lincoln: University of Nebraska Press.

Carroll, William K. 2005. 'Introduction: Social Democracy in Neoliberal Times.' In *Challenges and Perils: Social Democracy in Neoliberal Times*, edited by William Carroll and R.S. Ratner. Halifax: Fernwood Publishing.

Carroll, William K., and R.S. Ratner. 2005. 'The NDP Regime in British Colombia, 1991–2001: A Post Mortem.' In *Challenges and Perils: Social Democracy in Neoliberal Times*, edited by William Carroll and R.S. Ratner. Halifax: Fernwood Publishing.

Castoriadis, Cornelius. 1991. 'Power, Politics, Autonomy.' In *Philosophy, Poli-*

tics, Autonomy, edited by David Ames Curtis. New York: Oxford University Press.

Clarke, John. 2001. 'Short History of OCAP.' Accessed 19 July 2005 from www.ocap.ca/archive/short_history_of_ocap.html.

Clarke, Tony. 1997. *Silent Coup: Confronting the Big Business Takeover of Canada.* Ottawa: Canadian Centre for Policy Alternatives.

Cleaver, Harry. 1998. 'The Zapatista Effect: The Internet and the Rise of an Alternative Political Fabric.' *Journal of International Affairs* 51(2): 621–40.

Cleveland, John W. 2004. 'New Left, Not New Liberal: 1960s Movements in English Canada and Quebec.' *The Canadian Review of Sociology and Anthropology* 41(1): 67–84.

Cloward, Richard, and Frances Fox Piven. 1977. *Poor People's Movements: Why They Succeed, How They Fail.* New York: Vintage Books.

Coalition of Immokalee Workers. 2005. 'Coalition of Immokalee Workers, Taco Bell Reach Groundbreaking Agreement,' 8 March. Accessed 28 July 2005 from www.ciw-online.org/we%20won.html.

Cockcroft, James D. 1998. *Mexico's Hope: An Encounter with Politics and History.* New York: Monthly Review.

– 2006. 'Imperialism, State and Social Movements in Latin America.' *Critical Sociology* 32(1): 67–81.

Collier, George A., and Elizabeth Lowery Quaratiello. 1999. *Basta! Land and the Zapatista Rebellion in Chiapas.* Oakland, CA: Food First Books.

Crotty, William. 1991. *Political Participation and American Democracy.* New York: Greenwood Press.

Day, Richard. 2005. *Gramsci Is Dead: Anarchist Currents in the Newest Social Movements.* Toronto: Between the Lines.

De la Colina, José. 2002. 'As Time Goes By: "Marcos," or the Mask Is the Message.' In *The Zapatista Reader,* edited by Tom Hayden. New York: Thunder's Mouth Press. Originally published in *Letras Libres* (1999).

de Marcellus, Olivier. 2001. 'Peoples' Global Action: Dreaming Up an Old Ghost.' In *Auroras of the Zapatistas: Local and Global Struggles of the Fourth World War.* Brooklyn: Autonomedia.

Debord, Guy. 1994. *The Society of the Spectacle.* Translated by Donald Nicholson-Smith. New York: Zone Books.

Deleuze, Gilles, and Felix Guattari. 1987. *A Thousand Plateaus: Capitalism and Schizophrenia.* Minneapolis: University of Minnesota Press.

Dyer-Witheford, Nick. 1999. *Cyber-Marx: Cycles and Circuits of Struggle in High-Technology Capitalism.* Chicago: University of Illinois Press.

Eber, Christine. 2003. 'Buscando una Nueva Vida: Liberation Through Autonomy in San Pedro Chenalhó, 1970–1998.' In *Mayan Lives, Mayan Utopias: The*

Indigenous Peoples of Chiapas and the Zapatista Rebellion, edited by Jan Rus, Rosalva Aída Hernández Castillo, and Shannan L. Mattiace. Toronto: Rowman and Littlefield. Originally published in *Latin American Perspectives* 28(2) (2001): 45–72.

Ejército Zapatista de Liberación Nacional. 2001a. 'Opening Remarks at the First Intercontinental Encuentro for Humanity and Against Neoliberalism.' In *Our Word Is Our Weapon,* edited by Juana Ponce de León. Toronto: Seven Stories Press. Remarks originally given on 27 July 1996 in Oventik, Chiapas.

– 2001b. 'Second Declaration of La Realidad for Humanity and against Neoliberalism.' In *Our Word Is Our Weapon,* edited by Juana Ponce de León. Toronto: Seven Stories Press. Communiqué originally issued August 1996.

– 2001c. 'The First Declaration of the Lacandón Jungle.' In *Our Word Is Our Weapon,* edited by Juana Ponce de León. Toronto: Seven Stories Press. Communiqué originally issued 2 January 1994.

– 2001d. 'Votán Zapata or Five Hundred Years of History.' In *Our Word Is Our Weapon,* edited by Juana Ponce de León. Toronto: Seven Stories Press. Communiqué originally issued 10 April 1994.

– 2005. 'Sixth Declaration of the Lacandona, Part 3.' Translated by Irlandesa. Received 1 July 2005 from Chiapas-95 (English) E-mail Listserve chiapas95-english@eco.utexas.edu.

Epstein, Barbara. 1991. *Political Protest and Cultural Revolution.* Berkeley: University of California Press.

Esteva, Gustavo. 2003. 'The Meaning and Scope of the Struggle for Autonomy.' In *Mayan Lives, Mayan Utopias: The Indigenous Peoples of Chiapas and the Zapatista Rebellion,* edited by Jan Rus, Rosalva Aída Hernández Castillo, and Shannan L. Mattiace. Translated by Carlos Pérez. Toronto: Rowman and Littlefield. Originally published in *Latin American Perspectives* 28(2) (2001): 120–48.

Evans, Peter. 2000. 'Fighting Marginalization with Transnational Networks: Counter-Hegemonic Globalization.' *Contemporary Sociology* 29(1): 230–41.

Federici, Silvia. 2004. *Caliban and the Witch: Women, the Body, and Primitive Accumulation.* Brooklyn: Autonomedia.

Ferguson, Sherry Devereaux. 2002. 'A Cacophony of Voices: Competing for the Future.' In *Civic Discourse and Cultural Politics in Canada: A Cacophony of Voices,* edited by Sherry Devereaux Ferguson and Leslie Regan Shade. Westport, CT: Ablex Publishing.

Flood, Andrew. 2003. 'Dreaming of a Reality Where the Past and the Future Meet the Present.' In *We Are Everywhere: The Irresistible Rise of Global Anti-Capitalism,* edited by Notes From Nowhere. New York: Verso.

Fo, Dario. 2003. *Accidental Death of an Anarchist.* London: Methuen Drama.

Foucault, Michel. 2003. 'The Subject and Power.' In *The Essential Foucault: Selections from the Essential Works of Foucault, 1954–1984*, edited by Paul Rabinow and Nikolas Rose. New York: The New Press.

Foweraker, Joe. 1990. 'Popular Movements and Political Change in Mexico.' In *Popular Movements and Political Change in Mexico*, edited by Ann Craig and Joe Foweraker. Boulder: Lynne Rienner Publishers.

Galeano, Eduardo. 1973. *Open Veins of Latin America: Five Centuries of the Pillage of a Continent*. New York: Monthly Review Press.

García Márquez, Gabriel, and Roberto Pombo. 2004. 'The Hourglass of the Zapatistas.' In *A Movement of Movements: Is Another World Really Possible?* Edited by Tom Mertes. New York: Verso. First published in English as 'The Punch-Card and the Hourglass,' *New Left Review* 9 (May-June 2001): 69–79.

Gilbreth, Chris, and Gerardo Otero. 2001. 'Democratization in Mexico: The Zapatista Uprising and Civil Society.' *Latin American Perspectives* 28(4): 7–29.

Gilly, Adolfo. 1998. 'Chiapas and the Rebellion of the Enchanted World.' In *Rural Revolt in Mexico: U.S. Intervention and the Domain of Subaltern Politics*, edited by Daniel Nugent. Durham, NC: Duke University Press.

Giroux, Henry A. 2004. *The Terror of Neoliberalism: Authoritarianism and the Eclipse of Democracy*. Boulder, CO: Paradigm Publishers.

Glick Schiller, Nina. 2005. 'Transnational Social Fields and Imperialism: Bringing a Theory of Power to Transnational Studies.' *Anthropological Theory* 5(4): 439–61.

Global Exchange. n.d. 'Global Exchange in Chiapas.' Accessed 19 July 2005 from www.globalexchange.org/countries/americas/mexico/chiapas/program.html.pdf.

– 'Program Summary. Accessed 19 July 2005.' www.globalexchange.org/about/programSummary.html.pdf.

Goodwin, James, James Jasper, and Francesca Polletta. 2001. 'Why Emotions Matter.' Introduction to *Passionate Politics: Emotions and Social Movements*, edited by Jeff Goodwin, James Jasper, and Francesca Polletta. Chicago: University of Chicago Press.

Grace, Joan. 2005. 'Challenges and Opportunities in Manitoba: The Social Democratic "Promise" and Women's Equality.' In *Challenges and Perils: Social Democracy in Neoliberal Times*, edited by William Carroll and R.S. Ratner. Halifax: Fernwood Publishing.

Graefe, Peter. 2005. 'The Dynamics of the Parti Québécois in Power: Social Democracy and Competitive Nationalism.' In *Challenges and Perils: Social Democracy in Neoliberal Times*, edited by William Carroll and R.S. Ratner. Halifax: Fernwood Publishing.

Hardt, Michael, and Antonio Negri. 2000. *Empire.* Cambridge, MA: Harvard University Press.

– 2004. *Multitude: War and Democracy in the Age of Empire.* New York: Penguin.

Harvey, Neil. 1998. *The Chiapas Rebellion: The Struggle for Land and Democracy.* Durham, NC: Duke University Press.

Hayden, Tom. 2002. 'Conclusion.' In *The Zapatista Reader,* edited by Tom Hayden. New York: Thunder's Mouth Press.

Hellman, Judith A. 2000. 'Real and Virtual Chiapas: Magic Realism and the Left.' *Necessary and Unnecessary Utopias: Socialist Register 2000:* 161–86.

Hernández Navarro, Luis. 1994. 'The New Mayan War.' *NACLA Report on the Americas* 27(5): 6–10.

– 2002. 'Mexico's Secret War.' In *The Zapatista Reader,* edited by Tom Hayden. New York: Thunder's Mouth Press. Originally published in *NACLA Report on the Americas* (May-June 1999).

Higgins, Nicholas. 2000. 'The Zapatista Uprising and the Poetics of Cultural Resistance.' *Alternatives* 25: 359–74.

Hodgins, Peter. 2002. 'A Truly Comic History: Central Canadian Nationalism and the Politics of Memory.' In *Civic Discourse and Cultural Politics in Canada: A Cacophony of Voices,* edited by Sherry Devereaux Ferguson and Leslie Regan Shade. Westport, CT: Ablex Publishing.

Holloway, John. 2002a. *Change the World without Taking Power: The Meaning of Revolution Today.* London: Pluto Press.

– 2002b. 'Zapatismo and the Social Sciences.' *Capital and Class* 78: 153–60.

Huizer, Gerrit. 1970. 'Emiliano Zapata and the Peasant Guerrillas in the Mexican Revolution.' In *Agrarian Problems and Peasant Movements in Latin America,* edited by Rodolfo Stavenhagen. Garden City, NY: Doubleday.

Huyer, Sophia. 2004. 'Challenging Relations: A Labour-NGO Coalition to Oppose the Canada-U.S. and North American Free Trade Agreements, 1985–1993.' *Development in Practice* 14(1&2): 48–60.

Jasper, James. 1997. *The Art of Moral Protest: Culture, Biography, and Creativity in Social Movements.* Chicago: University of Chicago Press.

Johnston, Josée, and Gordon Laxer. 2003. 'Solidarity in the Age of Globalization: Lessons from the Anti-MAI and Zapatista Struggles.' *Theory and Society* 32: 39–91.

Katsiaficas, George. 1987. *The Imagination of the New Left: A Global Analysis of 1968.* Boston: South End Press.

Kearney, M. 1995. 'The Local and the Global: The Anthropology of Globalization and Transnationalism.' *Annual Review of Anthropology 1995* 24: 547–65.

Keck, Margaret, and Kathryn Sikkink. 1998. *Activists Beyond Borders: Advocacy Networks in International Politics.* Ithaca, NY: Cornell University Press.

Khasnabish, Alex. 2004. 'Moments of Coincidence: Exploring the Intersection of Zapatismo and Independent Labour in Mexico.' *Critique of Anthropology* 24(3): 256–76.

– 2005. '"They Are Our Brothers and Sisters": Why Zapatismo Matters to Independent Labour in Mexico.' *Anthropologica* 47(1): 101–14.

Kingsnorth, Paul. 2003. *One No, Many Yeses: A Journey to the Heart of the Global Resistance Movement.* London: The Free Press.

Klein, Naomi. 2002. 'Rebellion in Chiapas.' In *Fences and Windows: Dispatches from the Front Lines of the Globalization Debate*, edited by Debra Ann Levy. Toronto: Vintage Canada. Originally published in *The Guardian*, 3 March 2001.

Knudson, Jerry. 1998. 'Rebellion in Chiapas: Insurrection by Internet and Public Relations.' *Media, Culture and Society* 20: 507–18.

Laclau, Ernesto, and Chantal Mouffe. 1985. *Hegemony and Socialist Strategy.* London: Verso.

Lal, Vinay. 2002. *Empire of Knowledge: Culture and Plurality in the Global Economy.* London: Pluto Press.

Laxer, Gordon. 2003. 'Radical Transformative Nationalism Confront the U.S. Empire.' *Current Sociology* 51(2): 133–52.

Leyva Solano, Xóchitl. 1998. 'The New Zapatista Movement: Political Levels, Actors, and Political Discourse in Contemporary Mexico.' In *Encuentros Antropologicos: Politics, Identity and Mobility in Mexican Society*, edited by Valentina Napolitano and Xóchitl Leyva Solano. London: Institute of Latin American Studies.

– 2003. 'Regional, Communal, and Organizational Transformations in Las Cañadas.' In *Mayan Lives, Mayan Utopias: The Indigenous Peoples of Chiapas and the Zapatista Rebellion*, edited by Jan Rus, Rosalva Aída Hernández Castillo, and Shannan L. Mattiace. Toronto: Rowman and Littlefield. Originally published in *Latin American Perspectives* 28(2) (2001): 20–44.

Linebaugh, Peter. 2003. *The London Hanged: Crime and Civil Society in the Eighteenth Century.* New York: Verso.

Linebaugh, Peter, and Marcus Rediker. 2000. *The Many-Headed Hydra: Sailors, Slaves, Commoners and the Hidden History of the Revolutionary Atlantic.* Boston: Beacon Press.

Lomnitz, Claudio. 2001. *Deep Mexico, Silent Mexico: An Anthropology of Nationalism.* Minneapolis: University of Minnesota Press.

Macdonald, Laura. 2002. 'Globalization and Social Movements: Comparing Women's Movements' Responses to NAFTA in Mexico, the U.S. and Canada.' *International Feminist Journal of Politics* 4(2): 151–72.

Mansbridge, Jane, and Aldon Morris, eds. 2001. *Oppositional Consciousness: The Subjective Roots of Social Protest.* Chicago: University of Chicago Press.

Mark, Jason. 2001. 'At the Millennium, a Broader Definition of Human Rights: Justice, Democracy, and Dignity.' Accessed 19 July 2005 from www.globalexchange.org/about/newhumanrights.html.pdf.

Mattiace, Shannan. 1997. 'Zapata Vive! The EZLN, Indigenous Politics, and the Autonomy Movement in Mexico.' *Journal of Latin American Anthropology* 3(1): 32–71.

– 2003. 'Regional Renegotiations of Space: Tojolabal Ethnic Identity in Las Margaritas, Chiapas. In *Mayan Lives, Mayan Utopias: The Indigenous Peoples of Chiapas and the Zapatista Rebellion*, edited by Jan Rus, Rosalva Aída Hernández Castillo, and Shannan L. Mattiace. Toronto: Rowman and Littlefield. Originally published in *Latin American Perspectives* 28(2) (2001): 73–97.

McAdam, Doug, Sidney Tarrow, and Charles Tilly. 2001. *Dynamics of Contention*. New York: Cambridge University Press.

McBride, Stephen. 2005. '"If You Don't Know Where You're Going You'll End Up Somewhere Else": Ideological and Policy Failure in the Ontario NDP.' In *Challenges and Perils: Social Democracy in Neoliberal Times*, edited by William Carroll and R.S. Ratner. Halifax: Fernwood Publishing.

McCarthy, John D., and Mayer N. Zald, eds. 1979. *The Dynamics of Social Movements: Resource Mobilization, Social Control, and Tactics*. Cambridge, MA: Winthrop Publishers.

McKay, Ian. 2005. *Rebels, Reds, Radicals: Rethinking Canada's Left History*. Toronto: Between the Lines.

Mexico Solidarity Network. 2005. 'MSN Response to the Sixth Declaration of the Selva Lacandona.' Received 29 July 2005 from Chiapas-95 (English) E-mail Listserve chiapas95-english@eco.utexas.edu.

– n.d. 'Alternative Economy Program.' Accessed 19 July 2005 from www.mexicosolidarity.org/Alternative%20Economy/.

– n.d. 'History.' Accessed 19 July 2005 from www.mexicosolidarity.org/About%20MSN/History/.

– n.d. 'Zapatista Solidarity.' Accessed 19 July 2005 from www.mexicosolidarity.org/Zapatista%20solidarity/.

Meyer, Jean. 2002. 'Once Again, the Noble Savage.' In *The Zapatista Reader*, edited by Tom Hayden. New York: Thunder's Mouth Press. Originally published in *Letras Libres* (1998).

Meyer, David S., Nancy Whittier, and Belinda Robnett, eds. 2002. *Social Movements: Identity, Culture, and the State*. New York: Oxford University Press.

Meyer, David S., and Sidney Tarrow, eds. 1998. *The Social Movement Society: Contentious Politics for a New Century*. New York: Rowman and Littlefield.

Midnight Notes, eds. 2001. *Auroras of the Zapatistas: Local and Global Struggles of the Fourth World War*. Brooklyn: Autonomedia.

Mintz, Sidney. 1998. 'The Localization of Anthropological Practice: From Area Studies to Transnationalism.' *Critique of Anthropology* 18(2): 117–33.

Miyoshi, Masao. 1993. 'A Borderless World? From Colonialism to Transnationalism and the Decline of the Nation-State.' *Critical Inquiry* 19: 726–51.

Monsiváis, Carlos. 2002. 'From the Subsoil to the Mask that Reveals: The Visible Indian.' In *The Zapatista Reader,* edited by Tom Hayden. New York: Thunder's Mouth Press. Originally published in *Proceso,* 3 March 2001.

Nash, June. 2001. *Mayan Visions: The Quest for Autonomy in an Age of Globalization.* New York: Routledge.

Nevitte, Neil. 1996. *The Decline of Deference: Canadian Value Change in Cross-National Perspective.* Peterborough: Broadview Press.

Notes From Nowhere, eds. 2003. *We Are Everywhere: The Irresistible Rise of Global Anti-Capitalism.* New York: Verso.

Nugent, Daniel. 2002. 'Northern Intellectuals and the EZLN.' In *The Zapatista Reader,* edited by Tom Hayden. New York: Thunder's Mouth Press. Originally published in *Monthly Review* (July 1995).

Olesen, Thomas. 2005a. *International Zapatismo: The Construction of Solidarity in the Age of Globalization.* New York: Zed Books.

– 2005b. 'Transnational Publics: New Spaces of Social Movement Activism and the Problem of Global Long-Sightedness.' *Current Sociology* 53(3): 419–40.

Oppenheimer, Andres. 2002. 'Guerrillas in the Mist.' In *The Zapatista Reader,* edited by Tom Hayden. New York: Thunder's Mouth Press. Originally published in *The New Republic* (June 1996).

Peoples' Global Action. n.d. 'Brief History of PGA.' Accessed 19 July 2005 from www.nadir.org/nadir/initiativ/agp/en/pgainfos/history.htm.

– n.d. 'Hallmarks of Peoples' Global Action.' Accessed 19 July 2005 from www.nadir.org/nadir/initiativ/agp/free/pga/hallm.htm.

– n.d. 'Peoples' Global Action in a Nutshell.' Accessed 19 July 2005 from www.nadir.org/nadir/initiativ/agp/gender/desire/nutshell.htm.

– n.d. 'Peoples' Global Action Organisational Principles.' Accessed 19 July 2005 from www.nadir.org/nadir/initiativ/agp/cocha/principles.htm.

Polletta, Francesca. 2002. *Freedom Is an Endless Meeting.* Chicago: University of Chicago Press.

Ponce de León, Juana, ed. 2001. *Our Word Is Our Weapon.* Toronto: Seven Stories Press.

Portes, Alejandro, Luis E. Guarnizo, and Patricia Landolt. 1999. 'The Study of Transnationalism: Pitfalls and Promise of an Emergent Research Field.' *Ethnic and Racial Studies* 22(2): 217–37.

Ratner, R.S. 'Conclusion: Canadian Social Democracy at the Crossroads.' In

Challenges and Perils: Social Democracy in Neoliberal Times, edited by William Carroll and R.S. Ratner. Halifax: Fernwood Publishing.

Rediker, Marcus. 2004. *Villains of All Nations: Atlantic Pirates in the Golden Age.* Boston: Beacon Press.

Reinsborough, Patrick. 2004. 'Decolonizing the Revolutionary Imagination: Values Crisis, the Politics of Reality, and Why There's Going to Be a Common-Sense Revolution in This Generation.' In *Globalize Liberation: How to Uproot the System and Build a Better World*, edited by David Solnit. San Francisco: City Lights Books.

Robinson, William. 2005. 'Global Capitalism: The New Transnationalism and the Folly of Conventional Thinking.' *Science and Society* 69(3): 316–28.

Ross, John. 2000. *The War against Oblivion: The Zapatista Chronicles.* Monroe: Common Courage Press.

– 2006. 'A Report from the Red Alert: Zapatistas at Critical Crossroads.' In *Counterpunch*, edited by Alexander Cockburn and Jeffrey St. Clair. Available online from www.counterpunch.org/ross07312006.html.

Ross, John, and Al Giordano. 2006. 'John Ross' "Twenty Questions for Big Al, the Other Campaign, and the Zapatista Army of National Liberation."' In *The Narco News Bulletin*. Available online from www.narconews.com/Issue41/article1907.html.

Roudometof, Victor. 2005. 'Transnationalism, Cosmopolitanism and Globalization.' *Current Sociology* 53(1): 113–35.

Rus, Jan, Rosalva Aída Hernández Castillo, and Shannan L. Mattiace, eds. 2003. *Mayan Lives, Mayan Utopias: The Indigenous Peoples of Chiapas and the Zapatista Rebellion.* Toronto: Rowman and Littlefield.

Russell, Adrienne. 2005. 'Myth and the Zapatista Movement: Exploring a Network Identity.' *New Media and Society* 7(4): 559–77.

Schools for Chiapas. 2005. 'An Open Letter to Tom Hanson and the Mexico Solidarity Committee.' Received 2 August 2005 from Chiapas-95 (English) E-mail Listserve chiapas95-english@eco.utexas.edu.

Selbin, Eric. 2003. 'Zapata's White Horse and Che's Beret: Theses on the Future of Revolution.' In *The Future of Revolutions: Rethinking Radical Change in the Age of Globalization*, edited by John Foran. New York: Zed Books.

Solnit, Rebecca. 2004. *Hope in the Dark: Untold Histories, Wild Possibilities.* New York: Nation Books.

Stavans, Ilan. 2002. 'Unmasking Marcos.' In *The Zapatista Reader*, edited by Tom Hayden. New York: Thunder's Mouth Press. Originally published in *Transition* (Spring 1996).

Steinberg, Marc. 2002. 'Toward a More Dialogic Analysis of Social Movement Culture.' In *Social Movements: Identity, Culture, and the State*, edited by David

Meyer, Nancy Whittier, and Belinda Robnett. New York: Oxford University Press.

Stephen, Lynn. 2002. *Zapata Lives! Histories and Cultural Politics in Southern Mexico*. Berkeley: University of California Press.

Subcomandante Insurgente Marcos. 1998. 'First Declaration of La Realidad for Humanity and Against Neoliberalism.' In *Zapatista Encuentro: Documents from the First Intercontinental Encounter for Humanity and Against Neoliberalism*, edited by Greg Ruggiero. New York: Seven Stories Press. Communiqué originally issued January 1996.

- 2001a. 'A Storm and a Prophecy – Chiapas: The Southeast in Two Winds.' In *Our Word Is Our Weapon*, edited by Juana Ponce de León. Toronto: Seven Stories Press. Communiqué originally issued 27 January 1994.

- 2001b. 'Another Cloud, Another Bottle, and Another Letter from Durito.' In *Our Word Is Our Weapon*, edited by Juana Ponce de León. Toronto: Seven Stories Press. Communiqué originally issued 30 September 1996.

- 2001c. 'Flowers, Like Hope, Are Harvested.' In *Our Word Is Our Weapon*, edited by Juana Ponce de León. Toronto: Seven Stories Press. Communiqué originally issued September 1995.

- 2001d. 'In Our Dreams We Have Seen Another World.' In *Our Word Is Our Weapon*, edited by Juana Ponce de León. Toronto: Seven Stories Press. Communiqué originally issued 1 March 1994.

- 2001e. 'Ten Years Later: Durito Found Us Again.' In *Our Word Is Our Weapon*, edited by Juana Ponce de León. Toronto: Seven Stories Press. Communiqué originally issued 25 December 1995.

- 2001f. 'Tomorrow Begins Today: Closing Remarks at the First Intercontinental Encuentro for Humanity and Against Neoliberalism.' In *Our Word Is Our Weapon*, edited by Juana Ponce de León. Toronto: Seven Stories Press. Remarks originally given on 3 August 1996.

- 2001g. 'Who Should Ask for Pardon and Who Can Grant It?' In *Our Word Is Our Weapon*, edited by Juana Ponce de León. Toronto: Seven Stories Press. Communiqué originally issued 18 January 1994.

- 2002a. 'Testimonies of the First Day.' In *The Zapatista Reader*, edited by Tom Hayden. New York: Thunder's Mouth Press. Originally published in *La Jornada*, 19 January 1994.

- 2002b. 'The Fourth World War Has Begun.' In *The Zapatista Reader*, edited by Tom Hayden. New York: Thunder's Mouth Press. Communiqué originally appeared in *Le Monde Diplomatique*, September 1997.

- 2004a. 'A Death Has Been Decided.' In *¡Ya Basta! Ten Years of the Zapatista Uprising*, edited by Žiga Vodovnik. Oakland, CA: AK Press. Communiqué originally issued July 2003.

- 2004b. 'Durito and One about False Options.' In ¡Ya Basta! Ten Years of the Zapatista Uprising, edited by Žiga Vodovnik. Oakland, CA: AK Press. Communiqué originally issued March 2003.
- 2004c. 'The Death Train of the WTO.' In ¡Ya Basta! Ten Years of the Zapatista Uprising, edited by Žiga Vodovnik. Oakland, CA: AK Press. Communiqué originally issued 12 September 2003.
- 2004d. 'The Seven Loose Pieces of the Global Jigsaw Puzzle (Neoliberalism as a Puzzle).' In ¡Ya Basta! Ten Years of the Zapatista Uprising, edited by Žiga Vodovnik. Oakland, CA: AK Press. Communiqué originally issued June 1997.
- 2004e. 'Three Shoulders.' Available online from http://flag.blackened.net/revolt/mexico/ezln2004/marcosshoul dersAUG.html. Communiqué originally issued August 2004.
- 2004f. 'To the Solidarity Committees of the Zapatista Struggle in All the World.' In ¡Ya Basta! Ten Years of the Zapatista Uprising, edited by Žiga Vodovnik. Oakland, CA: AK Press. Communiqué originally issued March 1997.
- 2005. 'A Penguin in the Selva Lacandona Part 2.' Translated by Irlandesa. Received 25 July 2005 from Chiapas-95 (English) E-mail Listserve chiapas95-english@eco.utexas.edu.
Tarrow, Sidney. 1998. Power in Movement. Cambridge: Cambridge University Press.
–2005. The New Transnational Activism. Cambridge: Cambridge University Press.
Taylor, Charles. 2004. Modern Social Imaginaries. Durham, NC: Duke University Press.
Tenuto-Sanchez, Mary Ann. 2006. 'My Thoughts on the John Ross Article "A Report from the Red Alert."' The Narcosphere: A Project of the Narco News Bulletin. Available online from http://narcosphere.narconews.com/story/2006/6/19/94748/1573#3.
Tutino, John. 1986. From Insurrection to Revolution in Mexico: Social Bases of Agrarian Violence, 1750–1940. Princeton: Princeton University Press.
Vance, Chris. 2001. 'Canada and Zapatismo.' In Auroras of the Zapatistas: Local and Global Struggles of the Fourth World War, edited by Midnight Notes. Brooklyn: Autonomedia.
Vertovec, Steven. 1999. 'Conceiving and Researching Transnationalism.' Ethnic and Racial Studies 22(2): 447–62.
–2001. 'Transnationalism and Identity.' Journal of Ethnic and Migration Studies 27(4): 573–82.
Virno, Paolo. 2004. A Grammar of the Multitude. Translated by Isabella Bertoletti, James Cascaito, and Andrea Casson. New York: Semiotext(e).

Warman, Arturo. 1976. *'We Come to Object': The Peasants of Morelos and the National State*. Baltimore: Johns Hopkins University Press.

Warnock, John W. 2005. 'The CCF-NDP in Saskatchewan: From Populist Social Democracy to Neoliberalism.' In *Challenges and Perils: Social Democracy in Neoliberal Times*, edited by William Carroll and R.S. Ratner. Halifax: Fernwood Publishing.

Weinberg, Bill. 2000. *Homage to Chiapas*. New York: Verso.

Whittier, Nancy. 2002. 'Meaning and Structure in Social Movements.' In *Social Movements: Identity, Culture, and the State*, edited by David Meyer, Nancy Whittier, and Belinda Robnett. New York: Oxford University Press.

Wilson, Peter Lamborn. 2003. *Pirate Utopias: Moorish Corsairs and European Renegadoes*. Brooklyn: Autonomedia.

Wolf, Eric. 1969. *Peasant Wars of the Twentieth Century*. New York: Harper.

Womack Jr., John. 1968. *Zapata and the Mexican Revolution*. New York: Vintage.

– 1999. *Rebellion in Chiapas*. New York: The New Press.

Wood, Lesley J. 2004. 'Bridging the Chasms: the Case of Peoples' Global Action.' In *Coalitions Across Borders: Transnational Protest and the Neoliberal Order*, edited by Joe Bandy and Jackie Smith. Lanham: Rowman and Littlefield.

Yegenoglu, Meyda. 2005. 'Cosmopolitanism and Nationalism in a Globalized World.' *Ethnic and Racial Studies* 28(1): 103–31.

Yeoh, Brenda S.A., Katie D. Willis, and S.M. Abdul Khader Fakhri. 2003. 'Introduction: Transnationalism and its Edges.' *Ethic and Racial Studies* 26(2): 207–17.

Zinn, Howard. 2003. *A People's History of the United States: 1492 – Present*. New York: Perennial Classics.

Zournazi, Mary. 2003. *Hope: New Philosophies for Change*. New York: Routledge.

Index

Abbs, Maryann: 209–10, 213
Adorno, Theodor: 166–7, 169
affinity, politics of: 44–5
anti-free trade movement: 75–83;
    Action Canada Network (ACN),
    80; Coalition Against Free Trade
    (CAFT), 78; Common Frontiers,
    80–1; decline of, 79–80, 81–2; for-
    mation of, 75–6, 78; International
    Citizens' Forum, 81; legacies of,
    82–3; Mujer a Mujer, 80–1; Mujeres
    en Acción Sindical, 80–1; National
    Action Committee on the Status of
    Women and, 76–80; New Demo-
    cratic Party and, 79; Pro-Canada
    Network (PCN), 78–9; tensions
    within, 78–80
anti-power: 53
Appadurai, Arjun: 130, 159–63, 184
autonomist Marxism: 40–2, 163

Bakhtin, Mikhail: 122
Bandy, Joe: 215
Barthes, Roland: 32–3
Big Noise Tactical: 13, 139, 182, 259–
    70
biopolitics: imagination and, 159–63,
    184–5; immaterial labour and, 42,
    43; socio-political struggle and, 43
Bleakney, Dave: 143–4, 175–6, 239–42
Bloch, Ernst: 176–8, 277
boomerang effect, the: 218–19
Brennan, Tim: 47–51
Buck-Morss, Susan: 35–6, 154, 157–8,
    163, 184–5
Building Bridges: 13, 148, 165, 195,
    209–14, 218, 222
Bull, Malcolm: 46–7

Callahan, Manuel: 125, 134
Canada–Colombia Solidarity Cam-
    paign: 167, 217
Canadian Labour Congress (CLC):
    76, 78
Canadian Union of Postal Workers
    (CUPW): 143, 239
Canadian Union of Public Employ-
    ees (CUPE): 226
Carroll, William: 64
Castoriadis, Cornelius: 178
Cauca, Colombia: 168, 170
CCF/NDP: 62–5. See also Co-opera-
    tive Commonwealth Federation;
    New Democratic Party

Chiapas, Mexico: agrarian organizing and, 102, 107–11; Article 27 and, 101, 111; corporatism in, 100–1, 109; federal electoral fraud and, 110; First Indian Congress, 107–8; González Garrido, Patrocinio, 110; guided social reform and, 98–9; independence and, 88; independent organizing in, 107–11; Indigenous politicization, 107–10; Lacandón Jungle and, 102, 114; land distribution, 102, 109; Mexican Revolution and, 98; modernization of, 89–91; National Solidarity Program, 110–11; Plan Chiapas, 109; Programa de Rehabilitación Agraria (PRA, Program of Agrarian Rehabilitation), 109; Ruiz, Samuel, 108
Chiapas Media Project: 13–14, 141, 227
Clarke, John: 178–9, 247–8, 255–6
Cleaver, Harry: 130
Communist Party: of Canada, 60–1; U.S., 57–8
Co-operative Commonwealth Federation (CCF): 61–2. See also CCF/NDP; New Democratic Party

Day, Richard: 44–5
de Marcellus, Olivier: 236, 239
Debord, Guy: 161–3
Deleuze, Gilles: 19–20, 34–5, 38–9, 40, 86, 187–9
DesRoches, Mike: 180–1, 251–4, 258
Dobson, Stephan: 226–7, 228–9
Doherty, Eric: 148, 165–6, 210–3
Dyer-Witheford, Nick: 36–7, 40–1

Enlightenment, the: 166–7

Epstein, Barbara: 56, 67–8, 72
EZLN (Ejercíto Zapatista de Liberación Nacional). See Zapatista Army of National Liberation

feminism: socialist and radical, 71–2. See also National Action Committee on the Status of Women
Fo, Dario: 152–3
Food for Chiapas: 13
forward dream: 176
Fourth World War, the: 37–8, 266, 273–4
Fuerzas de Liberación Nacional (FLN). See Zapatista Army of National Liberation, Fuerzas de Liberación Nacional

Gilly, Adolfo: 107, 113, 117–19
Giroux, Henry: 74–5, 156, 158, 163, 175
Global Exchange (GX): 13, 147, 195, 199, 205–9, 214, 218, 222–3, 224
groundless solidarity: 44
Guattari, Felix: 19–20, 34–5, 38–9, 40, 86, 187–9

Haberman, Friederike: 146–7, 236–8, 243–4
hacktivists: 13
Halkin, Alex: 141–2, 227–8
Hardt, Michael: 17, 18–19, 41, 42, 43–4, 160–1, 163, 220
Holloway, John: 39–40, 53
Horkheimer, Max: 166–7, 169

immanence: globalization and, 35; neoliberal capitalism and, 36–7; plane of, 34–5
immaterial labour: 42; socio-political

struggle and, 43; subjectivity and,
160–3
infinite responsibility: 44
Intercontinental Encuentro for
Humanity and Against Neoliberalism: First, 145, 146, 235, 242; Second, 146, 236; Third, 14, 221, 226

Jeffries, Fiona: 145, 175, 235, 242–3

Katsiaficas, George: 66, 68
Keck, Margaret: 214–15, 218, 223, 270
Kingsnorth, Paul: 134, 235
Klein, Naomi: 135–6
Knudson, Jerry: 129–30

labour movement, U.S.: AFL-CIO
and, 58; American Federation of
Labor and, 57–8; radical tendencies
in, 57–9
Laclau, Ernesto: 145, 173–4
Lal, Vinay: 11, 22, 32
Leyva Solano, Xóchitl: 116–17
Linebaugh, Peter: 51–3
lines of flight: 38

Marcos, Subcomandante Insurgente:
birth of the EZLN and, 108; Delegate Zero, 274–5; Durito and, 30–1;
on the nature of the EZLN, 5; relationship between civil society and
the Zapatistas, 215–17, 272; Zapatismo's resonance and, 18, 26, 119,
134–6, 274–5. See also Zapatista
Army of National Liberation; Zapatismo
Marques, Jessica: 148–9, 191, 195–6,
223–4
McKay, Ian: 56, 59–60
McKay, Kevin: 183–4

Mexican independence: annexation of Chiapas and, 88; Hidalgo,
Miguel, 88; history of, 87–90; Morelos, José María, 88; Reform Laws
and, 89; Wars of, 87–8
Mexican Revolution, the (1910–17):
Aguascalientes convention government and, 97; Carranza, Venustiano, 97–9; Chiapas and, 98–9;
Díaz, Porfiro, 90; history of, 90–8;
Madero, Francisco, 92, 94, 97;
Morelos and, 93, 98; mythology of,
22, 84–7, 105, 106; Plan of San Luis
Potosí, 92, 94; Precursor Movement and, 91–2; Villa, Pancho, 92,
97; Zapata, Emiliano, 92–5, 97–8
(see also Zapata, Emiliano); Zapatismo and, 93–4
Mexico, post-revolutionary: Alemán, government of, 101; Article
27 and, 100; Cárdenas, Cuauhtémoc, 106, 110; Cárdenas, government of, 100; corporatism and, 99–
100, 106; Cuban Revolution and,
103; De la Madrid, government of,
109; Democratic Opening Law,
105; Echeverría, government of,
105; electoral fraud and, 106; indigenismo, 99–100; institutionalized
party-state and, 101; liberation
theology and, 102–3; Mexico City
earthquake (19 September 1985),
106; National Liberation Movement (MLN) and, 103; neoliberal
financial restructuring, 105–6; new
leftist actors and, 102–5; Partido
Revolucionario Institucional (PRI,
Institutional Revolutionary Party),
102, 105, 109; Political Reform Law,
105; Portillo, government of, 105;

Salinas, Carlos, 106, 110; student movement and, 104–5; Tlatelolco massacre, 104–5

Mexico Solidarity Network (MSN): 13, 148, 164, 191, 194–205, 214, 218, 222–3, 225

Mouffe, Chantal: 145, 173–4

multitude, the: biopolitics and, 43, 220; criticisms of, 45–51; historical currents of, 51–3; nature of, 44; resonance of Zapatismo and, 53–4, 273–4, 279

National Action Committee on the Status of Women (NAC): 76–8, 80

Negri, Antonio: 17, 18–19, 41, 42, 43–4, 160–1, 163, 220

neoliberalism: as a new phase of capitalism, 74–5; Enlightenment rationality and, 166–7; proto-fascism and, 74–5

netwar: 127–8

New Democratic Party (NDP): 62–5. See also CCF/NDP; Co-operative Commonwealth Federation

New Left: Canadian, 68–9; decline of, 67–8; legacies of, 69–73; U.S., 67–8; world-historical movement, 66–7

North American Free Trade Agreement (NAFTA): 80–1, 110–11, 116, 118–19

Notes from Nowhere: 134–5

Not-Yet: 176–7, 277

Not-Yet-Become: 177

Not-Yet-Conscious: 177

Novum: 177

Nugent, Daniel: 86–7

Old Left: 56–65

Olesen, Thomas: 131–3

Ontario Coalition Against Poverty (OCAP): 14, 178–81, 230, 244–59

Partido Liberal Mexicano (PLM). See Mexican Revolution, Precursor Movement

Partido Revolucionario Institucional (PRI). See Mexico, post-revolutionary, Partido Revolucionario Institucional

Peoples' Global Action (PGA): 14, 144, 146, 175, 235–44

Pickard, Carleen: 147, 207–9, 224–5

Podur, Justin: 230–1, 245–6

political imagination: characteristics of, 7, 154–5; political action and, 152–85; possibilities for change and, 153; socio-historical and, 177–85; source of, 176–8; Zapatismo and, 154, 273

Polletta, Francesca: 56–7

radical pacifists: 57, 59

RAND Corporation: 127–8

Rediker, Marcus: 51–3

Reinsborough, Patrick: 138–9, 142–3, 172–3, 174–5, 261

research methods: geographical focus and, 10–11; political imagination and, 10–15; research partners and, 11–14; theory and, 15; transnational resonance and, 10–15

resonance: bases and consequences of, 15–18, 23, 24–8, 126–50, 275–7; criticisms of, 17–18, 137–8; 'dark side' of, 23, 199, 201–2, 204–5, 214–32; dimensions of, 7, 123–4; means and mechanisms of, 14–15, 275, 278; most rhizomatic manifestations of, 13–14, 233–70; of Zap-

atismo, national, 116–21; of Zapatismo, transnational, 122–51, 274;
political dissatisfaction and, 8–9,
25; power relations and, 17, 27, 220;
radical socio-political change and,
9; reimagining political struggle
and, 9; rhizomatic histories of, 23,
186–270, 278–9; romanticism and,
26, 189, 215, 222–31; socio-political
analysis and, 7–8; traditional solidaristic responses to, 13, 194–214
rhizome: characteristics of, 19–20,
187; communication and struggle,
18–21; conceptual and analytical
tool, 20, 187–8; social movement
theory and, 188
Rowley, Rick: 140–1, 144–5, 147–8,
150–1, 182–3, 260–2, 265–9, 270
Rozental, Manuel: 167–71, 217–18,
219–20
Russell, Adrienne: 130

Schools for Chiapas: 204–5, 229–30
Scott, Mac: 179–80, 250, 257
Selbin, Eric: 83, 133
Sienkowska, Carrie: 199–200,
225–6
Sikkink, Kathryn: 214–15, 218, 223,
270
Skydragon Community Develop-
ment Co-operative: 183
smartMeme Strategy and Training
Project: 14, 138, 172, 261
Smith, Jackie: 215
social democracy: 49, 63–5; Keynesi-
anism and, 63–4
social imaginary: 171–2, 173, 178
Solnit, Rebecca: 136–7
Soohen, Jacquie: 139–40, 183, 262–5,
270

spectacle: 152–3; society of the, 161–3;
Zapatistas and, 154
state apparatus: 38–9
state illusion: 39–40

Tabobondung, Rebeka: 164, 221–2
Tarrow, Sidney: 128
Taylor, Charles: 171
transnational: 6
transnational advocacy networks
(TANs): 214–15, 270

utopia: 156–8, 184–5
Utopian Marxism: 176–8

Virno, Paolo: 42–3

war machine, the: 38, 40
Warman, Arturo: 93, 97–8, 100

Zapata, Emiliano: Agrarian Law, 95;
assassination of, 98; Liberating
Army of the South and, 92–8; origins of, 92–4; Plan de Ayala, 94–5.
See also Mexican Revolution
Zapatista Army of National Liberation: Alianza Nacional Campesina
Indipendiente Emiliano Zapata
(ANCIEZ), 111; birth of, 108–9;
community bases of, 114; First
Declaration of the Lacandón Jungle, 112–13, 122–3; Fuerzas de Liberación Nacional (FLN, Forces
of National Liberation), 108, 114;
General Red Alert, 192, 274–5;
Indigenous Revolutionary Clandestine Committee-General Command (CCRI-CG), 125, 192–4;
legacy of Emiliano Zapata and,
114; Mexican Revolution and, 115;

México Rebelde and, 116–17; origins of, 112–15; Second Declaration of La Realidad for Humanity and Against Neoliberalism, 236; Sixth Declaration of the Lacandón Jungle, 192–4, 202; uprising (1 January 1994), 112; Votán Zapata and, 114–15. *See also* Chiapas, Mexico; Marcos, Subcomandante Insurgente; Zapatismo

Zapatismo: democracy, liberty, and justice, 125; dimensions of, 124–6; EZLN and, 125; Indian Question and, 120–1; Juntas of Good Government and, 198; lead by obeying, 125; walking questioning, 125. *See also* Intercontinental Encuentro for Humanity and Against Neoliberalism; Marcos, Subcomandante Insurgente; resonance, of Zapatismo, national; resonance, of Zapatismo, transnational

Znet: 230, 245

Zournazi, Mary: 153, 159, 173